1966 and Not All That

1966
AND NOT
ALL THAT
Edited by
Mark Perryman

Published by Repeater Books

An imprint of Watkins Media Ltd

19-21 Cecil Court
London
WC2N 4EZ
UK

www.repeaterbooks.com
A Repeater Books paperback original 2016
1

Distributed in the United States by Random House, Inc., New York.

Cover design: Johnny Bull
Layout and typesetting: Jan Middendorp
Typefaces: Marbach and Supria Sans

ISBN: 978-1-910924-08-2
Ebook ISBN: 978-1-910924-09-9

For the Kingswood, Walton
and Tadworth Summer Flower Show 23.07.66.
Proof positive of the "all that" of 1966.

Contents

Introduction

The Not All That

Mark Perryman

THE OFFICIAL FILM OF 1966, *Goal!* – with commentary by Brian Glanville and narration by actor Nigel Patrick – is a linear, not entirely uncritical, cinematographic portrait of a singularly special three and a bit weeks of English football. The ambition of *1966 and Not All That* is for the first time in fifty years to try to do something similar on the printed page.

The title is adapted from the irreverent and much-loved history of England, *1066 and All That* by W.C. Sellar and R.J. Yeatman, who described it as "a Memorable History of England, comprising all the parts you can remember, including 103 Good Things, 5 Bad Kings and 2 Genuine Dates." Published in 1930, its spirit survives via the children's TV favourite *Horrible Histories*. Our history of 1966 is irreverent too, but never disrespectful. Whatever the changed circumstance of world, and English, football from then to now, for any country to win the World Cup remains a remarkable achievement. And in early July '66, make no mistake, England were, as they remain since, World Cup quarter-finalists at best. *1966* therefore refers to the achievement, and *Not All That* refers to all that it has since been forced to represent, or as our writers largely argue, misrepresent.

The book opens pre-match, quite rightly, with the voices of those who were there to see England make it happen. For the first time an oral history, a people's history, of the 1966 tournament, expertly compiled by Amy Lawrence. And to provide a half-century of context, Mark Perryman's chapter reviews all that has followed, on and sometimes off the pitch.

Our writing styles mix the reflective and analytical with real-time reportage. Asif Burhan and Joe Kennedy provide a 1966 tournament guide written as if they were there in '66 – in actual fact neither were even born then – but in a way that readers of modern World Cup handbooks would be familiar with. Well-informed broadsheet digests of key facts mixed with fanzine-type satire.

As kick-off approaches, football historian John Williams surveys the state of English football in the mid-1960s. Cultural historian Richard Weight does the same for the rest of the country beyond the touchline. Alan Tomlinson reports from the final as a teenage fan, while reflecting fifty years later on how the tournament was organised, with all that he has learned as one of the world's leading experts on the politics of FIFA. German football writer Claus Melchior reminds English readers that despite England's failings at previous World Cups the West Germany team in 1966 were very much the underdogs.

One very particular approach to '66 that this book has adopted is to provide space for the "other." To this end each of England's games, from group stage to the final, is reported on by a writer of the opposition nation. Once more this is in 'real-time' style, complete with how their team came to England, what they made of the nation and team, and what happened to them next. A Mexican, a Uruguayan, a Frenchman, an Argentine, a Portuguese and a German: sounds like the line-up for a poor-taste joke, but in our book it provides an international range of highly innovative writing to turn the familiar into the unfamiliar. Do they mean us?

The first half is time to drill down into the detail of how the tournament was played, and consumed. Writer on stadia architecture Simon Inglis recalls the state of the venues, some gone, some rebuilt, some much as they then were. Sportswriter and lecturer in sports journalism Rob Steen revisits the ways in which the tournament was covered by the media. Simon Kuper, co-author of the book *Why England Lose*, explains Why England Won. Literary historian Claire Westall unpicks the meaning behind the near industrial production of 1966 nostalgia.

Our second half provides a bout of much-needed reflection. Acclaimed critic of the modern game David Goldblatt answers some vital questions on whatever happened to football in the past fifty years. Sociologist Mark Doidge compares the English and German models for organising their football. For a wider view on a very English hang-up on the longevity of years of hurt, Scottish political commentator Gerry Hassan and German sportswriter Markus Hesselmann provide their perspectives.

In extra time cultural theorist and '66 World Cup spectator Steve Redhead argues for a dialectical approach if we are to truly appreciate the liberatory potential of football. Football travel writer Stuart Fuller celebrates his very own liberation from the limitations of the domestic game via a budget airline destination guide with fixture list at the ready. Nick Davidson, author of a history of cult German club FC St Pauli, explores how in both Germany and England fans are founding common cause against their modern and our modern football. Football Beyond Borders activist Sanna Qureshi looks beyond national identity politics to locate the subversive side of the game.

No penalty shoot-out in our book; that would be just too painful. Instead we go straight into post-match with a unique charting of World Cup achievements since 1966. Football statistician Philip Cornwall has done the numbers to produce a result that will have readers arguing the toss forever and a day.

Goal! was directed by the Turkish artist Abidine Dino and produced by the Chilean Octavio Señoret, with a distinctly un-English soundtrack of discordant, almost ambient jazz provided by John Hawksworth. Almost nothing is traditional or predictable about this film that famously ends with the Groundsman locking up after the final has ended, kicking the litter and debris off the steps, and Brian Glanville's concluding words from his commentary: "And at Wembley Mr McElroy locks up." It's taken fifty years to catch up with the whole meaning of what happened at Wembley on that day; isn't it time we did so?

Pre-Match

A People's History of 1966

Amy Lawrence

WORLD CUPS CAN BE such profoundly formative things. As a football supporter, the scale and sense of history and every-four-years pattern (all the more thrilling for the wait) just seems to strike a chord that resonates outside the regular football experience.

I can still flash back in a heartbeat to big moments in my personal World Cup past. Watching Maradona's Hand of God in 1986 in the lounge at dad's and trying to make sense of an injustice that was incomprehensible to a fourteen year-old who had never seen anything like it. In 1990, I set off by train with two friends, a sleeping bag and a couple of hundred quid for Genoa to spend a week at Italia '90, where the romance of Roger Milla and Toto Schillachi, and the glorious Italian hospitality, rendered us all spellbound. USA '94 bought a quandary – whether to go as planned, or forgo attending that World Cup to take up the offer of an actual real job as a football journalist starting in the office immediately (quite the dilemma). By France 1998, I was an accredited member of the travelling press pack, so privileged to witness the drama of England-Argentina in St Etienne, Dennis Bergkamp's wondergoal in Marseille, Croatia coming of age in Paris, and Zinedine Zidane earning the soubriquet of "President" during the final. Fast-forwarding to the most recent edition, in 2014, a pilgrimage to the Maracanã for the first time took my breath clean away. I love World Cups, fully and unashamedly. Whether we can continue to love them in the same way as they travel under FIFA's peculiar direction remains to be seen. I'll try anyway.

The thing that struck me thinking about 1966 – not having been old enough to know about it other than through literature and old video clips – was a desire to know how it felt to experience that World Cup. This set in motion a search for stories. Moments. Memories. Happenings. Influences. The result is a story of wonder, a period piece provided by first-hand accounts of what ordinary folk were doing during that World Cup. It is time travel of sorts. I do hope you enjoy this journey as much as I did.

Somewhere in these musings is my dad's recollection of what he was doing on the day of the 1966 World Cup final. He was actually en route to meet my mum, who had gone with her family to Italy. They got engaged at the end of that holiday, had my brother in time for 1970 and I was a toddler in 1974. Not that we measure staging points of our lives by World Cups or anything...

World Cup Fever

As a young lad aged thirteen I went to all the World Cup games played at Goodison Park. In those days before all-seated stadiums I would get into the ground early and stand by the wall next to the pitch. For most of the games I stood next to one of the big glass dugouts either side of the players' entrance. The first game between Brazil and Bulgaria was held on a really balmy night and I remember Kenneth Wolstenholme standing at the side of the pitch before the game talking about the Brazilian support in the Bullens Road stand. It was fantastic to be able to get that close to the players and see them close up. During the match when Brazil were 2-0 up the Brazilian fans started "ole" chants when Brazil kept the ball. I joined in and was rewarded with a slap from the Bulgarian coach who leaned out of the dugout to deliver it! He was admonished somewhat by some of the adults stood next to me and kept his head down after that.

— **Michael Jones**

I was eight years old and lived in Hendon, North London, about eight to ten miles from Wembley. I went to the local school and just down from it is the Hendon Hall Hotel. It was the place where

Cup Final teams used to stay, and where the England team stayed before internationals. We would go down after school and get autographs. One day during the World Cup my dad took me to the pictures to see *Those Magnificent Men in Their Flying Machines* at the Hendon Gaumont. I can remember going up to the circle and there, waiting for the doors to open for the next screening, was the whole England squad. I sat down next to George Cohen and gazed over to Jack Charlton. For an eight year-old boy it was mesmerising. After a few minutes the doors opened and everyone filtered in for their seats. I can't remember anything about the film.

— Ian Marshall

I was thirteen during the 1966 World Cup and living in Durham City, which welcomed the Italian and Soviet squads for two weeks, the latter training at the spanking new University sports centre with the Italians over the road on the grounds of the agricultural college. So my routine for a fortnight was to spend all my days there between the training sessions. Remarkably there was no security at all, but then there were remarkably few of us trying to hang out with these world greats.

My abiding memories (backed by photos and autographs) are of befriending Facchetti, Mazzola and Rivera, and Lev Yashin who never seemed to tire of pesky autograph hunters.

I still have this image of the ferocity of the shots and Yashin shuffling a couple of giant steps to the right or left to prevent a "goal" into the top corner and, at least as I recall, punching them back from where they came well into the other half of the pitch. Of the Italian training sessions I only recall the dramatic shouting and how they would bite into whole lemons, the likes of which I have never seen since.

From the Korean victory, our French teacher, who was in the seats, claimed that Rivera – who had been dropped – jumped to his feet when Pak Doo Ik scored and screamed "Mamma Mia."

My dad and I saw all the six group matches, plus the Soviet-Hungary quarter-final. A true feast capped by getting tickets to the final. I can also remember prior to the final making a St George's cross flag, bigger than I was and pinned to a large broomstick, and being allowed to take it into Wembley.

— **John Bevan**

My parents lived in Edmonton – four children under eight in a two-bedroom flat, like so many they took a punt on a New Town. Our house was close to Harlow Common where there were a few football pitches. In the summer of 1966 I was six years old. Portugal had their camp a few hundred yards away in what is now the Moat House Hotel, back then known as The Saxon Inn. My brothers and I spent so many hours watching as the squad trained on the common. Eusébio of course was a magnificent athlete and a lovely man, as they all were. The locals got to be very fond of them all as I recall.

Another early memory as a young child is my Father "losing it" during the Uruguay game and me quizzing my mother relentlessly as to what these strange unfamiliar new words really were...

— **John Kenealy**

We got our first television when I was ten, so that my dad could watch the World Cup. Even though it was only black and white, it totally changed our lives. We watched snooker (balls in shades of grey), Formula One motor racing, major series like *Civilisation* and *The World at War*, animal documentaries and dramas – *The Forsyte Saga*.

— **Jackie Carpenter**

In 1966 I was thirteen years old and lived in Wembley. Myself and a couple of friends had been "bunking" into the stadium to see various matches for the previous year or so. To the side and fairly high up on the walls besides all the steps leading up to the turnstiles were apertures with what looked like the archetypal prison bars set vertically into them. I assume the apertures were there to let light into the inner stairwells. We found that there was one place where the bars permitted a very tightly-squeezed entry and we always got through those, usually to the cheering of the older supporters queueing up. Once through there was another squeeze through a folding gate and it was just a question of finding a sympathetic-looking official at the bottom of the steps leading into the arena. We did not go to the first game but saw all the other games played in England's group. We also saw the quarter-final against Argentina (when Rattin was sent off), semi-final against Portugal, third/fourth place game and the final against West Germany. For the final there were four of us and we spent the first half sitting high up in a gangway (would definitely get moved nowadays). There had been four empty seats nearby and no one came for them so we occupied them throughout the second half. High up behind the television gantries, on the halfway line.

— **Kevin Hall**

I was competing in a swimming gala in Telford (then known as Dawley) when England played Portugal in the semi-final. I toyed with the idea of crying off from the swimming, but Alan, our volunteer coach, made it clear that no one would have a cold or cough that week! I have memories of confused messages/"chinese whispers" from friends whose other friends had brought along transistor radios when Eusébio scored the penalty. It was a wee while before it became clear that England had not lost. Would that I could say the same about my swimming!

— **Steve March**

I had tickets for the group matches at Goodison, where Brazil was based. After a match that Brazil won, I remember coming away from the ground and seeing Brazilians celebrating in and on cars in the street by hooting horns and sitting on the bonnets. It seemed extraordinary in the rather grey, dull British culture of the time.

— **Stephen Perry**

"Bliss was it in that dawn to be alive. But to be young was very heaven!" That quote from Wordsworth sums up for me the summer of 1966.

I was sixteen. My friends and I had arranged to meet up in Ashbourne, the market town one mile from where I lived with my parents. We usually met on a street corner and then decided where to go. Sometimes the Rec, sometimes around the shops, and sometimes we sat in a pub garden with a lemonade or went to the Green Man, the hotel where my dad worked, and had a free orange squash.

On this particular day, Ashbourne was buzzing with people. More than we had ever seen at that time of day. In fact more than we had ever seen at any time of day. And what's more, they were all MALE. What on earth was going on? There were more young men and boys than we had ever seen in our entire life!

And so the World Cup had come to sleepy Ashbourne with the arrival of the West German supporters who were staying for a month near where the team were staying at the Peveril of the Peak hotel just outside Ashbourne. The next four weeks were absolutely wonderful. Every day we would go to town and hang out with the supporters who were really friendly.

After the first week we decided to go for the bigger fish and so, in our friend's Mini, we headed up to the Peveril to see if we could catch a glimpse of the players. Some of the older girls who were hanging out caught more than that! On Sunday there was always a disco at the Dog and Partridge pub nearby and it was there we encountered members of the team. We danced with them and then had quick snogs outside. I got quite close to a player who was in the final (not THAT close, I was only sixteen) but my friend, who was twenty, got very close to another player, who fathered a child, unbeknownst to him. I think he died forty-odd years later without ever knowing.

By the last week and the final, we had been with the players quite a lot and were told that if they won we would be invited to the party at the hotel. We must have been the only English people who wanted West Germany to win, although deep down I was glad England won in the end really.

— **Brenda Livingston**

I was six. There were nougat bars which cost sixpence and had a free World Cup Willie badge with each bar. The boys at school competed to cover their blazers in these badges. The headmistress made us take them all off for class photos but apart from that she didn't mind them.

— **Pete Green**

I was in the Sixth Form at the time, at St Mary's College, when we were offered the opportunity to watch all the matches held at Ayresome Park, selling ice cream for tenpence a match (fifty pence for post-metrication). I took up the offer and spent each match climbing up and down the stairs in the seating area.

Most of the Middlesbrough supporters were disgruntled at first that we were to only see North Korea and felt that Roker Park had stolen a march on us and would get all the better games. However, after the typical minnows' display against an aggressive Russian team which they lost 0-3, we began to warm to the new Red Devils. The first chants of "Viva Korea" began to appear during the next game with the ground erupting in the last two minutes with NK's equalising goal.

The final game produced good sales of ice cream as I remember it as very warm, though the Italians failed to rise to the occasion. I found myself yelling "Viva Korea" after their goal, only to realise that I was in the middle of a hoard of Italian supporters – I didn't sell any in that section but I did get out alive. The tension, volume and hope rose steadily during the second half, with support for the underdog rising to fever pitch. We even wanted the Russians to win to let NK through to the quarters. The keeper became a local hero for his saves which held the Italians at bay just long enough to give the whole crowd an unexpected feeling of joy.

— **Tony King**

I was thirteen in the summer of 1966, old enough to remember the World Cup clearly but young enough to enjoy pasting newspaper clippings into my *World Cup Willie* scrapbook every day of the tournament. Whether I would have remained so enthusiastic had we been knocked out, I don't know, but by the end of July I had pasted in introductions to each team and reports of every game, and carefully written lists of all the games and results.

Looking through it now, it's the hints of a then unknown future that make me smile most. The first sentence in the *Radio Times* introduction to England, quoting Alf Ramsey, "Yes, England will win the World Cup," echoed in the first sentence of the last article, post-final; the diplomatic "blind eye" to North Korea's flag at the Opening Ceremony; "Greaves has stitches in Leg Injury" after the French game; the list of officials for the final. What also strikes me is the lukewarm assessment of England's performance up until the semi-final, and the beautiful unadorned simplicity of England's kit.

— **Alastair Kidd**

My first memory was how easy it was to get a ticket. I was at Marsh Hill Boys' School in Birmingham. From the top floor we could see Villa Park. One day a few of us went down to the ground and simply went up to the ticket office and bought tickets for the West Germany vs Argentina game. My over-riding memory was that it was the only 0-0 game of the tournament.

I'm now retired and living in France. On arriving here I joined a local veterans' football team. Talking one night I told my tale of going to the World Cup match and another ex-pat turned round and said that he had been at the match. He had travelled from Leicester to see the game.

— **Bill Rhodes**

Went to all the matches on my Lambretta Cento 100cc (and very underpowered) scooter. I lived at home in Edgware and worked in

Harrow. You could buy a foot-long hot dog at the stadium for a shilling (five pence today).

— **Derek Andrews**

I remember being very miffed when we drew 0-0 with Uruguay in the first game, which I watched through a crack in the living-room door halfway down our stairs of our terraced house in Thornton Heath as it was a night game (I was seven).

— **Keith Hoult**

I was five years old and I went on holiday that summer with my family to a Butlins Holiday Camp where I dressed up as the mascot World Cup Willie – and won First Prize. I seem to remember that the prize was a plastic sub-machine gun. There was a tremendous sense of optimism about the future and the "greatness" of the nation. Looking back now it seems an incredibly innocent age.

— **Simon Banks**

I was only ten years old. I met the North Korean team who were staying at a Jesuit retreat next to the school I attended. They stayed at least for a time at Loyola Hall in Rainhill near Liverpool. The school was run by nuns who I remember urged us to be cautious as they were communists. We were told that they had asked for the crucifixes to be removed from their bedrooms. I understand the team presented a chalice to the priests before they left.

— **Steve Johnson**

I was six at the time, and have vivid memories of the run-up to the World Cup as it was when we got our first black-and-white second-hand telly! My two sisters and I were so excited and the day my uncle's friend, Norman, came to install it was like all our Christmases came at once. When the World Cup began, we started scrapbooks and collected tea cards and I became fascinated by all the funny names of the players.

— **Christine Osgood**

I was a young girl living in Sunderland and my friend and I got wolf-whistled by some foreign footballers who were sightseeing in the area. Twenty-odd years later I organised a celebrity golf tournament, Bobby Moore took part, he was the most perfect gentleman, what a marvellous human being he was.

— **Jan Scott-Collier**

I was fourteen, travelling on a bus along Lord Street in Liverpool in the days when buses still travelled from there and along Church Street. I had just finished my exams at school and the weather was scorchingly hot and sunny. The city seemed to be full of exotic people, mostly Brazilians because Brazil and the great Pelé were playing at Everton's ground at Goodison Park. The crowded street seemed to have more than its fair share of handsome dark-skinned men who stood out from the crowd. I remember feeling really proud that my city and my Dad's team's ground were playing host to such important guests.

— **Kathleen Pimlett**

The Soviet Union was playing Hungary in my hometown of Sunderland and several Russians (players or supporters, I don't know) approached us – a bunch of ten year-olds – at the Barnes Park tennis courts. They handed out Lenin badges all round, which, of course, we wore to school the next day.

— **Paul Shapiro**

My Dad somehow managed to get both of us mini-season tickets for the games at Goodison Park. Portugal, Brazil, Hungary and Bulgaria were the Home teams in this group. Fresh from seeing Everton win the FA Cup in May, the thought of seeing such world-class stars as Pelé, Garrincha, Eusébio, Simoes, Beckenbauer and Jairzinho was a dream come true for a fifteen year-old like me. Brazil were the ones everyone wanted to see though and their game against Portugal drew 62,000.

— **Fran Kearney**

I went to two group games at Old Trafford. It was twenty years later that my parents let slip they knew Mr and Mrs Stiles and Nobby, who holidayed at my mum's home farm in Ireland in the early '50s! "Well, it was really only his mum and dad, not Norbert."

— **Ged Parker**

Myself and a mate went to Goodison Park to savour the atmosphere of the World Cup, all the streets around Goodison Park were decorated with bunting and flags amidst a great carnival atmosphere when all of a sudden a drunken old man (probably about my age now) thrust a ticket in my hand for that night's match. Brazil vs Bulgaria, Pelé and all that... Then the dilemma hit home. One ticket and two ten year-old lads, what do we do? Democracy kicked in, we'd have to sell the ticket and split the proceeds between us, which we truly did. After selling the ticket for five shillings and getting blitzed on "Schofields lemonade," crisps and Mars Bars we thought we'd hit the jackpot.

— **Roy Darby**

I watched the opening match, then went off to do my evening's stint as a barman. The bar in question was at a place called Scalby Mills, which is at the northern end of the North Bay in Scarborough, Yorkshire. It was the summer before I went to Uni in the September. I was stacking clean pint glasses on the under-bar shelf, three per hand, hot from the glass washer, when one of them started to topple. No problem, I could nudge it back on with my knee. No, I couldn't. It broke, sending me to get eight stitches across a dazzling white patella and immobilising me for the duration of the competition. As the Buddhists would say, we get the accidents we need...

— **Peter McDonald**

For me the best match of the tournament was the semi-final between England and Portugal. Great goals and unbelievable tension after Portugal had brought the score back to 2-1. But perhaps most remarkable was something else entirely – one of my father's friends, working late in central London that day, had on a whim decided the World Cup semi-final wouldn't be a bad evening's entertainment. So he took a tube to Wembley, paid for his ticket at the turnstile and arrived in the stands about five minutes after the game started. He confirmed what a wonderful game it was but it was the casual nature of the whole thing that always made me marvel. I can't imagine you could have wandered into a World Cup semi-final without a pre-booked ticket on many occasions since!

— **Andrew Cole**

I remember the event simply because I wasn't allowed to watch it. The "men" had the TV and cans of Watney's Party Sevens. The women were sent out shopping for the afternoon – and had to take the children (including me) out with them. So I remember vividly this event that I really wanted to be part of – but was banished from!

— **Jon Keen**

I was fifteen at the time and two of my friends and I went to London for the Stampex exhibition to see the Jules Rimet trophy. It was stolen that night. Friends at school joked that we had stolen it.

We lived in Harlow at the time. Uruguay were staying at a hotel in the town. When the semi-final stage was reached, Portugal moved into the same hotel. Some friends and I walked about two miles to the hotel in an attempt to catch a glimpse of Eusébio and his teammates. I don't know what we expected, but we didn't manage to see anything. I do think, though, given that we were never going to see a match live, it made us feel a little more involved, rather like seeing the Olympic Torch did in 2012.

— **Colin Phelps**

I didn't watch any of it. I recall being out on the window-cleaning round with my dad when the big matches were on but have to say I was completely disinterested as were the majority of my young mod mates at the time. More interested in going to the Mecca Highland Rooms [in Blackpool], listening to and dancing to the latest soul and I think by that time ska records, and trying to pull girls. I was also waiting for my O-Level results. I seem to recall copious amounts of snakebite at this time, which is of course bitter mixed with cider.

— **Graham Jackson**

What an experience, I have many fond memories to this day. I still tell anyone who cares to listen "I was there"! I saw every game at Wembley and one Friday evening game in the rain at the now disappeared White City Stadium. I believe the game was played there to avoid a Greyhound meeting at Wembley, unbelievable! Although it is nearly fifty years ago I still recall the atmosphere, colour and emotions as though it were yesterday.

— **David Payne**

Stuart, Chris and I, staying up at night,
Live the World Cup on the telly
See Hungary, in black and white
Eclipse invincible Brazil and Pelé.

Three students, end of our first year,
My car, an open-top A40,
It's Saturday with time to spare,
We are driving down to Wembley.

A summer's day in Harrow
Looking for a place to park
A suburban street, so narrow,
At least not too far to walk.

We buy our tickets at the gate,
Find standing room behind the goal,
Lots of room to stretch out straight,
The crowd lethargic on the whole.

England are playing Argentina,
The match kicks off at three o'clock
We are said to be much cleaner
But the others are prepared to shock.

A quiet game until half-time
Now there's action we can see
It's all about the Argie captain
Remonstrating with the referee.

These days, players whinge for show,
Then, the small bald-headed ref
Took umbrage, and the whistleblow
Sent Rattin off to football death.

At last England score a goal,
A glancing header by our star
The match won, off we shuffle
Will we be able to find our car?

Fifty years on, I e-mail Chris
How was it for you in sixty-six?
We don't recall any national bliss.
Memory plays the strangest tricks.

   — Patrick Harvey

The Final

I was at a wedding on the day of the 1966 World Cup final. The ceremony was scheduled for late afternoon, which allowed the guests to watch the first 45 minutes of the game. At half-time with the score at 1-1 most of the guests were hooked and, unable to continue watching the game on television, they sat clustered around one of the guests sitting at the back of the church with a transistor radio pressed to his ear. Any attempt to pretend that this wasn't happening was blown away mid-service when the man with the tranny announced England's second goal by bellowing "We've scored!" This outrage was further compounded when the vicar called across to him "Who got it?" I'm not making this up. There was more to come. Outside the church the photographer gathered everyone together for a group shot and called for a cheesy smile at which point a familiar voice came from the huddle, "They've equalised." This resulted in a shot of people turning round in some dismay for confirmation of this. I'm pretty sure that photo didn't make it into the wedding album. What it also meant was that a fair proportion of the guests were missing for the soup course at the wedding reception as they'd sloped off to watch extra time on a telly in the nearest pub. Guess what the only topic of conversation was when the match was over? The bride looked ready to kill.

— **Barry Purchese**

My parents had tickets for the first-round matches at Aston Villa and went into a draw for the finals and got tickets. Dad always insisted that the disputed goal went in because he could see it from where he was in the stand. I took the match programme to school. Everyone wanted to touch it.

— **Chris Yapp**

I was eighteen at the time and remember being on holiday for two weeks prior to the final at what we'd now call an old-fashioned holiday camp. The organiser would announce the dances on match evenings with the phrase – "ladies, enjoy yourselves!" I drove home in a Ford Popular and got in five minutes after the start.

— **Bob Harrold**

The match was played on my thirteenth birthday. I got a new transistor radio for my birthday and as I didn't feel well listened to it in my bedroom. But it became too exciting so went downstairs to watch with my mum and dad so saw the best bits. I'm always so proud to tell people we won the World Cup on my birthday.

— **Jackie Owens**

My dad was at the final and got his ticket because one of his mates had to work on that day. But more interesting – in my view anyway – is that the brother of one of my dad's workmates owned Pickles, the Dog that Found the World Cup.

— **Julie Cattell**

The best day of my life. I found out my girlfriend at the time was not pregnant, saw the game live standing behind the Hurst non-goal end (saw every England game) and then went to Reading to see The Who at an early Reading Festival. Back for Trafalgar Square revelry, then home to my rented Ilford flat.

— **Ian Dewar**

In July 1966, I had just turned twenty-one years old on the 12th of July. I was working in Bradford for J H Langtry Langton as a Junior Quantity Surveyor. We were entitled to two weeks paid holiday and could take these when we wanted. I had chosen the last week in July and the first week in August, which was known as "Baildon and Shipley Tide weeks." For the last two or three years I had been "hitch-hiking" abroad, usually not getting too far but seeing the sights of France, Germany, Belgium and Italy. In 1966 I once again set off, with a mate called Alan Turner, who later was to be my Best Man. We set off to hitchhike to London on the Friday night prior to the day of the final, London was our first destination.

We wanted to watch the game on TV, so at first we thought about standing outside a TV shop. We decided against that and thought maybe of trying to find a pub with it on, but ruled that out as back then pubs couldn't stay open all day and usually closed at 3pm and reopened at 5.30pm, which is when the game was being played.

One of us had the idea of going to Wembley in the hope that as it would be busy, there might be a cafe open with a TV showing the match. So we left our rucksacks/kit bags in a left luggage office at Kings Cross station and got the tube to Wembley station. The train was full of people of different nationalities, many heading for the game.

When we got off at Wembley station and headed down the platform we were approached by men trying to sell tickets for the game. We each bought a ticket but they weren't for the same section, so once we were through the turnstiles, we waited outside one of sections until we found someone on their own who would swap their ticket for one of ours. Someone came along on their own who agreed to do us a favour and we gave him five shillings as an inducement to exchange tickets. So there we were inside Wembley at about 2.30pm and the 1966 World Cup final between England and West Germany was about to kick off.

— **Paul McNicholas**

I was seven in the summer of '66 and we had no TV so we used to walk round the corner to my aunt's house to watch the games. I still have my World Cup Willie badge and can remember all the words to the song "Red, white and blue, World Cup Willie." During the final I was very excited and fidgety and my dad kept telling me to sit still or leave the room! Most of all I remember the unbridled joy of my dear dad and my uncle dancing round the room when we won.

— **David Lloyd**

It was the day we were married in Wilmslow, Cheshire. The service was in the morning and towards the end of the reception the maître d' suggested that if we wanted to watch the second half we should be leaving in about fifteen minutes. My new wife and I went to a friend's house and the rest of the crowd went to my mother-in-law's to watch.

— **David Flower**

I was twenty-one years old, and attended the Final with my father and a group of other Spurs supporters. Dad and I lived near Wembley Stadium, just the other side of the North Circular Road. We'd been to several of the preceding games at Wembley. The atmosphere was fantastic. I remember seeing the Queen for the first time, albeit from a distance. She wore a yellow coat and hat. When it was finished, and we were walking down the outside steps, just in front of us was a German woman and I assumed her two teenage children, a son and daughter. All three were wearing German Rosettes. The woman opened her handbag and without altering pace, took out three red, blue and white England Rosettes. She kept one for herself and handed the other two to her children, they each removed their German ones, which she placed into her handbag, and pinned on the English ones. I thought that they didn't want to be seen as supporting the losing side, which I thought was bad, as West Germany played very well, especially to go to extra time. Many of us walked to The Harrow Tavern, (as it was known then). It was absolutely jam packed, singing and chanting the team's names. My father wasn't much of a drinker, but he had a couple of G&Ts that day.

— **Richard Merlin**

I was seventeen, living in Cornwall. A friend invited me to London to look at the "Modern Architecture." During the day we went to the South Bank and some other places. That evening we watched the 1966 World Cup on a small black-and-white TV. Afterwards we went to Soho and had a meal with this amazing red wine "Bulls Blood," pretty naff by today's standards but all the rage back then. Afterwards I remember walking down the street shouting at some Germans supporters how we had beat them. All good fun.

   — **Adam Purser**

As a young Scot (nineteen years of age) I was living in the Hornsey YMCA in North London during the World Cup in 1966. I watched the final on television in the hostel's viewing room. Myself and a young German were the only two non-Englishmen in the room. Not surprisingly, we were the only two who cheered Germany's goals. At least we had the grace not to boo when England scored the winner, but we did question its legitimacy. Needless to say, we weren't the most popular of the hostel's residents that day.

   — **Bob Hall**

My mother bent down in front of the TV to pick up the tray with the teapot on it just as Germany scored to send the match into overtime...

   — **Tony Locke**

Very strong memory of the anguish of the 2-1 lead, heading for half-time. It felt like an equaliser was coming. Dying for a pee during extra time but refusing to leave the sofa. Then Geoff Hurst smacked in the fourth. I was so impressed the keeper hadn't seemed to move at all, just watched it fly in. Longest pee I can remember followed.

   — **Michael Woodward**

I was sixteen and it was my first holiday without my parents and I went with three school friends to a chalet in Maldon in Essex. It was on the River Blackwater and one of the friends had a dinghy which we sailed. I spent the week of the final looking for somewhere to view the final. These were not the days where every pub in town had a TV and advertised that they showed live football and anyway I was only sixteen and lived in fear that if I ever did go to a pub I would soon be spotted and a policeman would come in and arrest me!

I found a TV shop in Maldon high street that had their TVs fairly close to the door so I stood in the doorway to watch the game. The salespeople didn't seem all that bothered about the game and eyed me with a little suspicion as I stood there and watched. At no point did they invite me into the shop so I could get a better view.

When Geoff Hurst scored the winner I couldn't contain myself any longer and I threw my hands in the air and cheered loudly. I had forgotten that I was in a doorway and I stubbed my thumb on the doorframe directly above my head and recall that it was painful for several days afterwards.

— **Tony Masters**

Eighteen months before the World Cup was to be played around a dozen of us applied for a Book of Tickets – ten games in all including all the England group games. The camaraderie, the joy, the feeling of being free, even for a short time, from the drudgery of our jobs was truly intoxicating. At least eight times our section (to the right side behind the goal – where the players came out) started the mighty "Clap clap, clap clap clap, England" chants and thrilled as the chant swept around the ground. We were witnessing and were part of something so very special. All of us remember every game we saw. Come the final – what a day! Our band of happy lads went to the West End that evening. Shook hands with many German fans. We swam in the fountains at Trafalgar Square and had as many beers as we could afford.

— **Peter Olsen**

I watched it on our TV, but left pretty quickly because I had arranged to meet a boy I fancied in the centre of Birmingham. I was wearing bell-bottom trousers and a skinny rib top – and I think I had a little crochet beret. A woman at the bus stop told me I was sinful for wearing trousers. We were the only ones getting on at the stop but she insisted on sitting next to me. The city centre was eerily quiet until a couple of hours later, when it became very merry. It was the first and last time I had Black and Tans with whisky chasers.

— **Ros Napier**

My dad had a friend in Germany, who got tickets for the final, then couldn't make it – so he took me. I was eleven. We had £5 seats right opposite the royal box, amongst lots of German supporters given the origin of the tickets. They had small German paper flags to wave, with a bear printed on in brown with a red tongue. Every time England scored they threw some on the floor and ground them up. I've seen a quick flash of me in the film *Goal!* as we were just below the camera gantry in the roof.

— **Charlie Hislop**

I was at Wembley with my dad and uncle. We left before the end because my dad was worried about missing the train back to Leeds.

— **Terry Macalister**

I was a student then. It was the end of term, and my family had nobly volunteered to collect me and my luggage from my digs in Birmingham and drive me back home down the then-comparatively-new M1 motorway. We didn't have anything fancy like a car radio to tell us what was going on. It was only when we hit

London – hearing car hooters going off en masse, and then in Central London seeing jubilant crowds capering about – that we realised something spectacular must have happened. A thrill and a bit. Glorious.

— Elisabeth Kimber

I am one of an elite group in my generation. When others recall England's victory in 1966, it is through the phrase "It is now" that they heard uttered live on TV by Kenneth Wolstenholme. But I didn't hear those words until much later, because I WAS THERE. And for any sceptics, I have the tickets to prove it.

— Alan Preskett

I was a seventeen year-old in 1966. I managed to buy a ticket for all the matches being played in London for a cost of just over £4 each! The highlight was of course being able to attend the final and seeing England win. I had been invited to attend my first formal black-tie dinner that evening and was in a quandary whether to stay until the finish as it would make getting to the function very rushed. In the end it was certainly worth staying. After the dinner, where I was by far the youngest guest, the ladies adjourned and I was left with cigar-smoking older gentlemen. I felt very out of my depth until someone asked "Does anyone know who won the football?" I could answer that I had actually been there and share the wonderful story of us winning.

— Geoff Session

1966 was the year in which I became engaged and subsequently married on 16th Sept. However my most exciting day in that year, and probably my whole life, was watching England win the World Cup at Wembley. My first visit to Wembley had been for the Cup Final between Portsmouth and Wolves in 1939. I had been back many times since then for international matches both during and after the war watching stars such as Matthews, Mortensen and Lofthouse. Another memory along the way was England's defeat by Hungary. Nothing however matched the excitement of beating Germany and seeing the Geoff Hurst hat-trick – and to top it off my friend Lawrie at the end of the game producing a bottle of champagne and two glasses just like a magician with a white rabbit out of a top hat.

— Peter Jones

I was eighteen and had just left school in July 1966. I was a keen West Ham supporter and had already been at Wembley in 1964 and 1965 to see West Ham in the FA Cup and European Cup Winners' finals. Bobby Moore was my favourite and had been for several years so it was very emotional to see him take the World Cup for England from the Queen.

The iconic photo of Bobby Moore supported by his colleagues holding the cup aloft is framed and hanging on my wall. And in addition I have the programmes for the three Wembley matches (signed later by Geoff Hurst) framed together with the two rosettes I wore on the day. England & West Ham – a unique piece of history.

My diary for 1966 (which I still have) records the day: "Went with Dave (he was a school friend and had managed to get the tickets) to see World Cup final – England won 4-2 after extra time Geoff 3, Martin 1 & Bobby collected cup – a West Ham final." Later that evening I went with my boyfriend to see *Those Magnificent Men in Their Flying Machines*. The following day another friend (Alan) arrived with all the Sunday newspapers (also recorded in my diary) and I cut out and saved all the articles in a scrapbook.

— Marjorie Hume

I was nine. I watched it at home with my dad and sister. My dad bet me sixpence Germany would win – that's 2.5p in "new" money. A few weeks later I went to watch it again at the cinema with my football friends from school. They turned the whole game into one glorious technicolour film. You don't get that nowadays!

— Charlie Swan

I remember meeting the Spanish team in Erdington, Birmingham when they used the Delta Metals social club in Holly Lane for training, my dad worked at the Delta at that time. We watched the final with my pal Steve on a black-and-white set in our living room. I was eleven. When the last goal went in I remember dad got so excited he upended the settee with me and my mate on it.

— **Gerry Tuckley**

On the morning of 30th July 1966 I was at home looking after my two young children. My husband was getting ready to go to the final by train with his friends. He had been to all the matches. My husband was just leaving when the phone rang. He told me that there was a spare ticket and that this would be a memory of a lifetime for me. I had never seen England play or been to Wembley before. Having got the children ready we left in our car and went to my mother's to leave the children. We parked at Wembley Town Hall and got to the ground just in time. We stood behind the goal and I had a clear view of that goal – the ball was well over the line!! We are avid West Ham supporters and remain season-ticket holders.

— **June Tilley**

After the World Cup my wife June met Bobby Moore on many occasions as our children went to the same nursery school as his and he was often there to pick them up so had many chats with him.

— **John Tilley**

My sister and I were allowed extra money for sweets on the day (usually we had to make our shilling's worth of sweet ration last a week!) probably to help keep us quiet. The clearest memory for me was of Nobby Stiles skipping and the final goal plus my Mum and Dad dancing after the match to a medley of Beatles, Everley Brothers and Elvis records (on the Dansette). The best thing about it all is that my brother who is six years younger than me can't remember it at all! If you have a younger brother, you'll know what that means.

— **Lauren Hughes**

The episode I remember the most (and it's never been seen since) was my quiet mild-mannered dad getting up from his seat when the final whistle went at the end of extra time and running around the house shouting his head off.

— **Joseph Morgan**

I was the only one watching at home. Mum, dad, gran and sister were in the garden as they could not bear to watch it.

— **Graham Stephenson**

We flew from Cyprus to the UK to watch the World Cup at my aunt's house in Grove Park, London. All went well until her walnut-cabinet television developed a faulty tube which reduced the grainy 601 lines of the black-and-white picture to a compressed strip six inches (fifteen cm) high. We decamped to another aunt's home this time in Pontypridd, Glamorgan. I watched all the matches (as a fourteen year-old girl I had never watched football on TV previously) but couldn't bear to watch the final, so I recall making chocolate mousse with my aunt in the kitchen, but could hear the roars and groans coming from the lounge. The results – dessert and the final score – were brilliant.

— **Daisy Fearns**

We watched it on the telly at home. As extra time approached, there was a thunderstorm and my mum insisted on the TV being turned off and the aerial unplugged (given that lightning would strike one house out of millions in south London). We listened to the only World Cup England are ever likely to win on a dodgy transistor radio. With hindsight, I think being struck by lightning has higher odds than an England World Cup win...

— **Gary Messer**

Before the contest started one of my friends said, "If England win the World Cup I'll take off my trousers and shit in the road." Afterwards we were curious to see if he would. As far as I know he didn't.

— **Bob Fox**

I was eleven and watched it on TV with my older sister in Tunstall, Stoke-on-Trent, and remember the great excitement. It was the first and only football match I've ever seen and I suspect that's true for my sister too.

— **Annie Rhodes**

I was only three and a half at the time living in York but my mum wanted England to win and my dad, an American, had put a bet on Germany winning. My only memory is that of my dad laughing and laughing hard when Germany scored at the end of normal time, and my mum punching him over and over on the back, saying "Shut up! Shut up!"

— **Nicholas Alvarez**

I was six at the time and remember most of all my mum turning on the radio about ten minutes after the final finished; first record on: "The taxman's taken all my dough..."

— **Richard Withnell**

My sister and I grew up in Wembley and were aged seven and five respectively at the time of the match. We watched the match with our parents on a black-and-white TV in our parents' bedroom as mum had flu. As soon as the match finished we walked down towards Wembley stadium. The road leading up to the North Circular was lined with people and we joined the cheering and joy when the England team drove past in a coach.

— **Cathy Burnstone**

On this Saturday my father, a lifetime football fan and one-time player, agreed to drive me and three friends to Windsor for the music festival. We were all sixteen at the time. Football? We did no care a jot. The Who were topping the bill. Cream were playing their first set the next day.

In the middle of the music there was an announcement with the result. Greeted by a single cheer. Then the music continued.

My father's memory of the day says it all. "Not one of the miserable buggers even said thank you."

— **Chris Queree**

I was there! With my father, Robert, and my wife Marjorie. Because we had tickets for a West End show that evening we had to leave the ground immediately after the final whistle. Hurrying down to the underground we managed to board the first tube train away from Wembley. Imagine our amazement when we sat down to the cries from the other passengers (at least a dozen or so) of "What was the final score? Did we win?" They had left their seats before the end to ensure they missed the "the crowd."

I wonder what they tell their grandchildren?

— **George Thompson**

From Afar but Still There in Spirit

I was in the Royal Navy and watched it in a pub in North Queensferry, Scotland, just me and the landlord.

— **Ken Coombs**

I watched most of the games on TV but missed the final as I went on my first holiday with a couple of friends camping near Bowness-on-Windermere. That afternoon I remember seeing a couple of brief glimpses of the match in a butcher's shop. My compensation for missing the match was meeting my first serious girlfriend, the beautiful Audrey from Windermere.

— **Ian Pounder**

Having booked my summer holiday months ahead, without thinking for a moment that England had a hope of getting to the final, England vs West Germany coincided with our Dover-Calais crossing. With my friend Richard, we were driving to Italy in his sister's MGB. We found ourselves on deck during a pretty rough crossing listening to the running commentary around a very basic transistor radio with scratchy reception. There were lots of England supporters and a fair number of Germans too. As the game progressed, more and more people congregated around the radio. Half-time coincided with us being halfway across the Channel. The second half was anguish for everybody, accompanied by the fact I was feeling increasingly seasick. More and more beers were being bought by everybody. As we came into the harbour the Germans equalised. Groans all round. When we disembarked we found the guy with the radio and all hung around on the quayside. At one point the radio cut out and we frantically dashed about trying to pick up reception. When England won we all piled off to a local hostelry, probably twenty or thirty of us, our new friends who we met on the boat. We celebrated England's win over several hours at which point we realised we were not in a fit state to commence our long drive to Italy. We hung around to sober up, big smiles on our faces.

— **Peter Lawrence**

I went to Derby Baths in Blackpool as usual on that Saturday afternoon with my friend Marion. We were expecting to meet up with the usual gang and I was particularly looking forward to seeing a boy I fancied but there were no boys there at all. No lifeguards either or indeed any other adults so we amused ourselves by running around and doing all the things normally not allowed. Weirdly magical and certainly unforgettable.

— **Bee Wyeth**

When the World Cup came round my dad bought two books of tickets, one for me one for him. We went to a couple of early games and then I was playing cricket. When England got to the final I got a call saying would I play a cricket match? I was trying to establish myself. Nobody wanted to play this bloody game but I'd do anything for a game of cricket. So I didn't go to the World Cup final. I gave my ticket away to play in a game instead.

My dad went. He was a very straight bloke, a civil servant, liked everything orderly. He didn't like the hassle of queues and things. If we ever went to see a film we'd go in after it had started and sit down to watch it from halfway through to the end and start again until we went back to the bit we started at. It wasn't until I was older that I ever watched a film properly.

My dad, not wanting to get stuck in the crowd at Wembley, left the final with five minutes to go. It was 2-1 when he left. I missed the game for a game of cricket, my dad missed extra time because he didn't like queuing.

Thirty-seven years later, when England got to the 2003 Rugby World Cup final in Australia, it was transmitted back in England at 9 am on a Saturday morning. My little girl had a gymnastics class so we decided to record it, we went off to class trying to avoid everything. We got back and turned on the video. But we had only set it for 80 mins and after that it went cccssshhhhh and turned off. So the only two World Cups England have won, the Selvey family have missed both of them.

— **Mike Selvey**

Driving back from our holiday in north Wales listening in to the car radio a Radiomobile valve set. I got my Dad to flash everyone coming the other way after we won.

— **Richard Jones**

I remember the tournament as a seven year-old. I'd kept my World Cup wall-chart up to date each morning as most of the games were concluded after my bedtime. The real memory though is the final. Come the glorious day my sports-apathetic parents decided the day of the final would be a great day to take my little sister and myself to Chester Zoo as it would be nice and quiet. They were 100% right – we were about the only people there and my grumpiness was compounded by the fact that the animals seemed as fed up as I was at missing the big day.

Ever since, I've not liked zoos. For some people it may be a view based on animal welfare but for me I can't see a lion without thinking of Bobby Moore.

— **David Carrington**

I was fourteen years old. On the day of the final we were going on holiday, driving from London to Southampton, the port where we were to set sail to Lisbon. As West Ham supporters we had an added interest in the match as the trio of Martin Peters, Geoff Hurst and of course Bobby Moore were playing. We listened to most of the game on the radio in the car and reached Southampton ahead of departure with extra time to go. So, we drove hectically around the town, looking for a television shop that had a television turned on in the window, which luckily we found and together with a crowd of other people saw England win 4-2 over West Germany. A super start to our holiday!

— **Clare Handrup**

My dad was eleven in the summer of 1966 and grew up in Ponders End, Enfield, what was then your typical white, working class London suburb. He lived with his two older brothers and his parents in a rather loveless, joyless home filled with mutual unhappiness. So the day of the World Cup final, my dad and several of his relatives are watching the match in the living room on their rented television. (A year later on the 1967 FA Cup final day, Spurs playing Chelsea, a poor sap from the TV rental store came to collect the telly due to unpaid rent. My grandad chased him out the house with an axe. He wasn't the kindest of individuals was my grandad, as you'll see more proof of later.)

The game duly goes to extra time. Now, my grandad at the time did an afternoon paper round and extra time in the game clashed with when he was supposed to be delivering newspapers. What does he do? Goes up to my dad and tells him he has to do it. So it's extra time in the 1966 World Cup final and my dad, age eleven, is delivering newspapers rather than watching the game. He would hear people cheering in their living rooms when England scored which just made him feel worse. He never saw England win the World Cup. He never saw Bobby Moore lifting the Jules Rimet Trophy.

Even now, it's a topic I daren't bring up.

— **Jack Howes**

The day England won the World Cup was the same day that my parents and I were going to Italy on our first package holiday. Needless to say we just made it in time to catch our plane and celebrated with a crowd of young taxi drivers from the East End of London when we arrived in Riccione.

— **Lucille Grant**

I was nine when England won the World Cup. I still remember the day.

My brother and I had the Saturday job of collecting our pre-ordered boxes of groceries from the village shop. As we walked down I commented that the village was strangely silent and deserted. It was a warm summer day but there was nobody in their gardens – not even any cars. The shop was open but the shopkeeper wasn't there. When we called out the old man came running out, bundled the boxes onto the counter then disappeared with hardly a word. When we got home I asked dad what was going on. "Oh, I think it's the football World Cup today," he said. "Oh," I said. And we got on with our normal Saturday things.

— **Andy Williams**

I was on holiday on the Clyde Coast at a place called Millport on the Isle of Cumbrae. I was there with my parents, and unlike me, my dad had little interest in football. Although television was fairly widespread throughout the country back then, Millport was a holiday town and hardly anyone had a television set in their rented property. This wasn't a problem normally. People were active outside most of the time. No one wanted to waste their holiday watching TV.

This year was different, though. We knew that the World Cup was being televised live and a few of us wanted to see some of the games. One particular cafe, the Swiss Cafe, had a television set and people piled in to see the first match, but rather mysteriously, the set went on the blink and never worked again for the entire tournament.

The World Cup was frequently discussed by my holiday mates but we never saw any of it – and then England reached the final. I asked my mum and dad if they knew anywhere that was showing it and eventually they told me I could watch it at a nearby guest-house, but I'd need to be on my very best behaviour. When the big day came, I was ushered into a room where fifteen to twenty people – boys and men – were waiting to see the action. I wanted West Germany to win.

As a twelve year-old, the thing that I became aware of as the goals were scored was the different allegiances of those in the room – all of us Scots. I noticed support for England from the dads, but all the boys desperately wanted England to lose. The adults, like my own dad, had been through a war against Germany. They had stood side by side with their English comrades. There was no way they wanted West Germany to beat England but youngsters like myself just wanted to see our football rival beaten.

— Gordon Semple

It was the last but one day of our caravan holiday in Wales. No television. My father and me and my brother wanted to drive back to our Birmingham home to watch the match. My mum refused to cut her holiday short. Words were exchanged. We had to listen to the match crouched around a tinny transistor radio.

Never mind, we shared in the drama and excitement of an unforgettable occasion. What my mother did I do not remember.

— **Steve Keeling**

Greg and I had Subbuteo that year and had had several World Cup finals of our own. But, this was the real thing. You know those days when you just feel "this is special"... this is a special day. We all crowded into the front room, even grandad Taylor came to watch the match. "Bloody Jerry you can't trust him, he's either at your feet or your throat," grandad quipped. He had been through the first war and saw action at the Somme, just over fifty years before. I loved my grandad. Greg and I lay on the floor, with our hands supporting our chins, we were transfixed.

Extra time came. "Greg, it's time for you to do your paper round," mum said as she went into the kitchen. We just looked at each other; surely mum was having a laugh? We decided to switch into "invisible mode" and simply merge with the carpet, surely mam would forget. It's the World Cup final, its extra time in the World Cup final!

We watched the Germans sitting on the pitch. They were done... surely they were done? Alf Ramsey and the coach told the England lads to get up, stand up, let's show them we are fine, we are English and now we will finish them. Suddenly, piercingly, our peace was threatened... "Gregory... get your bag and get yourself to that paper round." I turned to Greg and said, "Don't worry... I'll tell you all about it when YOU get back from your round." Ooooooops... He turned to mum and said... those immortal words: "It's NOT FAIR!" I was adamant that I was staying put. Then mum turned to me and said, "You can go with him, you'll be back soon, you won't miss much."

And, that is how Greg and I missed England's finest hour. We went, the only two lads in Braunstone... in England... in the World... in the bloody UNIVERSE to miss extra time. Walking up Pollard Road towards the end of the round, it was a ghost town.

Then there was a huge outbreak of sound. England had scored! Some neighbours invited Greg and I in to see the final few minutes of the match. We ran out of the neighbours' house, and ran all the way home. That evening we played and replayed England's World Cup win like thousands of kids. What a moment in time.

— **Adrian Wait**

I was fourteen and saw a lot of the matches on TV. I remember thinking Farkas' goal for Hungary against Brazil was the best goal I'd ever seen. The World Cup final was the day we left for Boys Brigade camp so I didn't see it.

— **Jon Dean**

I was eight and a half months pregnant and as vast as a barrage balloon. My husband and I didn't even know the World Cup final was on – we had other things on our mind, like buying a spin dryer before the baby arrived. So, there we were, in the electrical goods section of our nearest department store when we realised we were completely alone. It was like the *Marie Celeste*. Eventually we came across the staff – all watching the largest TV in the store. They took one look at me and two of them wordlessly wheeled up a huge settee...

— **Jacky Steemson**

I was eight years old and stuck on an extremely hot and cramped coach returning from a weeks' break at a Pontins' holiday camp on the south coast. I remember all the men on the coach with pensive faces trying to catch the commentary on a tin-can tranny drowned out by the growl of a struggling engine. They kept asking the driver to stop for a wee every ten minutes, during which time they crowded around grainy black-and-white TVs in Little Chefs. I think the six-hour journey took about ten that day!

— **Reg Bull**

I was ten years old, and a glasses-wearer since the age of two. A new pair was ready to be picked up at the opticians but I hung on as long as possible watching the final. Eventually the end of full-time was approaching, and dad said I had to go. I trudged through deserted streets to the edge of town, to find a bored optician, who asked me the score. I told him we were losing. "Oh well," he replied, "at least I'm not missing anything."

Back home, again the only living soul on the street, I rang the doorbell. No one came. A second ring, still no response. Yelling through the letterbox, I could hear the excitement mounting. Dad opened the door. "You'll just make the extra time whistle – we've won!"

I push past towards the living room and the black-and-white screen. There are people running onto the pitch. No one even noticed my new glasses.

— **Rosalind Atkins**

I was six, my brother four. We were so excited by all the talk about the World Cup final that, instead of actually watching the game, we played football in the hall with a rolled-up sock. England won the main game, I hear, but there was some debate about who won the game between me and my brother. Probably him because he had a good engine and more of a will to win than me. You can't teach that.

— **Mike Dunne**

Watching From Over Land and Sea

I remember as a teenager in Montevideo listening to the games during class at school (four hours difference from GMT) from an earphone cupped in my hand and artfully connected via my sleeve to a portable Spica in my blazer pocket. The opener was a goalless draw with England (they never could beat us in a World Cup).

The day of the opener we were on a farm (estancia) in upcountry Uruguay, where we woke up to the sound of heavy rainfall. As we were breakfasting in the kitchen the foreman popped his head through the doorway to say, "Doesn't look good for the game, this is going to carry on all day." We all giggled while dad patiently explained that London was thousands of kilometres away, and then invited him to come and listen to the match on the radio with us at midday. Sure enough, he turned up about five minutes before kick-off just as the commentator was informing us that both teams were coming on to the pitch at Wembley under a steady downpour. As he sat down to remove the mud from his boots he gave us children a complicit wink and turned to dad to say: "Told you it was a big'un."

God's truth.

— Kenneth Gilmore

I remember this with such clarity. I was in Lyon, France and my French wife-to-be, Martine, had left the apartment to buy her wedding dress. Her grandmother and I watched the game together sitting on a sturdy sofa bed. Memories of the war and occupation were still raw and everyone I knew in France supported the England of Mini cars, Beatles and Carnaby Street. When Hurst scored that last goal I jumped with delight landing back heavily on the sofa which duly collapsed, splintering in all directions and enveloping "Grandmaman" in a mayhem of wood and cloth. The event became a much-embellished family story.

The wedding took place a few days later and nearly 50 years on survives. Vive la France!

— Bob Moon

My memory of the 1966 World Cup final was from the perspective of a ten year-old football-mad kid living in Singapore, where my dad was stationed with the RAF. We had to listen to the game in the wee hours of Sunday morning on the World Service, by means of a crappy short-wave radio that we owned. No footage of the final reached Singapore for about two or three months, until *Goal!*, the feature film of the '66 finals, was finally released and made it out to Asia. I then finally saw what I had heard on that fateful and brilliant day in July.

Many years later as a young sound technician at the BBC I had the great pleasure of working alongside Bobby Charlton and regaled this tale to him over a game of Subbuteo (which he won with great aplomb). I did however get to deliver the immortal commentary line, "Charlton shoots and Charlton scores" as the greatest No. 9 ever to pull on an England shirt bore down on my goal. Happy days indeed.

— **Paul Kennedy**

In the summer of '66 I was a recently graduated art student with all the prerequisite Left Bank posturing and pretensions (very big at the time). I wasn't that into football, despite having played for my school. French cigarettes (Gitanes), Thelonious Monk and an existential scowl was my thing. Football didn't solve the true meaning of life, man. I was too cool to fool. But it was hard to miss the excitement building around London.

A friend insisted on giving directions in terrible Spanish to a group of Brazilians on the top of the Fulham Broadway bus. They thanked him in excellent English. I hoped England would win of course. But really, did I care? I was off on a soul-searching quest, hitch-hiking around the Aegean to soak up classical antiquity. Was a man throwing a discus superior to a man kicking a ball? Would Praxiteles have chipped out a great Bobby Charlton?

Through the preliminary rounds I had made my way to Athens and admired all the naked goddesses and frozen athletes that I was supposed to admire. My idea was to make the full circle. Istanbul down to Rhodes, across to Crete and back to Athens. I moved on, thumbing my way up to Thessaloniki, where at the Youth Hostel I was warned getting to Istanbul could be dodgy. Enmity between the Turks and the Greeks severely restricted cross-the-border traffic. They were right, the first day I tried there was nothing. I don't mean nothing stopped, I mean there was no traffic at all. The second day a couple of other travellers showed up at my spot, a Swede and his girlfriend. And by the time the flatbed lorry pulled up a Swiss kid had joined us. We climbed onto the back and hung on for life as the beast bounced and sped along the empty pockmarked roads. As the day got hotter we took off our shirts, even the girl, and cooked ourselves in the Aegean sun. For the whole day! It was a very long trip.

By the time we arrived in Istanbul, late afternoon, I was all too aware of my crisply burnt back. The kind of pain that makes you cry without realising you are crying. I could only cringe at the weight of my shirt on my shoulders. The cafes lining the ancient streets were crowded with noisy men huddled at tables, too focused on little transistor radios to notice us. From the ebb and flow of the Ooos and Ahhhs and muted cheers it was obvious they were following a match. I had lost track of the World Cup schedule, and not speaking a word of Turkish, I had no idea who was playing. Then finally there was a unanimous cheer, a thunderous roar as cafes up and down the street erupted. Men jumped from their seats hugging and shouting and waving.

They saw us, me in particular, and with mob instinct immediately focused their frenzy. Was it my long hair? My arty clothes? Then I realised my skin – by now boiled lobster pink – gave me away. Was that good or bad? I couldn't tell when they rushed me, I was too freaked to read their expression. It was only when they began to pound me on the back while jubilantly shouting "Engleesh! Engleesh! Engleesh!" that I understood. Their delight was so great they took my tears and howls of pain to be an English expression of joy.

— **Michael Harvey**

The "morning" England won the World Cup... I was sitting in a room with fifteen or so others listening to the World Service broadcast... in Borneo! It was about 3 o'clock in the morning, ceiling fans whirring, mozzie nets tucked in! We were serving with the Army Air Corps by Kutching airstrip. Twelve years later, I met up with Bobby Moore in Terminal 3 bar at Heathrow. I was on my way to the desert in Abu Dhabi. He was heading for Singapore. Funny old life?

— **Roddy Kyle**

The World Cup final 1966 was not just watched by millions in England, people all over the world cheered England on and celebrated the victory. I was eight years old and my family lived in Paris. We always went to my grandfather's house in deepest rural Brittany (Tremel, population three hundred) for our summer holidays. It was barely twenty years since the German occupation had ended and many families, including mine, had suffered greatly. Needless to say, the *Boche* were not forgiven. The English, on the other hand, were extremely popular, especially in my family.

My grandfather lived in a small house with no running water, but in 1966 he had just had the electricity connected. On the day of the final he hired a black-and-white TV, which was incredibly exciting, for us kids especially. It sat on a sideboard in the kitchen and the whole family (my grandfather, parents, aunts – there were about ten of us) crammed into this room and sat on wooden benches to watch the game.

England's goals brought screams of delight, my normally very severe grandfather, my parents, my aunts, all jumping up and down, hugging each other, clapping and laughing. I remember this so well, because I had never seen my entire family so happy, and so united. However, when Germany scored the second time, one of my aunts left the room in floods of tears. She didn't come in again for ages, but she was standing outside listening, I could see her through the window. When the third goal was awarded by the Soviet linesman, we totally knew it was for all the Russians who had died in the war – there were cries of "Bravo les Russes!"

I had not experienced anything like it before. It got me and my brother into football.

— **Sophie Tarassenko**

The game wasn't shown live in Canada. Rather, we had to wait till later in the day to see the tape. I settled down in front of the TV to watch; five minutes before kick-off the phone rang. My mother said, "Hello, Willie, isn't it wonderful about England winning the World Cup!" Her and her bloody radio.

— **William Moore**

Meanwhile… in Germany

What a year 1966 was, I was sixteen, just left school and got my first girlfriend (or should I say she got me!). Then, big blow, my father was posted to RAF Rheindahlen at HQ RAF Germany, where I got a temporary job in the NAAFI, stacking shelves. I had never been interested in football, but everyone at work was trying to watch the World Cup final in the stock room on a small, grainy, black-and-white TV. When England actually won the Cup, I joined in the celebrations and was sacked soon after. That evening, to mark England's win, myself and some friends went into the local town of Mönchengladbach and put washing liquid in the fountains. Such fun!

— **Ken Cross**

I watched the final in a bar in Germany with my mate Geoff. We were students hitch-hiking around Europe and were trying to get to Denmark to watch it, when someone told us – and I never found out whether or not this was true – that it was not being shown live there. The bar was packed. We were the only English people there and the atmosphere was quite hostile. We couldn't understand why the place erupted when the white shirts scored. We then realised that England must be playing in the dark shirts! (The television was both small and black-and-white.)

The bar emptied a bit when England took the lead in extra time, and once the last goal went in it emptied completely. By the end, there was only Geoff, me, and three Norwegians who joined us for a celebratory beer – not as easy as it sounds as the solitary barmaid was sobbing her heart out behind the bar!

When we left, there was a major traffic jam and a group of British soldiers – not exactly on their first drink of the day – were doing their bit for Anglo-German relations by walking up and down the road banging on car roofs and shouting out the score.

— **John English**

On the day I was sixteen and with a Venture Scout group camping in West Germany near Freiborg. We found a local inn with TV and took over a section of the bar to watch the final as we had done to watch the semis. When Hurst scored that disputed goal there was a bit of reaction from the other customers but apart from that the reaction was always friendly towards our group and philosophical about the result.

— **Laurie Goldberg**

I was on my first trip abroad on a school coach trip to Belgium and Germany. 30th July was my eleventh birthday and we were staying at a hotel in Konignswinter on the Rhine. The tour schedule for the 30th was a visit to the Drachenfels and on the way back the German coach driver had the radio tuned in to the final. There was a communication problem and by the time we got back to the hotel we believed that England had lost the final 3-2. It was only the next day that we found out the truth. Maybe the coach driver was scared of being mocked by a bunch of unruly school kids.

— **Steve Carroll**

My school had a Scout group. In 1966 we were camping in Bavaria, hardly following the World Cup. It was the 70th Birmingham Scout group based at King Edwards School. We were camping near Mittenwald. On the day of the final we went to a local hostelry to watch the match. The Germans were very generous and came over to shake our hands when the final whistle went. The next day a couple of them came and challenged us to a game of football. There was quite a crowd the following day to see us play. We lost 0-3. They felt they had restored German pride (in a friendly way). We didn't tell them that at our school, we did not play football. Rugby was our game.

— **John Sommer**

I was a fifteen year-old on holiday in Germany for the duration of the World Cup. I saw the final on a black-and-white TV in a bar in Michelstadt. I went outside at the end and the whole village was quiet, and I of course celebrated. The shutters opened and heads looked out, "Englander!" they all shouted. Great fun.

— **Mike James**

My friends and I were travelling in Germany at the time in a little red Mini and it had a GB plate on it. We were South Africans but had hired the car in the UK. When we came to the Austrian border there was a long queue but when someone spotted our GB plate there was much cheering and we were invited with a loud cheer to join the head of the line! This was in spite of the fact that we four girls were blissfully unaware of the World Cup, were not football fans and not British. We kept quiet however and gratefully accepted the accolades!

— **Judy Hargraves**

I travelled through Germany on a train on the day of the World Cup final. I was nineteen in 1966 and had left my home city of Sheffield busy erecting flagpoles for the World Cup along the front of Sheffield Wednesday's Hillsborough stadium. I didn't give them a second glance. Football bored me silly, still does. I was doing something far more exciting; off to join a group of complete strangers in London for an international youth working holiday in East Germany, or the GDR as I quickly learned to call it. Behind the Iron Curtain! That sounds such an obsolete phrase nowadays but then it caused a real frisson of apprehension and disbelief when I told people where I was off to. It was part of Project 67, organised by CND to promote friendship, peace and understanding between young adults.

It certainly promoted that along with muscles and exhaustion as we worked twelve-hour days on a collective farm a few miles from the Polish border alongside others from the USSR, Sweden, Denmark, Malta, and other places I've forgotten. Collapsing onto our bunk beds when we got back at the end of the day we found to our dismay that a relentless programme of social and political education awaited us. A quick shower and meal of some variety of sausage and potatoes and we were off again. We visited schools, factories, nurseries, coal mines ("the first socialist nursery," "the first socialist coal mine…").

The trip was a powerful experience which did lead to friendship and understanding, but it was the journey home that I remember so clearly. We travelled back on a train through West Germany on the day of the World Cup final. The football enthusiasts in our group were glued to their transistors, as indeed were most of the other passengers. There was just the small problem that we were on opposing sides to each other. International friendship, peace and solidarity were suddenly off the agenda. Naked nationalism just as quickly took their place. As the match progressed to its conclusion the entire train could be heard to groan collectively. Sobbing on manly German shoulders took place.

Our football enthusiasts were beside themselves, until the more savvy members of our party picked up on the vibe coming towards us in waves from the other passengers. It was clear that things could take a nasty turn as some male passengers got up and advanced towards us shouting. I didn't need to understand German to get the drift. We beat a tactical retreat and regrouped in another carriage. But feelings were running high throughout the train and we silently communicated with each other that speaking English out loud was not a great idea. We spent the rest of the journey through Germany in complete silence nervously looking over our shoulders for any looming German football supporter. It was a genuinely threatening situation to be in.

Several weeks spent working alongside Germans and others, sharing experiences, learning about each other's life and countries, making friends, all gone, all wiped out by ninety minutes of football. So yes, I do remember the 1966 World Cup, and the lesson I learned on the homeward journey has stayed with me over the years. So has my intense dislike of football.

— **Chris Scarlett**

I am from Germany and my family bought a TV just for the World Cup. My grandma could not grasp the concept of people on a screen and insisted that we all put on our Sunday best just in case the people inside the TV could see us. When it came to the end of the game and Germany lost we heard an almighty row next door. Our neighbour had thrown their TV out of the window, followed by various bits of furniture. The wife and kids were crying and so everybody came out of their houses trying to help and calm down the very irate TV thrower.

Six years later I married an English man and have lived in the UK ever since. I watch the final whenever it's replayed on TV enjoying these memories, realising that the rivalry between England and Germany has never really stopped. It's just a game?

— **Aggie Smith**

In 1966 I was living in West Berlin, my sister lived in East Berlin. I was a frequent visitor to East Berlin, with my British passport I could easily obtain a 24-hour visa at Friedrichstraße border crossing. From Friedrichstraße I took the S-Bahn to Schöneweide station, from there I walked to Oberschöneweide to my sister in Fontanestraße. As I did on this particular Saturday but there was no one in the streets. Oh, yes, it's Cup Final Day.

I found Sonja, my sister, Kurt, her husband, and Hilda, from Bridge – forerunner of the Britain-GDR Society (this was before the GDR was recognised by Britain) – in the sitting room watching the game. I joined them, supporting England, of course. Hilda, who was over from London, gave me a dirty look when I got excited during the singing of "Rule Britannia." It makes me cringe now thinking about it, it didn't at the time. Come to think of it, we weren't really supporting England, we just didn't want the other side to win.

Heads kept popping round the door at regular intervals: "How are we doing?" answered by the refrain "We're not in it," which of course "we" weren't, it was the West German team playing.

— **Irena Fick**

And Now, Fifty Years On

Our parents decided television in the home was stultifying for children. It must have been halfway through the 1966 World Cup coverage that despite this they decided watching the games would be educational. They went out and bought what was probably one of the first portable TVs so that we could "watch England win." I'm not sure what was the most amazing: England winning, or a box in the corner of our sitting room.

Once the tournament ended, the TV went up into the attic, to come out about three years later, so that me and my brothers could witness a man walking on the moon.

— **Diane Mathewson**

My grandad was there, behind the goal where Geoff Hurst thundered in the fourth. My grandad's name is Dennis Wells but he is affectionately known to everyone as Wilbur. He has dementia now so not too many clear memories. I do recall asking him why he never kept the programme. He gave it to a little boy outside Wembley who couldn't get in.

— **Jordan Conte**

In 1966 I was at boarding school. My exams were over but the school didn't break up until sometime in the week of the 18th July. I pleaded extenuating circumstances to go home a few days early;

my mother was away and my father – a GP – needed someone at home to take messages from patients. It was exciting to have football on the television every day, see all these different countries although the commentator would remind you who was playing from left to right across your screen as there was no colour TV then. At the start of the final there was just my ten year-old sister and I watching. However by the time the second half progressed I think all my three sisters and both parents were watching. The injury-time equaliser drained us all.

There was for me a sad sequel to that weekend which many have forgotten. As a family we used to go every August to the Roseland Peninsula in Cornwall. On the Monday following we learnt of a pleasure-boat disaster off the Cornish coast costing many lives. For some people that victory sadly was the last bit of joy they would have known.

— **Richard Carton**

I was sixteen in 1966 and went with my dad to the group games at Goodison and the final at Wembley. I have three abiding memories.

First, we got one of our two tickets for the Final through a lottery. Everyone who went to the group games was part of the draw to qualify for a final ticket. What could be more democratic? What could be further away from the football of today?

Second, I saw two unforgettable games that were symbolic of the time. One was Hungary's defeat of Brazil and in particular the goal scored from a cross on the right wing. I was in line with the winger and the forward in the centre who together conjured up one of the best moves I have ever seen. The other game was the remarkable recovery of Portugal against North Korea. Eusébio worked miracles to overcome a 3-0 deficit and became one of my great heroes.

Third, the final. A great match which for us began with a Wembley steward willing to let my dad and me into the same enclosure, despite having tickets for different parts of the ground.

Perhaps the oddest part of the day was that, for reasons I cannot explain, my dad decided to support Germany and wore a German rosette. I acted as if I did not know him on the journey to and from the ground!

All in all, football experiences that have remained amongst the most vivid of my life, matched only by just escaping being crushed in Block Z at the Heysel nineteen years later.

  — **Michael Shackleton**

In 1966, aged fifteen, I was at Villa Park to see Argentina, including the notorious Rattin, beat Spain (Gento, Suarez and all) 2-1, but watched the rest, including the final, on TV. When I came to Azerbaijan as an English teacher in 2000, one of the first thing my students were anxious to talk to me about was the great Tofiq Bahramov's role in the 1966 final – of course, like most other people, I'd assumed the famous linesman was Russian.

I didn't meet Tofiq but, with my Azerbaijani wife Saadat, I interviewed his son Bahram, and held the golden whistle that his father was presented with. In the action pictures that Bahram keeps with pride, his father is invariably smiling, enjoying the game, a fan of football. "What was in his soul was on his face," is how his family remembers him.

  — **Ian Peart**

I drew World Cup Willie for my friends. I grew up to be a graphic designer.

  — **Joseph Scerri**

My brother was in Aden at the time. When the Post Office issued World Cup stamps overprinted with "England Winners" they quickly sold out in England and were attracting a premium from collectors. BFPO in Aden however had plenty in stock so my brother was able to source a lot of them and the sales earned enough to keep us both in beer money for many months.

  — **Ken Smith**

It was the first thing that really bonded my father and I together.

— **Legh Davies**

Never forget my wedding anniversary – married on the day that England won the World Cup!

— **David McInally**

I was six and my brother ten. Our dad took us to the England vs Mexico game. I remember waving my Union Jack flag lots. That summer we went on our first foreign holiday to Tangier in Morocco flying from Manston airport on an Air Ferry DC6. Our hotel was in the middle of the souq and when the local kids found out we were English they just shouted "Bobby Charlton, Bobby Charlton" at us.

— **Ric O'Connor**

I got married in March 1966. Winning the World Cup was the best wedding present I had. It was just wonderful the feeling I had for Alf Ramsey who proved all his critics wrong. I have the greatest admiration for Bobby Charlton for his achievements in football, his demeanour and his part-tragic history. I love that man and he doesn't know it.

— **Len Sugarman**

I was born during the match; my dad watched it and mum was a bit fed up because she couldn't.

— **Mrs Maxted**

I was born the day after.

— **Simon Turner**

They Thought It Was All Over

Mark Perryman

"**S**OME PEOPLE ARE ON THE PITCH…" There you have it in the words of the most famous English sporting commentary of all time: the definitive proof. Never mind the dispute over the third England goal – did it or did it not cross the line and why did the linesman think he could tell from at least fifty yards away? – the fourth and final goal is scored by Geoff Hurst while an England pitch-invasion is underway. It is now? No referee on earth should have allowed a goal under such circumstances. To question the status of '66 isn't to devalue or undermine it. 30.07.66 remains English football's greatest ever moment, winning a World Cup in whatever circumstances in whichever era remains no mean feat and absolutely deserves to be celebrated as such. It is however the fifty years afterwards of only once coming close again and mostly nowhere near close that elevates '66 to such lofty heights.

The future though could wait on the morning after the 4-2 the day before. "Health Minister's Dilemma", screamed the front-page headline of the *Sunday Telegraph*, edition dated 31 July 1966. Ian Waller, the paper's political correspondent, reported: "The Government's freeze on incomes and prices has already provoked an acute Ministerial conflict and brought the Minister of Health, Mr Kenneth Robinson, to the brink of resignation." Meanwhile in other news "London Goes Wild After England's 4-2 Cup Triumph." Not quite the overblown treatment for England's post-1966 under-achievers say beating Switzerland or Croatia, and qualifying for a Euro or World Cup, getting out of their group, making it to the quarter-finals, and the rest of the football fare we've become used to accepting as good as it gets. On the sports pages of the same edition, "That slim gold cup is ours" has to compete for space with a report on George Scadgell having a successful bowls tournament, Warwickshire playing well against Worcestershire in the County Championship, and all the thrills of the first day of racing yachts at Cowes Week.

I grew up devouring my parents' early-morning copies of the *Daily Telegraph* and *Daily Express* with an overly precocious interest in news, politics and sport. But this particular front page I have no distinct memory of. Rather I'm reliant on a facsimile edition given away at a local newsagents a decade and a bit ago, to coincide with England at France '98 if I remember correctly, just in case any of us were in danger of forgetting what happened in '66. Fat chance.

Of 1966 I have precious few memories. I was six and a half at the time though strangely enough it was the death of Churchill the year previously that did stick in my then five year-old's memory. My father was of the wartime generation, a Sergeant Instructor in the RAF, my middle name is "Alan" after his best pal, one of the Battle of Britain few to whom we owed so much. My sister, Penelope, seven years older, went up to queue with my father to show their respects where Churchill's coffin resided. It was a momentous occasion for so many, a kind of passing on from the post-war era to something new. A year later not only '66 but also the landslide victory of Harold Wilson's Labour Party with all the promise of a "white-hot technological revolution" combined to usher that changing era along. And another year on there was the '67 Summer of Love, swiftly followed by '68, the Tet Offensive, "London, Paris, Rome, Berlin, We Shall Fight We Shall Win," the Civil Rights Movement, Women's Liberation, the Prague Spring. Meanwhile for some the events of May '68 consisted of a Red Army victory over a colonial power of a quite different sort – Charlton, Law and Best spearheading Man United's defeat of Portugal's Benfica. Eusébio's return to Wembley an unhappy 4-1 thrashing, with United the first English club side to lift the European Cup.

Politics, economics, the cultural and the social, what's an -ology got to do with celebrating the fiftieth anniversary of 1966? More than some might imagine. As World Cup 2010 came to an end, a great road trip across huge expanses of South Africa, spoilt only by the intermittent and incontrovertibly pitiful performances of the England team, I popped into see *Halakasha!*, an art exhibition celebrating all things African football. One of the panels accompanying the exhibits carried these words from Prishani Naidoo: "The field of play football produces stretches far beyond the boundaries of its goal posts and pitches – fields of play that sometimes bring into question the 'taken-for-granted', 'the natural', the ways in which 'we are meant to be' in society." Naidoo was using the self-same notion as C.L.R. James a generation earlier in his classic book on Caribbean cricket, *Beyond a Boundary*. The touchline representing not where the pitch ends but where the game's impact begins. On the day of England's final group game against Slovenia in Port Elizabeth, I'd picked up a special edition of the *Sun* printed in South Africa which illustrated the point perfectly. This must-win match was being played twenty-four hours after George Osborne's first Budget speech as Chancellor in the Con-Dem coalition. The *Sun* front page had it all hopelessly mixed up, "Action over Nation's Crisis... Recovery Masterplan Revealed... Taxing Time Ahead For All... Country Must Pull Together... Heskey Could Be on the Bench."

The best World Cup film ever features not England's '66 victory but Germany's in '54. This was a truly epic performance, West Germany still reeling from the war, an amateur team, 0-2 down in the final to Puskás and his Hungarian Mighty Magyars who a year previously had famously thrashed England 6-3 at Wembley, 7-1 in Budapest (not to mention West Germany 8-3 in the tournament's earlier group stages). The Germans came back to win 3-2, the story celebrated in Sönke Wortmann's film *The Miracle of Bern* released in 2004 for another fiftieth anniversary. The film depicts a nation coming to terms with defeat, division and slow progress towards global rehabilitation. West Germany and Japan banned from taking part in both the 1948 London Olympics and 1950 Brazil World Cup. After the joy of winning the final against all reasonable odds the closing credits of the film draw this most remarkable story to a close. "A year later the last prisoners of war came home... At the same time the German Economic Miracle began... The Bern Eleven never played as a team again." With such an ending the film locates the legend of '54, the greatest upset of any World Cup final, absolutely in those twin themes of a divided and despised nation restoring its self-belief and this being expressed more than anything else via economic recovery on the scale of the miraculous. See, it's not just a particular fraction of the football-obsessed English liberal left intelligentsia who make these kinds of connections.

It is from such quarters that for me comes the single best quote to explain why '66 does matter – the words of historian Eric Hobsbawm: "the imagined community of millions seems more real as a team of eleven named people." Hobsbawm explains his line of analysis by recounting a childhood growing up as an English expat in 1920s Vienna listening with dread alongside Austrian school-friends to an Austria vs England international on the radio. The dread was caused by the fact he knew any England goal would result in blows being rained down upon him. Luckily for him the game remained scoreless. But it clearly didn't prevent the idea forming in the young Hobsbawm's mind, adding a final sentence to his line of thinking decades later: "The individual, even the one who only cheers, becomes a symbol of the nation himself."

To date 1966 is not just the only year England has won the World Cup but also the only time England has hosted it. One of my few memories of this greatest of years was being bought a *World Cup Willie Pocket World Cup Guide* from Short's newsagents in Tadworth, Surrey as an after-school parental treat. For some reason the one page that has stuck with me was a picture profile of Just Fontaine, the French striker who held (and still holds) the record for the most goals scored in a single World Cup, an astonishing thirteen at Sweden '58. I was certainly not aware enough to make any comment at Willie's attire on the cover. World Cup Willie was one of those fabled three lions, dressed in a singlet with the flag of the host nation splashed across it. Except it wasn't. The one and only time England get to host the World Cup and the FA managed to get our flag wrong, St George replaced by the Union Jack of Great Britain. It's a case of mistaken national identity few Scots were likely to make even back then, the "Battle of Britain" Home Nations match at Wembley a year later with Scotland triumphing and promptly crowning themselves World Champions ample enough proof of that. The Welsh likewise have been comfortable with their own national footballing identity dating back to at least the 1960s too, though without the subsequent World Cup appearances the Scots could boast and be bolstered by. There is no obvious Welsh equivalent of the "Tartan Army" though the pride and passion in following their own *national* team is just as potent despite that. The Northern Irish for a while suffered from a similar confusion to the English, the Unionist baggage of all things red, white and blue a vital part of their self-definition in the face of Irish Republicanism; but this melted away too when Northern Ireland qualified for World Cups '82 and '86 and became a "Green and White Army" of their own that was certain of being anyone but England.

Today the English St George has entirely replaced the Union Jack of '66 and thereafter as England fans' flag of choice. But it took a long time coming and elements of this mistaken identity persist. Pictures from Italia '90 of England fans, just about the halfway point towards the fiftieth year of hurt, show the Union Jack was still the dominant flag supporters flew, wore, hung. It took another six years, thirty years on from '66, and England hosting Euro '96, for the fashion to change. This time round, perhaps aided by the fact that unlike in '66 Scotland managed to both qualify and be drawn in the same group as England, the FA dressed the tournament in the St George's Cross flag of England. More broadly the pressures towards breaking up Britain had already begun too. Blairist New Labour was a year away from their 1997 General Election landslide but riding high in the polls, and with John Major's Tory administration clearly on its last legs Labour had pledged to offer Scotland and Wales an almost immediate referendum on devolution once the election had been fought and won. Unsurprisingly then, a Union Jack would no longer do to dress our support for England in. England's successful run to the semis featured a barnstorming thrashing of Holland 4-1, arguably England's best tournament performance since '66 and at Wembley too, plus a never-to-be-forgotten settling of his Italia '90 demons when this time Stuart Pearce put his penalty away in the quarter final shoot-out against Spain. But it was the game with Scotland, the first competitive encounter since the long-abandoned Home Internationals last played in 1984, that would for many England fans not only define their tournament but their identity too. With "Three Lions on a Shirt" providing that summer's English anthem and an England shirt our national dress, a distinct Englishness was emerging that was barely discernible in those grainy black-and-white shots of the '66 crowds. In 2002 this was a process awarded official recognition when the England home shirt for World Cup 2002 incorporated for the first time a subliminal St George Cross in the shape of a single vertical red stripe.

The period 1996-2010 marked England qualifying for every summer tournament they entered, with the only failure Euro 2008. England made it to semis, quarters, last sixteen in every one except Euro 2000, but even there the thirty-four years of hurt were temporarily ended with England defeating Germany, even if both were knocked out at the group stage, a poor England team beating an even worse German one. Captained by David Beckham for a decent chunk of this period, this was a team that at World Cup 2002, Euro 2004 and World Cup 2006 with Sven-Goran Eriksson in charge promised just enough to keep the hope of something better next time when the plucky exit in the quarters started to become an unwelcome habit. In parallel Britain was experiencing as close as we'd got to a break-up even if the constitutional details were yet to be sorted out. Northern Ireland for as long as most of us could remember had been a different polity to the mainland, the principle fissure being Unionism vs Republicanism rather than Tory vs Labour that we were used to. Now the same was happening in Scotland via the civic national-ist and broadly social-democratic Scottish National Party just as new Labour beat a headlong retreat from anything resembling its Labourist past, never mind socialism. And to a lesser extent a similar process occurred in Wales, too, with Plaid Cymru increas-ingly positioning itself as Labour's leftish critics. On the pitch this resurgent Englishness kind of came to a grinding halt at the hands of a humiliating German defeat, 4-1, which knocked England out at the Group 16 stage at World Cup 2010 after a deadly dull Eng-land campaign to squeeze past Algeria and Slovenia and finish second to the USA in the group. Things improved at Euro 2012 with the more customary quarter-final exit to eventual finalists Italy. But caught between the London 2012 hoopla and Wiggoma-nia following his *Le Tour* win scarcely anybody noticed England were back to their modest best. In the Sunday night annual TV extravaganza that the BBC Sports Personality of the Year awards have become, England's Euro 2012 barely merited a minute such was its obvious insignificance to a sporting year that was decid-edly Team-GB British, with Wiggins sporting a mod-era Union Jack roundel on his bike and cycling jersey.

As the 2000s came to a close then the biennial splurge of St George began to ebb, reaching perhaps its lowest point in the summer of World Cup 2014. In November 2013 captain Steven Gerrard, after the first back-to-back home defeats since 1977, had declared with an admirable dose of optimism, "There's not too much expectation and pressure on us. I'm sure that will help us." The following June however England managed to exceed even the lowest of expectations, going out at the group stage with just a single point, the worst performance since England's first appear-ance at a World Cup in 1950.

In the early 2000s the biennial football tournaments, Euros

and World Cups, had promised so much, even if the final score confirmed those epic words in the English comedy *Clockwise* from John Cleese: "It's not the despair, I can take the despair. It's the hope I can't stand." Outside of football there was a Rugby World Cup in 2003, the Ashes at home in 2005 and 2009, and down under in 2011 – all in the name and colours of England.

It was off the pitch and wicket in the 2000s however that developments took place which would ensure a resurgent Englishness. In 1988 Jim Sillars had spearheaded an earlier surge in SNP support as the party's victor in the dramatic Govan by-election, overturning a rock-solid Labour majority of 19,509 with an astonishing 33.1% swing. This was an era when Scotland would still qualify for most, if not all, summer tournaments: Spain '82, Mexico '86, Italia '90, Euro '92, Euro '96, and France '98. And since Spain '82 the Scots support went out of its way to define itself as anything but British, never mind English. In his book *Football: A Sociology of the Global Game*, academic Richard Giulianotti has a neat way of explaining the actions of his fellow countrymen:

> An important aspect of the Scots' new carnival identity was their cultural nationalism, specifically their desire to differentiate themselves from the English. During the 1980s, as the English became notorious for hooligan behaviour, the Scots adopted a simple binary opposition when presenting themselves abroad: they were 'Scottish fans not English hooligans'.

All well and good, but with the SNP failing to make any kind of electoral breakthrough in the 1992 General Election, when Sillars lost Govan, Sillars derided the Scots supporters as "ninety-minute nationalists." By the 2000s the situation was reversed. No Scottish team has qualified for a Euro or World Cup since 1998 while support for the SNP has rocketed. Those "ninety-minute nationalists" of Jim Sillars' imagination had turned their attentions outwards, beyond the touchline, their nationalism now a full-time pre-occupation.

South of the border, despite the worst efforts of some, there remains no obvious political expression of English nationalism outside of England's increasingly feeble summer campaigns. Without Hobsbawm's "team of eleven named people" we'd be hard-pushed to come up with a convincing example of a public face of Englishness; it is a national identity being shaped by an otherness north of the border.

In '66, World Cup Willie got away with wearing the wrong flag unscathed. When England lined up against West Germany in that year there was a scarcely a murmur of discontent when England's National Anthem was belted out as part of the pre-match pleasantries. It was ever thus. England, home or away, the only football team that doesn't have its own national anthem. Eh? *God Save the Queen* is of course the anthem of the United Kingdom. Most former British Empire countries when they become independent promptly junk it, while Scotland and Wales have jumped the gun and dropped it already. England cling to an anthem which isn't even its own as a source of great comfort, despite getting the words wrong on every occasion I've heard it sung at a game. The lines, according to my dog-eared copy of George Courtauld's *The Pocket Book of Patriotism*, are "God Save the Queen," most certainly not "God Save Our Queen." A pedant writes? Or is a not-too-subtle point being made, if half the Commonwealth and an indecent chunk of the Scots, Welsh and Northern Irish no longer care very much for the Windsors and their public-subsidised hangers on we'll have them to ourselves thank you very much. Long to Reign Over Us? Happy and Glorious! Enough said, though I prefer to hold fast to the notion that there's an alternative Englishness lurking in the margins whose anthem topped the charts eleven years on from '66. "The flowers in the dustbin" of the Sex Pistols' version, "and there is no future in England's dreaming."

Football, imagined communities, framing a national identity. World Cups provide a global platform for this potent mix. 1966 was one stop on that journey. There simply isn't any single other means of providing such a ready and universal means to explain national identity and cultural globalisation as football. In the 1960s when the sport didn't enjoy the kind of planet Earth popularity it enjoys now, a case could have been made for rock music; or at various times in history the rules of mathematics and scientific formula, though both are largely accessed by national and international elites rather than the people. World religions? No one religion unites the globe, instead of course the opposite applies, they serve to divide instead. American author Franklin Foer summed this up in his handy book *How Soccer Explains the World*, subtitled "an unlikely theory of globalisation." Foer points to the irrefutable evidence; the players on the pitch, in the technical area the managers, coaches and backroom staff, the ownership of the bigger, and some smaller, clubs, the audience in the stands and via TV, club and national team tournaments, the exchange of playing styles and tactics. In European terms never mind the Euro, the single cultural currency is without doubt football. In global terms no international governing body comes close to FIFA in terms of its purchase on foreign affairs populations actually give a damn about. The United Nations doesn't even come close.

Foer makes a key point about soccer (sic) and culture: "Of course, soccer isn't the same as Bach or Buddhism. But it is often more deeply felt than religion, and just as much a part of the community's fabric, a repository of traditions." It is in this sense that '66 comes to mean so much alongside the five decades of Britain in the twin processes of decline and separation.

My other memories of 1966, apart from that World Cup Willie tournament handbook, are next to non-existent. My father was a member of our village horticultural society and on a World Cup Saturday the Kingswood, Walton and Tadworth Horticultural Society held their flower show. I was daddy's little helper checking tickets on the gate, nobody came, and it rained. That Saturday World Cup football meant nothing to this particular rain-soaked six year-old. As for the rest I can't recall. What stuck more in my mind were two great British, or should that be English, historic anniversaries. The three-hundredth anniversary of the Great

Fire of London was the cause for a huge firework display on the River Thames and a rare Perryman family outing by car to the capital to get a good view from the riverside. The nine-hundredth anniversary of 1066 was celebrated with a set of special stamps and the start of my childhood First Day Cover collection. A year of anniversaries; at the time few would have thought along the lines of Franklin Foer to put a mere football match, of whatever stature, alongside events of such historic significance. Fifty years later, for better or worse, his observation borders on the new common sense.

By the time of Mexico '70 garage forecourts had become a battleground for collectables, not that we called them that at the time. Fill up with enough petrol and get all manner of goodies to complete collections. The Esso offer was "The 1970 World Cup Coin Collection." I've still got mine, the greats from '66, Banks, the Charlton brothers, Moore, Hurst and Peters alongside the thrusting new stars with Leeds United to the fore – Allan Clarke, Terry Cooper, Norman Hunter, Mick Jones and Paul Reaney. Leeds were in their pomp, Division One Champions the previous season 1968-69, runners-up to Everton 1969-70. They lost the FA Cup final that year, too, the first I can properly remember, to Chelsea, and a historic Cup Final too because it was the first to be settled by a replay. The World Cup? My memories are only slightly better, the final watched live in colour on the TV, another first, round a friend, Grant Ashworth's, house.

Fragments of childhood memories, a mix of history, family, changes in consumption, technological developments affecting how we enjoyed our leisure time, a sense of some kind of north-south divide played out on a football pitch. Flash Chelsea, most of whose first team seemed to live in the leafy suburbs just like me, versus a Leeds of grainy, hard-faced northern-ness. Then the whole lot of them coming together for the common cause, fighting the heat and the altitude of Mexico in England's name. The squad made heroically wholesome and real via my much-treasured and, by the time of the tournament, complete coin collection.

The 1970s meant secondary school and England's failure. The '73 game against Poland was the beginnings of proper football memories, or should that be nightmares? A youngish and incredibly cocksure Brian Clough in the studio with others of this verbally pugnacious sort, Malcolm Allison, Derek Dougan, Paddy Crerand, giving it their all. I seem to remember a year or so later a BBC *Play for Today* telling the story of watching the game from the point of view of a Pole living in England. The first mutterings, post-Powellism, of a multicultural conversation. Not on the pitch, mind. Another research resource from my adolescent collectables is "The 1973 Esso Top Teams," the four home nations' squads united to form one Top 22. Not one of the players from the England, Scots, Welsh and Northern Irish line-ups pictured is black. It would be facile to suggest that the exclusion was anything to do with racism, there simply weren't the top black players to pick in those days. However it would be equally facile to pretend that the memories and celebrations of '66 are entirely disconnected from a contest around the racialisation of Englishness. The vocabulary is important here. The Parekh Report, *The Future of Multi-Ethnic Britain*, published in 2000, attempted to carefully navigate the differences between racism and racialisation:

> Britishness, as much as Englishness, has systematic, largely unspoken, racial connotations. Whiteness nowhere features as an explicit condition of being British, but it is widely understood that Englishness, and therefore by extension Britishness, is racially coded... Race is deeply entwined with political culture and with the idea of nation, and underpinned by a distinctively British kind of reticence – to take race and racism seriously, or even to talk about them at all, is bad form, something not done in polite company. This disavowal... has proved a lethal combination. Unless these deep-rooted antagonisms to racial and cultural difference can be defeated in practice, as well as symbolically written out of the national story, the idea of a multicultural post-nation remains an empty promise.

Ramsey chose an all-white 1966 squad not because he was racist but because these were the best players at his disposal. Likewise when Roy Hodgson announces his squad selections he is hardly indulging in the proverbial "political correctness gone mad" when a majority of his players are Afro-Caribbean and mixed race. The fans? In almost all cases couldn't give a damn, a winning performance is all that matters. The issues perhaps get a tad more complex, not to mention fraught, when as a result of globalisation and migration players increasingly are qualified to play for more than one national team. The loudest booing of a black player I've ever witnessed at Wembley was when England hosted Ghana and Danny Welbeck, whose parentage meant he could have played for either team, came on as an England substitute. The moment he crossed that touchline in a senior international the chance of him ever representing Ghana was gone and the away fans let him know the depth of their disappointment.

Not much of this applied in '66. Not only no black England players, no African teams. The black stars of the tournament, Pelé but more especially Eusébio, embraced as the exotic and most of all celebrated for their sublime skill. Meanwhile in one corner of the North East the North Koreans became everybody's favourite second team. These are deep and genuine impulses not to be lightly rejected. Football at its best making cross-cultural connections long before any kind of popular understanding of globalisation. Yet two years later Enoch Powell burst onto the political scene with a speech that detonated any kind of consensus around race and immigration. Satnam Virdee describes the essence of Powellism as:

A powerful re-imagining of the English nation after empire, reminding his audience it was a nation for whites only. In that historical moment the confident racism that had accompanied the high imperial moment mutated into a defensive racism, a racism of the vanquished who no longer wanted to dominate but to physically expel the racialised other from the shared space they occupied, and thereby erase them and the Empire from its collective memory.

It is to football's eternal credit that the England team has been such a powerfully symbolic barrier to inclinations towards exclusion and expulsion. Of course racism persists, football can only achieve so much, contradictions and contestations remain in and out of the game, but to dismiss the achievement only nurtures the pessimism about the human condition that allows racist attitudes to flourish and grow.

To this extent the "years of hurt" could legitimately be reconstructed instead as decades of healing. Not enough to shape a winning football team out of a rapidly changing society, mind. And given the scale of these changes the multicultural team remains scarcely representative. There remain no players from an Asian background within sight of selection, Danny Welbeck is one of the few players of an African heritage selected, if Jack Grealish makes it into the team he will be the lone representative of one of England's largest migrant communities, the Irish (though many others obviously choose to represent Ireland; perhaps the question should be asked why), another significant migrant community, the Chinese, remains unrepresented, as do the Turkish, and apart from Phil Jagielka none with Polish or other East European family connections, and unlike the '66 squad no players of the Jewish faith, either. None of this is to advocate that much-misunderstood practice, positive discrimination. But it does reveal the narrowness of the particular version of multiculturalism the England team has come to symbolise. And at an elite level the narrowness of the communities from which football recruits, a weakness that Simon Kuper and Stefan Szymanski in their essay "Why England Lose" contrast with the much wider recruitment base of modern German football; not that they're anything to worry about mind, what have the losing side in '66 ever won? Answers on a big postcard please.

Englishness has a formidable relationship with football. To fully understand the meaning of '66 and the fifty years after demands an appreciation of this. Football more than almost any other single cultural formation has helped shape a modern national identity for England. With pluses and minuses. Events on the pitch becoming hopelessly confused with historic events off it – such is the terrain on which a contest between a "soft" inclusive patriotism and a "hard" exclusive version takes place.

At the time of the 1982 Falklands War Stuart Hall staked out with passion the lines of division:

> We are up against the wall of a rampant and virulent gut patriotism. Once unleashed, it is an apparently unstoppable populist mobiliser – in part because it feeds off the disappointed hopes of the present and the deep and unrequited traces of the past, imperial splendor penetrated into the bone and marrow of the national culture.

World Cup Spain '82 was a mere sixteen years into the five decades' worth of hurt, distinguished though by England at least qualifying for a World Cup unlike the disastrous failures to qualify consecutively for Germany '74 and Argentina '78. It was a tournament that opened the day before Argentine forces surrendered to the victorious British armed forces. Argentina's military escapade coming to a bloody end, theirs and ours. Hall's "rampant and virulent gut patriotism" was there for all to see almost every time England kicked a ball. But despite that Hall had the intellectual courage to describe a more hopeful vision of what England might become:

> The traces of stone-age ideas cannot be expunged. But neither is their influence and infection permanent and immutable. The culture of an old empire is an imperialist culture: but that is not all it is… Imperialism lives on – but it is not printed in an English gene… bad ideas can only be displaced by better, more appropriate ones.

From a near-identical intellectual and political trajectory as the sociologist Stuart Hall, the historian Eric Hobsbawm boldly summmarised his vision of English post-Falklands popular triumphalism: "We have won a little war, involving few casualties, fought far away against foreigners whom we can no longer even beat at football, and this has cheered people up, as if we had won a World Cup with guns." At World Cup '82 by luck, careful planning or FIFA skullduggery England and Argentina were kept well apart in the draw. Four years later at Mexico '86, twenty years on from Argentine captain Rattin's sending-off in the '66 quarters, it's Maradona's Hand of God that does for England at the same stage. In the stands and for many back home the football becomes entwined with the Falklands, our No. 3 transformed into 3 Para, the pitch becoming Goose Green, goals for bullets.

We cling on to this legacy of imperial valour and military conquest in the doomed belief that it somehow makes up for all those upstart nations overtaking us. In '66 we could beat Argentina, since then they've won two World Cups and have made it to two other finals, too.

And Germany? Four World Cups and no World Wars. Twenty years of hurt from 1954 to 1974, another sixteen to the Italia '90 triumph, with a further gap of twenty-four to the most recent victory, Brazil 2014. We have a half-century of hurt to endure, the Germans get away with a couple of decades interspersed with semi-final and final appearances plus the odd European Championship thrown in for good measure, 1972, 1980, plus Euro '96, won at Wembley still under the shadow of the old Twin Towers of '66 vintage.

In many ways the turning point in the England vs Germany rivalry and the "all that" which comes with it wasn't '66 at all, rather it was Italia '90. This was a tournament at the height of what became known as "The English Disease." For the preceding five years all English club sides had been banned from European competition, an unprecedented punishment following crowd trouble involving Liverpool fans at the Heysel European Cup final resulting in the death of thirty-nine Juventus fans. This was an era when going to football required an unavoidable clash with trouble. Mass arrests, games dominated by what FA Chairman Sir Andrew Stephen described in 1972 as "the madness that takes place on the terraces." Pitch invasions, games halted and abandoned. Riots accompanying European away trips. After one riot in 1974, Spurs Manager Bill Nicholson famously pleaded with his supporters: "This is a football game – not a war." Not for some it wasn't. Mounted police deployed on the pitch to keep some semblance of order. In 1977 Man Utd forced to play a "home" European tie at Plymouth Argyle's ground, the furthest away possible from Old Trafford but still in England, as punishment for their rioting fans. The FA fined because of the riotous misbehaviour of England fans at tournaments. Players knocked unconscious by missiles thrown from the terraces. Games forced to be played behind closed doors. Fatalities. In 1985 the Bradford stadium fire, fifty-six deaths. On the same day a teenager dies at St Andrews when fighting breaks out between Leeds and Birmingham City fans.

Not nice, but hardly a surprise, that the *Sunday Times* after the Bradford fire should describe football as "a slum sport played in slum stadiums increasingly watched by slum people, who deter decent folk from turning up." It had taken less than two decades for English football's golden moment to lose almost all its shine. Following the failures to qualify for the 1974 and 1978 World Cups, England on the pitch finally made it to the 1980 European Championships hosted by Italy. The team were more or less back to the pre-1966 standard, finishing third in their group and thus failing to make it to the semi-final played between the two group winners and runners-up. It was off the pitch that the huge change in what England had become since '66 was most evident. Other countries had a domestic hooliganism problem. In this era England was virtually unique in exporting it to make trouble at Euros and World Cups. It was an unwelcome sideshow that would more or less persist through to Euro 2000, twenty years later, until a seismic change in England fan culture occurred faraway amongst the 10,000 England fans who travelled out to Japan 2002. And England abroad has never been the same old, bad old, ever since.

One of the architects of the successful organisation of World Cup 1966, now Shadow Minster of Sport, Denis Howell found himself describing England fan trouble at Euro '80 as a "National Disaster." He wasn't alone; when asked to comment on his team's fans England Manager Ron Greenwood described them as "Bastards," suggesting "I hope they put them in a big boat and drop them in the ocean half-way back." FA Chairman Harold Thompson added his own description of England supporters: "Sewer-rats." This was the dominant discourse around what it meant to follow England for the fifty years' middle two decades, 1980-2000. For a long time few would challenge it in the way Stuart Weir bravely did, writing in the then sociology house journal *New Society* in his report from the England away end at Italia '80:

> The Italian police were slow to react, but made up for that by the extreme nature of their reaction. First, squads of police ran out of one of the tunnels and waded into any English fan within reach, regardless of whether they were involved in the affray or not. Shortly afterwards, riot police lined up on the other side of the moat and fired tear gas canisters into the great mass of English supporters in red, white and blue, who were nowhere near the original fracas.

Weir accurately locates the skewering of the discourse in terms of the class relations already underpinning modern football twelve years before the abomination the Premier League would become:

> Football is a popular sport, but it belongs to the world of Mrs Thatcher, Howell and Sir Harold, not to the fans. Though workers formed and ran many of the leading clubs, they and the game's major institutions - the FA and Football League - are now remote from the fans who keep the game going. The clubs are under the

control of local business elites who restrict the participation of their followers to separate supporters' clubs. The young fans get the worst deal. They are herded about with scarcely any respect. If they travel to away games, they are kept strictly segregated at all times and often end up in a pen at the home ground, with a poor view of the match.

James Erskine's superb documentary film of Italia '90, *One Night in Turin*, heavily based on the peerless Pete Davies book of the same tournament, *All Played Out*, memorably opens with a long sequence of violent crowd trouble. Except this wasn't anything to do with football, it was the Trafalgar Square Poll Tax riot of earlier that summer. I can still remember this Saturday afternoon. Shamefully as someone who prides himself on his left-wing principles I can't claim to have been marching and demonstrating myself. Instead I was in a West End cinema and when the closing credits rolled a concerned box-office manager appeared on stage to announce it was unsafe for anyone to leave. The West End was in flames with every plate-glass window in the vicinity smashed to smithereens. Later that night on the tube home I listened in to conversations of groups of lads who'd also been held up, this time from leaving home games across the capital and regretting they'd missed out on all the violent fun.

The football violence of the 1980s cannot be entirely divorced from a period not just of increasing social division but mass mobilisation and more-than-occasional public disorder. Huge CND marches and associated direct action, 1981 inner-city riots at Brixton and Toxteth but elsewhere too, Derek Hatton in Liverpool, Ken Livingstone at the GLC, David Blunkett's Socialist Republic of South Yorkshire, the 1984-85 Miners' strike, followed by the weekly night-time siege of the new HQ of Rupert Murdoch's News International at Wapping. There was an ongoing mainland IRA campaign with the Brighton Grand Hotel Bombing in 1986, arguably its most breathtaking operation of all. In 2009 the *New Statesman* published a special edition to mark the thirtieth anniversary of 1989, which it dubbed "The Year of the Crowd." It ranged over the fall of the Berlin Wall, the Tiananmen Square Massacre and the frenzy in Tehran amongst the huge numbers turning out for the Ayatollah's funeral.

And England? Hillsborough, just another Liverpool FA Cup semi-final but a day that ended in tragedy. Andrew Hussey contributed the Hillsborough essay in which he makes the following key point to describe the images and memories of Liverpool's Kop and the fans who stood and sang their hearts out for their team:

> This was the mob, the crowd, the working class in a group and in action, but it was nothing to be feared. The humour and dignity of this crowd were iconic. These images announced to the world the cultural vibrancy of ordinary people and their pleasures. To this extent, Liverpool fans were as crucial a component of 1960s pop culture as the Beatles.

And as everyone knows the Beatles were bigger than God. But that depth of warm appreciation had been hollowed out by the harsher climate of the 1980s as Hussey succinctly explains:

> By the end of the Thatcherite 1980s this same crowd had become the object of scorn and derision. To be working class, to be a football fan, to be unemployed and northern was to be scum.

And ninety-six died.

During the 1980s fans' behaviour was met with legislative and media mood-swings between the uselessness of platitudes and inertia to moral panic and the clamour for the punitive. Those who were in a position to do something ended up doing nothing. The worsening conditions at grounds just got worse, the policing not much better, crowd safety measures close to non-existent, the rising tide of racism looked away from in the hope that it might go away, or not even caring if it did or didn't. To go to football at least for some was to know something was seriously wrong.

Andrew Hussey, writing this time on Heysel, describes it as "a deadly metaphor for the gathering destructive culture that brought English football to its bloody knees." Most significantly, Heysel marked the culmination of a long trajectory of violence and neglect in England's football culture, which, despite the 1980s success of its clubs in Europe, was heading inexorably towards self-destruction.

Of course Heysel and Hillsborough, despite the same club being involved in both tragedies, are entirely different episodes of condition and circumstance. There should be absolutely no doubt about that. But at the same time unless we include and address both in this middle period we cannot understand how football then went on to change, what drove that change and where we have ended up.

One year after Hillsborough, five years after Heysel, Italia '90 was the largest ever World Cup with 24 nations taking part, and the longest at fifty-two matches, since the tournament began in 1930. This was the beginning of the change in all recognition from the kind of competition '66 was. On the eve of Italia '90 critic and writer Stan Hey predicted: "The World Cup will inevitably become not a sporting event, but a completely commercial package - no longer the peasant game, but sanitised, trussed up and priced for corporate consumption." Having experienced all that has changed since then few today would disagree. The football has changed too – the players, managers and tactics which in 1966 were for many fans unfamiliar have become part and parcel of how we consume the domestic game. There are far fewer surprises, a player or nation bursting onto the tournament we've never heard of or seen before. Hey again tracks this change towards 1990: "Teams became more homogenous, national styles blurred by the diaspora of players moving around the world in search of a club to pay their astronomical wages." A process that has accelerated ever since.

Globalisation is too often described as a single process with only one, invariably neoliberal, end result. The multinational concentration of economic power and a corporate culture of homogeneity. Of course there are different kinds of models and thus consequences of globalisation. Football is in part illustrative of that variety of choices and outcomes. It was never inevitable that football should choose the neoliberal model, this was a political choice and whilst individuals are to blame the error was systemic. Italia '90 is in this regard the tipping point, domestically and internationally. Hey is incredibly prescient on this as well:

> The global success of football has almost certainly sown the seeds for the game's corruption. There is now a momentum which seems to be beyond control. Those of us who have retained an optimism for football's capacity for survival and ability to re-invent itself are already checking our watches. It's starting to feel like we're in injury time.

We are now well past that point: we have gone through the agonising wait for extra time to come to an end, suffered a resounding defeat in the penalty shoot-out, drowned our sorrows in a post-match drinkathon and woken up with the most almighty hangover, as the last remnants of what we once thought was the people's game are flogged off to the highest bidder.

Italia '90 however also offered some cultural pointers towards alternative outcomes. New Order's *World in Motion* provides the soundtrack. A compulsive mix of Mancunian cockiness, pumping American House beats, Euro-pop synths and Jamaican rap. And most of all, you could dance to it. This was an era when young men became interested in fashion on an unprecedented scale, styles relocated from their mainland European belonging and worn instead in the stands while being celebrated in the newly launched style magazines *The Face* and *Blitz*, or the football/fashion crossover fanzine *The End*. Pet Shop Boys in the charts, Italian Euro-Disco and House music on the dancefloor, queues round the block to get into the Hacienda in Manchester, the same outside lesser-known clubs up and down inner-city England. Cultural commentator Steve Redhead dubbed this combination "football with attitude," providing the space for "a stylish Euro-citizenship in marked preference to what was on offer in Britain."

The World Cup was fast becoming an international celebration of the only sport which can legitimately be described as a cultural universal. The common cause in football is of global proportions and despite their worst efforts no corporation or TV company can entirely monetise the popular passion it inspires.

In England there was a changing context of how football was consumed. In the immediate bloody aftermath of Heysel, Liverpool fan Rogan Taylor helped found the Football Supporters Association and emerged as a highly articulate figure to represent those both most affected by this changing context and those most prepared to challenge it. Rogan said of this constituency: "A new wave of post-fanzine football fans is emerging. They combine a genuine enthusiasm for the game with a raised critical awareness of its past mismanagement and recognise the new role they might play in the future." This wasn't a reactive movement simply wanting to preserve the past, rather it was pro-active with at least the beginnings of a vision for football's future. Rogan described this moment: "There is a new agenda for the game, much wider than before. The sooner it is adopted, the sooner the real work can begin."

England's campaign at Italia '90 stood in such stark contrast to the tragic outcome of Hillsborough '89, Euro '88 when England exited the group stage without winning a single game, and the deaths at Heysel and the Bradford Fire in '85, it could hardly fail to provide sime sense of hope. A relatively successful campaign at Mexico '86 didn't provoke anything like the same level of public support. A quarter-final too little, too early. Italia '90 for England, twenty-four years after '66, had all the makings of a new beginning.

By 1990 there was at least some recognition that "fan = hooligan" wasn't a particularly useful equation. Football was enjoying unprecedented mass-media exposure. The boundaries of masculinity and race around the sport were showing signs of being redrawn. The domestic game was becoming Europeanised, to be followed shortly afterwards by a wider globalisation.

English football however remained fundamentally trapped in this period of being defined as a source of disorder and violence. The writing-up of the Italia '90 story before it happened is important in understanding the wider process of the production of images of "postmodern football." 5 June 1990 report, the *Sun*: "Shamed Already. 3 yobbos jailed before the Cup starts." 6 June, the *Sun*: "Superyob booted out of Italy." 14 June, the *Daily Mirror*: "England fans shot in row over pizza." 19 June, the *Daily Mirror*: "Watch out, fans! Cops warn of new bust-up." 27 June, the *Daily Mail* headline: "Get out, animals!" 28 June, the *Sun*: "Labour backs deported riot fans." 30 June, the *Daily Mirror* back-page headline: "We face a war if England win." 5 July, the *Sun* front page: "Soccer yobs in war of Turin." 6 July, editorial in the *Sun*: "Give thugs 5 years. Our way of life is at the mercy of morons." England fans were not alone in provoking a spiral of media amplification to produce a moral panic. Earlier in this World Cup summer the *Sun* had produced a handy cut-out-and-keep guide, "How to avoid those Lager Louts," with star ratings of the hot spots: "there's bovver, bad bovver, bedlam."

In these circumstances it took until the semi-final for the football violence story to be finally overtaken by the football being played. As England's campaign progressed it was followed on TV by millions, with football showing off its capacity to mobilise a national audience that no other sport comes close to matching. A casual, new audience with a softness of touch to their fandom that stood them apart from the hardcore, the already committed. There were a few little Englanders of course, but this was their noisy last stand. A soft patriotism was taking over, a growing female fan-base, the growing numbers, and recognition, of black players transforming the racialisation of England's support we were more used to enduring. This was football consumed as being part of a European, global community. Steve Redhead linked what we were watching on the pitch to what was happening in the stands, down the pub, on the sofa that summer. "Just as the old national differences in styles of play are gradually being erased by the globalisation of football so the cultures around spectatorship are undergoing a period of intensified mixing and matching."

Unarguably Italia '90 is to-date England's greatest ever World Cup achievement. Away from home, a 24-team not 16-team tournament, two knock-out rounds before they reached the semi, Holland to contend with at the group stage, and going into the tournament off the back of Euro '88 where England had failed to win a single game. None of the circumstances that favoured England in '66 applied. The hurt in failing to match '66 only increased by failing to get close to match '90 in the years after either. The Euro '96 semi doesn't count I'm afraid; same favourable conditions as '66, 16-team tournament, at home, England allowed to play all their games at Wembley, again. If you need reminding who England lost to in that semi, and how, you're probably reading the wrong book.

Italia '90 wasn't only significant for the English, this was a turning point for the tournament too and all who played in it and watched it the world over. The USA qualified for the first time since 1950 (who they famously beat then escapes me, sorry); they've qualified for every World Cup ever since. Cameroon burst on to the world stage; never again would African nations be treated as World Cup makeweights. Costa Rica and Colombia ensured Central America would henceforth be recognised as containing decent football-playing teams alongside the South American powerhouses we were more familiar with. South Korea followed qualification for Mexico '86 with Italia '90 after a long gap since their first World Cup, Switzerland '54; they have an unbroken run of qualifiers since 1986. And like the USA, while not quite acquiring "Group of Death" status to be avoided in the draw, the South Koreans are nevertheless quite capable of springing a surprise as so-called big teams have sometimes discovered to their cost.

This was also the last World Cup Yugoslavia were to compete in, the USSR team as well, and the last trophy to be won by West Germany. A world, not just a World Cup, on the verge of something new and different. Or so we thought at the time; now perhaps we're not so sure. A tournament remembered by viewers in England at least for the great booming voice of Luciano Pavarotti singing *Nessum Dorma*. Football popularising opera, or was it the other way round, who would have thought that ever possible? Today such ventures have become well-worn broadcasting clichés every time a Euro or a World Cup comes around but back then it seemed fresh, original, daring.

Pete Davies in his book *All Played Out* had a wonderful way of explaining the significance of not just one night but more like three and a bit weeks with Gary Lineker. "Planet Football - it's a place where the simple dreams of boys kicking a ball between coats on the ground are force-nurtured, under floodlights and cameras, to the most mutant and enormous dimensions." And that's what makes these tournaments *World* Cups. Four years later Pete Davies produced another book for the USA '94 American audience; he rather waggishly titled it *Twenty-Two Foreigners in Funny Shorts*. Not any more we aren't; since the early 1990s football has conquered those remaining parts of the world, the USA, Australia and the oil-rich Middle East in particular, that up to then had failed to fall under its spell.

To understand football's global spread is to appreciate the social dynamics that affect, and are affected by, globalisation. It is a sport requiring no expensive kit or facilities. A tin can will do for a ball, jumpers for goalposts, a bit of chalk and a street makes do for a pitch. OK the offside rule can serve to confuse the bastard in the black but for the rest of us the rules are simple, put a ball between two upright posts and one horizontal bar. Almost any body shape can play, from those who ate all the pies to skinny beanpoles. And there's a world of professional leagues to provide a rich route out of poverty for the lucky few. Thus is explained football's appeal across the globe and the truly international contest the World Cup has become. One of the good things FIFA has done has been to spearhead this spread from the previous enclaves of Europe and South America. Taking the tournament to Central and Northern America, Asia and Africa, and re-organising the qualifying groups as well to help ensure the finalists are at least to some degree representative of the world game.

England reaching the semi-final at Italia '90 ushered in a scale of change that it would be hard-pushed to suggest actually winning the thing in '66 came close to matching. Football in the mid to late '60s was only at the very beginning of marketisation. In Marx's epic words the process that ended with "all that is solid melts into air, all that is holy profaned" had barely begun. By the 1990s almost anything that could be sold off didn't have any problem finding a seller and a buyer. Shirt sponsors, stadium-naming rights, kick-off times and days, cup competitions in association with the highest bidder, entire tiers of grounds given over to executive boxes and corporate hospitality areas.

Much of this degenerate people's game was already in place prior to Italia '90. What the tournament did was to convince the game's governing body in England, the FA, that England's TV audience was ripe for monetisation by creating an elite level where television would be king and via this become the game's paymaster. In politics Thatcherism had already come to an end earlier that summer, her treacherous understudy John Major simply prolonging the death agony of the Conservative Party. The Tories in government but no longer capable of ruling public opinion. Instead from the mid-1990s onwards Tony Blair's New Labour offered up a fresh-faced modernisation which draped itself in the garb of Britpop and football. Blair's last Labour Conference speech before the '97 Labour landslide illustrates this playing footsie with football and music perfectly. According to the official transcript:

Labour's coming home! (*Applause*) Seventeen years of hurt never stopped us dreaming. Labour's coming home! (Applause) As we

did in 1945 and 1964, I know that was then, but it could be again
– Labour's coming home. (*Applause*) Labour's coming home.

Cringeworthy doesn't even begin to do those words justice.

Football helped to provide the gloss for a New Labour model
of modernisation that chose to leave the rapaciousness of neoliberal globalisation essentially unscathed. Academic David
Held has described New Labour's conception of globalisation
as follows: "Internationalisation of economic processes – this
is, both of production and of financial transactions – is the central force of our times." The economic task of government thus
becomes limited to ensuring the conditions for a low-inflation
economy rather than challenging structural inequality, making
investment as attractive as possible and never mind most of the
consequences for employment conditions, actively weakening
workers' right to organise, minimising labour cost via a low-wage,
casualised workforce that isn't unionised, subsidising via public
expenditure infrastructure improvements to benefit the private
sector. From 1979 onwards this more or less describes government policy via Thatcher, Major, Blair, Brown, and Cameron.

This is the vital political context in which to understand the
period 1990 to the present. When in 1990 and thereafter the FA
decided to modernise football, their first and only inclination
was to open it out, entirely unguarded, to the market. England
remains a deeply unpoliticised society. The two most recent
World Cup hosts, Brazil and South Africa, stand in almost total
contrast. In the latter a mass Communist Party holds important
posts in government, trade unions can take action that stops
South Africa in its tracks, ex-guerillas lead political parties, the
legacy of Nelson Mandela is alive, if politically not very well.
Brazil on the other hand won its third Jules Rimet Trophy for the
team to take it home to a nation ruled after a coup by the military.
That period of murderous misrule was ended thanks to popular
pressure, not at the ballot box but in the streets. Those movements would eventually see militant trade-unionist and Workers

Party leader Lula elected president. It was as if instead of losing the Miners' Strike in 1984 Arthur Scargill had led Labour to win the General Election. You get the idea? So it was hardly a surprise that FIFA's shameless exploitation of the single biggest popular cultural formation in both countries, football, should be the subject of not just the odd moan down the pub but social movements, mass protests and the fundamental rejection of the neoliberal model of football. "Fick Fufa," as the South Africans I met in 2010 would rather brilliantly put it.

And Germany? Despite Merkel and her Christian-Democrat government this is a society that is fundamentally social-democratic. Regulation and labour protection, social partnership and public investment, setting political and economic boundaries the multinationals are expected to observe are part and parcel of German politics across the parties. A very different centre ground to our own.

It is in this regard not such a surprise the FA did something no other governing body in world sport at the time had done. It surrendered its governance of football at an elite level.

It was the FA with breathless enthusiasm following Italia '90 that made the decision to float off the First Division in hock to TV contracts. The mistaken belief was that this would somehow strengthen its hold on the game. It proved of course to be the precise opposite. The division of responsibilities of the FA vs Football League had always been somewhat tenuous and based on a combination of class conflict and north-south resentment. Added to this was the localised sectionalism of the clubs and their fans, their own glory mattering for many every bit as much as England's. The formation of the Premier League however massively weakened any control the FA had until it is close to non-existent.

This coincided with a development internationally which simply worsened the situation. The creation of the Champions League in 1992, despite its name over-populated by the rich runners-ups and wealthy third and fourth places, served to create a top tier within England's elite-level clubs now guaranteed European competition at least from September through to December via the replacement of a knockout cup with group stages. UEFA's decision to abandon both the UEFA Cup and Cup Winners' Cup and replace their knockout formats with yet another group-stage format guaranteed the same extended period of European football for the next level of English teams below the top four.

Landlord for the loss-making Wembley Stadium, renting it out to all and sundry, administering the rules of the game, representing English football within UEFA (though the clubs do a large measure of this themselves when it comes to their competitions) and FIFA, protecting the commercial interests of the FA Cup's corporate sponsor, maintaining the bureaucracy of County FA's. There's plenty to keep the FA busy but not much most would actually define as the governance of the sport they are responsible for. And when the numbers of adult men playing eleven-a-side football reveals a rate of decline bordering on the cataclysmic it is surely time to ask how an organisation that came up with the original rules of football, the first FA, got into this mess? Football writer Barney Ronay helps provide us with a very reasonable answer:

> The real problem for the FA is that it has no real power. It is essentially a front, a fluttering ceremonial brocade of a national sporting body. Football may be rich and powerful, but the FA exists at one remove from this, like Prince Charles complaining pointlessly about architecture from the sidelines.

And he makes the point that the health of a football nation depends on the forceful co-operation of forces beyond the sport:

> The FA neither owns nor controls the mechanics of grassroots football. It has no power to dictate what Premier League clubs do with young players. It isn't the nation's PE teacher. It is instead something of a patsy. One of the FA's significant functions is to act as a kind of political merkin for the wider problem. Which is,

simply, access for all: the right to play, a form of shared national
wealth that has been downgraded by those in power for decades.

Absolutely, as testament to these fabled years of hurt the state
of the country's playing fields and publicly owned sports facilities portrays a football nation that doesn't know how to look
after itself. The FA have proved to be the architects of their own
destruction but it wasn't their gross negligence that concreted
over the pitches, privatised council leisure facilities to turn them
into middle-class domains, refused to control fast food and
sugar-heavy drinks leaving them to spike up obesity levels and
turned childhood into a daily fright-zone killing off three-and-in
and pavement kickabouts within a generation of '66. Street football? Makes for a half-decent TV unreality show, the reality is it
barely exists in England today.

The FA without any doubt does a lot of good work for the England cause that rent-a-quote critics too quickly disavow. England
games continue to attract crowds far in excess of most other European nations. Our Under-21 games are often better supported
than senior internationals being played across Europe in the
same week. Ticket prices for both are kept admirably low. The
support remains and as supporters we are cared about too, an
FA free-to-join home-supporters club, senior management at the
FA attending forums to listen to the views and experiences of our
previously maligned and ignored travelling support. I've chaired
enough of these forums to know the relationship can sometimes be tense and nervous but at least we're no longer ignoring
one another. The FA after World Cup 2002 recognised that any
efforts to build on our off-the-pitch popularity over there had to
be fan-led not celebrity photo-calls and the like. They've bravely
and imaginatively backed that approach ever since, so much so
we hardly now think of England as trouble anymore. This means
in turn the attention shifts, quite rightly, to performance on the
pitch at tournaments, not off it. To that end the FA now has a
state-of-the-art national training centre, St George's Park, the

only pity is it finally opened more than a decade after other countries, France's Clairefontaine most notably, opened theirs. We're playing twenty-year catch-up but at least we're moving slowly in the right direction. There's growing investment in the age-group teams. The England DNA project led by the FA's Technical Director Dan Ashworth is hugely impressive. Anybody who has heard Dan's presentation couldn't fail to be impressed, his appointment one of the most important the FA has made in the years since '66, providing a vision and strategy for how England teams should play the game to compete at the highest level they are capable of reaching.

In women's football we have a league run by the FA with the national team at its apex. England players centrally contracted. Internationals played all around the country. Extended international breaks to compete in mini-tournaments outside of the World Cup and Euro cycles. A level of investment in the sport on a par with our immediate rivals. Linking tournament success directly to a drive to increase levels of participation. It's early days yet but in a short space of time England have gone from exiting at the Euro 2005 group stage when they were enjoying home advantage, to World Cup semi-finalists in 2015. Beating reigning European Champions Germany in the third-place match as well to make the achievement even sweeter.

A half-century on, marking the fiftieth anniversary of 1966 will no doubt reflect that familiar trait in Englishness, holding on to past glories, ignoring present predicaments and never mind the future. The "not all that" since Kenneth Wolstenholme was able to pronounce in the BBC's post-match commentary, "It is only twelve inches high… It is solid gold… And it undeniably means England are the champions of the world" makes a feast of backward-looking a near inevitability. So what might looking forward instead resemble, seeking to make the next lot of years of hurt a tad less painful, or even better end the decades of non-achievement altogether? This is a responsibility that lies fairly and squarely with the FA; the self-destruction has robbed them of most of their powers, the national team remains their biggest responsibility. To turn that into a responsibility to be proud of and in turn help shift the balance of power and influence from football's business to sporting interests, the project has to be to re-establish the England team at the pinnacle of our sport. This is not only the right thing to do – to challenge sectional and commercial interests for the common good, to project the vision and ensure the reality of an inclusive England that belongs to all, to celebrate being part of a world game which at its very best is founded on equitability – it is the only thing to do; the FA has precious little else it can achieve with any kind of measure of certainty.

Happy birthday, 1966. Without wishing to spoil your fiftieth, here's my team of eleven presents to make getting to your one-hundredth a whole lot less painful than your last five decades.

✻

1. Fifty @ 50

Fund fifty grassroots football coaches, based in city and regional clusters, to provide free coaching support for prima-ry-age children, boys and girls. Each to be trained up to UEFA pro-licence standard. One of the wisest statements I've heard on England's post-'66 predicament was from Trevor Brooking when he was the FA's Technical Director. Trevor was bemoan-ing the fact that despite their obvious commitment it is the least qualified coaches we let loose on our children's football-ing development, and he linked this specifically to the failure to think long-term. Fifty @ 50 would start to address both failings. The funding to extend to these fiftieth-anniversary coaches would be able to service fifty hours of high-quality coaching a week. And as a support network, approach every player who has represented England from '66 onwards, every manager, assistant and backroom staff too, offer them a mentoring role for coaches, the kids and their families, with an agreement to provide fifty hours of such support a year. These are those who have given so much to the English game; a seat on the TV punditry sofa or a spot chipping in on the radio is a terrible waste of their experience and talent. Build such a commitment into joining up with present and future England squads. Establish a trust fund to ensure Fifty @ 50 has the finances to still be around in 2066.

2. The Bobby Moore Centre at Wembley

Right next to Wembley Stadium, almost directly below the Bobby Moore statue, is one of those facilities providing a number of five-a-side pitches. What a great location, except it's privately owned, of no benefit to the FA. There is no link to any kind of coaching programme, its bar is well-used when there's an international but apart from that nothing to show off what the FA is trying to do with England DNA, its walls plastered with adverts for energy drinks that rot your teeth and make you fat. What a wasted opportunity. Purchase it outright as the FA's Bobby Moore Centre, use it as a showpiece whenever England are at home to introduce kids, their parents, their club coaches to all that England are trying to achieve at the Under-11 level, and in between use it as a seven-day-a-week coaching centre specifically to develop the kind of ball skills Bobby Moore was a past master at.

3. Take England Back on the Road

Never mind the politicians, the greatest ever venture in English devolution was when England went on the road. From 2000 when the old Twin Towers Wembley was closed for demolition until 2007 when the new version finally re-opened, England internationals were played not just at Anfield, Old Trafford, Villa Park and St James' Park but also Ipswich, Leicester, Derby, Southampton, Middlesbrough and Leeds. Cities which with the greatest respect would not normally have expected to have been included; but England's tour of the regions was all-embracing. For once an England game became a local event and all the more special for that, the support more genuinely national than ever before. The enthusiasm for England up and down the country at World Cups 2002, 2006 and Euro 2004 was surely in part caused by this. Reopening Wembley squandered all of this. In the intervening nine years no home England international has been played away from Wembley and if the stadium contracts are abided by none will be for the foreseeable future, keeping England locked into Wembley for another twenty-one years. There are some signs the FA may relent and play the odd home game away from Wembley but they should simply rip these contracts up and make going back on the road an annual trip. Those contracts were only ever signed to keep the people who fill the Club Wembley tier and the executive boxes happy, most of whom can't be arsed to make their way back from their half-time cocktail bar for the kick-off. Wembley-only is made even worse by the near total absence of Saturday 3pm kick-offs for internationals, qualifiers or friendlies. North of Watford that means leaving work mid-afternoon, back in the early hours, kids left at home. Commit to a minimum of two Saturday or Sunday 3pm kick-offs, and extend the generous family discounts offered for some sections of the ground to the whole ground for these games.

4. Schoolboys and Schoolgirls Double-Header International

For no obviously good reason, when the old Wembley closed the tradition of the annual schoolboy international ended with it. Usually played against Scotland, I can well remember motorways being jam-packed with coaches full of kids wildly excited about their big footballing day out. Bring them back but with a few twists. Alternate between Wembley and one of the top club grounds in the North. A double-header, boys and girls. Play a wide variety of international opposition with linked school projects to learn about football in these coun-tries, Brazil and Argentina, Ivory Coast and Ghana, Japan and

South Korea, Germany, Italy and the like. Reduce the size of the pitch and goals, as almost all experts in age-level football advise. Use the experience to contribute towards a culture of the national collective where playing for and supporting England matters.

5. Bring Back the Home Nations but More Too

An FA success story is the growing popularity of Under-21s matches – regularly attracting crowds of 30,000 plus, where other countries rarely attract attendances into four figures for their same games. On the road around England, mainly Championship and League One (or second and third divisions in old money as I still prefer) grounds, reasonably priced tickets. The crowds are growing for the next age-group down too, the Under-20s. At finals the results haven't been so good but that's not what we're immediately concerned with here, rather reclaiming the primacy of the national team to our national sport. Bringing back the home nations as an end-of-season tournament in non-Euro years for the Under-21s would contribute towards this with the added spice of a guest nation. Germany or Argentina for starters, Poland or Australia would attract large expat support, an African team would provide experience of coping with unfamiliar playing styles. Giving such opportunities to our young players, many on the verge of playing for the senior team, would provide them with invaluable experience comparable to a Euro or World Cup group stage, and would only help the England teams of the future. Modelled on England's proven success with support there's not much doubt the Home Nations would be enormously popular. Plenty of other countries hold mini-tournaments, France's longstanding Toulon tournament amongst the best known; the Algarve hosts loads of them, men's and women's football, Cyprus too, so why not the supposed "home of football"? For both men's and women's Under-20s, -19s and -17s, why not each play a regionally based end-of-season tournament against the other best three sides at their level from Europe and beyond? Award to the likes of the North-West, Midlands, Yorkshire, where there's a variety of grounds and a huge appetite for football; with imaginative promotion and cheap tickets, the crowds would turn out. More ways of supporting England for the fans, more invaluable tournament experience for the players.

6. Bid to Host Age-Group World Cups and European Championships

England has had a sorry recent record of spectacular failure in bidding to host World Cup 2006 and once more for World Cup 2018. We have to go back to 1996 for the last men's Euros we hosted, 2005 for the women's. So why not broaden the scope to bid for World and European age-group championships? Given half a chance we've proved across sports and Olympics to be rather good hosts, and for football we already have the facilities in place and all the evidence suggests decent-sized crowds, certainly much bigger than other countries might expect. It's not unusual for the competitions to be played in front of virtually empty stands; not in England they wouldn't be. Large and varied diaspora communities would help too for the away teams' support. Use any success as a platform to bid for the "real" thing, encourage an understanding of being patient as young talents develop into senior stars, and once more place the England team in the frame for the nation's sporting affections with a reach no club side could match.

7. Football at the Commonwealth Games

There's another reason why playing Home Nations and mini-tournaments are important. Apart from England, and the other GB nations, every other country gets to play in two global football competitions, the World Cup and the Olympic Games, should they qualify of course. Most of the top World Cup teams do make it through to the Olympic football finals providing invaluable experience when most of those players graduate

into their World Cup squads a year or two later. England don't
of course because Olympic representation is under the banner
of "Team GB." Nothing reveals better the lingering reluctance of
the FA to give up on England being a kind of Greater Britain
than their cackhanded efforts to create Team GB men's and
women's football teams despite the outright opposition of the
Scots, Welsh and Northern Irish FAs, an opposition loudly
amplified by all their fans too. Not many England fans were all
that keen either; at a meeting I chaired with then-FA Chairman
Dave Triesman, well-known for being a Tottenham fan, one
supporter made the great point that it was a bit like asking
Spurs and Arsenal to form a North London team. Sadly, despite
the success of the England team at the 2015 Women's World
Cup, leading voices in the game have called for a Team GB
women's football team. All of this flies in the face of a history
dating back to 1870 and that first-ever football international,
England vs Scotland, a dull 0-0 draw. The intention is understandable however; tournament football is unlike almost any
other experience footballers have of playing the game. Three
group games in the space of ten days or thereabouts. England
don't have the strength in depth generally to rotate and in any
case the strength of the opposition plus what is at stake
wouldn't allow it. Games in another country, often enough not
on our own continent either, travelling between games,
sometimes an unfamiliar climate, altitude even. And that's
before we get to the knockout stages. The focus on the team's
performance is huge, unprecedented even for Premier League
players, the expectations sky-high, well until recently at any
rate. There is though another global tournament both England
and the home nations could enter to experience all of this, the
Commonwealth Games. Except football unlike rugby sevens
isn't a Commonwealth Games sport. Why on earth not? No
need for qualifiers, using rankings with pots drawn across
Europe, Africa, Asia, Australasia and the Americas with the
Caribbean might see the likes of Cameroon, Ghana and Nigeria

line up alongside Australia and Jamaica. For a women's
tournament Canada would be serious contenders too. OK,
outside of the home nations and Cyprus European teams
would be under-represented unless Gibraltar was asked to
make up the numbers, or as a Commonwealth Games nation
Channel Island teams? Nevertheless, a 16-team tournament
could be quite a tasty proposition, men's and women's,
age-group based like the Olympics. Something that, if campaigned for by the English, Scots, Welsh and Northern Irish
FAs, would unite us while preserving our independent status
of each other. Of shared benefit for our individual World Cup
ambitions, working towards this would be a useful step in the
right direction away from the pettiness our various national-
isms too easily descend into.

8. A Squad Penalty Shoot-Out League

All the experts say that penalty shoot-outs cannot be practiced.
Still that doesn't seem to stop some countries being better than
others at them, and England are close to worst of all. We can
safely assume that as international footballers our players are
fiercely competitive; it's how they have reached the top of their
sport. Once England have qualified, establish a weekly
training-ground penalty shoot-out competition officiated by
FA staff, for a dedicated website with a league table of results.
The pressure would be on to come out on top. And for the final
round the last home friendly before a tournament ends with a
penalty shoot-out. Fans are asked to help by doing everything
they can to put our players off. OK, it's not the same as stepping
up to the spot in a World Cup quarter-final, but it does at least
encourage practice in a pressured environment.

9. Put England Games First in the Fixture List

Here's a challenge the FA should issue to the clubs, the Premier League, and TV broadcasters. Whenever England games are due to be played, the preceding weekend's fixtures should all kick off Saturday at 3pm. Currently some will be played Saturday late afternoon, others Sunday, and the remaining few as late as Monday evening. Shift them all back to Saturday and the players get up to two extra days both to recover and to be part of the England coaching set-up and pre-match preparation. Other countries manage to do this, why not England? And with England now based at their coaching HQ St George's Park near Burton, feed that data into the fixture computer so that as many as possible Premier League games are played within an hour or two's drive of Burton on that Saturday too, thus reducing tiring travelling time. And if the Premier League et al won't play ball, expose their selfishness.

10. No More Pride, Passion, Belief

Other countries have winter breaks; our players arrive at tournaments knackered. Yet the main cause of the relatively poor physical condition of our team is how we play our football. "Pride, Passion, Belief" used to be the big-screen message at Wembley immediately before kick-off for England internationals. Thankfully it's been taken down but the sentiment remains. Admirable qualities of course – with a bit of luck they'll get a team to a World Cup quarter-final – but by now we should have learned that they're not enough to win trophies. For that you need most of all technical ability to play the tactics required, with top physical condition the platform on which to build. We actively celebrate the physicality of English football, up and at 'em, non-stop action, and deride other playing cultures which don't match up. This is how the Premier League is marketed worldwide. It is what the fans want. The globalisation of our football in this regard remains on our terms. The foreign influence if anything hasn't gone far enough. Admitting our deficiencies in this regard requires a cultural shift that has to come from below, but a start could be made with the England "Man/Woman of the Match" being awarded by a panel of experts for technical skill. At the very least it might help provoke a debate.

11. A National Anthem We Can Call Our Own

This isn't about being anti-monarchy; it's not for football to sort out that arcane institution. Rather it is about owning up to the responsibility English football has for carving out a modern version of what it is to be England. The Scottish FA only adopted *Flower of Scotland* as their anthem in 1997; there are no centuries of tradition, the song itself originated in the 1960s. I can remember a poll on the FA website after World Cup 2002 asking fans if they'd like an anthem of our own. Without any campaigning, no offering of suggestions, 36% plumped for yes. A song, ancient or modern, that comes to represent the England we want to become, on the pitch, as a nation, no longer about an institution, but about us. It would be a courageous move, one that announces that England is as much about the present and future as our past. It would make the moment when the Anthem is sung unique to football, a special moment rather than one draped in the otherness of officialdom.

*

Does all this add up to England winning the World Cup at some unspecified – or as FA Chairman Greg Dyke foolishly put it, specified – date in the future? Quite possibly not, but the issue here is there is only so much an FA that has given up all its powers to govern the game can do. This grand plan – and the ideas are not that grand in terms of size of budget or scale of ambition required – could be activated by the FA even in their much-reduced role. And that would signal a start towards reclaiming the primacy of the national team. In terms of where we'd then end up come future World Cups, that estimation demands a humble recognition that Germany, Brazil and Italy have won a hatful of World Cups since Italy's first in 1934 to Germany's latest in 2014, whereas England has just the one, an historic lead which is not going to be easily overcome. Our defeated '66 quarter-final opponent, Argentina, have since then also put our World Cup record to shame. New World Champions have emerged too, France and Spain, going from perennial under-achievers to winners and finalists. But England has managed to regularly to reach the quarter-finals, both before 1966 and since. In 1986 and 2002 we went out at this stage to the eventual winners, which gives an added measure to the achievement. Upgrading to becoming regulars in the last four shouldn't be entirely beyond us. Since the last time we reached that stage Croatia, Turkey, Bulgaria, South Korea, Uruguay, Holland and Sweden have all matched that achievement; why, with some modest improvements to our situation, shouldn't England? Because after '66 the FA utterly failed to act to build on that success, instead assuming there would be more of the same to come. There wasn't. And then after coming so close again in '90 the FA did act but with results that proved to be of no help to the England team at all. Many would argue these resulted instead in diminishing whatever prospects it might continue to have.

Simon Kuper and Stefan Szymanski have produced the definitive explanation of England's failings in their essay with the self-explanatory title "Why England Lose". Their case is that England are natural World Cup quarter-finalists and we really haven't much reason to expect anything better. Theirs is an empirical analysis; mine is more of an idealist account. I would periodise the fifty years since '66 as follows.

From 1966 to 1978: England in decline. First we revert to type at Mexico 1970, failing to beat a top-tier nation in our group. We come up against another top-tier nation in the quarters and lose, pluckily. Then unable to rebuild or reform for the first and only time we fail to qualify for two World Cups on the bounce. The current excuse of too many foreign players in our top division hardly applied in '74 and '78.

Second, 1982 to 1990: England in trouble. Things improve enough to get us back to the previous standard from 1982 to 1990, when we manage to excel, but off the pitch all things England become barely distinguishable from the hooliganism that accompanies them.

Third, from 1998 to 2006: We become England in recovery. Two consecutive quarter-finals in 2002 and 2006 with the Euro 2004 quarter-final in between. The hooligan reputation almost entirely expunged. The appointment of Sven Goran-Eriksson a masterstroke despite dyed-in-the-wool conservatism opposition. The makings of a world-class squad at different times including David Seaman in goal, Gary Neville and Sol Campbell at the back, Paul Scholes, Steven Gerrard, Frank Lampard in midfield, Wayne Rooney and Michael Owen up front. With that lot the argument goes we should really have been capable of equalling '90 at least. But the trouble was once one or two of them were injured, out of form or suspended, the squad cupboard was too bare to compete at the level required. The saving grace from 1998 to 2006 was David Beckham. Supremely gifted, scorer of the most exquisite goals at the most extraordinary of moments, an industrious captain who led by example confounding even his most embittered critics. Like Bobby Moore and Paul Gascoigne, though, his greatest achievement was to represent more than his footballing parts, and in era when this occurred with maximum effect. In his book *Beckham* cultural analyst Ellis Cashmore summed this up superbly:

Beckham is not just well suited to the requirements of a culture in which consumption is of paramount importance: he is perfect. Without knowing it, he conveys ideas that have become germane: that They, the celebs, are both different and yet the same as Us; that we could be like them, at least theoretically – if only we had a little more talent and a tad more industry; that this is a system that rewards and punishes according to just principles and that

we all end up with what we deserve. Only one deserves to be
Beckham, of course. But by consuming him, we can all share in
the experience.

The trouble was once he had gone, by World Cup 2010, there was
no one who came remotely close that most would want to share
their experience. For a fleeting moment perhaps the impossibly
youthful Theo Walcott, but apart from one magical night, Zagreb
2008, when he single-handedly destroyed Croatia with a glorious
hat-trick, not much afters to lift him to superstar status. So in this
regard Becksmania simply served to mask a period of stabilisation.

Fourth, 2010 to 2014: England in decline, again. Following the
run of quarter-final appearances the team edges towards stagna-
tion and then what looks increasingly like a return to the age of
England in decline.

Of course, like Eric Hobsbawm's periodisation of ages of industry, revolution, empire, and extremes the borders between one
and another are porous, they overlap. But for me they serve well
to help explain the last fifty years and in turn the status we should
afford '66.

On the thirtieth anniversary of '66 novelist Kim Newman wrote
a richly humorous short story *The Germans Won*. In the story,
Ramsey was sacked immediately. Germany over-confident in
Mexico imploded while England made it to the semis and up to
'94 had appeared in no less than four finals, on the losing side of
each. In politics Peter Walker succeeded Edward Heath as a Conservative Prime Minister, Denis Healey succeeded Harold Wilson
as a Labour PM. The troubles in Northern Ireland settled via pow-
er-sharing, in the South Atlantic a peace settlement was signed
with Argentina over the disputed territory of the Falklands after
Argentine warship the *Belgrano* was allowed to return to port
unharmed. At USA '94 England under Bobby Robson, who'd
stayed around after beating Germany on penalties at Italia '90
before losing to Maradona's Argentina in the final, led England to
World Cup glory. It's a credible alternative account.

The original *1066 and All That* was a gentle debunking of the conventional view that great men and women make history. Instead the forces for change lie with people, the social movements they create, the ideas that inspire them, the conditions under which they live and choose on occasion to resist. My account of the fifty years since '66 is rooted in such an approach. But to mimic Kim Newman for a moment I would re-imagine three key moments. After Mexico '70 the FA approaches Bobby Moore to open a discussion about what role at the FA might suit him when he retires in a few years' time. (The German FA found a role for Franz Beckenbauer – Bobby had all the potential to at least match Franz's achievements but was never given the chance.) In 1980 following Nottingham Forest's back-to-back European Cup wins the FA swallows its pride and reservations to plead with their arch critic in the TV studios, Brian Clough, to manage England. In 1990, with Bobby Robson resolved not to continue in the job, the FA appoints the sole member of the '66 team to make a success of managing an international team, Jack Charlton, to come home and manage the team that he wants to run more than any other in the world.

Fanciful, perhaps, but as the song says, nothing can stop us dreaming. Or if you prefer a more materialist analysis to conclude this fifty-year account, an early version of a populist soundbite from the media-savvy Harold Wilson: "Have you ever noticed England only ever win the World Cup under a Labour Government?" It was true then Harold; it's true now.

Introducing the England 1966 Squad

Asif Burhan

ENGLAND, TWICE QUARTER-FINALISTS, go into the eighth
World Cup final series as one of the favourites to win on
home soil. This elevated status seems to be mainly derived from
their position as host nation rather than any recent football pedigree. England have only won three of the fourteen matches they
have played at the World Cup and never reached the semi-finals
in four attempts. Home advantage can be exaggerated too. Even
double-champions Brazil failed to cope with the pressure and
expectation of playing in front of their own public in 1950.

To progress to the latter stages, England must finish in the top
two of what, on paper, is a difficult opening group. Mexico have
lost all but two of their World Cup games and should be there for
the taking. However, no one has won the World Cup more than
England's first group opponents, the formidable Uruguayans.
England have only beaten Uruguay once and their only World
Cup meeting in Berne in 1954 ended in humiliation for a team
including Stanley Matthews, Tom Finney and Nat Lofthouse.
France did not feature in the 1962 tournament but finished third
in 1958, defeating Scotland and Northern Ireland along the way.
Only three years ago in Alf Ramsey's first match in charge, France
demolished England 5-2 in Paris. It is likely England will need to
defeat them in their final group game to stay at Wembley for the
quarter-finals.

Since that defeat, the last England team to be selected by an
FA Committee, Ramsey has gradually reorganised the team on
his own terms. Under previous manager Walter Winterbottom
at World Cup '62, everything went through the mercurial Johnny
Haynes but Ramsey's England is no longer reliant on a single

player. Haynes himself, widely acknowledged as the finest passer in English football, has not been picked since a serious car accident in 1962.

It was Ramsey who gave a debut to Leicester City's Gordon Banks, who has emerged as England's first choice goalkeeper. Without a win in Ramsey's first three matches, West Ham's Bobby Moore was appointed captain for the fourth and has retained the armband ever since. Bobby Charlton, a previously inconsistent winger for Manchester United and England, has been moved centrally and now seems better equipped to display his undoubted natural talent in what will be his third World Cup. Up-front, hopes will rest on the hugely talented Jimmy Greaves. A prodigious scorer for every team he has played for, will he now prove he can score the important goals England will need at the sharp end of a World Cup?

Although not first choice to succeed the long-serving Walter Winterbottom, Alf Ramsey has settled into the job after a difficult start. His management credentials cannot be questioned having guided Second Division Ipswich Town to promotion and then a first-ever League Championship in 1962. Without him they were soon relegated back to the second tier.

Some would call Ramsey England's first "professional" manager, as he is the first to select the team without any input from the FA Selection Committee, who picked the England squad for Winterbottom. Gone is the preference for merely a selection of the best players in England. Now it is all about choosing the best team of players. A former international with thirty-two caps, including the fateful 1950 World Cup in Brazil, Ramsey knows what it takes to play at the highest level and has earned the respect of his players.

Certainly, this will be the best-prepared England team at a World Cup. Ramsey will be assisted by his two coaches, Harold Shepherdson and Les Cocker. Shepherdson, a survivor of the previous regime, is Ramsey's most trusted lieutenant. The more abrasive Cocker is the fitness trainer, ensuring the England squad reaches a peak of physical fitness at the tournament. In addition, for the first time the squad will have a recognised doctor along-side them, the Harley Street consultant Dr Alan Bass. Attention to detail is the management's policy, even down to the way the players cut their toenails.

During an intensive two-week training camp at the spartan Lilleshall retreat, the team has fostered more of a club spirit. The squad have been living in each other's pockets, rarely allowed out into town and estranged from their families. It is hoped that this closeness will stand them in good stead when the pressure and confinement created by the World Cup competition will ensure that their every move is scrutinised by a worldwide audience – for the first time, able to watch every match broadcast on television.

The Nearly Men

Alf Ramsey initially named a squad of forty on 7 April before the 1965-66 season ended. A month later he named a reduced squad of twenty-eight to join him for pre-tournament training. The twelve players omitted at this stage and put on stand-by were:

Gordon West (Everton)
Tony Waiters (Blackpool)
Chris Lawler (Liverpool)
Paul Reaney (Leeds United)
John Hollins (Chelsea)
Tommy Smith (Liverpool)
Terry Venables (Chelsea)
Peter Osgood (Chelsea)
Derek Temple (Everton)
John Kaye (West Bromwich Albion)
Joe Baker (Nottingham Forest)
Gordon Harris (Burnley)

From the twenty-eight remaining players Alf Ramsey picked to join him at Lilleshall at the start of June, twenty-seven reported for duty. Everton captain Brian Labone asked to be excused as he was preparing for his wedding and had pre-booked a honeymoon for the summer. Five more players were cut by Ramsey on 18 June before the final squad embarked on their pre-World Cup tour of Scandinavia. The following players had been asked to stay match-fit with their clubs in case of emergency:

Johnny Byrne: "Budgie" first appeared for England as a Third Division player in 1961, earning him a British record transfer to West Ham the following year. Seven goals in his first six internationals proved his ability but he has failed to score in his last five England games and not played for his country in over a year. This season he has been eclipsed at West Ham by his young strike partner Geoff Hurst who has scored forty goals in all competitions compared to his seventeen. Having narrowly failed to make the squad for the 1962 World Cup, Byrne can count himself doubly unfortunate to have missed out again.

Gordon Milne: The Liverpool wing-half played fourteen times for England in 1963 and 1964 but not since. His club form in helping Liverpool win a second league title in three seasons kept him in Ramsey's thoughts but at twenty-nine, the Preston-born midfielder has surely lost his chance of playing at the highest level again for his country.

Keith Newton: The Blackburn right-back made his England debut against West Germany in February 1966 but was carried off injured. He played again in April in the win over Scotland. His club season ended in disappointment as Blackburn finished bottom of Division One. The twenty-five-year-old Newton will now face the tough job of trying to prolong his promising international career while playing in the Second Division.

Bobby Tambling: The Chelsea captain this season scored twenty-three goals in all competitions to help his club finish fifth in the league. He started England's last game at Wembley against Yugoslavia alongside Geoff Hurst and the man he replaced at Chelsea, Jimmy Greaves. His only international goal remains in his previous cap three years earlier in Ramsey's first game in charge, the 5-2 defeat to France in Paris.

Peter Thompson: The exciting Liverpool winger helped his club win the League Championship this season but has failed to score in his twelve England appearances to date, the last of which came against Northern Ireland last November. At twenty-three, Thompson can look forward to playing in the European Cup next season and becoming an England regular in time for the 1970 finals.

The Final Selection

 **Gordon Banks, aged 28, 27 caps
Leicester City FC, Goalkeeper**

With Chesterfield since the age of fifteen, Leicester City signed him for £7,000 in 1959 after only twenty-three appearances for the first team. By the end of his first season he had established himself as first-choice goalkeeper and thereafter played in four Cup finals, winning the League Cup in 1964 but otherwise on the losing side in the same competition, 1965, and the FA Cup 1961 and 1963. Banks broke his wrist before the start of this season but recovered to play thirty-seven games in all competitions for Leicester. Alf Ramsey brought in Banks for only his second match in charge, a 2-1 defeat to Scotland, but retained faith in his choice. In 1964, Tony Waiters made five appearances to briefly threaten Banks place but his greatest rival for club and country could eventually come from promising teenager Peter Shilton, who made his Leicester debut this May. However for this summer at least, Gordon Banks is undoubtedly his country's No. 1 and, faced with the greatest forwards in the game, may have to prove his world-class status if England are to win the tournament.

 George Cohen, aged 26, 24 caps
Fulham FC, Right-back

Made his Fulham debut in 1957 and helped them reach the FA Cup semi-finals the following season and promotion to the First Division the next. Since replacing Jimmy Armfield in the England side against Uruguay in May 1964, Cohen has been virtually ever-present at right-back, playing in ten internationals this season. One of five right-backs chosen by Ramsey in the preliminary squad of forty, Cohen has seen off considerable competition to wear the No. 2 shirt this summer. His speed and determination are qualities that will be put to the test against the world's best wingers this summer, his ability to overlap and support the attack perhaps crucial in breaking down massed defences.

 Ray Wilson, aged 31, 45 caps
Everton FC, Left-back

A former railway worker, Wilson was recommended to Huddersfield Town in 1952 but only became a regular for his club five years later after Bill Shankly had converted him into a full-back. After twelve years in Yorkshire he joined Everton in the summer of 1964, recovering from a torn muscle in his first season to help the Merseysiders win their first post-war FA Cup this year. First capped in 1960, Wilson did not taste victory with England until his sixth match. He played in all four of England's games in the

1962 World Cup and ten of the twelve this season. A hard tackler and supremely fit, Wilson is undisputed first choice at left-back.

 Nobby Stiles, aged 24, 14 caps, 1 goal
Manchester United FC, Midfield

An England Schoolboy International before he signed for Manchester United as an apprentice, Stiles was given his club debut by Matt Busby in 1960 aged eighteen. He did not play in the 1963 FA Cup final but only missed one game all season when Manchester United won the First Division in 1965. His ability to win the ball and effectively complement Bobby Charlton for his club has now been utilised by Ramsey at international level ever since Stiles' debut against Scotland in April 1965. He has played all but three of England's games since, even scoring the only goal in the win over West Germany in February earlier this year. Although lacking the skill and flair of more-vaunted midfielders, Stiles nonetheless seems a certain starter in the World Cup.

 Jack Charlton, aged 31, 16 caps, 2 goals
Leeds United AFC, Centre-back

With Leeds United since the age of fifteen, Jack Charlton's fortunes have ebbed and flowed as much as his club's in the intervening years. When John Charles was pushed into attack, Charlton came into the defence on his debut in 1953. Twice promoted and once relegated with Leeds, he is now the lynchpin of a young defence for a club which has finished second in the First Division for the past two years as well as reaching the FA Cup final in 1965 and the semi-finals of the European Fairs Cup this season. Nonetheless, at the age of twenty-nine, it was surprising when Jack was given his first England cap against Scotland last year. Alongside younger brother Bobby, they became the first siblings to play for England this century. It is felt his strength in the air and tough tackling adds something to defence alongside the more refined Moore. Charlton has been Moore's regular partner ever since, even scoring on his last two appearances.

 Bobby Moore, aged 25, 41 caps, 2 goals
West Ham United FC, Centre-back

England's youngest-ever captain when appointed in 1963, Bobby Moore is the man England hope will raise the Jules Rimet Trophy at Wembley on 30 July. Since his West Ham debut aged seventeen, Moore has never looked out of place, whatever stage he has performed on. A ball-playing central defender of rare ability and composure, seemingly destined to perform at the highest level. He led West Ham to their first major honour in 1964, lifting the FA Cup, and then returned to Wembley the next spring to lift the European Cup Winners' Cup, although it was to prove third time unlucky as the Hammers were defeated this season in the League Cup final. Impressive as an England Youth and Under-23 international, the uncapped Moore was chosen to travel with the 1962 World Cup party. His stand-out debut in a warm-up match against Peru alongside Maurice Norman led to the pair forming the defensive partnership for England in every game at the tournament. With Johnny Haynes and Jimmy Armfield both recovering from injury, Moore first captained his country against Czechoslovakia aged twenty-two and is now full-time captain. He has scored his first England goals this year against Poland and Norway. There remains press speculation over his long-term future at West Ham, but Moore will be looking to put that to one side this summer if he is to lead his country to victory on the greatest stage.

Alan Ball, aged 21, 10 caps, 1 goal
Blackpool FC, Midfield/Forward

Rejected by Wolves and Bolton as a schoolboy, Ball eventually signed for Blackpool and became their youngest-ever player in 1962. In three successive seasons he has scored more than ten league goals, recording a career best sixteen from forty-one games 1965–66. Ball made his international debut in Belgrade just over a year ago aged nineteen and remains the youngest member of the England squad this summer. Whether utilised as a winger, a right-sided forward or part of a three-man midfield, his stamina, work rate and adaptability are valued by Ramsey to such an extent that he is likely to play ahead of more seasoned internationals.

Jimmy Greaves, aged 26, 51 caps, 43 goals
Tottenham Hotspur FC, Forward

England's all-time record goalscorer, can Jimmy Greaves now prove this summer he is the best striker in the world or will the bout of hepatitis he suffered this season prevent him from showing his true potential on the greatest stage? A prolific goalscorer from his days as a schoolboy, he was signed by Chelsea aged fifteen, scored on his first team debut aged seventeen in 1957 and finished the season as the club's top scorer with twenty-two goals in thirty-seven appearances. Another 102 league goals in 124 appearances over the next three seasons persuaded AC Milan to sign him for £80,000 in 1961. Greaves failed to settle in Italy and despite scoring nine times in fourteen games, returned to London with Tottenham Hotspur. Greaves continued where he had left off, scoring a hat-trick on his debut and helping the club retain the FA Cup in 1962. The following season he scored twice in the final as Spurs became the first English side to win a European competition, the Cup Winners' Cup against Atlético Madrid.

The First Division's leading goalscorer in five seasons, Greaves goes into the World Cup having failed to score twenty goals this season for the first time in his career after missing three months due to illness. Greaves made his England debut aged nineteen in Peru, scoring in a 4-1 defeat in 1959. He scored one goal in four appearances at the 1962 World Cup but failed to shine. His recent form for England has been called into question having not scored for his country in over a year, but four goals in the recent game against Norway, a record sixth hat-trick for England, seem to have ensured his starting place.

 **Bobby Charlton, aged 28, 68 caps, 38 goals
Manchester United FC, Midfield/Forward**

The most experienced member of Ramsey's squad, Bobby Charlton heads into his third World Cup looking to finally prove he is the world-class footballer many believe him to be. By the time he had scored twice on his Manchester United debut in 1956, Charlton had already won the FA Youth Cup three times. A league champion in 1957 and 1965 and an FA Cup winner in 1963, Charlton's performances this season, helping Manchester United reach the semi-finals of the European Cup, have earned him the Footballer of the Year award. A survivor of the Munich Air Crash in 1958, Charlton made his international debut the same season, scoring a spectacular goal against Scotland. He has rarely stopped finding the net since, becoming England's highest goalscorer in 1963 before Greaves overtook him the following year. Originally a left-winger, Ramsey seems to have at last found his best position, central and free of any defensive duties. His rare ability to beat a man and shoot powerfully with either foot will be crucial to England's hopes in a tournament where they are likely to come up against packed defences.

Geoff Hurst, aged 24, 5 caps, 1 goal
West Ham United FC, Forward

The son of a professional footballer, Geoff Hurst is a late addition to the squad. In 1960 Hurst played a first-class cricket match for Essex against Lancashire and seriously considered giving up football until Ron Greenwood took over at West Ham, converting him from left-half to centre-forward in 1962. Since then he has developed into an old-fashioned English target man, strong in the air, adept at holding the ball up and bringing others into play. He scored in the Hammers' 1964 FA Cup final win over Preston North End and played throughout their successful 1964-65 European Cup Winners' Cup campaign. This season has been Hurst's most prolific, scoring forty goals in all competitions, twenty-three of them in the league. That form persuaded Ramsey to give him his first England cap in February for the friendly against West Germany; he opened the scoring in his next game, the 4-3 win over Scotland, but struggled to look convincing in the recent matches in Scandinavia and will start the tournament behind the more prolific Greaves and Hunt in the pecking order. Barring injury it is unlikely he will play a significant part in this tournament.

 John Connelly, aged 27, 19 caps, 7 goals
Manchester United FC, Winger

Able to score with either foot, Connelly has won league titles with two different clubs, Burnley in 1960 and his current team, Manchester United, in 1965. Spotted playing for St. Helens at the age of eighteen in the Lancashire Combination League, Connelly remained an amateur even after signing for Burnley until he finished his apprenticeship as a joiner aged twenty-one. In seven years at Turf Moor, Connelly scored over one hundred goals from the wing, nearly one every other game, before joining Manchester United for £56,000 in April 1964. This season, he has helped Man-

chester United reach the semi-finals of the European Cup. First
capped in 1959, Connelly has never quite cemented a starting
place in the England team. An unused member of the 1962 World
Cup squad, Connelly will be hoping to start this time around
having played six games this season, scoring twice.

 **Ron Springett, aged 30, 33 caps
Sheffield Wednesday FC, Goalkeeper**

Spent five years at QPR before joining Sheffield Wednesday
in March 1958. Although relegated in his first season there, he
helped them win the Second Division championship the following year. This season, he helped Wednesday reach the FA Cup
final where after leading 2-0 they lost 2-3 to Everton. First capped
in 1959, Springett went to the 1962 World Cup as first choice,
playing every game. At fault for two of the French goals in the 5-2
European Nations' Cup defeat, Ramsey's first game as manager
in 1963, Springett was soon replaced in goal by Gordon Banks.
Springett has played only four times since but remains Banks's
first deputy for the time being.

 **Peter Bonetti, aged 24, 1 cap
Chelsea FC, Goalkeeper**

Nicknamed "The Cat," Bonetti made his club debut aged nineteen
in 1960 and has been Chelsea's No. 1 since the 1960/61 season. He
helped his club win the 1965 League Cup final with an inspired
performance in the goalless second leg away to Leicester City.
This season, Bonetti played every game as Chelsea reached the
semi-finals of the European Fairs Cup in addition to thirty-eight
League appearances. The last of the squad to be capped in the
penultimate game against Denmark, Bonetti is unlikely to feature
in this tournament but the experience gained this summer may
prove invaluable if he is called upon in 1970.

Jimmy Armfield, aged 30, 43 caps
Blackpool FC, Right-back

Originally a left-winger and a keen rugby player, the former England captain was voted best right-back in the world at the 1962 World Cup. Since making his debut for Blackpool aged nineteen, and helping them to finish second in the league in 1955/56, Armfield has stayed loyal to his boyhood club despite their lack of success. Young Player of the Year in 1959, he finished second in the main award behind Bobby Charlton this season. Such form earned him his first England caps in two years, returning as captain in the absence of the injured Bobby Moore.

 Gerry Byrne, aged 27, 2 caps
Liverpool FC, Left-back

A Liverpool player since he was fifteen, it took a few years, and the arrival of Bill Shankly, for Byrne to break through as a first-team regular. In the 1965 FA Cup final, Byrne suffered a broken collarbone after only three minutes but played on throughout the game, even setting up Roger Hunt's goal in extra time. An ever-present in Liverpool's Second Division title campaign in 1961-62, Byrne has just repeated the feat, playing every minute as Liverpool won the First Division for the second time in three seasons. His club form led to a second international cap against Norway in June, three years after his first in 1963. Byrne is capable of providing cover in either full-back position.

 Martin Peters, aged 22, 3 caps, 1 goal
West Ham United FC, Midfield

Uncapped until May, Peters has impressed so much since, he may have forced his way into Ramsey's World Cup team. Having first appeared for West Ham in 1962, he was pivotal in the Hammers' successful 1965 European Cup Winners' Cup campaign playing in a three-man midfield. Peters scored in this season's League Cup final to add to a career-best eleven league goals. He has taken that form into the international arena, starring on his debut against Yugoslavia before scoring in his second appearance against Finland. His versatility and technique make him one to watch this summer.

 Ron Flowers, aged 31, 49 caps, 10 goals
Wolverhampton Wanderers FC, Centre-back

The oldest member of the squad, the former RAF airman first played for Doncaster Rovers academy before joining Wolves' nursery side, Wath Wanderers. Signed by Stan Cullis in 1952, Flowers initially made his name as an attacking midfielder winning three league titles in the 1950s and the FA Cup in 1960. Three years after making his debut back in 1955, Flowers played in forty consecutive internationals between 1958 and 1963, scoring two penalties in the 1962 World Cup and England's first-ever goal in the European Nations' Cup the following year. No longer first choice, Flowers provides experienced cover should injuries or suspensions occur.

 Norman Hunter, aged 22, 4 caps
Leeds United AFC, Centre-back

With Leeds from the age of fifteen, Hunter has been Jack Charlton's defensive partner since 1962, winning the Second Division title in 1964 and narrowly missing out on the league and cup double in 1965. This season, Hunter has added goals to his fierce tackling, scoring five times in forty-one matches. Having made his international debut in 1965 as England's first-ever substitute, he has started three games this year alongside club colleague Charlton and some would have England utilise this partnership in the World Cup at the expense of captain Bobby Moore.

 Terry Paine, aged 27, 18 caps, 7 goals
Southampton FC, Winger

A man who originally made a living building coaches for the British Railway Depot, Paine has just helped his club win their first-ever promotion to the First Division, scoring sixteen times. Signed by Third Division Southampton from Winchester City, Paine is a crowd favourite at The Dell, renowned for his pace, crossing ability and goalscoring, having found the net 137 times in ten seasons at the club. In 1961, he was appointed captain and led them to promotion this season. An established international, Terry, alongside Ron Flowers, is one of two members of Ramsey's squad playing outside the top division. Having made his debut in 1963, he became the first right-winger since Stanley Matthews to score an England hat-trick against Northern Ireland later that year. The last of his seven international goals was the winner against West Germany in 1965. He has only appeared four times this season for England and is likely to be battling Ball and Connelly for a starting position in the World Cup team.

 Ian Callaghan, aged 24, 1 cap
Liverpool FC, Winger

Callaghan joined Liverpool as a member of the groundstaff aged fifteen before signing on as an apprentice five years later. He made his debut in 1961 but didn't make his breakthrough until Liverpool's promotion-winning season in 1963, appearing twenty-three times. He was an ever-present for Liverpool in both of their recent title-winning campaigns, scoring eight times in 1963-64 and five times this season. In between, Callaghan played a pivotal role in Liverpool's first FA Cup win in 1965, crossing for Ian St John's extra-time winner against Leeds United. Ramsey called him up for the pre-tournament European tour in which Callaghan made his debut in the 3-0 win over Finland. Inexperienced at international football he may be, but Callaghan goes into the World Cup brimming with confidence as an English champion and having experienced European club football for two successive seasons.

 Roger Hunt, aged 27, 13 caps, 12 goals
Liverpool FC, Forward

Signed by Liverpool from Stockton Heath as a twenty year-old, Hunt had to wait a year before making his debut for them in the Second Division. He scored then and has rarely stopped since, finding the net forty-one times in forty-one games as Liverpool won promotion in the 1961-62 season. Liverpool's top scorer in their 1963-64 championship-winning campaign with thirty-one, Hunt repeated the feat this season, scoring another twenty-nine for the champions. In addition Hunt scored in Liverpool's 1965 FA Cup final win and their 1966 European Cup Winners' Cup final defeat to Borussia Dortmund. He made his international debut as a Second Division player in April 1962, scoring on his debut against Austria and earning a place in the 1962 World Cup squad. Somewhat overlooked at first by Alf Ramsey, he has now cemented his place with a series of impressive performances this season, particularly away from home, including a goal in the win away to Spain, two in Glasgow against Scotland, and England's last goal in the victory in Poland.

George Eastham, aged 29, 19 caps, 2 goals
Arsenal FC, Midfield

The son of a former England international George played along-side his father at the Northern Irish club, Ards, before joining Newcastle United in 1956. When Newcastle refused to allow him a transfer, Eastham went on strike at the end of his most prolific season, 1959-60 scoring twenty, in 1960 eventually securing a move to Arsenal. He has never hit such heights for Arsenal, only twice reaching double figures and scoring six from thirty-seven appearances this season. Called up for the 1962 World Cup squad, Eastham didn't make his debut until the following year against Brazil. Barring injuries to others, it is unlikely he will see action this summer.

 Alf Ramsey, aged 46
The Manager

Born in Dagenham, Ramsey served in World War II, playing for the British Army XI before embarking on a professional career with Southampton and Tottenham Hotspur as a diligent right-back, nicknamed "The General." Capped thirty-two times for his country, including at the 1950 World Cup, Ramsey retired from playing in 1955 and entered management with Ipswich Town, then in the Third Division South. Within seven seasons, Ramsey had incredibly led Ipswich to the First Division title. He was appointed England's first full-time manager in charge of selection, succeeding Walter Winterbottom in October 1962.

Meet the 1966 Teams

Joe Kennedy

Group One

England

Anthem: "God Save the Queen." As ever, the notorious monotony of the anthem has led some to suggest a more rousing number, such as "Jerusalem," "Land of Hope and Glory" or "Drive My Car".

Qualification: England qualified by virtue of hosting, giving Alf Ramsey's players plenty of time – some would say too much – to put their feet up and relax.

Coach: Ramsey promised that England would win the next World Cup upon taking over from Walter Winterbottom in 1962. It's a big claim, although his achievement in turning Ipswich Town from Third Division makeweights to champions of England in just under seven years simply can't be overstated. Much has been made of his tactics, although scepticism remains about their usefulness at this level of the game.

Star player: Bobby Moore succeeds Johnny Haynes as captain and the graceful West Ham defender should do more than enough to justify the decision.

Prospects: Between Tottenham's Jimmy Greaves and the West Ham trio of Moore, Martin Peters and Geoff Hurst, this team feels a little more London-centric than previous squads. It's hard not to feel that Swingin' London is due its sporting version at Wembley. Portugal, West Germany and Brazil look more dangerous on paper, but England have a higher than average chance of success.

Want to distract them?: A young England squad based in London should have more than enough to distract them, thanks very much.

Sing when they're winning: The Who, "My Generation." Ramsey's new England will be looking to shrug off the complacency and naivety which saw the national side stall in the 1950s.

France

Anthem: "La Marseillaise," known more commonly on the English side of the channel as "Why Can't Our Anthem Be More Like Theirs?"

Qualification: Despite a surprisingly stiff challenge from the amateurs of Norway and the presence of the ever-dangerous Yugoslavia, France qualified with points to spare. A defeat in Belgrade was their one setback, but they won all their other games.

Coach: Henri Guérin took the top job after leading St-Étienne to the 1962 Coupe de France.

Star player: Defensive midfielder Robert Herbin was a star of Guérin's cup-winning side of 1962 and provides bite and abundant experience, despite being only twenty-seven at the time of writing.

Prospects: France are solid but lack spark. Big questions remain about whether their naturalised Argentinian forward Nestor Combin will come good after an inconsistent season at Varese. He proved his talents at Lyon, but has made a slow start in Italy.

Want to distract them?: "Non, vous ne pouvez pas apporter votre propre chef cuisinier à l'hôtel!" – "No, you can't bring your own chef to the hotel!"

Sing when they're winning: Herman's Hermits, "I'm Into Something Good." The uphill challenge for the French will be staying there.

Mexico

Anthem: "Mexicanos, al Grito de Guerra" – "Mexicans, at the Cry of War." A really quite impressively aggressive anthem.

Qualification: Overcame difficult, for CONCACAF, opposition in the first round of qualifying in the form of the USA and Honduras. In the second round, a trip to Jamaica proved trickier than expected, but the Mexicans left Kingston with a narrow away win and were then able to gain a decisive victory over Costa Rica.

Coach: Ignacio Trelles is in his second spell as head of the national team, having previously masterminded a first-round victory over eventual finalists Czechoslovakia in 1962.

Star player: Javier "Chalo" Fragoso is the up-and-coming prospect in attack, and scored twice in the 8-0 thrashing of Jamaica in Mexico City.

Prospects: Mexico, you'd expect, will be solid without being spectacular. They'll be looking to take points off France in particular, as defeating England at Wembley should prove beyond them. Quarter-finals at best.

Want to distract them?: "No ganar aquí! 1970 va a ser mucho más divertido si usted tiene algo que esperamos!" – "Don't win here! 1970 will be much more fun with something to look forward to!"

Sing when they're winning: The Honeycombs, "Have I the Right?" Possibly waiting to enjoy their privileges as hosts.

Uruguay

Anthem: "Orientales, la Patria o la Tumba" – "Orientals, the Fatherland or the Grave!" A favourite for trivia fans as it's the world's longest anthem.

Qualification: A flawless performance, taking maximum points from an admittedly easy group also containing Peru and Venezuela.

Coach: Ondino Viera, a seasoned campaigner who took Paraguay to runners-up spot in the 1963 Copa América.

Star player: Playmaker Héctor Silva got a few goals in qualifying and should be one to watch. Also look out for young striker José Urruzmendi.

Prospects: Mixed. Qualification was clinched, but they didn't have much to deal with, and Viera only took over last year so may not have fully bedded in his tactics. Nevertheless, the two-time winners can never be written off.

Want to distract them?: "Muy bien, así rayo puede caer dos veces, pero no lo hará por tercera vez." – "Okay, so lightning can strike twice – but it won't a third time."

Sing when they're winning: The Walker Brothers, "The Sun Ain't Gonna Shine Anymore" – although perhaps it will if the Uruguayans can stretch their luck in the competition that little bit further.

Group Two

Argentina

Anthem: "Himno Nacional Argentino" – "National Hymn of Argentina." A quintessential piece of blood-and-soil romantic nationalism from the *Cono Sur.*

Qualification: Argentina cruised past Paraguay and Bolivia, taking seven of the eight points available and finishing with a +7 goal difference from their four games.

Coach: Juan Carlos Lorenzo, one of the elite group of managers who have worked eponymously – his last job was at San Lorenzo.

Star player: An entirely home-based squad will look to Boca defender Carmelo Simeone for leadership and his club teammate Alfredo Rojas for goals. River Plate's Ermindo Onega might add some creative spark.

Prospects: A decent technical side, but Argentina seem to have a little less about them than South American rivals Brazil and Uruguay. West Germany will offer them a stern test in the group stages, so much will come down to the Transatlantic Hispanophone "derby" against Spain in Birmingham.

Want to distract them?: "¿De verdad parece que pueda llegar a ser un Pelé Argentian? Suena un poco exagerado para mí." – "Do you really think there'll be an Argentinian Pelé one day? Seems far-fetched to me."

Sing when they're winning: Cliff Richard and the Shadows, "Summer Holiday." A squad with very little European experience might indulge in a little sightseeing while in Birmingham. Hopefully, they find canals interesting.

Spain

Anthem: "Marcha Real" – "Royal March." The current version of the lyrics contains some provocative celebration of Spain's imperial adventures, which may not be quite *de rigeur* in the current climate of decolonisation.

Qualification: With only Syria and the Republic of Ireland to play, this should have been simple, and became even more so when the Syrians withdrew in protest at FIFA. A 1-0 defeat in Dublin coupled with a 4-1 win over the Irish in Seville, however, meant that a play-off was required. This was to have been held in London, but concerns were raised that, given the English capital's large Irish population, this was not really a "neutral" venue. Cue a switch to Paris, and a 1-0 Spanish victory.

Coach: José Villalonga, who has previously coached both of Real and Athletico Madrid.

Star player: Inter's Luis Suárez is the star of an inventive supply line laying on opportunities for Francisco Gento.

Prospects: Several of Spain's stars – not least Suárez and Gento – are slipping into the twilight years of their careers now and it's fair to see this as their last crack at securing the Jules Rimet Trophy. It's unlikely that they'll do so, but expect them to squeeze past Argentina into the quarter-finals.

Want to distract them?: "Un montón de canas por ahí, muchachos!" – "Lots of grey out there, guys!"

Sing when they're winning: The Beatles, "Can't Buy Me Love." Spain seem to have stopped appropriating players from other countries these days. Let's see how a reliance on homegrown players works out for them.

Switzerland

Anthem: The "Swiss Psalm," known alternatively as the *Schweizerpsalm*, the *Cantique Suisse*, the *Salmo svizzero* and the *Psalm Svizzer*. As ever, one wonders how the Swiss team communicate on the field.

Qualification: Switzerland topped a group in which only Northern Ireland were expected to offer much, although an away draw to the amateurs of the Netherlands in Amsterdam threatened to put a spoke in the wheel.

Coach: Alfredo Foni, born in Udine, played as an international for Italy and later managed the *Azzuri*. Fortunately, the earliest the Swiss could meet the Italians is in the semi-finals, so there's unlikely to be any conflict of interest.

Star player: Goalkeeper Karl Elsener has been around for a few years now and has previous World Cup experience under his belt.

Prospects: Switzerland will be thankful they have the creativity of Köbi Kuhn to create chances, but there's little to suggest that this rugged and reliable team can reach the next level.

Want to distract them?: As remarked upon above, the multilingual Swiss will surely be capable of confusing one another on your behalf.

Sing when they're winning: Nancy Sinatra, "These Boots Are Made For Walkin'" – Swiss footwear is better for hiking Alpine trails than for besting West German defenders.

West Germany

Anthem: The "Deutschlandlied," or "Song of Germany." Nothing if not emphatic.

Qualification: Minnows Iceland withdrew, so the task of the boys from the Federal Republic was to beat Cyprus – which was done without breaking sweat – and Sweden. Although the Swedes took a point home from West Berlin, goals from Werner Krämer and Uwe Seeler allowed the *nationalmannschaft* to come from behind to win in Stockholm.

Coach: Helmut Schön, who had the distinction of coaching the Saarland representative side at the 1952 Olympics, and has recently moved out from under Sepp Herberger's wing to take full control.

Star player: Young midfielder Franz Beckenbauer has pulled Bavarian nobodies Bayern Munich into the national limelight and, at only twenty years of age, has staked out a role of some significance in the national side. Up-front, Seeler and Helmut Haller are one of the deadliest partnerships going into the tournament.

Prospects: If their 1954 victory was carried to some extent by good fortune, a West German triumph in England will almost certainly come down to class. Strong in all areas of the pitch, they are the beneficiaries of the stable management of Herberger and Schön, and it does look like their time might have come once again.

Want to distract them?: Used to insulting Germans in cod-Deutsch, it might surprise them more to not say anything.

Sing when they're winning: The Kinks, "Tired of Waiting for You." Germany have been waiting for an indisputable star for years now; Beckenbauer is that man.

Group Three

Brazil

Anthem: "Hino Nacional Brasiliero" – "National Hymn of Brazil."
A song about an "intense dream," which may have been one in
which Pelé stays fit.

Qualification: As you are probably aware, the 1962 champions
were not required to participate in qualification. If you want a
measure of their form, they came fourth in the last Copa
America, but even that was three years ago.

Coach: Vicente Feola, who led the *seleção* to their first World Cup
victory in 1958, returns after a spell at Boca Juniors hoping to
give the Brazilians their third consecutive title.

Star player: It's obviously, even boringly, Pelé, but his injury
problems in Chile have raised a few doubts about whether he's
a big-tournament player. Absurdly, the prodigy who took the
world by storm in 1958 will arrive in England with something
to prove.

Prospects: Despite a hard group, Brazil should, and probably will,
prosper. There's plenty of hype about their youngsters,
including Jairzinho and Tostão, while Pelé, Garrincha and
Gerson offer a level of class far beyond what most of the
opposition can lay claim to in their entire squads.

Want to distract them?: "Eu não quero preocupá-lo, rapazes, mas
Pelé parece estar mancando." – "I don't want to worry you,
lads, but Pelé appears to be hobbling!"

Sing when they're winning: The Rolling Stones, "Get Off My Cloud."
It would be three wins in a row, but they wouldn't find it lonely
at the top.

Bulgaria

Anthem: "Mila Rodino" – "Dear Native Land." Adopted only recently, the current version includes a verse about Bulgaria's brotherhood with the USSR. Good thing they weren't drawn together, then.

Qualification: Tricky. They finished behind Belgium on goal difference, but the fact the two teams were level on points meant that the Bulgarians were able to go through after winning a play-off 2-1 in Florence.

Coach: Rudolf Vytlačil, who some will remember leading Czecho-slovakia to the final in 1962. He will be hoping to repeat the trick this year.

Star player: Undoubtedly Georgi Asparuhov, the twenty-two year-old striker whose quickfire brace in Florence secured passage to the finals.

Prospects: With Asparuhov leading the line, you'd expect Bulgaria to have a fighting chance in one of the other groups, but it's hard to see them progressing against the holders plus Portugal and Hungary, two of the leading European contenders at the tournament.

Want to distract them?: "Mozhete dori ne mozhe da nameri svoi sobstveni menidzhŭri!" – "You can't even find your own managers!"

Sing when they're winning: Elvis Presley, "Good Luck Charm." They'll be hoping back in Sofia that Vytlačil can be one of these for his adopted nation.

Hungary

Anthem: "Himnusz," meaning, simply, "Anthem." Functional in title, but a little nostalgic in its callback to "the plundering Mongols' arrows."

Qualification: Following their swaggering Gold at the 1964 Tokyo Olympics, the Hungarians will have been pleased to do the double over their Austrian neighbours. Máté Fenyvesi's winner on the stroke of half-time in Vienna was the turning point in the group. Arguably the greater achievement, however, was taking three points from the East Germans.

Coach: Lajos Baróti comes to England with an Olympic Gold, an Olympic Bronze and a third-place finish in the 1964 European Nations' Cup on his CV. To say he's done a good rebuilding job after the disintegration of the Puskás-led "Golden Team" is an understatement.

Star player: Ferenc Bene (Újpesti Dózsa). Not quite twenty-two, the Olympic Golden Boot just edges out the more familiar Flórián Albert here. Bene is a lean, graceful, predatory forward who, as Morocco discovered in Japan, thinks nothing of notching two hat-tricks in a game. Added points for his widow's peak, which makes him appear quite the rake.

Prospects: Hard to call. While not quite the team that periodically embarrassed England in the '50s, the Magyars come bearing trophies and their youngish side brims with potential and attacking élan. Nevertheless, they're in the Group of Death and must beat either Portugal or Brazil. If they can do that, they're an outside bet.

Want to distract them?: "Magyar sütemények nem rossz, de másolta őket az osztrákok!" – "I don't mind a Hungarian cake, but you copied them all from the Austrians!"

Sing when they're winning: Spencer Davis, "Keep on Running." Baróti, Bene and co. need to keep their Olympic momentum for their visit to Lancashire.

Portugal

Anthem: "A Portuguesa" – "The Portuguese." They'll hope its imperative to "hoist the undefeated flag" rings true at Wembley on 30 July.

Qualification: Pipped 1962 finalists Czechoslovakia to the post, largely thanks to Eusébio's winner in Bratislava in April last year. No mean feat.

Coach: Otto Glória, an experienced Brazilian who had previously done the business in his home country and with Marseille as well as with the Portuguese Big Three.

Star player: This is a squad hitting its prime, but the undoubted star is Eusébio, the Mozambique-born Benfica striker. There's not much he can't do, and he arrives in England as the reigning holder of the *Ballon d'Or*. Seriously good.

Prospects: Regardless of the fact this is their World Cup debut, pretty good – *if* Eusébio and Benfica strike partner José Torres can reproduce their club form.

Want to distract them?: "Ele é brilhante, mas ele pode fazê-lo em um dia chuvoso em Liverpool?" – "He's brilliant, but can he do it on a rainy day in Liverpool?"

Sing when they're winning: Tom Jones, "It's Not Unusual." Actually, it would be – Portugal are very much rising stars of world and European football, and will be hoping to make history here.

Group Four

Chile

Anthem: "Himno Nacional de Chile" – "National Song of Chile." Talks of the "protection" offered by the snow-covered Andes, which they unfortunately won't be able to bring with them to hide behind when they encounter the vengeance-fixated Italians.

Qualification: Finished level on points with Andean rivals Ecuador so played off in Lima to decide who'd be coming to England. A relatively easy 2-1 victory saw the 1962 hosts book their tickets.

Coach: Luis "El Zorro" Alamos. He'll need the cunning of his namesake to escape a group with both Italy and the Soviets in it.

Star player: Captain and inside-forward Leonel Sanchez is only thirty but has eleven years' experience of playing for the national side under his belt, along with about nine million goals for Universidad de Chile.

Prospects: Chile are competent but it's hard to see their entirely South American-based squad prospering under the winding gears of Wearside and the smokestacks of Middlesbrough. Third in the group and back to Santiago, despite their third-place finish as hosts.

Want to distract them?: "Prefiero tener un Pennine que un Ande cualquier día de la semana, lo siento compañero." – "Give me a Pennine over an Ande any day of the week, sorry mate."

Sing when they're winning: Bob Dylan, "Subterranean Homesick Blues." What they'll have if Zorro takes them on a teambuilding visit down a Durham mine.

Italy

Anthem: "Il Canto degli Italiani" – "The Song of the Italians." The chorus has four iterations of the phrase "we are ready to die," which is entirely plausible based on their "combative" antics in Santiago in 1962.

Qualification: The second-highest scorers in European qualifying after group rivals the Soviet Union, despite their growing reputation for defensiveness. A 1-0 defeat in Glasgow in their penultimate qualifier put what had hitherto been a cakewalk in jeopardy, but the *Azzuri* recovered to thrash the Scots 3-0 in the return in Naples.

Coach: Tasked with rebuilding after the chaos and recrimination of the Chilean sojourn in '62, Edmondo Fabbri previously took Mantova from Serie D to Serie A in four years. He could be one to watch.

Star player: The glamour players are Inter's Sandro Mazzola and Milan's Gianni Rivera, who Fabbri notoriously struggles to accommodate in the same team. Them aside, Giacinto Facchetti is the proverbial Rolls Royce at left-back, an elegant and accomplished performer both defensively and going forward.

Prospects: Who knows? Resolve the Mazzola–Rivera issue and limit the scope for temperamental meltdowns and this squad really could go all the way, but the disastrous Battle of Santiago continues to loom large in Italian sporting consciousness. They're meeting Chile again, too.

Want to distract them?: "Cospirazione? E' tutto nella vostra testa, ragazzi!" – "Conspiracy? It's all in your heads, lads!"

Sing when they're winning: The Beatles, "We Can Work It Out." This is a side who need to resolve their issues.

North Korea

Anthem: "Aegukka" – "Patriotic Song." The line "glory of a wise people brought up in a brilliant culture," which is a pretty forward introduction for this most unknown of quantities.

Qualification: Largely a formality after the anarchy of withdrawals and disqualifications in the Africa, Asia and Oceania qualifying round. Ultimately, Australia were the only other contestants for the one place allocated to these three continents, and they were dispatched 9-2 on aggregate over two surreal legs in Phnom Penh. FIFA need to rethink qualification in these regions sharp.

Coach: Myung Rye-hyun. Must help his players acclimatise to unfamiliar settings, although the unkind might draw certain similarities between Teesside and Pyongyang.

Star player: One of the youngest sides at this World Cup, the player to watch is probably striker and captain Pak Seung-zin, although his Moranbong teammate Pak Doo-Ik is a corporal in the North Korean army and therefore, one presumes, disciplined in training.

Prospects: Absolute no-hopers who got here almost entirely because of technicalities. If they have a lifeline, it's that they're playing all of their group games in one city, Middlesbrough, which might give them a home advantage of sorts.

Want to distract them?: "Soljighi , seungli neun maeu buleujua ida!" – "Frankly, isn't winning a little bit bourgeois?"

Sing when they're winning: Cilla Black, "Anyone Who Had a Heart." Everyone loves an underdog.

Soviet Union

Anthem: "Gosudarstvenny Gimn SSSR" – "State Anthem of the USSR." Replaced the "Internationale" with this during the war, much to the chagrin of the international workers' movement. Explicitly celebrates Lenin and Stalin, so don't sing along unless you want your kitchen refitted by MI5.

Qualification: The highest-scoring team in European qualifiers, albeit with relatively timid opposition from Wales, Greece and Denmark. Dropped points only in Cardiff, but they'd already qualified when they fell to Ivor Allchurch's late winner there.

Coach: The not particularly high-achieving Nikolai Morozov took Torpedo to third place in the Soviet League back in the '50s, and took over the national side in 1964 after guiding Lokomotiv to promotion. Hardly a stellar record, but impressed in qualification.

Star player: Holding midfielder Valery Voronin, who will know Morozov from Torpedo, is the man to watch. An all-rounder, his passes are as searching as his tackles are bruising.

Prospects: Good to strong. More than likely to find sympathy amongst the miners of County Durham, and may feel that their time has come.

Want to distract them?: "Kommunizm yavlyayetsya bol'shim v teorii, no on nikogda ne rabotayet na praktike!" – "Communism is great in theory, but it never works in practice!"

Sing when they're winning: The Dave Clark Five, "Glad All Over." They'll be celebrating from the Baltic to the Pacific if they can pull it off in England.

Kick-Off

This is England '66

Richard Weight

THE ENDURING POTENCY of England's World Cup victory is not mere pride in a unique sporting achievement but is bound up with a deeper legend of the 1960s as an age of modernity, cultural vigour and social change.

The Labour Party was re-elected in the General Election of 31 March 1966 with an increased majority of 96 MPs. Harold Wilson's hope that a "white heat" of technological progress would erode class barriers was already foundering on the entrenched influence of public schools. Britain's economic fragility was apparent in manufacturing decline and the devaluation of the pound in 1967. Yet, overall standards of living continued to rise while the gap between rich and poor narrowed. Wilson's governments also gave civil rights to women, gay men and ethnic minorities, as well as abolishing capital punishment and increasing university places.

However, conservative ideas about race and gender were still widely held, especially among older people shaped by the Empire and two World Wars. The World Cup therefore took place when a new, post-imperial British identity was being constructed and contested, forced to compete with the resilience of Victorian attitudes to what being British – and English – meant.

The coffin of the old Britain and the cradle of the new were on display at the state funeral of Winston Churchill held on Saturday 30 January 1965. There were mass expressions of grief and gratitude to the late war leader but many people wanted the country to move on, among them Colin MacInnes, author of *Absolute Beginners*, the 1959 novel about modern, cosmopolitan youth. As MacInnes wrote in "The Week he Died" for a *Sunday Telegraph* supplement following the State Funeral: "[Churchill's] death may finally liberate us from our obsession with 'the war', from our stupid hatred of Germany, our futile jealousy of America, our daft illusion that the Commonwealth is the Empire he admired and sought, impossibly, to maintain."

Liberation was only partial. Few Britons saw themselves as European when Harold Wilson began the nation's second attempt to join the European Economic Community shortly before the tournament. To sweet-talk the Germans, the Queen was dispatched to the Federal Republic soon after Churchill's funeral. It was the first State visit to Germany by a British monarch since 1913 and she was greeted by jubilant crowds in Hanover, the seat of her ancestor George I. But the Labour Foreign Secretary, Michael Stewart, reported that the Queen found the rhythmic chanting of "Elizabeth! Elizabeth!" disturbing. According to papers in the National Archive he reported to the Cabinet: "I think she thought it was too reminiscent of ritual Nazi shouting." Stewart, with some degree of foresight, concluded: "Two world wars and the horrors of Nazism have left such a legacy of bitterness that we cannot be sure that Anglo-German reconciliation will last."

That legacy was apparent when England played their democratic, capitalist ally in the final. The *Daily Mail* explicitly linked war and football in the minds of its readers: "If Germany beat us today at our national sport," it declared, "we can always point out to them that we have recently beaten them twice at theirs." In Roger Hutchinson's book *It Is Now!* Bobby Charlton recalled that "for six years we had waged a war against Germany; now we were preparing to do battle on the football field. A strange thought just before a vital match. But that's how it was."

However, while anti-German sentiment was raw and rife among older people it would be wrong to see the tournament as a crude expression of English xenophobia. Attitudes to Europe were softening; according to polls at the time almost two thirds of the public were in favour of joining the EEC by 1966. It was a profound shift based on a pragmatic view that entry would be good for business and consumers. Bitterness about the war competed with envy of West Germany's post-war economic success, the *Wirtschaftswunder*, which had delivered a higher standard of living in the Federal Republic. Despite the French veto of Wilson's application to join in 1967, support remained high after entry in 1973 under Edward Heath and into the Referendum of 1975 when Labour were back in power, in which two thirds of voters opted to remain in the EEC.

Several factors drove this fresh engagement with Europe. Continental holidays, once the preserve of the wealthy, were becoming affordable for ordinary Britons, with 4.2 million people taking foreign breaks by 1971 – up from 1.5 million in 1951. The influence of travel was soon apparent in British culture. Sales of wine doubled between 1960 and 1970 as the drink lost middle-class associations that had previously inhibited working class Britons from drinking it. Supermarkets were an American import of the '60s, but ironically they brought Europe a bit closer by making wine – and food from garlic to pasta – more available and affordable as people acquired a taste for the exotic on holiday. This was a time when Heinz-tinned Spaghetti Bolognese was still marketed as the "exciting new Italian dish."

Another aspect of Europeanisation was the evolution of Britain's youth culture from a pale imitation of the United States in the 1950s into a hybrid of American, European and Caribbean style called "Mod." The Mod-Rocker seaside disturbances of 1964-65 were a precursor of the tribal football hooliganism that blighted Britain a decade later. But those who fought on the beaches were a minority on the edge of the generation gap. Mod had become a broad commercial youth movement by the time of the World Cup and its adherents, more interested in style than combat of any kind, saw Continental Europe as a place of sharp suits and scooters rather than the dictators and collaborators their parents had fought in the War.

While their clothing style was mostly French and Italian, the music they listened to – from soul to rhythm & blues – was mostly African-American. Refracted through the lives of upwardly mobile white Britons, it too reflected a new cosmopolitanism that went hand in hand with a fresh confidence in British pop culture, which had been dominated by the United States since the 1920s. In the week that the tournament began, eighteen of the artists in the top thirty of the British pop charts were native acts, ranging from "Sunny Afternoon," The Kinks' satire of an overtaxed aristocrat at number one, to Dusty Springfield's version of "Goin' Back" at number thirty.

FA executives were so out of step with this new music that they commissioned Lonnie Donegan to compose England's tournament song, "World Cup Willie." Victory on the field could not save it from failure in the charts. Although the 1950s Skiffle king had influenced the likes of Lennon and McCartney, his "jaunty New Orleans brass band and banjo" number was a chart flop in the year that *Revolver* was released. No wonder when it was neither traditional enough to appeal to the middle-aged and elderly English, nor modern enough for the youth market.

Despite these efforts from the FA, British pop music seeped organically into football stadiums as young fans turned songs by their favourite groups into tribal chants. Traditionally, football songs had been dominated by hymns like "Abide with Me." These refrains continued to be sung but by the mid-'60s the football hymnal competed with tunes like another 1966 Kinks hit, "Dead End Street." Originally written about working class poverty, according to the Adrian Thrills book *You're Not Singing Anymore*, the lyrics were changed by Stoke City fans to have a pop at rivals Port Vale: "What are we living for? To see Port Vale in Division Four."

The decline of the football hymnal also testified to the fact that mainland Britain was becoming one of the world's most secular countries. More people still went to church on Sunday mornings than to football matches on Saturday afternoons and the audience figures for *Songs of Praise* remained higher than those for *Match of the Day.* However, church attendance fell by 19% to around four million people in the decade 1960-70. The number of baptisms and religious marriages fell by 50% to less than a third of the population; cremation, still seen as a heathen practice in the 1950s, became the most popular way of dispatching the dead by 1967.

When John Lennon said "We're more popular than Jesus now" in an interview in March 1966, most Britons (despondent church leaders included) accepted it as a fair assessment of the fact that the Beatles had more fans than the Saviour did. God was not dead. 70% of the population still believed in Him even if most no longer practiced their faith. Belief was buttressed by the high levels of religiosity among new Commonwealth immigrants, from Christian West Indians to Muslim Pakistanis. However, while God was far from dead, religion retreated from the public arena into the private spheres of British life where it was less able to police attitudes and behaviour. One result of this new secularity was a more liberal attitude to sex and family life, accompanied by the gradual emancipation of women.

The number of women going to university and into professional work began to rise in the '60s. In just five years up to 1966, the overall number of women in work rose from 37.5% to 42.2% of the female population, as a result of which they made up 34.3% of the British workforce by the time the World Cup began. In the second half of the '60s, women were given the right to contraception and abortion as well as easier divorce and the right to half a family estate if their marriage ended. Marriage remained a popular institution but expectations of it rose as women demanded more sexual and intellectual satisfaction than their mothers had enjoyed. According to the historian Penny Summerfield, the number of Britons who thought extra-marital sex was immoral fell from 66% to just 10% in the period between 1963 and 1973. Sex was liberalised in law and in popular culture but the way that women were depicted during the World Cup showed how much their new expectations and opportunities were contested by men of all ages.

During the tournament England's female fans were seen as enthusiastic bystanders, caught up in the patriotism of it all for a time but ultimately excluded from a resolutely male culture. This was symbolised by the fact that the players' wives were segregated from them at the victory dinner held at the Royal Garden Hotel in Kensington High Street on the night of the final. Even the *Sun* newspaper compared their treatment to "slave girls in an Arab bazaar." The *Sunday Mirror*'s triumphant report on England's "GOLDEN BOYS" included a photo of their wives in "a ground floor lounge bar" of the hotel while the victory dinner took place on a floor above them. Under the headline "As always – women have the last word," the *Sunday Mirror* said "they sipped drinks and chatted about the game... judging by the absorbed expressions of the wives, it should never be said again that women cannot get excited over football."

Inside, the *Sunday Mirror* carried an article on micro skirts in Paris and two pictures of topless women. Above a photo of the French model Clotine Lange was printed "Auberon Waugh's ABC of Beauty." The journalist son of the novelist Evelyn Waugh gave *Mirror* readers the following advice on dating and mating in his entry "D for Dramatic":

> Plain girls who want to cut a dash have to paint their eyelids blue, whiten their lips and cut inches off the smallest mini-skirt they can buy. If nothing else works, they can always faint. Or scream... [But] dramatic girls are dangerous. Their message for men is unmistakeable – stick to the homely types. One act of folly leads to unbelievable suffering for all concerned until the final catastrophe.

Quite what constituted a dramatic girl or a final catastrophe was unclear. But Waugh's message was not: sexual freedom was a dangerous, double-edged trend for men. Male anxiety about female emancipation, whether sexual or economic, meant that despite being given more control over their lives, women had more power in the bedroom than in the boardroom. Two years after the World Cup, sewing machinists making car seats at Ford's Dagenham plant fought a battle for equal pay with male car workers – a campaign that was supported by the Employment Secretary Barbara Castle and led to the 1970 Equal Pay Act. The resistance they encountered came as much from their trade union as from their employer and it showed that although the "permissive society" was sexually liberating for all, men were more willing to permit shorter skirts than bigger pay packets.

Bigger pay packets for footballers were transforming the British game when the World Cup was staged, following the abolition of the players' maximum wage in 1961. The glamorous affluence of football stars reflected two changes in post-war British society: the growth of a more American-style consumer society in which class cultures, and their political affiliations, became more blurred; secondly, the growth of a more American-style celebrity culture of which footballers were now a part. In March 1966, George Best and his friend Manchester City's Mike Summerbee opened up a male boutique in Manchester. Best was photographed carrying boxes of what he called "our new Mod stock" into the shop. Four hundred female fans who'd turned up for the opening nearly smashed the front window trying to get in.

An *Observer* colour supplement feature published to mark the tournament, called "The Game That Came Out of the Gutter," charted the changing role of football in British life. It was accompanied by an interview with Jimmy Greaves in which the England star said, "My pleasures are a film, a few pints at the local, a game of tennis on Sunday – maybe at the Savoy. Not so long ago, the Savoy would have made me shudder. I vote Tory." He continued with this defiant reassurance to readers:

> Football's still very much a working class game and traditions die hard. Every footballer I know comes from a basically working class background... but it goes deeper than that – the crowd, the

whole surroundings. It's not like Wimbledon with strawberries and cream, and women with frilly drawers on. It's a hard, dirty game. You go out on the field and you come back covered in mud. Football's a man's game.

On the one hand Greaves, like other star footballers of the day, represented the rise of ambition among the working classes, which made a few of them stars in the '60s without troubling the institutions that helped to perpetuate the class structure. His revelation that he voted Conservative also showed that the Labour Party would not always be the beneficiary of the increased opportunity over which Harold Wilson's reforming governments presided.

Greaves' view that despite money and status he remained working class also revealed the British tendency to see class in a restrictively cultural way rather than in the more fluid economic terms with which Americans pursued their Dream. In other words, acquiring wealth and the trappings of taste did not make you middle class as it did in the United States. The survival of deference to the Establishment was displayed when Bobby Moore wiped the sweat from his hands before receiving the Jules Rimet Trophy from the Queen in order, as he later said, to avoid soiling her white gloves.

Although football remained a largely working class pursuit for players and fans it had become important to all social groups as a measure of national status, in an age when the United States and the Soviet Union had between them eroded British power. Harold Wilson used the tournament to score points about the state of the nation under Labour. His request to comment on the final at half-time was turned down by the BBC; but that evening he joined Ramsey and the team on the balcony of the Royal Garden Hotel in Kensington to milk the crowd. The Labour politician Dick Crossman wrote in his diary, later published as the *The Diaries of a Cabinet Minister*:

I must record a big change in Harold's personal position. Luck was running against him till the end of the week; now it seems suddenly to have turned. I would guess he has had a real success with President Johnson. But it is also a tremendous help for him that we won the World Cup on Saturday... When I told Anne [his wife] over lunch today that the World Cup could be a decisive factor in strengthening sterling, she couldn't believe it. But I am sure it is. It was a tremendous, gallant fight that England won. Our men showed real guts and the bankers, I suspect, will be influenced by this, and the position of the government correspondingly strengthened.

The day after the final the *Sunday Mirror* agreed, with the head-line "WORLD BANKERS PLEASE NOTE: Britain's reserves went up yesterday by one valuable gold cup." The Football Association agreed too. An assessment of England's win published by the FA in September 1966 used it to make a sly attack on militant trade unionists and radical students:

[The victory] raised our prestige throughout the world... [and] is indeed one of the few bright spots in the somber economic situation which faces the country this summer. We feel sure that many of our export industries will derive a welcome boost from this success. The players who have made it possible worked hard and made many sacrifices. They have set an example of devotion and loyalty to the country, which many others would do well to follow.

Black and Asian people's loyalty to the country was also being questioned in this period, at a time when immigration was making England the most racially diverse place in Europe. Decol-onisation continued in World Cup year when Guyana became independent on 26 May 1966 but gaining freedom from Britain did not stop people wanting to come here. Between 1961 and 1971, the combined ethnic-minority population rose from 500,000 (about 1% of the population) to 1.5 million (about 3%). Most of those arriving in the mid-1960s were from the Indian sub-continent. But it was the children of earlier West Indian migrants who formed the bulk of a new British-born ethnic-minority population. From 1961 to 1966, the number of British children of Caribbean descent rose from 35,000 to 133,000 out of a total of 402,000 ethnic West Indians living in the UK. Among those children were future England internationals like Nottingham-born Viv Anderson who celebrated his tenth birthday on the day before the World Cup final.

A Peckham doctor from the West Indies called Harold Moody had launched Britain's civil-rights movement as far back as 1931 with the formation of the League of Coloured Peoples, but anti-discrimination legislation was only passed a year before the tournament. Racists condemned the Race Relations Act of 1965 as an affront to free speech and free trade and they found tacit support among football fans, players and club owners. This was a period when the small number of black professionals in the domestic game was rising and when vocal racist abuse of them – a white working class tradition since the late nineteenth century – was as common on the terraces as it was on the streets. Popular culture was saturated with prejudice, notably the BBC's *Black & White Minstrel Show* and the Cockney anti-hero Alf Garnett in the sitcom *Till Death Us Do Part*, the first series of which aired in the summer of 1966.

Some cheered England's victory because it was achieved with an all-white team. Pundits and people eulogised great black players like Pelé and Eusébio with sincerity but also with ease because they were essentially visitors. Such players were an exotic temporary presence and not a resident, British-born citizenry who were challenging racial definitions of Englishness. The whiteness of the England team was not explicitly referred to in order to score points in the contemporary debate on immigration; but it gave comfort to those who needed it that England remained, symbolically at least, a white nation (the presence of the Jewish George Cohen could simultaneously be thought to affirm that the English were a tolerant people).

Cricket was not a global sport like football, having only been exported to parts of the Empire, but in the 1960s it symbolised multi-racial England more than football did. On 16 June 1966 Basil d'Oliveira, the South-African born "Cape coloured," made his Test debut for England against the West Indies, twelve years before Viv Anderson became the first black footballer to represent his country. In 1968 d'Oliveira's selection led to a tour of South Africa being cancelled by the white minority government, an act which mobilised anti-racist opinion and led to a worldwide sports boycott of the apartheid regime. This was in marked contrast to the fact that African nations boycotted the 1966 World Cup in protest at unfair qualification rules.

For almost three centuries "Britain" had been understood as an island of whiteness. Racial affinity was one of the cultural bonds that held together the testy, pragmatic union between England and Scotland – along with monarchy, Protestantism and an Empire that had been justified as the commercial and political expression of British racial superiority. Although Anglo-Scottish racial affinity still prevailed in the 1960s, the World Cup showed how fragile the Union was becoming.

The rise of Scottish nationalism began in the 1950s and not, as is commonly assumed, the 1980s. Almost two million Scots (two-thirds of the electorate) signed a petition calling for Home Rule in 1950, a cause driven by Scotland's industrial decline, which made its standard of living lower than in most of England. Discontent with the economic benefits of Union transformed a perennial cultural nationalism into a political movement for greater autonomy. Although desire for full independence remained a minority opinion, Scottish nationalism was gathering pace when the World Cup took place and was aggravated by it.

The oldest grievance of the Scots was the arrogant English tendency to elide "England" and "Britain." This had been common since the Victorian age of Empire – ironically, given Scotland's disproportionate role in colonial conquest and rule – and it was manifest in the resolutely British iconography of the 1966 tournament. World Cup Willie, the official mascot used to promote the tournament worldwide, was a lion wearing a Union Jack football jersey. As well as being used on royal coats of arms, the lion had become an imperial symbol in the nineteenth century, pictorially used to challenge the might of the French cockerel, the German eagle and the Russian bear. Willie was designed by the children's book illustrator, Reg Hoye, who had previously illustrated some of Enid Blyton's work. Hoye modernised him by giving him a mane that looked like a spiky Beatle mop-top, but Willie's jersey remained an affront to Scots.

More fans waved Union Jacks than St George flags at England matches (at the final they outnumbered George flags by twenty to one). Match programmes approved by the FA all displayed the Union Jack and even the BBC made the same cardinal error, despite having a devolved structure that was more sensitive than most institutions to cultural differences within the Union. The Scottish Edition of the *Radio Times* "World Cup Number" announced that the BBC2 channel would be launched in Scotland in the week the tournament began (having first been shown to England in 1964). Readers were told that "the sense of occasion for Scottish viewers should then be enhanced" by a dramatisation of Walter Scott's *Heart of Midlothian*. But that didn't stop the BBC printing a Union Jack on the *Radio Times* cover and next to "England" in its guide to the teams taking part.

Scottish resentment at England's victory was as much a testament to the contemporary state of Anglo-Scottish relations as it was to centuries-old rivalry. Commenting on the final in the *Observer* of the day after England's win, Glasgow-born Hugh McIlvanney noted that "Scottish supporters sat in a smouldering sulk in corners of the Press Centre and insisted they did not know what all the fuss was about." In a gesture that proved Scots do have a sense of humour, the Scottish Football Association sent a message of congratulation to its English counterpart, which described the victory as a great *British* achievement. Dennis Law simply described it as "the blackest day of my life."

The following year, Law scored one of the goals in Scotland's 3-2 defeat of England in a European Championship qualifier at Wembley on 15 April 1967. A pitch invasion by Scottish fans followed which, though less famous than the "Tartan Army" invasion of 1977, was just as symbolic in the context of British politics. Scots joked that they were now effectively World Champions and the British press acknowledged it. Beneath the headline "TARTAN TIGERS!" the *News of the World* commented: "Not only was the glitter of the world crown tarnished, but Scotland are now the international champions." In the same paper the match report also suggested that complacency was at the root of defeat: "The England forwards began as though they wanted to give an exhibition of football to recall the greatness of last July."

Complacency certainly prevailed at Westminster. Soon after Scotland's triumph on the pitch, Scottish voters delivered another beating in the polling booths of Hamilton in Lanarkshire. On 2 November 1967, Winnie Ewing won a by-election in a previously safe Labour seat to become the first SNP Member of Parliament since World War II, a shock that led to political devolution belatedly becoming Labour Party policy in order to blunt the appeal of nationalism.

The Scottish programme notes for the 1967 British derby, written by a Glasgow journalist called Gair Henderson, showed that for the Scots the "Auld Enemy" remained England rather than Germany:

> Folk with the Harry Lauder accent are [not] reputed to have a flair
> for throwing away their money... so there must be real magic in a
> football match that can make them pay up cheerfully and leave

the Highland glens, the crofts and the cities and head south for London and the green, green grass of Wembley. There is! ...The wars of the Thistle and the Rose are fought nowadays on a much more friendly basis, but for Scotsmen the greatest pride of all is to beat England. That, my dear Sassenach friends, is not just bitter Hie'land rancor showing itself in a twisted way... what greater glory could there be than humbling the greatest football team in the world?

Henderson denied that Scots had supported Germany but a Scottish "anyone but England" movement became a feature of tournaments that England played in from World Cup '82 onwards. This "bitter Hie'land rancor" mattered because football was a cultural bond that once held the Union together while providing an outlet for core national identities via the first ever international England vs Scotland match in 1870 and home internationals from 1883 onwards.

Published in time for Christmas 1966, the BBC commentator Kenneth Wolstenholme wrote an account of the tournament called *The Boys' Book of the World Cup* (girls' interest had apparently faded). In the introduction he wrote "the myth of English people being quiet and reserved died on Saturday 30 July 1966." Other English myths began to die too. Like all triumphs in a nation's history, the responses to 1966 tell us as much about underlying anxieties as they do about the thin layer of confidence on the surface of victory. World Cup Willie was a strange sort of lion who epitomised a nation in transition: On the one hand he was a vestige of male, Anglo-centric imperialism and on the other hand he was the cuddly symbol of a more democratic society.

At its best, thanks to the likes of David Bowie and The Specials, the popular culture of which the tournament formed a part continued to be artistically innovative and socially challenging into the 1970s and beyond. However, by the time England failed to qualify for the 1974 World Cup, the broad optimism of the '60s had turned into disillusionment amid political resistance to social change that slowed down progress and intensified anger among the millions who stood to benefit from it.

Consequently, 1966 came to be ever more romanticised in the folk memory of the English. For many people it remained a moment of triumph amid the thwarted hopes of the '60s and a lesson in what the nation might collectively achieve. But for other fans in the 1970s and '80s, the victory also became part of a xeno-phobic and at times racist populism, which saw Bobby Moore and his men as exemplars of white, male, working class triumph over foreign enemies. The cry of "Two World Wars and One World Cup" reflected the more conservative bent of the Union's most powerful nation, which struggled to come to terms with its declin-ing power more than its smaller compatriots. English national-ism remained a loosely aligned movement, freighted with ideas of war, empire and race that voiced rancorous discontent with devolution, the European Union and multicultural settlement.

Ironically, Scotland's relative footballing success dimmed in the 1990s as a new kind of Tartan Army emerged, whose mem-bers were more concerned with social justice than pitch inva-sions. Scarred by a Thatcherite project they never voted for, and captivated by the SNP's vision of a left-leaning multicultural European nation, more and more Scots voted for a party com-mitted to breaking up Britain (significantly the SNP recruited a majority of Scottish Asians to its cause). From the opening of the Scottish Parliament in 1999 to the Independence Referendum of 2014 and the General Election of 2015, Scots rebuked and buried complacent English assumptions about the nature and vigour of the British state.

Yet when England played both Scotland and Germany in the Euro '96 tournament another face of Englishness showed itself: one in which the lines created by "thirty years of hurt" hadn't dis-figured the left-liberal contours of 1966. Football was linked again to the vibrant pop culture of the day and to a more reflective, self-aware Englishness that admitted the importance of female fans

and the necessity of a multi-racial team, and which at least knew
the difference between England and Britain in the St George flags
the fans now flew. And as the quite successful England team of
the decade 1996–2006 was dismantled, a semi-final and three
quarter-finals, a new realism about the team's international prospects seemed to mirror a new realism about the extent to which
Britain was no longer a world power or a united kingdom. The
"Golden boys" had been tarnished by the bitter nationalism they
had been made to bear; but those eleven red-shirted men, and the
modern England of '66 that they ultimately represented, continued to shine through.

When Saturdays Came

John Williams

THERE IS LITTLE DOUBT that football clubs in England filled a huge emotional and social vacuum in the years immediately after World War II, perhaps especially for working class men still recuperating after the brutal conflict. The social geographer Nick Phelps has captured especially well the atmosphere, lived social reality, and the wider role of the game in the years of the post-war "golden age," with many football clubs revealing a "complex nesting of local, regional and national identities." The heady experience of post-war league champions was felt first in the North West, then relocated to London, and on to the south coast. After Liverpool had snatched the first post-war championship in 1947, followed by an Arsenal triumph in 1948, it was unassuming and largely unconsidered — but fiercely tough — Portsmouth FC who were to sweep to successive post-war titles, in 1949 and 1950.

Portsmouth FC, in these early post-war years, did its best to ape the football powerhouses "up north," not only in terms of its intensely physical style of play, but also in its austere stadium, the character of its players and the intimacy and warmth of the relationship established between the club's staff and its supporters after the war. Barrel-chested butcher's son and half-back, "Jolly Jack" Froggart, for example, was feted by local fans, reputedly for stocking up on match-days on his father's best beef. Club hard man Jimmy Scoular was prized for his chastening habit (for the opposition) of having his shorts "pulled right up, you know, showing his thighs." On the pitch, Scoular was described by Manchester United's Duncan Edwards, no mean judge, as "the finest tackler of the ball I ever saw." But Scoular was also the master of the strategic body check or sly trip when it was needed to gain advantage for his men. Even the *Liverpool Echo*, not averse itself to a bit of northern-style grit, commented in November 1948 that referees who chose to side with the Portsmouth way were liable to believe that football was indeed "a he-man's game."

In this celebration of the virtues of hard-nosed working class localism, Portsmouth's players, under beady-eyed manager Bob Jackson, were the subject of the sort of authoritarian paternalism that was well suited to the austerity of the immediate post-war period. As at many English clubs at the time, Portsmouth's playing staff were required to live near the home ground, keep out of trouble, and front up in local shops and pubs in the wake of embarrassing defeats or weak match performances. Control could be more easily asserted on "troublesome" types, of course, if the player and his family also lived in a clubhouse. But mostly these players exuded, perhaps above all else, a deep commitment to the collective; they were the antithesis of today's stars, or even northern footballing heroes of the time – Matthews, Finney, Lawton, Liddell – instead epitomising the conservatism and general lack of class-consciousness in the south of England when compared to some northern cities.

Indeed, like many professional players in England at the time, Portsmouth's players in these early post-war years echoed key aspects of their domestic habitus, the occupational culture they served; or the local "structure of feeling," to use a phrase invented by the radical literary theorist Raymond Williams. They reflected back to their followers, in this case, the values of patriotism and the competition that existed between the crafts and trades that dominated the local Admiralty Dockyards in Portsmouth. Most professional players in this sort of context and at this moment were essentially ordinary citizens; privileged workers likely to be spotted in a local pub or working men's club, or else taking their kids to school, albeit they were ones with an unusual craft and social position against which local male supporters could readily compare themselves.

Watching professional football in England, at a time when the major manufacturing cities of the north and south of Britain were slowly recovering after the privations and extensive damage of years of conflict, was, as one local fan in Portsmouth put it, like seeing "the bright light in the city." In many places in England the streets were still dingy and poorly lit, with towns and cities widely battle-scarred and riddled with demolition sites well into the late 1950s. Historian James Walvin has argued that going to poorly appointed football grounds in England at this record-breaking time for attendances was a cheap and comforting way of "shrugging off wartime restraint and drabness," a chance to return to more familiar pleasurable pursuits. It was simply something that many working men almost instinctively did, as a necessary buffer to the deep, infrastructural gloom around them and in the absence of other viable leisure options.

But post-war English football also fed, at least for a while, on the enduring spirit of the Blitz and the new solidarities and confidence established among working people. It did so in its role as an important site for the continuing cultural projection through sport of an illusory imperial power, something that had been left relatively untouched by developments in coaching and the playing of football abroad. Indeed, victorious Portsmouth players, the English champions, later recalled international football tours in the early 1950s, including to Brazil – visits which seem to have had no influence at all on the traditional ideals of British football managers or on the limited style of play of the classic English professional player. "British football was top dog in those far off days," said one. "Arrogance ruled supreme." He was right, of course, and later England manager Alf Ramsey seemed to have the same view about how little there was to learn about the game from Brazil. But a rude awakening was coming.

The year 1953 has been neatly described by Ronald Kowalski and Dil Porter as the year in which the British people finally shook off the grey "overcoat of post-war austerity." Rationing was easing – within eighteen months margarine, cheese, butter, meat and bacon would all be off the ration; a new young Queen had captured people's hearts; Crick and Watson dominated international science talk; Everest was conquered by a British-led expedition; and, in cricket, the Ashes were regained. The year is mainly remembered in English football circles, however, for two contrasting reasons: firstly, for the popular celebrations that followed the gentlemanly veteran Stanley Matthews' first and only FA Cup final win. The great northern master, a symbol of working class decency and respectability, finally received his long-awaited victor's medal from the newly crowned young Queen Elizabeth II, in front of – for the first time – a national TV audience. And, secondly, 1953 is remembered for the humiliation suffered by the national team (including Matthews and Ramsey of course) later in the year at the hands of a rampant Hungary, led by the imperious Ferenc Puskás.

As Martin Jones and Gavin Mellor have pointed out, the Matthews final symbolised a moment when the traditional, local roots of the sport in England – as epitomised by Matthews himself, as well as by the place and role of football in reviving exhausted post-war English cities such as Portsmouth – were beginning to be reshaped by the forces of a new, optimistic modernity, one that was to have a much stronger national providence. The game, in short, "intersected with the cultural spirit of the period, a time of celebrating both modernity and tradition."

The 1953 final, between Blackpool and Bolton Wanderers, was still celebrated in those northern football towns, of course, as a ripe old Lancashire clash transported down south. It had all the trappings of local pride and regional bragging rights that such a match implies. But its obvious TV popularity, franked by the presence of the new monarch – an estimated audience of 10 million watched the final at home – conferred on the contest a much more powerful national relevance at a moment of major social transformation. This was despite, of course, the English football authorities' continuing suspicions about television coverage, anxieties that would last pretty much undisturbed for the next forty years.

Matthews symbolised, in the eyes of the establishment, the kind of honest, modest and deferential figure that best characterised the decent and respectable working class men who had been so central to the history of the professional game and to the survival of the nation during the years of conflict. Media analyst Gary Whannel has argued that the lives of football stars during this period were often narrated in the press and elsewhere as "moral fables" in which good, embedded traditional values were routinely emphasised. Although Matthews had actually managed, even in the wake of organised protests about his proposed departure from the Potteries, to engineer a move from Stoke City to Blackpool, the persistence of the grimly defended retain-and-transfer system in England meant that smaller clubs could largely hold onto their prize assets in the 1950s.

Famously, Tom Finney, alongside Matthews unarguably the greatest English player of his generation, signed for Preston North End at fourteen years of age in 1936 and retired some twenty-four years later in 1960 after making 473 competitive appearances and scoring 210 goals for Preston. It was an astonishing record, but one that produced precisely no medals, nor titles won. Finney supplemented his meagre football wage with returns from his Preston plumbing business. The season after Finney retired, Preston were relegated from the top flight and have not been back since.

Although there are examples of a few more ambitious, less class-bound, English archetypes who went abroad to play from the 1950s onwards – Finney himself was wanted by Sicilian club Palermo in 1952 but his club refused to even discuss the matter – most domestic footballers of the time (like the FA and the Football League) still regarded "abroad" as an impenetrable and largely inhospitable foreign no-man's land. Not much changes. Elite English players of the day, in any case, were well-schooled in the practised art of being thankful for their £14 basic wage in England, earned for "doing what they loved" and something that they would happily do for free. And they were further grateful, of course, for being spared the options: the slow torture of the factory or the pit – or even worse.

The catastrophic first England international football home loss, 3-6 against Hungary in November 1953, was initially treated by sections of the press and the English football authorities as an aberration, something surely to be straightened out when the countries met in a return fixture in Budapest six months later in May 1954. The traditional virtues of the English game of "relentless chasing" and "tearing into the tackle" were argued by journalists to be the best means of revealing the lack of backbone among these collectivist foreigners and thus were the likely solution to the Hungarian puzzle. Some letter-writers to the national newspapers at the time even volunteered that their own club side would have been enough to see off the fancy Magyars. Instead, in the 1954 return leg England capitulated to Puskás and his men in an even heavier 7-1 defeat. It was "Disaster on the Danube" according to the alliteration-favouring *Daily Mirror*.

Jimmy Hogan, a revered Scottish tactician (at least abroad) who had spent much of his career coaching on the continent, told the newly football-obsessed *Daily Worker* in the aftermath of this latest fiasco that "our players have forgotten that the game is one of intelligent movement. Professional football in England has degenerated into a lazy and indolent life, for all but the few really conscientious players." This seemed harsh – no one could argue that English footballers were not working hard enough. But what exactly were they learning? Hogan's words certainly seemed to ring true for the 1954 World Cup finals in Switzerland one month later. Seeded England were knocked out by Uruguay at the quarter-final stage, registering one win, one draw and a defeat, to the South Americans, in the process. There were few signs of progress in the tournaments which followed: in 1958, in Sweden, England failed at the group stage; and 1962, in Chile, there was another quarter-final exit, this time to a strolling Brazil. "The Brazilians were so cocky and composed behind their 3-1 lead," England player Johnny Haynes said later, "that they were able to indulge in their victory dance in the last ten minutes, flaunting their superiority and their success."

When English league champions Wolves had beaten the Hungarian "people's army" club of Honved on a mud-heap at Molineux back in December 1954 – in a floodlit match covered live on radio and TV and billed as the club championship of the world – in some quarters the old order was thought to have been re-asserted. But not all were fooled. England international-in-waiting, Haynes, wrote later that the international defeats by the Hungarians had made a "tremendous" impact on football in England – but that it was short-lived. Midfield players began to play a little "shorter" for example, looking for return passes, he reported. English clubs also "tightened up" on training routines and everyone worked a little harder – for a time. Actually, Haynes reasoned that the English football elites had read the wrong lessons from the Hungarians. The mistake was thinking that it was their fitness, not skill, which was the key to the success of the men from Central Europe, so few English clubs radically changed their methods. The basic drag-back practiced so devastatingly by the Hungarians at Wembley in 1954, for example, was not widely seen in English football until the 1960s.

It was hardly surprising, perhaps, that the general technical quality of the English game improved relatively little in the years that followed. While the continentals were already talking about "science," tactics and variety in player preparation, the English approach to training, even into the early 1960s, was still incredibly basic, drawing largely on the brutal fitness regimes learned by club trainers and managers in the armed forces during the war. It was aimed at producing stamina and strength for the long slog ahead more than it was developing match awareness or ball skills. Directors at English football clubs – in tune with their training staff and still central at most clubs to player recruitment at this time – routinely reported to their board meetings on the hundreds of players they had scouted by referring mainly to their size, physique and weight of kick.

Training at a club such as Liverpool FC was a case in point. Monday was the day off, Tuesday was spent at the rudimentary Melwood training ground, on exercises, perhaps with a brief practice match. Wednesday and Thursday were usually days spent at Anfield, endlessly lapping the pitch under the eagle eye of disciplinarian trainer Albert Shelley, while Friday was back at Melwood, in spikes, for speed work. If it rained, the Liverpool players slogged up the covered terraces, or else did some basic gym work. This was the pattern at most clubs. There were still very few practical or creative activities undertaken with a football in training in the English game, and little on match tactics. When Bill Shankly arrived in December 1959 he introduced small-sided games and more ball work though, as elsewhere, fitness remained at the core of the Liverpool training regime.

Despite calls in sections of the quality press for a new direction, one prioritising skills and technique over fitness and brawn, most professionals in the game in England were still much more comfortable with the ideas of, say, a Stan Cullis over the young Matt Busby, and the "committed" game of a Jack Charlton over that of younger brother Bobby or – God forbid – the soon-to-emerge outrageous skill and wilful individualism of a George Best. When, in 1959, Denis Violett the technically gifted Manchester United captain argued that their "direct" style of play would make League champions Wolves poor ambassadors for the English game in the European Cup, he was strongly rebuked by the Football League for his insolence. The message was clear enough: the real strength of English football was to be found as much in character as in skill or technique. Moreover, the enduring sense of *entitlement* in the English game rang loud and clear in the late 1950s, even among the most ardent modernisers: that England and its domestic club football could – and *should* – regain its rightful place, at the very pinnacle of the world game.

As the decade rolled towards its close, the style of player autobiographies in England finally began to signal a shift in mentality from the player-as-good-servant model of the Matthews and

Finney era into a quite new tone and language that signposted changing attitudes among some younger British professional players and in the wider society. These "dissident voices," as Joyce Wooldridge has called them, began to become much louder, less reverential. They were reflecting the early signs of what would be a generally brasher, more confident post-war working class masculinity, one buoyed by the sensation-seeking ambitions of the Sunday papers, the emergence of distinctive working class youth cultures, new patterns of mass consumption, and a new popular realist literature – by Sillitoe, Braine and Osborne among others – which sympathetically depicted the aggressive aspirations of their frustrated working class anti-heroes. The inanity of National Service, the ignorance of most football club directors, and, according to Welsh international Trevor Ford in his 1957 book, the cunningly titled *I Lead the Attack*, the shame-free "fiddling" that was now a routine feature inside the English game orchestrated by players no longer willing to stomach the pitiful maximum wage, all increasingly featured in these no-holds-barred accounts of players' life stories.

Perhaps tellingly, in the same week in April 1957 that the English titleholders, Manchester United under Matt Busby, were playing in Spain in the new European Cup club competition against Spanish champions and cup holders, Real Madrid, the great Welsh player John Charles was also leaving Britain – to sign for Italian giants Juventus. He left for a fee reported to be in the region of £10,000. For those who had connected the trials of the English game in the 1950s to insular attitudes, a dearth of modern coaching, and a lack of proper financial rewards for professional players, this seemed like another watershed moment. Leslie Edwards in the *Liverpool Daily Post*, for example, railed against a potential English player drain, and the "pittance" that even top English players were still paid – £17 was now the maximum wage – compared to their continental equivalents. This meant, he argued, that in England "technicians of the highest class [were] set to work with labourers with the proviso that they should receive labourer's pay." In August 1957, the Liverpool players protested against low pay by refusing to pose for pre-season photographs unless they were paid, though they were soon brought to heel again as humble employees. But the strains were beginning to show in the battle, as the Football League liked to depict it, against the "greed" and "lack of respect" shown by a new generation of younger professional players who barely valued the "good of the game."

Matt Busby's early escapades in Europe with a young Manchester United side – explicitly, of course, against the wishes of the Football League – only added to the pressure for change in this and many other areas of the English game as the 1960s loomed. The British public's reaction to the Munich air disaster in February 1958, especially, began a sequence of developments that served, among other things, effectively to begin the long and incomplete process of the "de-localising" of football support in England. As Bobby Charlton, a survivor of the tragedy, put it, "Before Munich it was just Manchester's club, afterwards everyone owned a little bit of it."

The spread of television coverage of matches from the late 1950s and United's audacious attempts to take on the top clubs in Europe certainly brought the "Babes" thudding into the nation's living rooms. But the young United players under Busby seemed to have little in common with the flamboyant characteristics of the newly emerging national youth cultures of the day. They were far from self-confident, sneering teddy boys, either in action or appearance. Instead they seemed to epitomise the much more traditional values of the Matthews and Finney era – hard work, clean living, teamwork and bravery. The glamorous and much more individualistic United sides that eventually replaced the Babes – the teams of the early 1960s, of Denis Law, George Best and later Willie Morgan, for example – had rather more in common with the troubling generational changes and new youth lifestyles that would increasingly characterise the late 1950s and 1960s.

But what the public sympathy around Munich *did* do was to flag up United as a *national* club, perhaps the first in England that could legitimately claim support – and, for the same reason, also deep antipathy – from places well outside its host city. This development chimed with, and also reflected, new lifestyles characterised by increasing mobility and car ownership, growing working class affluence, and traces of new attitudes among younger fans, values that had been imported through the growing influence of American popular culture. Why support a loser local club when a successful national one was available and regularly on TV? From August 1964 BBC's *Match of the Day* beamed football highlights into British homes every Saturday during the league season. When the incendiary and glamorously subversive figures such as Best and Law emerged regularly on British screens soon after, this seductive circle of attraction was conveniently closed.

The glamour for this new United "brand" (as we would learn later to describe it) certainly appealed to younger fans. With attendances falling as the older, skilled working classes retreated to home leisure and Saturday afternoon's *Grandstand* and away from poorly appointed English stadia, so top football clubs in England in the early 1960s became much more aware of the need for self-promotion. A new generation of football managers would be key figures in this new era of the game as a putative TV show. "Personalities," such as Jimmy Hill, the irrepressible Bill Shankly and later the mischievous Brian Clough, became eminently quotable templates for others to try to follow. England's Alf Ramsey, of course, resolutely refused to play ball. As the new consumer culture and the lifting of the maximum wage for players in England in 1961 had begun to help transform managers from barely visible functionaries, and some younger players from model skilled workers, to commodified media and sporting stars, so on the terraces the English game also began to exhibit some of the traits – and some of the obvious problems – of the new age.

Football-fan culture and pop culture had first collided in England sometime in the early 1960s; claims about the exact time and place remain largely unsubstantiated. What we can say is that the blending of music and youth fandom – the Liverpool Kop's adaptation of Gerry Marsden's version of *You'll Never Walk Alone* in 1964 and their scrutiny of Beatles and Cilla Black songbooks to find other Kop Anthems, for example – began to delineate discrete spaces for older and younger fans inside English football grounds. Hooliganism at football in England had first surfaced as a public concern in the mid-1950s as younger fans began to travel in larger numbers and increasingly separately from older supporters. As seats and fittings were being ritually smashed at rock-and-roll venues, so Football Special trains began to suffer the same fate. Merseyside supporters again seemed to figure strongly here. Indeed, Liverpool's relegation to Division Two of the Football League in 1954 signalled a spate of serious incidents involving racism and fights with rival supporters and the police at the club's fixtures. By the 1960s it was joked that Merseyside fans were recognisable because they wore railway carriage doors as trophies on their lapels.

By the early 1960s the first versions of modern hooligan gangs were already forming in England, with young men regularly hauled before the courts claiming that they had read in local newspapers that rival supporters had planned to attack their spiritual home – the local stadium. In 1964 a spectacular moment occurred when a Millwall fan (historically, usual suspects these) threw a (dud) hand grenade onto the running track at a local derby match. "Soccer Marches to War," brayed the *Daily Express*. Indeed the English press worried loudly for eighteen months before the 1966 finals about the impression the world might take from these shores if the "hooligan outrages" now occurring in the domestic game transferred to the World Cup itself. They had no need to be afraid – *filling* World Cup venues in some of the English host cities (and even for some England matches) was to prove to be a much more pressing problem.

In the seventeen post-war league seasons up to 1962, Portsmouth (twice), Wolves (three times), Burnley (with a tiny population of around 85,000) and Ipswich Town all won league titles in England. Tottenham's title in the double season of 1961 was also to be the last to date for that decidedly "provincial" north-London club. In the fifty-four seasons that followed, only Derby County (twice), Nottingham Forest, Aston Villa and a briefly moneyed Blackburn Rovers in the mid-1990s (thus reviving this East Lancashire success story after a break of some eighty-one years) managed to resist the larger northern football strongholds of Leeds, Manchester and Liverpool and the London-based football aristocrats (Arsenal) and arrivistes (Chelsea). Effectively, the lifting of the maximum wage – as the men at the Football League had predicted – was the beginning of the end of the possibility of league success for provincial clubs from towns and smaller cities.

English football had been in a condition of some crisis, of course, in the years before the World Cup of 1966. Stadium facilities had long been underfunded by negligent and complacent directors and spectators were routinely treated appallingly. Incidents of hooliganism (and its coverage in the national press) were increasing and football crowds were falling annually. Almost five million league attendees were lost from the English game between 1960 and 1965 – though the creation of the League Cup from 1960 offset some of the travails of the League clubs.

Simmering crowd violence and falling attendances were very likely to be at least indirectly connected, but rising wages, and television and home-based leisure had also dealt serious blows to the established notion after the war that watching your *local* football club was what working class men did with their Saturday afternoons. Certainly, some members of the skilled working class in England were already beginning to strain at what had once been widely regarded as the standard ties of football, masculinity, family and place, connections that were further loosened as communities from war-damaged and simply worn-out British neighbourhoods were now decamped into new towns and garden cities, sometimes far away from their parents' traditional football bases.

Young people, dis-located in this way in the 1960s, would now do just a little more *choosing* of their favourite football clubs, and some of this preference work in the '60s would be more closely associated with the glamour and pop-culture "coolness" of specific football players – George Best's career at Manchester United began just months after Tom Finney's career ended – and the relative success of clubs now featuring more regularly on television and in the glittering new competitions of European football. The deference and intense localism of the 1950s, it seemed, had given way to a very new kind of sport.

Perhaps sensing growing inequality and the decline of smaller local clubs – there was certainly plenty of evidence around, not least in attendance figures – in June 1966, just before the World Cup finals began, Norman Chester, a warden of Nuffield College Oxford, a former member of the War Cabinet secretariat, and an expert in government and administration, was instructed by Labour Sports Minister Denis Howell to form a committee to "enquire into the state of the [English] game at all levels." This was something quite different from previous public inquiries in England, which had been variously into fan disorder and the range of "causes" of stadium disasters. Here the problem identified was a deep-seated, structural process of decline, focusing on the economics, culture and management of the English game itself. Nothing was off-limits, at least theoretically. This was decidedly one of those potential "take-off" points for English football, at a juncture when key members of the political class might be engaged by the game and at a moment when the sport itself was argued to lack real direction and focus – and the stomach for change.

Howell was both foul-mouthed and forceful, not a bad combination for getting some attention in football circles. He was already tired of the press obsession with hooliganism and policing (and his own ministerial responsibility for reacting to crowd violence) and was determined that the government could help harness what was expected to be the very positive impact (read "legacy" today) of finally hosting the World Cup finals in England: a means of turning around the fortunes of some English clubs that were, by now, in long-term and in some cases terminal decline. Howell knew that he also had some big back-up. Prime Minister Harold Wilson, Chester had noted later in his spidery handwriting, "is known to favour the round not the long ball and... he actively supports Huddersfield Town."

I think we might reasonably question the use of the word "actively" here, but at least football, not rugby or cricket, was on the political agenda for once. The new Labour government under Wilson from 1964 *had* of course worked very hard to tap into popular enthusiasm for an especially fruitful bout of creative young northern working class culture in the early 1960s. In football, both Liverpool FC and high-spending Everton, neighbouring Wilson's Huyton constituency on Merseyside, were near the top of the English game at this time and regional rivals Manchester United had been reviving fast under Matt Busby after the traumas of Munich. Wilson and his Cabinet colleagues were gambling on an electoral and national boost from a "feel-good" performance produced by England in the World Cup finals, and even a re-invigoration of the domestic game to follow. Wilson, perhaps fancifully, saw running the British Government as akin to managing a top football club – a matter he later discussed, with some animation, with ex-Huddersfield Town man Bill Shankly on the former's own, briefly favoured but excruciating, TV chat show.

Norman Chester was enthusiastic and highly competent for his new role, but he also had few illusions about the size of the task in hand. At least he was already well versed in the practised resistance in the English game to "outsiders"; to wiseacres and academics, "theory men" who were trying to tell their footballing betters how to suck eggs. So when he first met the press, Chester's hand-written notes for his opening statement revealed a clever determination to get his retaliation in first: to establish his solid football credentials as a supporter. "First watched M/c United in 1922," they read, "(long before Matt Busby)." United had actually finished rock bottom and were relegated from the First Division in 1922, so the young Master Chester could reasonably claim he was no glory hunter.

To confirm the point he also had notes on his current local club, Third Division Oxford United, who "wd have got into second [division] if they had one consistent goalscorer." This was simply publicity gloss. Finishing a distant fourteenth in 1966, Oxford were way off the promotion pace. But the point being made here was that his Football Enquiry Committee planned to examine the connections and synergies between the glamour boys at Manchester United and those men at the other more lowly Uniteds, and the various Citys, Towns and Athletics that were now wallowing and insecure down in the lower levels of the English Football League.

This eleven-man squad (not much changes in football in gender terms) of advisers pulled together by Chester was charged with examining something that the current generation of supporters and administrators might find rather more difficult to articulate and comprehend in the more divisive, knives-perpetually-sharpened era of the FA and the Premier League. The committee was required by the Minister to examine the means by which the game in England "may be developed *for the public good.*" As well as looking at the funding of local football, Chester demolished the theory that transfer fees benefitted smaller clubs – they didn't – he recommended more clubs be promoted and relegated, that clubs should be able to appoint salaried directors, and proposed a compulsory retirement age of seventy years for the eighty-four FA Council members, most of whom were already some way past this sell-by date.

In fact, Chester seemed to have plenty of footballing answers to the old Eric Hobsbawm question: "Where does the future come from?" He was something of a visionary, envisaging a future with paid TV, supporters on club boards, and more female spectators – "a major and largely untapped source of support." Writing to fellow committee member Clifford Barclay, Chester observed: "I imagine you may want to say something about amalgamation of grounds, the role of TV, and such stratospheric ideas as large

stadia catering for multi-sports activities." It was a strangely prescient moment, but it took the English game almost thirty years to
catch up. Although some areas highlighted by the Nuffield man
continued to get predictably short shrift, he would certainly have
recognised the supporter movements that eventually started to
sprout up from the mid-1980s and spread in the new century. As
usual, however, the report carried no legislative weight and when
Chester thought he had been invited to a League Management
Committee meeting to present his findings he found, instead, that
he was offered no more than lunch and a friendly chat. The game
stumbled on.

The report was finally published in 1968, with England as
World Cup holders and Chester's own Manchester United
about to become the first English club to win the European Cup.
Happy days. But, did winning the World Cup in '66 *really* benefit the development of the game in England? Ramsey's team had
limited ambitions, but a great spine – Banks, Moore and Bobby
Charlton were accomplished players, especially at home. But on
reflection the 1966 victory was also rather bloodless. Brazil and
Italy were ineffably poor, and England stumbled and kicked
their way out of their group, before sneaking past a ten-man
Argentina, and then disposing of a one-man Portugal – Eusébio
was plainly the only truly world-class performer at the whole
shebang. West Germany were talented, sure, but also a team in
transition. England winning in 1966 may have answered the critics of previous World Cup failures, but it did little to take the English game forward.

Nevertheless, English clubs soon had some unprecedented
success, winning seven out of eight European Cup finals between
1977 and 1984. However, much of this glory depended on forceful *British* players, and especially on fast-disappearing great
Scottish talent – Hansen, Dalglish and Souness at four-time winners Liverpool and Kenny Burns and John Robertson at double
European Champions Nottingham Forest, under a Brian Clough
once rejected by the FA. (Perhaps under Clough things might

have been different, but I doubt it.) By contrast the England team slumped in the 1970s, even failing to qualify for the 1974 and 1978 finals. Alf Ramsey's salary when he was sacked by the FA for the first offence, and after eleven years of remarkable service with the national team, was a pitiful £7200 pa.

Eternal schisms between the FA amateurs and the club game in England are often contrasted here with the more successful collectivist and centralised administrations abroad; did English clubs ever really care about national-team success? And, as international football became more cerebral and precise, and its top players became fitter and more athletic into the 1990s, so those typical English cultural traits that promoted tackling as a fine art, teamwork and high-tempo physicality, all became quite banal and much less effective. Given time and space in international football most English players proved to be poor decision makers. When Sweden beat England under the flapping Graham Taylor in the European Championships of 1992, the manager bemoaned the fact the Scandinavians were not only technically superior, they were now "even" more physical and better prepared than his own men.

Media pressure and the demand from fans for up-and-at-'em performances were also taxing problems for England on the international stage. Only once, in the latter stages of the World Cup finals in 1990 under Bobby Robson in Italy – and a full twenty-four years after winning the World Cup – have England looked once more like they really could belong at the highest levels of the international game. A team playing with both structure and freedom and containing Gascoigne, Waddle, Beardsley, Platt and Lineker outplayed the perennial foe West Germany in the semi-final in Turin – but inevitably lost on penalties. Even English hooligans stopped their antics to watch. A country and a culture that had seemed *All Played Out*, the title of Pete Davies's book about England at Italia '90, briefly appeared to be reborn. But it proved to be a fog, a mirage, merely the prelude to something quite different: the global reconfiguring of club football in England and the arrival of the bloated FA Premier League. We would soon be able to watch in our own backyards some of the greatest and best-paid players in the world – we just seemed to have forgotten, perhaps forever, exactly how, if at all, we had ever managed to produce them ourselves.

Stanley Rous, FIFA and the Making of a World Cup

Alan Tomlinson

> "England... closed their World Cup with a glorious bang that
> obliterated memories of its grey, negative beginnings."
> — Hugh McIlvanney, *McIlvanney on Football*

IT WAS SUPPOSED TO BE A WEEKEND of collective euphoria, spawning a sense of national pride that brought together the toffs and the louts, the gentry and the masses. But I've never recalled it like that, my Saturday excursion from Lancashire to London and back. Burnley had had an OK season; I'd done OK the summer before in my O-Levels; I was feeling OK about the History and English at A-Level, though not that keen on the French; and I had an OK job for the summer at the Smith & Nephew factory in Brierfield, just up the road from our house on the edge of town. And there'd been some OK games that I'd got to, the brutal treatment by Portugal of Pelé in its demolition of a fading Brazil, and then the astounding heroics (this was a bit beyond OK) of Portugal's Eusébio as he gazed in disbelief at his surroundings before dismantling the Pinball Wizards of North Korea and guiding Portugal, via a four-goal blitz, to a semi-final with England. The Koreans had earlier sent the fancy-dan Italians packing and we enjoyed the reported spectacle of their arrival home greeted by torrents of rotten tomatoes. Pizzas hadn't really come to Burnley by then, so we didn't see quite what a national insult this was for the Mediterranean prima donnas. But it's undeniable that tomatoes are easier to throw than mushy peas. We got that.

So with a ticket for the final in my pocket I caught the train from Burnley to Manchester, and then the electrified and rebranded

Inter-City, introduced just three months earlier (just in time for the World Cup), to Euston. It wasn't my first visit to Wembley. I'd been taken down there the season Burnley should have done the Cup and League double, but dawdled the championship title away to Alf Ramsey's Ipswich Town and then looked deflated and off the pace against Danny Blanchflower's Spurs in the 1962 Cup final. My father had taken me on that trip, and atop a sturdy pine stick was my brand new claret and blue rosette, made for the day by my mum. I wore it again at the new Wembley in 2009, when Burnley clawed its way past Sheffield United to get into the Premiership for the first time. But for this second trip to Wembley I was on my own, on the lookout for World Cup fever as England, at its fifth attempt and as host, tried to win the Jules Rimet Trophy, FIFA's World Championship.

I hadn't really concentrated too much on England's performances or form. We were club fans not patriots. The national side hadn't really looked very good as it initially stumbled on through the tournament before coming alive with two Bobby Charlton goals in the semi-final against Portugal. Ramsey had tried three wingers in respective matches – the first of them Burnley's John Connelly – before bringing in the high-energy unpredictability of Blackpool's Alan Ball, and using the misfiring Jimmy Greaves's injury scare as a way of replacing him with the hat-trick hero-to-be Geoff Hurst. An unusual-looking and increasingly effective shape was emerging. But England was down in London; in the North-West we'd had some really dazzling-looking sides in Group 3, and the application process for tickets to World Cup games delivered the opportunity to see some true international stars from Brazil, Portugal and Hungary. Plus the memorable Pak Doo-Ik at the heart of the North Korean challenge. But they all looked flawed – a bit of imbalance here, a vulnerable goalkeeper there – and gradually, England began to look like a serious, stable threat. When the family fluked a couple of tickets in the draw for the final allocation, and my elder brother prioritised domestic duties over footballing adventure, I said I'd have the ticket, and committed £1 and 5 shillings of my holiday earnings to see the game. I'd seen some great League and Cup games, and European Cup crackers, at Turf Moor since the later 1950s including in Burnley's championship year, 1960; this trip, I thought as I looked at my factory pay-slip, better be worth it.

What was the big deal then that Summer Saturday in the mid-'60s? Was England's 1966 triumph an end-of-an-era moment, a portent of more glamorous and dazzling, cosmopolitan-looking events? What did it mean politically, if anything, for a Labour-led United Kingdom whose Prime Minister was a bit of a football fan from Huddersfield, Yorkshire? And who was that tall bloke sandwiched between Queen Elizabeth and Prince Philip as Bobby Moore accepted the Jules Rimet Trophy from the young monarch?

That tall bloke, to give him his full name as presented in the Official Souvenir Programme for the tournament, was "Sir Stanley Rous, President of FIFA." Preceding him in the Programme were "Her Majesty the Queen, Patron: The Football Association," and "The Rt. Hon. The Earl of Harewood, LL.D, President of the Football Association." It looked like a line-up of grandees, though a more chiselled and rugged-faced chairman of the Football Association was also pictured, offering a "Welcome to England"; this was Mr. J.H.W. Mears, who had tragically died on 1 July, ten days before the beginning of the tournament. Sir Stanley knew what he was talking, or writing, about when he said that "when inviting The Football Association to organise the first World Cup Football Championship ever to be held in Britain, FIFA. knew that it would be well done." Because his long-term friend and colleague Arthur Drewry was at the time of this "invitation" in the FIFA presidential seat, Rous was secretary of the Football Association; and soon Sir Stanley himself would occupy that lofty position in world football. And so his message in 1966 was to all those associates in the FA and FIFA whom he knew had worked together to get, and plan for and stage, the World Championship Jules Rimet Trophy in England. Sir Stanley nodded a rather begrudging-sounding thanks towards the government too: "With the acceptable financial assistance from the Government and the services of many volunteers in the sub-seats as well as in London, visitors will be sure of seeing the matches in comfort and enjoying a warm welcome." So all told, the FA was seen as an ideal host for FIFA's showcase. "England is the original home of football," Sir Stanley reminded the players, national officials and fans of the world, but football "now has its home everywhere." Welcome to England, then, where our get-togethers will have "helped to make friends in sport."

Sir Stanley Rous, physical educator, international referee, 1948 Olympics organiser, football administrator, noted in his foreword to the 1963 *Encyclopaedia of Association Football* that there's "never been a more exciting time in football as an international game"; dozens of new countries formed in Africa and Asia "have clamoured for membership of FIFA and a place in the international football sun." It was FIFA's "great challenge," Rous added, to help "organise their game in every possible sense. And they have to be helped play the game in the very best spirit and to take their place in the international brotherhood of football nations above and beyond and apart from any political considerations,"

The English FA was awarded the hosting of the 1966 World Cup in August 1960. For the World Cups of the 1950s in Brazil, Switzerland, and Sweden the host countries had been the sole bidders. Chile defeated Argentina 32-11 in a Congress vote for the 1962 event, the German Federal Republic (West Germany) having withdrawn in recognition of a broad principle of rotation between Europe and South America. For 1966, West Germany was back in the frame alongside Spain and England. Spain withdrew before any vote, and in a tight contest England edged the decision over West Germany by 34 votes to 27. The 1970 World Cup event was awarded by an expanding Congress electorate at the 1964 Congress in Tokyo, Mexico getting the decision by 56 to 32 votes for Argentina. Rous was becoming concerned that putting such huge decisions in the hands of the Congress was "putting a strain on friendships," basing the choice of a host country "on not wholly relevant issues." He hatched a revolutionary plan for allocating and scheduling World Cup finals; Congress authorised that in future this decision should be allocated to the Executive Committee. It took some time to come to fruition. It was in 1966 that Rous presided over a pre-1966 World Cup FIFA Congress that allocated the three World Cups after Mexico to Germany (1974), Argentina (1978) and Spain (1982). Thereafter World Cup hosts were decided upon by secret ballots in the Executive Committee until May 2013 when the FIFA Congress, following the scandals and furore consequent upon the December 2010 allocations of the 2018 (Russia) and 2022 (Qatar) finals, transferred responsibility for these decisions back to itself.

It was all much lower-profile stuff back then, of course, and Rous himself recalled in his autobiography that at the Tokyo 1964 Congress he had persuaded FIFA to agree to these long-term allocations "so that the countries concerned could plan at leisure." His own involvement in the 1966 decision was influential on this long-term thinking once he gained the FIFA presidency in 1961. England had less than six years in which to prepare for the Finals, and little by the way of guidelines on how to do this. But Rous had been FA secretary from 1934, his long-term colleague Arthur Drewry was FIFA president when England won the bid, and Rous had been widely active in FIFA work from the 1930s, when he was co-opted onto FIFA's referees committee even though the FA was not at the time a member of FIFA. And in 1946 Drewry became, as a representative of the British Associations, a FIFA Vice-President. With the FA resuming membership and Drewry in that position, Rous was brought into FIFA's World Cup Organising and Olympic Games Committees.

So in some ways the location of the 1966 World Cup in England was a comfortable consequence of an overlapping set of interests within a network of football administrators and officials. Little abnormal was seen in this, and Rous's proximity to those staging the event was seen as a cooperative boon rather than any conflict of interests or collusion. "Buggins' turn," former England Coach Walter Winterbottom told me with an impish smile one wintry Sunday morning some 30-odd years later; a bonus of Rous's high esteem in the international football world of the time, he added. The politics of the UK were also generally conducive to giving any necessary support that hosting the World Cup would require. The newly elected 1964 Labour government had already created the country's first Minister for Sport, Denis Howell, and in his first meeting with the Prime Minister Harold Wilson he had an immediate list of his needs for this new junior ministerial post; Wilson's support for making nominations from the sporting world for the honours list, and for plans for a reception for athletes returning from the 1964 Tokyo Summer Olympics. Wilson had said "the country's broke" when Howell asked if he'd have any money in his ministerial role, but he suddenly brought the World Cup into the frame. The FA had had little support, he knew from conversations with its secretary Denis Follows, from the previous Conservative administration when asking for Government help to stage the tournament. Quintin Hogg, deputed by then Prime Minister Harold Macmillan to take some responsibility for sport-related issues, had promised no more than to provide police escorts for teams as they were driven around the country. Howell took his chance, "decided to return to the question of money," saying that the World Cup was on its way, a lot needed doing to guarantee its success, but a Minister for Sport and a World Cup coming up with "no money to organise it" wouldn't be much use. In his memoirs Howell recalled:

> Harold's response amazed me after what he had just said about money. "How much do you want?" he asked. I hadn't the faintest idea; there was no-one present to consult; I had yet to meet a civil servant or any other adviser, but I knew that I must not let the opportunity go. "Half a million pounds?" I suggested, which was a lot of money in those days. "Right," replied the Prime Minister, "I will agree to that, but no more."

So with a budget out of nowhere, and an emerging vision of the importance of the World Cup – "second only to the Olympic Games in international prestige" – Howell dedicated the whole of 1965 to preparations for the World Cup. He soon saw that implementation was way behind schedule. The FA had long decided which grounds would be used but had no details on what was required to make them adequate for the scale and profile of the event. He called in Rous, who had little to offer about ground improvements but alerted Follows to issues of media coverage, hospitality, modern facilities. None of which were remotely important to English football clubs in the early 1960s.

So Howell assembled a team "to form the core of this operation," including: himself, Sir John Lang (newly appointed government adviser on sport), Walter Winterbottom (former England coach), Sir Stanley Rous (FIFA president), Denis Follows (FA secretary) and Alan Hardaker (Football League secretary). It all seemed a bit *ad hoc*, a kind of bumbling through; if Howell is to be believed, though, without the snap judgement of Harold Wilson and the mobilisation of the old boys' network of football men, England 1966 could have been the dampest of squibs. In the book *Football and the Commons People*, Howell recalled as "a moment of inspiration" his appointment of Sir John Lang as Vice-Chairman of his "high-ranking committee," and with the undeclared half-million pounds of funding behind them – "a secret locked away in my Ministry" – this group toured the country seeing what upgrades were necessary to give the venues the necessary facelifts. The formula proposed by Lang was to fund 90% of temporary work requested by the clubs, and 50% of the more substantial upgrades, for instance new stands. Lang was recently retired from his post as Secretary of the Admiralty, a top-level public administrator. In the *Oxford Dictionary of National Biography* he is described as "endowed with a photographic memory" which "could recall, over several years, not merely the contents of a paper, but also its registered number"; he was also "always accessible and invariably calm and courteous" – a useful man to have around the less-sophisticated corridors of power of the professional clubs. Or to deal with sensitive issues of diplomacy such as the question of flags as they related to political protocol and the presence and name of North Korea. Lang was effectively an insider and middle-man, liaising when necessary between Rous or an FA figure, between FIFA and the Foreign Office from his own FIFA-related personal base in the Department of Education and Science in Curzon Street.

It looks remarkable in retrospect how little was known of what the challenge of staging the event was. What was it the countries and teams were actually competing for, for instance? Almost a year to the day before the event began, Rous wrote to his FIFA secretariat in the world-governing body's modest office in Zurich that housed its few employees, asking for some background information on the event and the trophy itself. This seems astounding, given that five years before his own FA had won the bid to host the Finals. FIFA assistant secretary Renee Courte's reply interpreted enquiries about the "Cup" literally, in a tone that is at best pedantic and at worst patronising. The letter itemises the history of World Cup hosts and winners, noting that the regulations would allow a team winning for the third time "to receive the cup as absolute property," necessitating the provision of a new trophy for the 1970 championship should Italy, Uruguay or Brazil win in 1966; provides the name of the sculptor of the Jules Rimet Trophy, Frenchman Abel Lafleur; encloses a photocopy of some passages from Rimet's book *The Marvellous History of the World Cup*; informs Rous that the Cup is made from 1800 grams of gold, weighs four kilos with the plinth, is thirty centimetres high, and though difficult to place a price upon was insured for 30,000 Swiss Francs.

The range of tasks that seemed to land on the FIFA president's desk before, during and after the event was astounding, from high-level diplomatic negotiation to scarcely credible transactions with commercial bodies. In Sir Stanley's personal archive can be found correspondence, directly to or from, Rous with companies on issues of the merchandising of replicas, in metal (a breach of FIFA regulations), of the Jules Rimet Trophy, to Arbiter Championship Trophies Ltd; and from Pedigree Dolls presenting him with two World Cup Willie dolls, "with the compliments of the management." These exchanges took place in October and November 1966 respectively, in the cycle of enthusiasm that followed the July victory. Prior to the event, exchanges between Rous, FIFA secretary Käser and the FA's Follows established image rights or advertising arrangements, on the basis of memory and recall of precedents. In one letter, 6 May 1965, to C. Vernon and Sons Ltd, London, a company seeking advertising rights related to the World Cup, Rous said that he would get hold of a bottle of Robinsons Lemon Barley "so that I may know what product I am talking about when I meet members of the committee, only one of which is British."

There were serious financial concerns as World Cup '66 was taking place in the context of an expanding media age and emerging consumer culture. Denis Follows wrote to FIFA, on 24 July 1964, requesting an advance of £25,000 from the £300,000 due to be paid to FIFA for the World Cup Television European rights; the issue was batted between FIFA and the FA, little if anything based in systematic documentation or contractual principles and commitments. But the most fascinating issues were not so much commercial as political.

The African issue was boiling up. On 8 February 1964 a member of the executive committee of the African Confederation (CAF), Chene Djan, contacted via telegram FIFA from Accra, with a stinging critique of the world body: "registering strong objection to unfair and unreasonable World Cup arrangement for Afro-African countries *stop* 25 Afro-Asian countries struggling through painful expensive qualifying series for ultimate only one finalist representation is pathetic and unsound *stop* at the worst Africa should have one finalist in London tournament *stop* urgent reconsider." Rous advised Käser to inform African colleagues that should an official protest emerge, FIFA may be able to help in some spheres, but that the rules were set, "the decisions reached

in Zurich can not be altered." Rous could recognise an impasse
when it stared him in the face, particularly as he had genuine
sympathy with some of the arguments coming from African associations. FIFA's Afro-Asian qualifying group was described by
Ethiopia's Ydnekatchev Tessema, future president of the African
Confederation, as "a mockery of economy, politics and geogra-
phy," in a powerful letter dispatched to CAF's then general secretary Mourad Fahmy on 19 February 1964, and copied to FIFA.
A boycott by almost all the African and Asian nations followed,
leaving FIFA to put together a plan to accommodate those countries that chose to remain in the qualifying competition.

And so it was left to North Korea to compete in a play-off with
Australia in Phnom Penh, Cambodia. In the end it had been
just these two who had chosen not to withdraw. Australia was
over-confident, ordering 200 neckties with "World Cup 1966"
imprinted alongside the Australian crest, but they were swatted
aside by the North Koreans, whose proposed inclusion in the
Finals was objected to by the West German and South Korean
ambassadors in London. Sir John Lang, E. Bolland (of the Far East
Department of the Foreign Office) and Rous worked to smooth
over such objections and arrive at acceptable compromises.
Lang's letter to Rous dated 28 March 1964 was crystal-clear. The
Foreign Office would permit competing countries' flags, including North Korea's, to be flown at all the matches, but on two conditions: North Korea must not anywhere "be described publicly
as representing the (so-called) People's Korean Republic"; and
no national anthems should be played at or during any match
"except those of the participants in the first match and the final
match series (both at Wembley)." Luckily enough *God Save the
Queen* was to get most plays; and Eusébio's goals against North
Korea in the quarter-final calmed the nerves of the diplomats.
The Foreign Office also insisted that this could not be seen as a
precedent for "dealing with East German participation in future
sporting events in this country." "Minimum publicity," Lang

added, all a bit hush-hush; just tell the venues what they can do nearer the day.

Alf Ramsey had been appointed as England manager just three and a half years before he would take his squad of World Cup hopefuls to their pre-tournament residential camp. Stressing English conditions in which the Finals would be played, "before our own people" and with a core of hardened internationals and younger talent yet to be identified, Ramsey called upon the attributes of ability, strength, character and temperament as the foundation upon which to build up confidence in both players and the public: "I say it again. I think England will win the World Cup," he reaffirmed in August 1963. This was not asserted with any romantic flourish, more a clipped, pragmatic, detached air, typified in his retort to Tony Pawson's enthusiasm after a five-goal thriller: "But you *cannot* have enjoyed it. There were so many mistakes, so much unprofessional play." Ramsey's imperative was to remove as far as possible, if not eliminate, risk, through identifying the appropriate players for the very specific roles he expected, ordered, them to perform on the pitch. A Ramsey side certainly had what John Moynihan described at the time as "admirable perseverance and collective will-power," particularly in the final, "a game of agony and tension." And it worked time and time again, as the narrative would have it, most effectively against the over-aggressive Argentines, fatally flawed Portuguese flair, and too-sporting-for-their-own-good Germans.

Inevitably, the England players who featured in the final victory over Germany were hailed as heroes of the day. Alan Ball dedicated around a quarter of his book *Ball of Fire* to the World Cup story, starting his tale with the confession that his winner's medal was his "most treasured possession," and the comment that the medal "signifies England's greatest moment in Soccer." The solid-gold medal on Ball's sideboard was said to be worth "about £25 in hard cash. But money would never persuade me to part with it. Indeed, so far as I am concerned, money couldn't buy it." In 2005, Ball sold his medal for the then record price of £164,800.

Jack Charlton in his 1967 autobiography described the final as "that fantastic July day" that would stay with the players for ever: "Neither the critics nor anyone else, for that matter can rob me of that moment of glory." His younger brother, Bobby, melancholic but athletically mellifluous survivor of the 1958 Munich air disaster in which so many of the great Busby Babes of Manchester United were killed, cried as he climbed the Royal Box at Wembley to collect his medal. This was surely, despite all his achievements with Manchester, the pinnacle of his footballing life: in Leo McKinistry's magisterial book *Jack and Bobby* the moment is described most eloquently by Bobby himself: "I've never cried before over a football match. But the sound of the public just got to me... Afterwards I thought that I was a wee bit unprofessional crying but now, when I look back, I don't see any other way I could have handled myself. It was lovely, a fantastic moment." The contrasting approaches and celebratory styles of the Charlton brothers symbolised a country's response, as Bobby mingled with guests at the official banquet at the Royal Garden Hotel, and Jack went on the booze at a West End club, waking up the following morning on the floor of a house in Leytonstone. The dedicated and the solemn; the wild and the hedonistic. Dutiful flair from Bobby on the pitch, behind him the ungainly determination of his elder brother.

Hat-trick hero Geoff Hurst, a relative newcomer to the national side, admitted in his 1968 book *The World Game* he had to adapt to "being always on show," unable to "take" his wife to their weekly shop at Romford supermarket: "The first time we went to this store after the World Cup was pandemonium. We were mobbed. Poor Judith was swept away, still waving her shopping list forlornly, while I was being backed up to the biscuit counter trying to shake a hundred hands at once." Hurst had enjoyed chatting to West Ham fans in the supermarket teashop just weeks before; now his goal-scoring heroics catapulted him into a different social world, one that would spawn agents and endorsements and riches that just half a decade before, when the maximum wage was still in place, would have been unthinkable. Hurst has much to say in praise of the celebrity life and the adulation of the crowd, in sporting terms too. Recalling the final, he wrote: "The crowd were bloody marvelous... you can sense instantly whether the stadium is with you or not... It was not so much they wanted you to win, it was the feeling that they were certain that you would succeed... The goals might have given us the game, but the crowd gave us the goals." Hurst's teammate Martin Peters in his 1970 book (with Peter Corrigan) *Goals from Nowhere* spoke about the role of the crowd. He'd sensed that by the quarter-final against Argentina that the Wembley crowd, nearer capacity than in earlier games, "was with us," wanting the team to win, "every man in the crowd, every Englishman that is... right behind us." For Peters, it wasn't likely that "you could ever get a crowd like that again." The "England–England" chant was for him "like a tidal wave" rolling up and down the pitch:

You could almost feel it pushing you along. And when they sang "When the whites go marching in" you felt like joining in. It really was a remarkable experience. I usually try to ignore the crowd, but no human being could have ignored that one.

The evening of the final, Bobby Moore led the players on to the balcony of the Royal Garden Hotel to accept the adulation of the public. Moore, unflappable defensive genius and golden boy of the English game, had difficulty coping with the end of the fairy tale. As his biographer Jeff Powell wrote:

As in most good fairy stories, the best moment came at midnight. Bobby came out of the hotel entrance to find thousands of people still waiting for a glimpse of their heroes. "I couldn't believe they were still there, still standing in the street after all those hours. It made me realise how much it meant to them. It really touched me. Moved me. I'd never felt, what can I say, such a bond with the fans. It was a real lump in the throat moment. Never forget it."

Afterwards the squad dispersed following close to two months of collective living and intense working together, and this hit Moore hard: "Then, suddenly it was all over. All breaking up... The spirit had been fantastic, I can't remember one moment of bad feeling. We'd all become part of each other. It left a funny, empty feeling." Moore had held aloft the FA Cup, the European Cup Winners' Cup, and now the World Cup in successive years. In the outpouring of tributes on Moore's early death in 1993, Michael Parkinson wrote an obituary for the *Daily Telegraph* that contrasted his memory of England's Golden Boy of 1966 with the expansive commercialism of post-Italia '90 English and European football. Parkinson's voice, like so many others then and now, was a lament for the noble simplicity of the achievements of the blue-eyed blonde captain:

> I am glad I saw him when I did, when the England shirt was pristine and not daubed with commercial graffiti, when there was still honour in the game, style, and most of all, humour. The lasting image of that time, will always be Moore, slim as a reed, holding aloft the trophy at Wembley. It was the moment when the boy from Barking became the golden icon of the Sixties.

Bobby Moore wiping clean his hands before contact with the monarch's white silk gloves and acceptance of the Jules Rimet Trophy has come to symbolise a moment when a collection of modestly paid artisans with a sprinkling of genius in their number could embody the emotions and aspirations of a population hungry for glamour, celebrity and success.

As England progressed unspectacularly via topping Group One and then through two thrilling knock-out stage games there was escalating popular support for the England team. And not just in the grounds; Arthur Hopcraft wrote in his classic 1970 book *The Football Man* of a "communal exuberance" that was released in the country: "The World Cup was carnival." The end of World War II was his only comparator; apart from then, he had "never seen England look as unashamedly delighted by life as it did during the World Cup." For Hugh McIlvanney, the "shabbiness" of Wembley was transformed from an "undistinguished concrete bowl"; "impossible to define the atmosphere precisely," he wrote, but it was nevertheless "palpable, and it was unique." The people looked "flushed, supercharged." A doorman gave McIlvanney the word: "It's bloody electric."

In terms of fair play, overall Sir Stanley could count himself satisfied with the Finals. The West German team never created a fuss about the "over-the-line or not" goal or the Soviet linesman Tofiq Bakhramov; this was a squad raised on a post-World War II sensitivity to the need for a younger generation to, as amplified in the lectures of manager Helmut Schön, "behave like gentlemen and sportsmen." In Uli Hesse's history of German football *Tor!* West Germany's goalkeeper Hans Tilkowski recalled that the main thing was to leave a good impression: "In 1966, the appearance and behaviour of the team were essential." He and other West German players remained close friends with several of the English players; Wolfgang Overath called England "a great side" and recalled that his own side's conduct "brought credit to the German team."

And more broadly the World Cup was certainly becoming more truly international, with seventy-four preliminary entries for 1966, double the number for France 1938. But dissatisfaction had been simmering for some time over qualification schedules and criteria, and allocation of number of Finals places to regions and confederations. This meant that far from all of Rous's developmental and internationalist ambitions were met in 1966. Apart from no African side participating in the 1966 World Cup, and just North Korea from Asia, the Argentines also believed themselves to be victims of European conspiracy. England played all its games at Wembley, allocated its semi-final there on commercial grounds. It wasn't quite the respectful form of intercultural exchange that Sir Stanley Rous believed to be the greatest quality of international football competition. And some criticism stung, coming from closer to home. Dr A. Foni, Switzerland's national team coach, penned his "Thoughts on the 1966 World Championship," arguing that top teams, the 1966 host England in particular, were in essence informally seeded to meet weaker teams, and had more rest than others between games. England had its single venue, a "definite ground," throughout the event, and even slightly favourable refereeing decisions, Foni added. Such little "nudges" were given, and certainly "not refused." On Rous's personal copy of Foni's article the Englishman wrote, in his minutely immaculate annotations, "disappointed – unfair, shows himself partisan attacks referees, officials, organisers, is *bitter*... is inaccurate, uninformed." Sir Stanley wasn't up for debate on this one. But Foni's tone was balanced and analytical; sometimes those with the most established sense of position and authority don't realise the hegemonic basis on which such authority has been assumed by their like, and is understood, however implicitly, to be reproduced.

The travelling and colourfully carnivalesque Brazilian supporters who lit up the host cities of Manchester and Liverpool returned home early after Pelé had been hacked from the tournament, despite intakes of painkiller administered during the match in an attempt to salvage the glory game of the two-time winners from the immediately preceding World Cups. Bill Murray wrote in his *Football: A History of the World Game* nearly thirty years later that "no player today would get away with what the Portuguese did to Pelé in the 1966 World Cup." Brazil would regroup for 1970 in Mexico, galvanised by a fit Pelé and younger recruits, to claim permanently the Jules Rimet Trophy as three-time winners. England wilted in the sun in Mexico in 1970, but could always blame the food that kept goalkeeper Banks out of the quarter-final game with West Germany (or even the substitutions made by an outof-touch Sir Alf Ramsey). The subsequent World Cup in Germany proceeded without England, and kicked off with a president-elect for FIFA, the Brazilian João Havelange, having ousted Rous from FIFA's top position in the pre-tournament Congress. And the following year an ambitious young marketing man, recommended to Havelange by international fixer and dealer Horst Dassler of Adidas, began work at FIFA: enter Joseph 'Sepp' Blatter, who with Havelange and Dassler soon took the World Cup Finals to twenty-four finalists at Spain in 1982, and to thirty-two in France 1998.

In this context England 1966 does look a tad cosy, the vision and accomplishment of the English interlocking elites of the FA, FIFA and UEFA. Argentina, Brazil, Chile and Uruguay represented the longest-established continental confederation, CONMEBOL. Mexico overcame Costa Rica and Jamaica to give the emerging North/Central American and Caribbean Confederation (CONCACAF) a single representative. The African and Asian confederations boycotted qualifying phases, arguing against the absurdity of their meagre allocations, so allowing the North Korean sensations a strolling eligibility in a 9-3 aggregate demolition of Australia. That left ten European nations: Bulgaria, England, France, West Germany, Hungary, Italy, Portugal, Spain, Switzerland and USSR. Not much of a global reach in this World Cup line-up at all. It has the look of a European party with some old family guests from the South American cousins, and the exotic unknown guest from (a part of) Korea. At its heart was Sir Stanley Rous, the FA secretary when the hosting bid was won, member of the Labour Government's World Cup committee, and FIFA president when the World Cup itself was won by his old employer.

Far from setting the standards for the future, England's red-shirted artisans immortalised in the official World Cup film *Goal!* gave the football establishment the ammunition to think that World Cup 1966 was a job well done on all levels. David Goldblatt describes the meaning of this fleeting moment of World Cup triumph in 1966: "The English, after twenty years of post-war imperial decline, felt themselves back where they belonged: victorious internationally, at peace at home." An alternative, German view is provided by Christoph Wagner describing the aftermath for the team as returning home to forget and rebuild while for England, '66 would become a burden, a cultural reference "that the English had to remember."

Academics Chas Critcher and John Clarke have pointed to the twin figures of Alf Ramsey and Harold Wilson, connected by a "commitment to rationalising modernisation," harnessing the "best of British" to new ways of working and operating in the world. Alf Ramsey began 1966 with around a hundred slim player files or dossiers, to cut these down to the twenty-two selections by the early summer. He was the only football pro in the building. His workplace was described in 1967 by Brian James as a "starkly furnished office, perhaps 13ft by 8ft," which in "the days of Regency riches... might have been part of the servants' quarters" in the imposing Lancaster Gate building: "a room utterly without character." And here, Ramsey undertook what James chillingly called "a job of terrifying loneliness." When Ramsey eventually lost his job after clearly losing his modernising and magic touch, it was because according to Critcher he was "becoming the victim of the rigidities of his own thinking." Ramsey himself put it differently, angrily declaring to football journalists Peter Lorenzo and Norman Giller that the "sad thing is that the bloody amateurs are back in command." Of course he was both wrong and right; the next England manager was the self-serving and untrustworthy mercenary Don Revie, an arch-professional and modernising innovator in many ways, but whose appointment can be seen as a mistake by a coterie of amateurs. Holding this balance between the old and the new, the "traditional and the modern" that 1966 seemed for many to represent, was a precarious business, for politicians and football managers alike. The heights of 1966 were followed by eight years of anti-climax that have fed into what the sports historian Tony Mason christened "a story of decline that we told ourselves about ourselves." We are still telling it fifty years on as a fragmenting national culture within England has to make do with an underachieving football culture. In that context the golden glow of '66 persists, buffed by the nostalgia that continues to sustain the golden moment in a mélange of myths, memory and recurrently desperate hope.

I'll certainly never forget my dad bobbing up and down with delight behind England's goal as the match finally ended, knotted handkerchief on his head as slender protection against the spasmodic squally rain, agreeing rapturously with the man close by shrieking that we'd "got the bastards again, for the third time." But I don't recall any spontaneous rendering of "Rule Britannia" when Hurst put England 3-2 up. I'd got a train to catch. I caught the train back North – admittedly it was pretty full – but there was little sense of jubilation, and fans back then were not dressed in replica kits and the like. Most of us just headed back to the routine greyness of everyday life and the anticipation of the new club season. London's offerings in the match-day souvenir programme included "The Fabulous Black & White Minstrel Show, Gorgeous Girls, Magnificent Minstrels in London's Most Colorful Spectacular!" Or Joe Brown and Anna Neagle were in "Charlie Girl." London's charms in the programme extended to Soho's "La Taverna" and its Italian musical quartet, The Golden Nugget Casino and "Mecca's Wonderful World of Entertainment." Maybe the match was part of a wider cultural diet of the Swinging Sixties, but none of that was of much interest, even if accessible, to this day tripper. England had won a match, lifted the World Cup, with six players from five northern clubs, a Leicester player in goal, and four more from two London clubs. It seemed like a good all-round effort, and I'd seen worse – but many, many better – matches.

In his book *The Sixties*, historian Arthur Marwick claims that England won the World Cup "with a genuinely entertaining team" and that this meant that football "crossed over to occupy the leisure time of people of all social classes as well as ordinary workers." Looking back at my Wembley day out, and the times that followed, I read that statement almost a half-century on with incomprehension. The entertainment element never stuck me as an asset or feature of Ramsey's English experiment; and a new British Rail brand and Inter-City livery couldn't change class cultures overnight.

So back in Burnley in the early hours of Sunday morning, then on the Monday shift in neighbouring Brierfield, I might have wondered what all the fuss about. Many of my fellow workers were Pakistanis, quite recent migrants, and working women – northern English women who'd had hard-working lives on unsociable shifts in a factory setting where there was little scope for social talk or gossip. My brother insisted that England had not won fairly, what with one unproven goal and a final goal that should not have been allowed as there were already fans on the pitch. He had a point, but maybe he was just annoyed that he'd passed on his ticket; for my part, I was thanking my lucky stars that I didn't have to get back down to Wembley for a Tuesday-night replay. I'd have probably lost my vacation job if I'd chosen to be a bit of that extended slice of World Cup history.

The German *Außenseiter*

Claus Melchior

ON 23 FEBRUARY 1966, England beat West Germany 1-0 in a friendly match at Wembley, the only goal scored by Nobby Stiles in the forty-first minute. Optimistic German fans may have looked at this match as a preview of the World Cup final to be played at the same location a little more than five months later. The rest of the football world, including bookmakers in England, decidedly did not, and had betting been legal in Germany at that time, local bookies would not have given much better odds on the *Außenseiter*, the underdogs, the German team winning the World Cup either.

Of course, in 1966 two German states existed (which at that time had not yet officially recognised each other): the Federal Republic of Germany, commonly referred to as West Germany; and the German Democratic Republic, GDR or East Germany. Except for people born in the GDR and old enough to remember it, in German collective memory German football in the second half of the twentieth century means West German football, which probably applies to football fans in the rest of the world as well. The GDR first tried to qualify for the World Cup in 1958 but finished behind Czechoslovakia and Wales. In 1966 the team could not get past Hungary; eight years later, in 1974, the GDR managed to qualify for the first and only time, followed by the high point in East German football history, a 1-0 win against West Germany in the final group match in Hamburg thanks to a legendary goal by Jürgen Sparwasser. The game of course had been styled as a battle of competing political systems, so this West German surrender probably was not part of a cheeky ploy to avoid Brazil, Holland and Argentina in the next phase.

Fifty years on from 1966 a now reunited Germany's reputation as a football powerhouse, expected to reach at least the final four in major competitions, and as a *Turniermannschaft* – a "never-say-die" team capable of harnessing its best qualities in the course of a tournament – is well established. Not so in 1966, in spite of West Germany having won the World Cup in 1954, finishing as semi-finalists in 1958 and reaching the quarter-finals in 1962.

Football in Germany began in the 1890s as mainly a middle and upper class pursuit, to some extent supported by the military. After World War I the introduction of the eight-hour workday allowed the working class to participate in the game as players and spectators. Only then did it gain a mass following, easily becoming the country's most popular sport. For two reasons, though, German football was hardly competitive on an international level. Firstly, the regional fragmentation of a highly de-centralised country led to the formation of a multiplicity of local leagues. The pyramid had no top, meaning that the best clubs would cruise through their local leagues and only had to crank it up towards the end of the season, when regional championships and the German championship were decided. Secondly, even in the 1920s the German football federation DFB (Deutscher Fussball Bund) remained staunchly opposed to professional football, partly as a commitment to the gentlemanly ideal of sport as a pastime practised by amateurs, partly out of fear that overtly paying players might cost the clubs certain tax breaks. For a while during that period German clubs were even prohibited to play against foreign professionals. All of this was a great big sham of course. Clubs soon began to lure away players from other clubs, which certainly involved some sort of financial incentive, and to keep their own players by financially compensating them too in some way for their efforts. On occasion clubs managed spectacular results in international friendlies, but more often they were on the losing side in matches against English professionals or top clubs from other central European countries like Austria or Hungary, often by a wide margin. Neither did German clubs compete in the Mitropa Cup, the most important international club competition in continental Europe between the wars.

The national team did not fare any better. Usually only playing three or four matches in a season, it was selected by DFB officials often guided by local considerations, picking a team of players from Northern Germany for a match in Hamburg or an away match in, say, Denmark, and conversely, players from the South for matches against Austria or Switzerland. In 1926 the DFB finally employed a coach, Otto Nerz, whose brief was to develop a team that could compete in the 1928 Amsterdam Olympics. After a promising start against Switzerland all medal hopes were dashed by eventual champions Uruguay in the second round, the result a hefty 4-1 loss. Two years later, like many other European countries, Germany skipped the first World Cup in Uruguay. The first official international against England ended in a surprising 3-3 draw in May 1930 in Berlin, but 0-5 and 0-6 losses against the Austrian *Wunderteam* in 1931 clearly demonstrated that German football was at best second-class.

After taking power in 1933, like just about everything else the Nazis also reorganised German football. The patchwork of small local leagues was replaced by sixteen regional leagues, thus reducing the number of clubs who could claim first-class status to a mere 160, but scuppering in the process all recent plans to introduce a national German league, which would have allowed the best players to practice their skills against strong competition week by week. Professional football was as much of a non-starter under the Nazi regime as it had been in the Weimar Republic, but the hidden professionalism continued.

However, the national team did now assume the status of a priority for the new rulers. The number of games was increased, international friendlies now serving as propaganda tools supposed to demonstrate Germany's good will as well as its strength as a sporting nation, and Otto Nerz was allowed to convene the country's best players for a number of training sessions. These measures seemed to pay off when Germany finished third at the

1934 World Cup in Italy, beating recent nemesis Austria 3-2 in the third-place match.

But this proved to be a flash in the pan. Winning the gold medal at the 1936 Olympics in Berlin was an ambition of the utmost importance and at the same time considered almost as a matter of course. The Nazi hopes – no doubt shared by the majority of German football fans – were shattered in an embarrassing 2-0 defeat by Norway in the second round, supposedly the only football match Adolf Hitler ever attended in his lifetime. Many participants later claimed the team had been tired, having been totally overworked in preparation for the tournament.

The new *Reichstrainer* Sepp Herberger was not going to make the same mistake for the 1938 World Cup. He had a promising team in place which, however, he had to reconstruct when after the annexation of Austria by the German *Reich* in March 1938 Nazi officials demanded the new greater Germany to be represented in equal parts in the line-up. Switzerland put paid to this experiment with a resounding 4-1 victory in a second-round World Cup replay in Paris, decidedly placing another German team amongst the also-rans.

According to a prevailing myth Germany's surrender and the end of World War II constituted some sort of a *Stunde Null* or Zero Hour, allowing the country to more or less start from scratch in 1945. But of course the attitudes and beliefs that had landed the country in that mess in the first place could not be eliminated with a flick of a switch, and while the majority of politicians who guided the rebuilding process were not tainted by involvement with the previous regime, this cannot be said of all levels of government, in particular the civil service and the judiciary system.

Certain continuities also existed in football and its administration. There were now only four regional leagues (and one for West Berlin) at the top level of the pyramid, but even in the smaller new state of West Germany resistance to the creation of a national league remained strong, despite such leagues having been established elsewhere across Europe between the wars. Although players now were officially allowed to receive limited payments from clubs, this was a far cry from full professionalism, the advocates of the old amateur ideal still standing their ground. And when the national team returned to the international stage in 1950 with a friendly against Switzerland, its coach was still Sepp Herberger, having mutated from *Reichstrainer* to *Bundestrainer*.

Herberger came from a poor family and was a talented football player. Early on in his career he realised that football might provide a way out of the conditions he grew up in. He was briefly suspended as a player for accepting illegal payments when changing clubs, and while still playing began to relentlessly pursue a coaching career that would allow him to make a decent living in football. To keep this dream alive he joined the Nazi party in 1933, though there is little indication that he actually shared its beliefs – an act of opportunism he had in common with millions of other Germans in the 1930s. As *Reichstrainer* he had served the regime in a public position (though with limited success), but in the eyes of the DFB and the public this certainly did not disqualify him from a similar job in the new democratic Germany. All in all, a typical German career path of that era.

Herberger easily met his first challenge as *Bundestrainer*, qualifying for the 1954 World Cup. The tournament in Switzerland then turned into his finest hour. Led by midfielder Fritz Walter, the best player Germany had produced up to that time, the team came through the group stage. A hard-fought 2-0 victory over Yugoslavia and an impressive 6-1 demolition of Austria then paved the way to the final, which saw one of the biggest upsets in World Cup history (certainly the biggest in a final) with Germany emerging as 3-2 winners over a heavily favoured Hungarian team that had dominated European football in the first half of the 1950s and still ranks among the greatest ever in football history.

The victorious players became heroes in a Germany starved of any sort of positive international recognition, but in truth the whole thing was a bit of a fluke. Rarely in the following years did the team perform like world champions, among the low points being a 1-2 loss to the Netherlands in Düsseldorf, this being considered the highlight of Dutch football up to that point. Qualification for the 1958 World Cup might have even proved a problem, had it not been for the automatic place then granted to the defending champions.

In Sweden the team performed better than could be realistically expected, beating South American champions Argentina in the opening match and Yugoslavia again in the quarter-finals, before succumbing to hosts Sweden in the semis in a game that created bad blood in Germany due to the supposed fanatical behaviour of the Swedish crowd. In the third-place match the team did not put up much resistance in a 6-3 loss against Just Fontaine's French team. Still, a respectable fourth placed finish. While the 1958 team had its moments, the 1962 squad proved to be a disappointment, going out to perpetual quarter-final opponents Yugoslavia. There was certainly no reason to assume a repeat of the successes of 1954 in 1966.

Beyond football in many ways the Swinging Sixties have to be considered as an important transitional period in German history. From a later perspective the 1950s have often been called a drab and boring period of restoration. Drab and boring maybe, but what exactly was being restored? Yes, cities were being rebuilt, but the political system that was being established certainly did not resemble anything that had gone before in Germany, not even the doomed first attempt at democracy, the Weimar Republic. So politically and economically there was a lot that was different about the Bonn Republic, even if culturally the 1950s may have been less interesting than glamorous 1920s Berlin.

It is often claimed that the 1954 World Cup victory played an important role in facilitating German acceptance of the new political order. Such claims seriously overestimate the cultural significance of football in 1950s Germany. Of course the World Cup presented a rare occasion to experience long-missed feelings of joy and pride, but the so-called *Wirtschaftswunder*, the "economic miracle" – providing full employment, readily available consumer goods and the benefits of the welfare state – arguably played a much larger role in reconciling Germans with parliamentary democracy than a winning football team.

This was an economic miracle that was heavily aided by the fact that West Germany started out almost debt-free, and by the influx of large sums of money provided through the US Marshall Plan. A lesson that seems to have been lost on the current generation of German and European politicians and economists dealing with the Greek debt crisis.

At that time football as a sport in Germany was not hijacked by politicians in the way it is now, a clear indication of how marginal the sport was considered to be in the general scheme of things. Chancellor Konrad Adenauer was never heard reminding people how Germany only ever won the World Cup with a Christian-Democrat government in power, and no cabinet minister attended the final in Berne. President Theodor Heuss sent the congratulatory telegram required by his role as head of state, but that was it. Adenauer's successor Ludwig Erhard, the architect of the economic miracle, was indeed a football fan, attending Bundesliga matches on occasion and known as an avid reader of *Kicker*, the pre-eminent German football magazine. But even he in 1966 was not willing to interrupt his summer vacation in order to attend the final at Wembley.

Generations who had lived through the Great Depression, the Nazi dictatorship with its totalitarian demands, and a devastating war were only too willing to settle in and enjoy the economic boom and the security it provided. Politics were kept at a distance, as long as the communists kept to their side of the Iron Curtain. Being able to buy a car and a television set and maybe even to afford a vacation in Italy were the pinnacles of earthly aspirations – no further thrills were needed. These generations knew they had never had it so good.

But change was on the horizon. Teenagers who had not experienced the turbulent times their parents and grandparents had lived through began to be affected by the sounds and images of a new youth culture that swept across the Atlantic. Actors like Marlon Brando and James Dean, singers like Bill Haley and Elvis Presley became stars the youngsters more or less had to themselves. Young men who modelled themselves on Brando and Dean wearing jeans and leather jackets quickly became termed *Halbstarke* ("half-strengths") and the music played by Haley and Presley, like jazz in earlier times, was ominously demonised as *Negermusik* ("negro music"). In the 1950s the term *Neger* (like *negro* in the US) was still a widely acceptable term for black people and did not have the clear racist connotations that *nigger* always had. Nevertheless it was often used in a derogatory way, as is clearly the case in the compound *Negermusik*.

The racism was indicative of a broader ambivalence, antipathy even, towards the US, common especially in the German middle classes. For more than a century America had been considered the promised land by many, and US military power was certainly highly welcome in order to keep the USSR at bay, but America was also judged to be superficial and uncultured. The idea that 8 May 1945, the end of World War II in Europe, had not just been a day of defeat but also and more importantly a day of liberation had not yet taken hold, and thus American mass culture in the form of Hollywood movies, rock 'n' roll, comic books and Coca-Cola was seen as a threat, especially after the occasional riot at cinemas or rock 'n' roll concerts. None of these riots were political in nature, but an indication of things to come nevertheless.

Ludwig Erhard had succeeded Konrad Adenauer as chancellor in 1963, his government still based on the coalition formed by the conservative Christian Democratic Union (CDU) and the liberal Free Democratic Party (FDP) which had ruled the Federal Republic since 1949. Adenauer's resignation was partly due to the unfortunate role the old chancellor had played in the *Spiegel Affäre* of 1962, an ill-fated attempt by the government to intimidate journalists who had reported critically about the state of the Bundeswehr, the new German army. Rudolf Augstein, founder and owner of *Der Spiegel*, Germany's pre-eminent news magazine, together with the main author of the offending article, had to endure several weeks in prison for treason before the government's case was thrown out in court. While this was going on demonstrators had taken to the streets all over Germany, an indication of the value Germans were now putting on the freedom of the press and the rule of law.

Erhard won the 1965 election, but his coalition dissolved in 1966 and was replaced by a Grand Coalition of Christian Democrats and Social Democrats (SPD). This was the first taste of government in the Bonn Republic for the Social Democrats, often vilified by Adenauer as soft on communism and a threat to German security. After the next elections in 1969 the FDP took a turn to the left and became the junior partner in a coalition government with the SPD under the charismatic Willy Brandt. In its twenty-first year the second German democracy had finally accomplished something essential to any democracy: a peaceful change of government forced by the results of a general election.

This gradual turn to the left in parliamentary politics was accompanied by political unrest all through the decade. 1962 had seen the *Schwabinger Krawalle* (Schwabing riots), another indication of things to come. On a summer night in Munich's Schwabing district police tried to arrest a group of street musicians. This led to skirmishes between police and young people opposing the police action all through the night, and then to four days of demonstrations around Munich University, the number of participants reaching an astonishing 40,000, among them a young Andreas Bader, later one of the leaders of the notorious terrorist Bader-Meinhof Group. Clashes with police turned violent on occasion and police methods were heavily criticised. As in the case with the *Halbstarkenkrawalle* of the 1950s there was no political agenda behind these actions, but young people in Germany obviously were no longer willing to accept misguided manifestations of authority.

The unrest soon turned political. More and more students took to the streets for a variety of causes. As in other parts of the world this movement was galvanised by opposition to the American war in Vietnam, but in Germany there was a different kind of generational divide behind it. A first generation of students who had grown up after the war now reached the universities, and while in the 1950s a veil of silence had been cast over Germany's recent past, this new generation began to ask unwelcome questions. Students in Germany were not just demonstrating against war, against autocratic regimes, for a better and more just world, but also against a society they perceived as largely unwilling to confront the demons of the past.

Again, as in other parts of the world, Germany in the 1960s saw not just a newly politicised generation of university students but a general shift in cultural and social attitudes. Rock 'n' roll had laid the groundwork and now pop culture began to provide the soundtrack to these changes. The Beatles ruled in Germany as everywhere else, young people began growing their hair, clothing became less uniform and sexual attitudes were loosening. But whereas educated young Germans like Astrid Kirchherr, Klaus Voormann and Jürgen Vollmer, who befriended the Beatles when they honed their musicianship in the clubs of Hamburg's *Reeperbahn* district, had looked to France and existentialist philosophy for inspiration, now London and England became the centre of attention. And since young Germans liked not only the Beatles and the Rolling Stones but football as well, it seemed appropriate that the 1966 World Cup was to be hosted by the country that both represented the cutting edge of popular culture and had also given the world its most popular sport.

Though they did not bring a World Cup victory the 1960s may be considered the most important decade in the history of German football, also seeing important transitions. It did not look like that early on. While coach Sepp Herberger considered winning the group at the 1962 World Cup a success, German fans begged to differ and viewed the quarter-final exit as a disappointment. And German clubs up to then had not exactly excelled in the new European Cup competitions, only Eintracht Frankfurt producing a decent run in 1960, eliminating Glasgow Rangers with impressive 6-3 and 6-1 wins in the semis, before losing a memorable final 7-3 to Real Madrid at Hampden Park.

Herberger knew that his players needed more demanding competition week-in week-out and had for a while been lobbying for the introduction of a nationwide league. In 1962 the DFB finally succumbed and launched the Bundesliga, play beginning with the 1963–64 season. Though players now could exist on the wages clubs were allowed to pay, there were still limits imposed on these payments. It took a match-fixing scandal uncovered after the 1970–71 season to finally introduce full professionalism. Nevertheless, the new league was a rousing success and seemed to pay immediate dividends internationally, when Munich 1860 in 1965 reached the final of the European Cup Winners' Cup, losing 2-0 at Wembley to a West Ham United team that featured three future World Cup heroes in Bobby Moore, Geoff Hurst and Martin Peters.

Herberger stepped down as *Bundestrainer* in 1964, leaving his successor Helmut Schön with the unenviable task of securing qualification to the 1966 World Cup. Up to then Germany had never lost a World Cup qualifier. (The record now stands at just two losses, the second of these coming on 1 September 2001, 1-5 in Munich against England when, as the song goes, even Heskey scored.) Nobody expected any problems against Cyprus (rightly so, it turned out, as Cyprus failed to score a single goal in four matches), but Sweden posed a severe threat to this unbeaten run. Memories of the 1958 semi-final were still fresh, with excessive German complaints about the hostile atmosphere in the stadium, unfair play by the Swedish players, and poor refereeing. In the aftermath there were widely reported incidents of Swedish tourists not being served in German restaurants and even cars with Swedish number plates being left with slashed tyres.

In the opening match in November 1964 in Berlin, Germany failed to hang on to a 1-0 lead, conceding a late equaliser by Sweden's Kurt Hamrin who had also scored in that notorious 1958 semi-final. Both teams then beat Cyprus easily at home, before they met again in September 1965 in Stockholm. The winner in all likelihood would go through to the World Cup; a draw would necessitate a play-off on neutral ground. In that match a young Franz Beckenbauer earned his first cap and old favourite Uwe Seeler celebrated his comeback from a torn Achilles tendon, at that time a career-threatening injury. Sweden took the lead in the forty-fourth minute, but Germany equalised before half-time. Nine minutes after the break Uwe Seeler scored the winner.

Nevertheless, a successful tournament for Germany in England was by no means assured. After the draw in early January the *Kicker* could not resist teasing its readers with the headline "World Cup: Final against England?" on the title page. The accompanying article pointed out that Germany's group was considered the second strongest among experts and how important it would be to win the group in order to avoid certain group winners Brazil and England in the quarters and semis. At the same time the magazine also began printing the weekly odds according to English bookmakers. After the draw Germany stood at 25:1, right in the middle of the pack, obviously not considered semi-final or final material. These odds were to remain remarkably unchanged well into June.

The build-up to the World Cup began with a 0-2 defeat against Czech club side Dukla Prague in January and that February loss at Wembley. The best match, according to Alf Ramsey, Wembley had seen in the last five years, an assessment considered English hyperbole in Germany. Ramsey, at least, seemed to have found his starting eleven already. From the team that played in the final only Martin Peters and Ray Wilson were not among the starters in the February match, Wilson coming on as a substitute. The German team on the other hand, still a work in progress, differed in six positions. At that time Germany had never beaten England; this game at least might have ended in a draw, had the referee not disallowed what seemed a certain equaliser, the ball supposedly already having passed the goal line before being crossed into the box. German players disagreed, but, well, they would, wouldn't they?

The loss at Wembley was followed by a 4-2 in Rotterdam

against the Netherlands, a good win for building morale, but not that significant considering the level of Dutch football in the pre-Cruyff era. What could not be known at the time was that the two Dutch goals were the last goals conceded by Germany until the third World Cup group game against Spain.

In April Borussia Dortmund eliminated holders West Ham United in the semi-finals of the Cup Winners Cup with 2-1 and 3-1 wins, four of the five goals scored by Lothar Emmerich. The national team on the other hand still did not inspire confidence with a meagre 1-0 win in an unofficial match against a selection from Hungary. Dortmund went on to beat Liverpool in the final at Glasgow, becoming the first German side to ever win a European trophy.

Without players from Dortmund who had business to attend to in Glasgow, Helmut Schön and his squad went on a tour of Ireland, beating the Republic 4-0 in Dublin and Northern Ireland 2-0 in Belfast. The Belfast win especially was viewed as a step forward, because the team had come out on top against a highly rated, very physical side. Three more games followed in June, a disappointing 1-0 against Romania, a 4-0 in another unofficial match against an Austrian selection, and finally a convincing 2-0 against Yugoslavia. By that time odds in England had changed to 14:1, but Brazil, England, Argentina, Italy and the Soviet Union, in that order, were still considered better bets to win the World Cup.

The German public on the other hand began to realise that this was not such a bad team and got their hopes up. In a special World Cup edition of *Kicker*, showbiz celebrities and some politicians (not Ludwig Erhard, though) made some pretty bold predictions about the team's chances. Editor-in-chief Robert Becker acknowledged in jest that he would reprint the January headline about a possible England vs Germany final if only he still believed in England. In his opinion everything between three and six matches was possible and he reminded his readership that getting out of the group stage should be considered a success.

The selection of the final twenty-two players to make the trip to England proved mostly uncontroversial. Some objected to Horst

Szymaniak being dropped. The experienced midfielder had been an influential part of the 1958 and 1962 squads. But he had clearly fallen behind players like Franz Beckenbauer, Helmut Haller and Wolfgang Overath, and many believed he would not take kindly to a reserve role. There was also criticism of Munich 1860 being represented by only one player, the team having snatched the championship away from Dortmund with a 2-0 win in Dortmund on the penultimate day of the season. But skipper Peter Grosser had never reached the level of his club performances with the national team and striker Rudi Brunnenmeier, an obvious choice for many, had already begun his infatuation with alcoholic beverages that was to hamper the rest of his career. As Uli Hesse points out in his history of German football, *Tor!*, Helmut Schön was well aware that only two decades had passed since the end of World War II and he wanted an uncontroversial, gentlemanly team to represent Germany.

The squad finally selected by Helmut Schön featured a nice balance between old hands (Uwe Seeler, Hans Tilkowski, Karl-Heinz Schnellinger, Helmut Haller) and young guns (Franz Beckenbauer, Wolfgang Overath, Wolfgang Weber and Sigfried Held), some highly gifted flair players and others who relied on a more physical game. Looking at a team photo it becomes clear that the rebellious fashion trends of the Swinging Sixties had not yet taken hold among German football players. No outrageous haircuts, not the slightest hint of long hair, no sideburns even – perfect son-in-law material all of them. Günter Netzer, the first German player to be considered some sort of a pop star, had received his first cap during the season but was never seriously in the running to join the World Cup squad.

On Friday, 8 July, four days ahead of its first match, the German team flew to England. According to an article in *Der Spiegel* on its way to Manchester the Lufthansa Boeing 727 passed over Wembley Stadium. The pilot drew the players' attention to the landmark and remarked: "This is where we want to see you play." Three weeks later he would get his wish.

Match Reports: Group Stage Games

Uruguay vs England

Leonardo Haberkorn

Uruguay Team Background

URUGUAY IS THE SMALLEST COUNTRY in South America, and its total population is barely that of a neighbourhood in the biggest cities of the surrounding countries. Nevertheless, by 1966 Uruguay has already won two Olympic football gold medals, two World Cups, and has lifted the Copa América ten times, far more than Brazil's three and just two less than the twelve Argentina has won. Moreover Uruguayan club side Peñarol can boast three Copa Libertadores de América (the South American equivalent of the European Cup) and a total of two Intercontinental Cups, the competition between the champions of South America and Europe. Shortly before the World Cup begins Peñarol have crushed Real Madrid in the 1966 edition 4-0 over two legs.

Peñarol have also just won their most recent Copa Libertadores. In the final in Santiago de Chile they had beaten mighty River Plate of Argentina 4-2, coming back from 0-2 in an unforgettable match.

Qualifying for the 1966 World Cup has been an easy job for a national team composed mostly by players from this immensely strong Peñarol line-up. During the qualifiers Uruguay have had to face Peru and Venezuela. Both were beaten, first at home in Montevideo, and then away at Lima and Caracas.

The Uruguayans are now in Harlow, where they have been received cheerfully. The South Americans feel extremely confident. During a visit to the local police station the players sing a *murga* song, typical carnival music from their home country, while the locals celebrate and applaud.

Uruguay, the *Celestes*, will be facing England for the fourth time and so far in these contests they have had the upper hand. In their first (friendly) match in 1953 Uruguay won 2-1 in Montevideo. One year after they met again in Switzerland during the 1954 World Cup. Once again, Uruguay prevailed, this time with a 4-2 score. In 1964 England had won a friendly match at Wembley, score 2-1.

The Uruguayan team stays at the Saxon Inn hotel. It is here that their coach, Ondino Viera, prepares the tactical scheme to be used in the first match against the strong English team.

In order to explain himself, he uses a table-tennis table to represent the Wembley pitch. On top of it he places eleven salt cellars that represent the Uruguayan footballers and eleven pepper cellars that will be the English ones. Salt must neutralise pepper, that's the key, he says. Ondino Viera moves the plastic salt cellars from side to side. He looks at his players and repeats: "If you do this, the English will not beat us!"

Evasive in front of journalists, Viera does not disclose the chosen strategy to the press. Neither does he reveal which players will be starting in his squad in the upcoming match. "Our labour must be silent and dark," he later confides to a journalist.

The morning of the match, in Harlow, beneath their national flag, the Uruguayan players swear to defend this blue-and-white emblem with all of their strength.

England vs Uruguay Match Report

Date: 11 July 1966
Kick-off: 19.30
Venue: Wembley Stadium
Uruguay line-up: Mazurkiewicz (GK), Troche (C), Manicera, Caetano, Ubiñas, Goncalves, Cortes, Rocha, Perez, Viera, Silva
England line-up: Banks (GK), Cohen, Wilson, Charlton. J, Moore (C), Stiles, Ball, Charlton. R, Greaves, Connelly, Hunt
Attendance: 87,148
Final score: Uruguay 0 England 0

Finally the moment has come. The *salt cellars* enter the pitch to take on the *pepper cellars*. The Uruguayans are astonished when they see their rivals wearing silk shirts and Vaseline rubbed into their faces so as to prevent sweat getting in their eyes. They have never seen something like that. Very sophisticated!

Wembley roars: "England! England!"

"People outside the pitch are made of wood," think the *salt cellars*, remembering the well-known phrase from Obdulio Varela, captain of the Uruguayan team that had clinched the 1950 World Cup in another mythical stadium: Rio de Janeiro's Maracaná.

Back home all of Uruguay listens to the radio. The match is not due to be broadcast on Uruguayan TV until two days later. The game starts. The first English attack already calls for goalkeeper Mazurkiewicz's intervention and ends up as the match's first corner kick, which is almost immediately followed by a second one. And only a few minutes later a third one that "Mazurka," as the Uruguayans call their goalkeeper, catches with elegance.

With the match just started a clear difference between both teams can be observed: Uruguay play slow; England, fast.

Mazurkiewicz always uses his hands to distribute the ball; this way he always manages to put the ball right at the feet of one of his teammates. That is the strongest point of the *salt cellars*: their great technique. The ball is passed accurately and low, it is played around with elegance and possession is treasured. The Uruguayans hardly miss a pass.

But the English are playing faster than them, a lot faster in fact, at speeds yet unknown for the *salt cellars*. At times it seems like each team is playing a completely different sport: salt on one side, pepper on the other.

Prior to the World Cup, Uruguay had played a friendly match against Spain; it ended in a 1-1 draw. After the match José Santamaría, the famous Spanish player, was asked for his opinion of the Uruguayan team: "Technically and as a whole, I found them awesome," he answered. "But their game is horribly slow. It's terrible. You just can't carry on playing like that nowadays."

This same issue is exposed now at Wembley.

The *salt cellars* fall back into their box in order to stop the *pepper cellars*. Eight minutes into the match Cortés lobs the ball over an opponent's head and a minute later, the *Celestes* manage to break through and reach the English box for the very first time. The crowd sighs with relief when Gordon Banks catches the ball.

The *salt cellars* are mainly defending their own half. In the thirteenth minute Milton Viera delights the overwhelmingly English support with an elegant dribble. Three minutes later Rocha steals the ball right off the feet of an English player with a very classy move and strikes forward in an almost artistic way. However, all that quality is made ineffective by the speed of the British game and the *Celestes* are not able to get close to their opponents' six-yard box and threaten England's goal. At times it feels as if there are twelve or thirteen *pepper cellars* on the pitch. "Uruguay play at walking pace," complains the BBC commentator from the TV screen and he is spot on.

The best moment for Uruguay in the first half: a nice long-distance shot by Cortés that Banks turns behind for a corner kick.

Thirteen minutes to go until half-time. Rocha pushes forward, stylishly, swiftly avoiding rivals, but when he is ready to shoot an English player appears out of nowhere at supersonic-jet speed and snatches the ball from him.

Almost half-time. Cortés gives a back-heel pass leaving an opponent on the floor. Quality versus speed. 0-0. Half-time.

Two and a half minutes into the second half Caetano commits a heavy foul against Bobby Charlton. There is some pushing and shoving. A minute later Ubiña tackles another English player. The England fans boo the *salt cellars*.

Uruguay keep hiding in their half, resisting the English attacks thanks both to the condiments' tactical scheme developed on top of a table-tennis table and the willingness, strength and talent of its players.

But the *Celestes* just do not have enough speed to challenge the English team. Ten minutes have passed now since the match resumed. Rocha passes the ball to blind-side an English player, and makes a one-two pass with Silva, but a fast *pepper cellar* stops the Uruguayan attack before Rocha can shoot on goal.

Four minutes later, Ubiña defends with an amazing bicycle kick. Wembley applauds.

With sixteen minutes of the second half gone something magical now occurs. Viera passes the ball to Rocha who controls it, his back to the English goal. The Uruguayan, without stopping the ball, lifts it over the English defender he has behind him as he turns around. Before the ball touches the ground Rocha hits a ferocious volley that misses the goal by just a few inches. It's the best shot of the whole match. The crowd applauds. "Pedro Rocha from Peñarol, twenty-three years old," says the BBC commentator, who feels the need to explain to his audience who that genius is.

England responds with its best weapon: fast and collective play. A succession of rapid passes dazes the Uruguayan defence. Nineteen minutes into the second half and it seems like an English goal is imminent. The Uruguayan defence manages to deflect the ball but it ends up right at Bobby Charlton's feet. Quality is not a *salt cellar* exclusive. The English star shoots without even stopping the ball. An astonishing save from Mazurkiewicz and the score is still 0-0.

The siege continues. More and more crosses land in the Uruguayan box. During a rare counter-attack from Uruguay Stiles elbows Silva, who dives and stays on the ground for a couple of minutes. Uruguay are now able to catch some breath for the fiunal part of the match.

There are only fifteen minutes to go now. Great attack in depth from the English, but Mazurkiewicz is able to make the saves that matter.

Next up Viera stops yet another attack from the *pepper cellars* with a foul. Almost the whole stadium turns against him. Five minutes to go. An English header hits the Uruguayan crossbar. One minute left. Another English header barely misses the goal this time.

Finally the referee whistles for full-time.

The Uruguayan team celebrate as if they have won. They effusively hug each other. Some English players leave quickly for the dressing rooms without thanking the referee, the crowd or their opponents. At the end of the game, with both teams expected to line up to sportingly shake hands, all of the *salt cellars* are there, but four or five *pepper cellars* are missing.

The Uruguayan What Happened Next

Back home in Uruguay people celebrate in the streets. The draw is received as a victory in the small country that is used to triumph.

"Another great feat of the Celeste" is *El Diario*'s headline, the first paper off the presses after the match. The article beneath tells of "a draw that tastes like victory against a mighty opponent... Cortés, Troche and Manicera performed brilliantly."

Some years later defender Manicera will say in an interview that everything that happened at Wembley was exactly what the coach had planned on top of the table-tennis table with the pepper and salt cellars: "Everything Don Ondino planned, happened. He was a genius, able to know what could happen in any match, and plan all moves of each single player in relationship to what the opponent would do."

Finishing second in the group, Uruguay moved on to the knockout phase of the tournament where they were beaten 4-0 by Germany in a quarter-final in which the *Celestes* suffered two controversial red cards shown by an English referee. (At the same time a German referee also made some questionable decisions during the quarter-final match in which England defeated Argentina.)

The *salt cellars* from 1966 would form the core of the Uruguayan team to achieve fourth place at the next World Cup, Mexico 1970.

However, as this brilliant generation started to retire, it was clear that slow-motion Uruguayan football had become obsolete globally.

The definitive confirmation arrived in West Germany at the 1974 World Cup when, during the opening match against Johan Cruyff's Holland, Uruguay were completely overwhelmed and lost only 2-0 thanks to one of the few *salt cellars* still playing, goalkeeper Mazurkiewicz, who had an excellent performance and helped prevent a far heavier defeat.

It was the *salt cellars'* curse: many years with lots of salt and very little sugar for Uruguayan football. It was not until the 2010 World Cup in South Africa that Uruguay would reach the semi-finals again.

Mexico vs England

Carlos Calderón Cardoso

Mexico Team Background

THE FIRST ROUND qualifiers for teams from FIFA's CONCACAF zone began on 28 February 1965. Mexico were in a qualifying group with Honduras, USA, Costa Rica and Jamaica. Qualification was secured with a 1-0 win over Costa Rica on 16 May, a match notable for a spectacular mass brawl.

Mexico's performance at the Chile 1962 World Cup gave home supporters hope of making greater progress in England. Mexico had beaten Czechoslovakia and would have replaced them as qualifying second from their Group for the quarter-finals if it hadn't been for the heartbreak of conceding a ninetieth-minute winner to Spain. The core of the '62 team made the squad for the England match including the coach, Ignacio Trelles, the first Mexico manager to lead his team successfully through qualifying campaigns for two consecutive World Cups. And Trelles, *Don Nacho*, had brought down the experienced squad's average age by bringing in a number of talented young players, including Enrique Bora, Gustavo Peña and Aarón Padilla.

Between the posts, ace-in-the-hole Ignacio Calderón was the man tasked with following in the footsteps of the legendary goalkeeper Antonio Carbajal, who was himself aiming to get a few minutes on the pitch as a substitute for a World Cup career that first began representing Mexico way back at Brazil 1950.

The draw wasn't kind to the Mexican team, putting it in Group One alongside host nation England, two-time World Cup-winners Uruguay, and the always competitive France.

Mexico's first game of the tournament was against the French at the historic home of English football, Wembley Stadium, on

13 July 1966. Playing calm and composed football, Mexico were able to take the lead thanks to a goal from Enrique Borja. But the joy was short-lived as the team lost its advantage when Gerard Hausser made the most of Mexico's sole defensive lapse of the afternoon and equalised. The score remained 1-1 until the final whistle from Israeli referee Menachem Askenazi.

England vs Mexico Match Report

Date: 16 July 1966
Kick-off: 19.30
Venue: Wembley Stadium
Mexico line-up: Calderon (GK), Hernandez, Mejia, Velasco (C), Gut-ierrez, del Muro, Diaz, Rizo, Monteon, Borja, Aguirre
England line-up: Banks (GK), Cohen, Moore (C), Wilson, Charlton. J, Peters, Stiles, Charlton. R, Hunt, Paine, Greaves
Attendance: 92,570
Final score: Mexico 0 England 2
Goals: Charlton. R, 37; Hunt, 75

With a bit less than half an hour to go before kick-off, Mexican flags can be seen waving at strategic points in the Wembley crowd. There are just over a hundred fans shouting for Mexico but they are eclipsed by tens of thousands of local fans booming out "England! England!"

The grass is perfect as the teams run out onto the pitch under a cloudy sky. Mexico have Ignacio Calderón in goal; a back line of Gustavo *Halcón* Peña (captain), Arturo *El Cura* Chaires, Jesús Del Muro, Gabriel Nuñez and Guillermo *Campeón* Hernández; Igna-cio Jaúregui, Isidoro *El Chololo* Díaz and Salvador Reyes in mid-field; along with Aarón Padilla and Enrique Borja up front.

We have no idea why Trelles allotted such a deep-lying defen-sive role to Chava Reyes who is more useful making sudden bursts forward in his more natural role in attack.

England's line-up is Banks, Cohen, Wilson, Stiles, Charlton. J,

Moore (captain), Paine, Greaves, Charlton. R, Hunt and Peters.

The Mexicans wear their classic kit of maroon shirts and navy-blue shorts, while England are in white tops and navy shorts. When the Italian referee Concetto Lo Bello signals the start of the game, the Mexicans take the kick-off and attempt to mount an attack.

We're barely into the second minute and England are on the verge of scoring through Greaves but the ball goes past the outside of the post. The England team is continually on the attack. Hunt decides to have a go and lets fly. Somehow, Calderón pulls off an unbelievable save, parrying the shot and eventually catching hold of the ball to prevent what looked a certain goal.

After fifteen minutes, the Mexicans put together their first attack but it peters out. England are well on top and the first goal could come at any moment. Nevertheless, an effort from Díaz in the twenty-fifth minute suddenly brings Banks into the game and it seems as if our boys are finally beginning to show glimpses of what they can do. Hopefully now they'll try to play further up the pitch instead of going backwards from the halfway line, as the coach has set them up to do.

Hunt eventually gets the ball in the net, but the referee disallows it, apparently for a foul by the English forward himself. We've barely recovered from the shock before the very thing we've been dreading – the first legitimate goal for England – occurs. And a great goal it is too, scored in the thirty-seventh minute by one of England's finest players, Bobby Charlton (of course!), who hits the back of the net with an absolute screamer from thirty yards out. "England! England!" rings out once more around the whole stadium and the Mexican players look crestfallen.

Now, Mexico have to respond positively; they can't keep on sitting back, waiting for the opposition to come to them. Hunt tries a volley from a corner and the ball flies out of play. Mexico counter-attack and Díaz is brought down just outside the opposition's penalty area. This is a great opportunity for the Mexicans to show what they're made of. Díaz takes the free kick himself but the

England defence do their job. We get a corner. That, too, is wasted. A new counter-attack from England threatens Calderón's goal. Mexico just about hang on and the Italian referee blows for half-time.

The second half begins with England pouring forward, cheered on by their supporters. With Calderón already beaten, Díaz clears a header from Bobby Charlton off the line.

The Mexicans attempt to break upfield and a tentative counter-attack produces a dangerous shot from Padilla that Banks manages to hold onto. He releases the ball to start England's next attack; Hunt runs free on the right and passes to Bobby Charlton who passes to Stiles, and then heads his teammate's lobbed return skimming past the post. The pressure from England is unremitting and the Mexicans have hardly got out of their own half, which leaves Borja and Padilla isolated up front, whereas England can have as many as six players in attack at the same time.

In the seventy-fifth minute, a space opens up in the Mexican defence as the team moves forward. Greaves nicks the ball and manages to get off a shot, which Calderón palms away. The ball lands at the feet of Hunt, who does not waste the opportunity and beats the goalkeeper to put England 2-0 up.

Once again, "England! England!" rings around the stadium. Mexico now have to go for broke if they don't want to leave Wembley as the losing side. England are quick to exploit the gaps opened up by Mexico's drive to score a pride-restoring goal and fire off shots from all angles but a packed defence keeps the score as it is.

In the final minutes of the game, Borja is just about to capitalise on a mistake by England when Banks bravely dives at his feet. There are fewer attacks now because, on the one hand, England know a win is close and, on the other, the Mexicans feel they're never going to score against the home side.

Regrettably, Mexico came out looking for a draw, and, as we all know, that's not how it works – if you don't go out to win, you end up losing. Which is exactly what happens. The Italian referee blows the final whistle. Now, Ignacio Trelles' squad will have to defeat a very strong Uruguayan team if they want to get through to the second phase of a World Cup for the first time in Mexico's history, but the task is already looking nearly impossible.

The Mexican What Happened Next

Mexico played its third Group One match against Uruguay. In the Mexican goal, Antonio *La Tota* Carbajal fulfilled his dream of ending his twenty-year World Cup career with an appearance in his fifth World Cup. Mexico came away with a 0-0 draw and a clean sheet for Carbajal, but it wasn't enough. The squad flew back without having achieved its aims of making it to the quarter-finals, but with the hope of greater success on home soil, since, in four years' time, Mexico would be hosting the rest of the world at the 1970 tournament.

France vs England

Philippe Auclair

France Team Background

The 1960s were not quite as dismal a decade for French football as is commonly thought. It is more that what France had shown at the 1958 World Cup, having played beautifully to finish third, did not mark the beginning of a new era, simply the peak of the Kopa-Fontaine generation. They still reached the quarter-finals of the 1960 European Championships and only just failed to qualify for the 1962 World Cup, falling to Bulgaria in a play-off despite "winning" their group ahead of the same Bulgarians (goal difference was not used to split sides who finished on the same number of points back then).

Two years later, they gained a place in the last eight of the Euros, and a place at the 1966 World Cup was secured when Henri Guérin's team finished top of a far-from-straightforward qualification group that included Norway and Yugoslavia. Yugoslavia, against whom France's record since 1951 read: played five, drawn one, lost four. And soon, lost five, as the first encounter between the two teams ended with the usual defeat.

Guérin took stock, and opted to experiment with a hitherto untested system, which he first tried out in a friendly against Argentina, a creditable 0-0 draw, June 1965 in Paris. The scoreline tells its own story: not conceding had become a priority. What was nominally a 4-4-2 morphed into 5-3-2 when France conceded possession, one of the defensive midfielders dropping to centre-back. The move infuriated French purists, but proved effective in the short term: Norway were beaten on their own soil, Yugoslavia at the Parc des Princes, both by a goal to nil. France had qualified for the World Cup.

Guérin did what seemed natural, and stuck to this ultra-cautious approach in England until the desperate situation of his team forced him to risk all against the host country. A mediocre opener against Mexico, in which Gérard Hausser, otherwise the brightest of a dull lot, missed a superb chance to put France in the lead and instead Mexico took the lead before Hausser redeemed himself with his second-half equaliser, the game ending 1-1.

Next, Uruguay, and an even more disappointing performance in an eerily silent White City stadium. A quite ludicrous foul by Uruguay's Jorge Manicera on Yves Herbet had resulted in a penalty, which Héctor De Bourgoing (formerly capped by Argentina) converted with great composure. After which France retreated into defence until the inevitable happened. The superb Pedro Rocha hit Uruguay's equaliser. Five minutes later, Julio Cortes lashed in a violent shot from an acute angle. 2-1 to Uruguay and the game despite still only in its 32nd minute was as good as over. An hour later, with the scoreline remaining the same, it was.

Qualification was still possible, however. All France had to do was to beat England at Wembley.

France vs England Match Report

Date: 20 July 1966
Kick-off: 19.30
Venue: Wembley Stadium
France line-up: Aubour (GK), Herbin, Budzinski, Bosquier, Arelesa (C), Herbet, Simon, Bonnel, Hausser, Djorkaeff
England line-up: Banks (GK), Cohen, Charlton. J, Wilson, Moore (C), Callaghan, Stiles, Peters, Charlton. R, Hunt, Greaves
Attendance: 98,270
Final score: France 0 England 2
Goals: Hunt, 38; 75

Just as implacably and inevitably as November winds rob trees of their leaves, France came to Wembley and were conquered as they had been nine years previously in the same stadium, when Finney, Edwards and Haynes had put Roger Piantoni's side to the sword. It will not blunt the regrets of Artelesa and his teammates that on this occasion the 100,000-strong crowd did not witness as complete an annihilation as then, when Taylor and Robson had both scored a brace. But regrets they have every right to harbour.

Facing elimination from the World Cup, the French had no choice but to abandon the safety-first approach that had cost them so dear against Mexico and, especially, Uruguay, and this they did with panache, until a lack of what the English call "the killer instinct" (a *leitmotiv* of our game since Just Fontaine's career was cut short by a knee injury four years earlier) in front of Gordon Banks's goal combined with bad luck and dubious refereeing to ensure there'd be no repeat of 1963's miracle – when a 5-2 win over the English at the Parc des Princes had given France a place in the last sixteen of the 1964 European Championships.

National team manager Henri Guérin, so widely and so justifiably criticised at home for his startling lack of ambition in France's first two group games, chose to change his team's shape rather than its personnel. Save for Nestor Combin and Di Michele, this was the same eleven that had drawn a dire opening match against Mexico. And except for Herbin, restored to the starting line-up in the place of De Bourgoing, the same eleven that had also lost against Uruguay.

This time, however, now that the French were up against a far more formidable opponent than those faced earlier in the tournament, Guérin did what he should have done from the outset. He deployed a 4-3-3 formation that played to the qualities of the skilful squad at his disposal, as was shown almost right from kick-off. He also dropped the sterile *béton* – literally, "concrete," the *béton* that had crumbled against Uruguay – to adopt a zonal defence system which, though barely rehearsed ahead of this game, gave greater freedom to defenders such as the adventurous Bernard Bosquier. What if Guérin had showed the same daring before it became a gamble?

Perhaps the English, having seen Mexico and Uruguay draw 0-0 on the same Wembley pitch twenty-four hours earlier, relaxed a little, knowing that a place in the quarter-finals surely beckoned. It certainly was an advantage to both England and France to know exactly what was required of them on that Wednesday evening.

England battled hard, too hard. Alf Ramsey had said when he took charge of England in 1962: "Some overseas sides control the ball better. I would say that players in the hotter countries move better, move quicker, perhaps think quicker than ours." Guérin's team certainly threw itself into the game as if to prove the English coach had a point.

First, Hausser stroked a beautiful cross from the left with the outside of his right boot, Herbin – who'd started the move – heading the ball powerfully just wide of Banks's right-hand post. The slight but vivacious Herbet, who moved from the wing to a more central position as early as the eighth minute, provided the zest and imagination that had been lacking until then, drawing attractive patterns deep in England's half – but without yet seriously threatening Banks.

There was the misfortune of the injury that Herbin was limping on from very early on. With no substitutes allowed it meant France were effectively playing with one man down. But they did not lose heart, and could consider themselves unlucky to go behind seven minutes before the pause, when, following a corner kick, Stiles crossed deep towards the far post, where Jack Charlton had unaccountably been left alone by the French defenders. His header struck the post, only to be fired home from point-blank range by Hunt. Was he offside, or was Jack Charlton? The French were convinced that this must have been the case and that Hunt's effort should be disallowed, as a Jimmy Greaves' "goal" already had been earlier in the game. Their protests were ignored. This wouldn't be the last time they'd have cause to complain about the decision-making of the referee, the Peruvian Arturo Yamasaki.

Perhaps fired by a sense of injustice, and despite what amounted to a numerical disadvantage, France played with even more purpose and vigour in the second half. Bernard Bosquier, one of the cleanest strikers of the ball in French football, was unlucky to narrowly miss the goal from a long way out on several occasions, whilst Simon, diving bravely to head from the penalty spot, forced Banks to turn the ball round a post.

Yes, Aubour had to parry a vicious swerving shot by Martin Peters, but France were still in with a chance – until the game's decisive moment, in the seventy-fifth minute, when Stiles' crude hack on Jacques Simon left the elegant Nantes midfielder lying in great pain right in front of the Royal Box. And it is while Simon lay injured that Hunt sprang to head Ian Callaghan's floating cross into Aubour's net.

Perhaps the Lyon keeper had been at fault; but not as much as the Peruvian referee. Stiles was punished by a caution; but that was too little, too late. His brutal intervention forced Simon to have his left knee strapped, not that it helped him much. He could hardly move after the Englishman's assault. France were *de facto* now playing with nine men – when England should have been reduced to ten.

There could, and would, be no way back. 2-0 it stayed. The inevitable had happened as expected, but not quite as feared. It did not constitute a redemption, as the despondency felt after the matches against Mexico and Uruguay could only be dissipated by a victory. But some pride had been restored, which was more than had been hoped for, if not enough.

The French What Happened Next

As could be expected, Henri Guérin did not survive France's worst World Cup campaign to date. A number of his players – especially the outspoken Robert Herbin – didn't hide their dislike of his character and his methods, and the general public didn't have a much more favourable opinion of the former Rennes and Saint-Étienne coach. But it still took well over a month for the French FA to act, following a twenty-four-hour-long meeting held behind closed doors at their Rue de Londres headquarters. Rue de Londres; Londres where France had failed. The irony was not lost on many.

At long last, on 3 September, Guérin ceased to be France's manager. Who would replace him? The FA's "crisis committee" came up with an imaginative solution: they chose not one, but two men, José Arribas and Jean Snella, respectively managers of FC Nantes and Saint-Étienne, France's biggest clubs at the time. The experiment proved short-lived, however, lasting only four games before an even shorter appointment, Just Fontaine, who lost both of the two matches for which he was France's manager.

French football was caught in a spiral of decline from which it would take well over a decade to escape. To most observers, the 1966 World Cup – the game against England in particular – had revealed the huge physical deficit of French players compared to almost all of their international opponents. We'd been left behind. Our academies – that of Nantes in particular – produced skilful players who could delight crowds with their imagination and their swift interplay. But what good was that when they had to face adversaries whose strength and fitness was so evidently superior to theirs and nullified their technical excellence?

In some ways, 1966 provoked a catastrophe in terms of the results that followed. French players – and spectators – developed an inferiority complex and a paralysing fear of failure which would only be conquered when a Michel Platini free-kick made sure that *Les Bleus* would be in Argentina for World Cup '78. A tournament that of course England failed to qualify for. 1966 had forced the game's administrators to address the systemic problems that had caused the catastrophe in the first instance, and this they did (nobody more than the FA chairman Fernand Sastre) in an almost visionary fashion from the early 1970s onwards, privileging the long term, paving the way for the successes to follow. *Un mal pour un bien*, a blessing in disguise, perhaps?

First Half

Grounds for a Celebration

Simon Inglis

COMPARED WITH ALL THE HYPE AND HULLABALOO that surrounds the staging of a World Cup since Italia '90 or thereabouts, England barely got into a sweat for 1966. No new stadiums. No great procurement scandals. Not even any last-minute construction scare stories.

Eight venues were used, all of them pre-existing and long established. At these venues, six of them club grounds, just two new stands were built during the build-up, both of which would have been built anyway (the North Stand at Old Trafford and West Stand at Hillsborough).

A few other stands were spruced up. Two terraces were covered (the Fulwell End at Sunderland and East End at Middlesbrough). Both end terraces at Everton were remodelled in order to accommodate an international-sized pitch. A protective steel grille had to be erected over the players' tunnel at Villa Park.

Just under 39,000 seats, around half of them wooden benches, were tacked onto existing terracing. Those on the Witton End at Villa Park were uncovered and used only three times. Middlesbrough's 8000 new seats cost 35s each (£1.75). Even in 1966 that was hardly pushing the boat out.

At Hillsborough a new gymnasium was built, to serve during the World Cup as a press centre. At Sunderland a new hospitality suite was constructed. At Everton, eight Victorian terraced houses (one of which had been home to Dixie Dean) were demolished to improve access. At Old Trafford a footbridge was built over the adjacent railway line.

At various grounds a few extra toilets were built and, where needed, "ladies rooms" provided for visiting dignitaries' wives (this being an era when women were still barred from the directors' lounges at most clubs). Flags and flagpoles were supplied for each venue (in sets of sixteen, to display the flags of the competing nations). A temporary hospitality centre was erected at Wembley. Actually, a marquee. Plus there was some bunting.

Total outlay on the 1966 World Cup grounds (excluding the two stands that were happening anyway): around £1m, or in today's money £17–18 million. Total cost to the taxpayer: just under £400,000, roughly £7 million today.

But if this might appear to the present-day reader to represent an admirable exercise in restraint, in stark contrast to the monstrous overspending that seemingly bloats each and every major international sporting event today, for the host clubs involved in 1966 the improvements were no small matter, and would not have been achievable without loans from the Football Association (who stood to make a decent profit on the tournament anyway).

However the FA's largesse, and its borrowing powers, went only so far, which is why the 1966 World Cup can go down in history as the first major sporting event in Britain ever to receive government funding – albeit not without a fight.

According to one official at the Department of Education and Science, under whose auspices sport then fell, the very idea of government loans being allocated to professional football clubs for hosting the World Cup was "utterly repugnant." If the government gave grants to those clubs, warned another official at the Treasury, there would follow a torrent of other claimants. And not only from football.

In 1906 the British Olympic Association was told, by King Edward VII no less, that if it wished to host the 1908 Olympics in London, it should be at no cost to the public purse. In 1948, Clement Attlee's Labour government cautiously welcomed the Olympics' return to London, but only if no public funds were required.

This was the British way, and given the success of the "Austerity Olympics," who could blame politicians in the 1960s for urging restraint? Sport was the province, surely, of voluntary organisations, of schools and benefactors, or at a stretch, of local councils and education authorities. As for professional sport, it could, and should look after itself. Especially as five-figure transfer fees were now the norm in football, while some players, like that Haynes fellow at Fulham, were on £100 a week.

If government did have a role in the provision of spectator facilities, went the argument, it was purely advisory, as demonstrated after the 1946 disaster at Burnden Park in Bolton. This led to a loose system of voluntary licensing and capacity limits (a system whose inadequacies would be cruelly exposed in the 1970s). Or it was fiscal. Thus the government happily taxed the football pools, but unlike several of its European counterparts, declined to put any of the proceeds back into stadiums or facilities.

So when, at a FIFA Congress in August 1960, the English Football Association beat, would you believe, the West Germans, for the right to host the 1966 World Cup (the vote was 34 to 27), the Conservative government of the day stayed well out of the equation. If "make do and mend" had worked in 1948 then it could jolly well suffice in 1966.

But the Britain of 1966 turned out to be a rather different Britain from the one of 1960 (just as the world changed dramatically between London winning its third bid for the Olympics, in 2005, and the actual staging of the Games, in 2012). Britain's last conscripts left the army in 1963, just as the Beatles were storming the world. Bookmaking had been legalised in 1961. Football fans were now starting to travel to matches on motorways. Footballers were no longer subject to a maximum wage. And whilst on the pitch the age of Stanley Matthews was giving way to that of George Best, at the 1964 General Election, Harold Wilson led the Labour Party to the narrowest of victories, thereby ending thirteen years of Conservative rule.

Harold Wilson personified this new age, not least because as a grammar schoolboy he had grown up supporting Huddersfield Town, in contrast to his Tory predecessor, Alec Douglas Home, an old Etonian aristocrat for whom "sport" meant hunting, shooting and the Long Room at Lord's. Under Labour, promised Wilson, the "white heat" of technology would forge a new economic prosperity. Under an initiative called "Leisure for Living," all manner of opportunities would emerge in the arts, culture, outdoor recreation and heritage.

For sport, the consequences of Labour's victory were to be profound. One of Wilson's first acts in government was to appoint Britain's first Minister for Sport, Denis Howell, a Birmingham MP who was also, remarkably, a Football League referee. Wilson also tasked Howell with the formation of the Sports Council twenty-plus years after an Arts Council had been formed in 1940. Now it was the turn of physical culture.

Not everyone was pleased. What did politicians know about sport? Sir Stanley Rous, former FA Secretary and since 1961, the FIFA President, might have been comfortable with all these goings on at Westminster. He was an operator. But for the butchers, bakers and candlestick makers in football-club boardrooms, these events represented a radical departure: the onset of the modern world in an industry still rooted in Victorian practices. Had it not been enough for them to have installed floodlights?

Nowadays, any country bidding for the World Cup has to draw up detailed bid books, outlining which cities and which stadiums will act as hosts. Strict stadia criteria must be met. Cities must vie with each other to make the shortlist, often at great cost to local taxpayers. (Anyone recall the expensive efforts of Bristol, Plymouth and Milton Keynes to be on the shortlist for England's doomed 2018 bid?)

In the run-up to 1966 no such criteria existed, and little civic involvement was sought. Instead, in November 1962 – nearly two years after England had won the bid – the FA finally announced a provisional shortlist of grounds.

The shortlist, split into geographical regions, was based on overall capacities, on the number of seats, the percentage of covered accommodation and the ability to house the international press and all the paraphernalia that even in the 1960s outside broadcasting brought with it. It read as follows: Goodison Park and Old Trafford (in the north west), St James' Park and Roker Park (north east), Villa Park and Hillsborough (Midlands and Yorkshire), Wembley and Highbury (London).

In reserve were the Victoria Ground (Stoke) and Ashton Gate (Bristol). Not chosen, despite having the requisite capacities, were Anfield, Maine Road, Bramall Lane, Molineux, White Hart Lane or Stamford Bridge. (Elland Road had yet to undergo its modern transformation courtesy of the Revie era.)

Yet truth be told, none of the chosen venues stood out as beacons of progress, nor could this be attributed solely to conservatism in the boardroom. During the years that followed World War II, when attendances hit record levels, football clubs had been prevented from improving their grounds by government restrictions on building materials. Schools, homes and hospitals had to take precedence.

Only those clubs that had suffered from war damage were allowed to rebuild. Hence during the 1950s only a handful of new stands appeared, and when they did, such as at Plymouth and Birmingham, their designs were rooted in pre-war thinking. Unlike today, no architects or engineers specialised in stadium design. Even the experienced firm of Archibald Leitch, which at various times between 1903–39 had a hand in the design of all six club grounds used in 1966, closed down in the mid-1950s. There just wasn't the work.

In fact at only one club, Manchester United, was there anything like a masterplan, and this too had been largely shaped by the war – during which Old Trafford was all but flattened – and by the necessities of the post-war period. Instead of building for the future, during the late 1940 and 1950s, just to get the ground up and running again, United effectively replaced all their bombed out stands and terrace covers with replicas of what had been there in 1939, up to and including the re-roofing of the Stretford End in 1959, columns and all.

Meanwhile clubs' income had also been hit by the Entertainment Tax. By the time it was lifted in 1957 the post-war attendance boom had ended, leaving most clubs content to do the minimum to patch up their aging facilities.

How antiquated English football grounds now appeared. (The same could be said of its athletics and aquatic facilities too.) In contrast, Barcelona's Nou Camp, inaugurated in 1957, appeared as a sleek concrete bowl, holding 90,000. In Sweden, in the run-up to the 1958 World Cup, two graceful, shell-like stadiums – the 52,000 capacity New Ullevi Stadium in Gothenburg and the 31,000 capacity Malmo Stadium – demonstrated the powerful grace of reinforced concrete and cable-suspension roofs. Plus of course there was the Maracanã, the peerless concrete bowl where Brazil had hosted the 1950 World Cup. Compared with these architectural and engineering icons, England's proposed venues for 1966 were a throwback to another age. All originated between the years 1892 and 1923.

There were, it is true, some pockets of modernisation. Sheffield Wednesday's concrete and steel North Stand, completed in 1961, was only the second cantilevered (or column-free) stand to have been built at a British football ground (after a smaller one at Scunthorpe three years earlier). That such stands were by then relatively commonplace on the Continent (and at British racecourses) did not detract from its genuine elan.

At Old Trafford in 1964, the directors at Manchester United, clearly tired of recreating the past, commissioned an even more daring, two tiered cantilevered stand on the north, or United Road side, costing £350,000 and holding 10,000. At its rear was a line of executive boxes, the first ever seen at an English football ground. They were there because United's new and forward-looking architect, Ernie Atherden, had installed boxes in a stand he had designed three years earlier at the Castle Irwell racecourse, just opposite United's training ground. (The racecourse closed in 1963 but the stand lives on, somewhat incongruously, as a student union.) Such facilities, he persuaded the United board, were the future. At the newly completed Astrodome in Houston they called them "skyboxes."

Wembley, too, had undergone a substantial refit in 1963, in time for the FA's Centenary. A new roof now covered the entire bowl, with state-of-the-art translucent panels closest to the pitch, and a new press gallery. Admittedly the sightlines were still lousy and the toilets hopelessly inadequate. But the twin towers retained their magic – in Britain and overseas – and the complex's new owners, Rediffusion Holdings, were major operators in the entertainment business. There was even a new ten-pin bowling alley next to the stadium.

Given the opportunity to host a World Cup today, every local authority in England would leap at the chance. Jump through barrels. Pull out all the stops. Sing the praises of their vibrant town centres. Rally local celebs. Go big on social media. Back in the 1960s, Newcastle tripped itself up at the first hurdle.

Originally scheduled to stage three matches, St James' Park was selected on condition that the Magpies build a new stand, add more seats and effect various other improvements, none of them unreasonable, all of them long overdue. But the club would not commit to the expense without a longer lease from its landlord, Newcastle City Council, and the Council refused a new lease without the club opening itself up to the community and modernising its whole management structure. Mirroring events at Westminster, here again was a battle between conservatism and modernism, between the traditional football establishment and the emerging Labour elite.

Not that Newcastle's replacement was any more propitious. Described in the *Daily Telegraph* as "an antique stadium if ever there was," Ayresome Park in Middlesbrough needed at least £45,000 to bring it up to basic readiness. Yet the club's bankers were refusing to extend the club's already sizeable overdraft, which had reached £60,000, not least because the new Labour government was urging caution in the midst of a credit squeeze.

Only after some "gentle" persuasion from Denis Howell and others did the bank relent so that the work could proceed. By the time it was completed, Middlesbrough had been relegated to the Third Division.

A second ground to fall by the wayside was Highbury. Very little explanation was offered publicly, but three factors were probably paramount. Firstly, the pitch at Highbury was one of the smallest in senior football, just 110 x 71 yards. Secondly, there was precious little space in the surrounding streets for all the broadcasting vehicles expected. But thirdly, Wembley had spent lavishly on maintaining its status as the national stadium and was well set up to cope as the sole London venue.

With just one, mind-boggling exception. One of the matches on the World Cup schedule, Uruguay vs France, was scheduled to take place on a Friday night (15 July). That was greyhound-racing night at Wembley, and the stadium company was unwilling to lose the income. So instead – even now it seems hard to take in – the FA switched the match to another greyhound stadium in west London, White City.

This giant hulk of a stadium, built originally for the 1908 Olympics, had been saved by greyhounds and speedway in the late 1920s, from 1932–64 was the main home of English athletics. In the 1931–33 and 1962–63 seasons White City had twice staged as an experiment the home games of Queen's Park Rangers, without ever gaining favour as a football venue, QPR preferring Loftus Road as their permanent home instead. That said, the attendance of 45,662 was sufficient to avoid any blushes. It also suited the World Cup Organising Committee, which maintained an office at the stadium throughout the tournament.

Of course 1966 all ran smoothly in the end. The English may not have excelled at stadium design but, as they had shown in 1908 and 1948, they were adept at putting on a show. Foreign fans seemed largely content with how they had been received at the grounds. English fans were amused by their banners and klaxons. The six host clubs undoubtedly benefited, not only from the grants and loans made by the FA and government, but also from the prestige.

Probably the least content were those on Teeside. Albeit they had the novelty of watching North Korea confound everybody's expectations. But after all their efforts to smarten up Ayresome Park, its new 42,000 capacity was not tested once. The opening games of USSR vs North Korea saw the stadium barely half-full, and in the other two games hosted not much more than a third of tickets were sold.

As for Denis Howell and his coterie of dynamic new sports administrators, their insistence on eliciting government support turned out to be wholly justified. When the final figures were announced in the House of Commons, there was, noted one Whitehall official, "not a word of criticism." Alf and his boys had made sure of that.

And even when, several months later, questions started to be asked in Whitehall about the exact nature of loans and grants made to the six League clubs – not the amounts so much as the legal conditions placed upon them – the FA took the wind out of all the sceptics' sails by repaying the government loans, in full, not only prematurely but, handily, just before a Public Accounts Committee was due to investigate in April 1967. Subsequently the Treasury issued a warning to Howell's department not to let such lax accounting happen again. But it agreed that the matter could "now die a quiet death."

By which time Howell was focused on Britain's efforts in the upcoming 1968 Olympics in Mexico. One of the star attractions at those games, and of the 1970 World Cup, was the newly completed Azteca Stadium, a giant three-tier bowl holding 107,000.

Back in Blighty, in January 1971 the frailty of Britain's "make do and mend" mentality was again exposed by the deaths of 66 fans at Ibrox Park. Now it was the Home Office's turn to get to grips with football.

And what is left today of the 1966 venues? Answer, precious little. Gone completely are the old Wembley (although the famed 1966 crossbar remains on display in the new stadium), White City (now the site of the BBC Media Village), Ayresome and Roker Parks (both now housing estates). At Villa Park none of the four stands or terraces that stood in 1966 survive. Similarly, Old Trafford has been almost entirely rebuilt (although a section of the South Stand is the original).

Only at Goodison Park and Hillsborough do complete stands survive. At the former, there is the Bullens Road Stand, built in 1926, still with its trademark criss-cross steel balcony, and the Gladwys Street Stand, built in 1938 (both designed by Archibald Leitch). Both stands have since been re-roofed however, and their terraces converted to seating. At Hillsborough, two stands have survived from 1966; the still sleek North Stand, dating from 1961, and the still unlovely West Stand, opened just before the World Cup in 1965. Many readers will know this stand better as the Leppings Lane End.

If the 1966 World Cup represented a breakthrough in the British government's awareness of professional football, the Leppings Lane End in April '89 was when the political class became transfixed by football and its consequences.

The final irony? Now that, post-Hillsborough, old England at last has a surfeit of stadiums befitting a modern World Cup, and sport enjoys a presence and an influence in Westminster that was unimaginable back in 1966, getting the World Cup back to these shores appears tougher than ever.

What would Denis Howell or Harold Wilson advise in the circumstances? Vote Labour of course. And don't stint on the bunting.

What the Papers Said

Rob Steen

A VISIT TO THE ELEGANTLY reupholstered St Pancras branch of the British Library is worth anyone's time. It is difficult, furthermore, to exaggerate the benefits of a spot of microfiching in the spacious newsroom to those unfamiliar with a world bereft of anodyne live press conferences, vituperative radio phone-ins or published interviews that conclude with the words "Wayne Rooney is the public face of Whiskas, the cat food footballers prefer." Browsing through the World Cup coverage supplied by The Credible Con-Artists Formerly Known Collectively As Fleet Street is guaranteed to throw up all manner of amazement at the way we were.

The 1960s, after all, was the last decade in which Britain's sporting media waves were ruled by the specialist newspaper correspondent, more often than not a hard-drinking soul perpetually in thrall to his (always his) own voice, and seldom constrained or contradicted by those intrusive, meddlesome cameras. Witness the verdict in the *Daily Mail* on England's nervy opening game from Brian James, along with the *Daily Mirror*'s Ken Jones one of the only two reporters Ramsey trusted and favoured: "But though we did not beat the unambitious and uncompromising team of Uruguay, let me add this: It was also part of my prediction that England could fail to win this first match, yet still take the trophy."

To read the procession of previews, match reports and news stories from the tournament is to be made vividly aware of the minimal input from those who merely played the game. Quotes are scarce, sparse and almost invariably unenlightening. In a recent article (for the magazine *Backpass*) Brian Scovell, then a young reporter at the sternly right-wing *Daily Sketch*, recollects ghostwriting the thoughts of Billy Liddell, the great Liverpool and Scotland winger who had retired five years earlier. Howard French, the "fobbish" sports editor, hadn't heard of him but was persuaded, wrongly, that signing Liddell would boost sales on Merseyside. Although columns "by" cricketers had long been a Fleet Street staple, Scovell, who ghosted several himself, cannot recall any other such contributions from ex-footballers during the tournament, much less contemporary practitioners. Only a handful of agents, tellingly, had begun to stick their oar in.

"There was no FA press officer," recalls Scovell, who is not at all embarrassed to remember being bracketed with two other red-top thrusters, Chris "Crash" Lander and Ian Todd, as "crocodiles." All light-hearted stuff, he insists, but there they were, sniffing around the fringes before "sliding quietly into the water ready to take a lump out."

Harold Mayes, a nice man with a moustache, was in charge for the media on behalf of FIFA and the outspoken Len Went had a similar job with Wembley Stadium. Any queries about the England team were addressed to Denis Follows, the FA secretary, who didn't have a footballing background... he had been the FA's treasurer. His former job was working for a union, handling pilots. The football writers had to go to Alf Ramsey himself if there was a story, but few of them had Ramsey's telephone number. The telephone at his office in the FA was answered by his secretary and Alf never rang back.

There were brief press conferences attended by around 40 people before matches, mostly held at the Bank of England sports ground where England trained, but Ramsey was a reluctant speaker. After matches he would come out of the home dressing room at Wembley Stadium and answered a few questions before going on the coach, which was parked in the tunnel outside with the engine switched on. The interviewers had to endure the fumes and no one had the temerity to ask the driver to switch off the engine. I think it was a device to keep these interviews short.

Popular as it was, football was not remotely close to a national obsession. From an all-time peak of 22,318 in 1948–49, average League attendances in 1964–65 had slithered below 14,000 for the first time in nigh-on three decades; the next season saw them decline further still. *Match of the Day* had only just completed its second season; the lone club game guaranteed a live screening was the FA Cup final; news of sacked managers, injuries and transfers was confined to radio and the press; daily newspaper sports sections were a quarter of a century away.

March 1966 had brought an encouraging omen when George Best inspired a stunning 5-1 romp in Benfica's Lisbon citadel, sweeping Manchester United past Eusébio et al and into the European Cup semi-finals. "El Beatle" had arrived. The bubble, though, was quickly pricked by Partizan Belgrade; the hippest new hip-swayer in town, moreover, was a Belfast boy destined never to grace a World Cup, not just with his outlandish skills but his audacity and daring. Just as those last two attributes were rarely glimpsed on English pitches that year, the notion of someone uttering the words "sexy" and "football" in the same sentence would remain fanciful for some time yet.

In the months leading up to the tournament Terry Cooper was embarking on a distinguished career as a sportswriter at the Press Association; he cannot recall any sense of gathering excitement whatsoever. "I was on the desk the night the trophy was stolen," he told me in 2015. "A colleague had been busy with a golf story and wasn't happy at all when he was told he'd have to drop it and cover the theft. But then that's journalists, isn't it? Always moaning."

Notwithstanding his relationship with Ramsey, Brian James's report in the *Daily Mail* the day after the England squad was announced was allotted an unprincely nine paragraphs; in the same paper, Terry O'Connor filed nearly twice that much on the GB vs USSR athletics meeting at White City – with the latter only half-complete. Priorities were no different elsewhere. Football had its place all right, but this was summer, and this was England, and there was competition aplenty.

The tournament was immediately preceded by Wimbledon and overlapped a Test series against Garry Sobers's mighty West Indies, as well as a Lions tour Down Under; county cricket and Flat racing, too, commanded oodles of space. That Albert Barham's report of England vs Uruguay in the *Guardian* spanned barely more column inches than a report of the Lancashire vs Hampshire county championship encounter spoke thunderous volumes. As did the same paper's previews of the Wembley final itself: not one quote from a participant on a page shared with a couple of stories from Kingston, stage for the impending Commonwealth Games in Jamaica, and another brace of bulletins from minor golf tournaments – Britain vs Europe in Bilbao and the Cheshire championships at Prestbury.

Viewed from an era that has seen daily sales slump well below 10 million, it is tricky to capture quite how crucial a role newspapers played in determining British opinion in the dying days of the pre-tabloid age. Fleet Street's average daily circulation tables were dominated, as now, by the so-called "populars," albeit in a vastly different order: the *Daily Mirror* (5.12 million), followed by the *Daily Express* (3.98 million), the *Daily Mail* (2.32 million), the *Sun* (1.24 million) and the *Daily Sketch* (857,000). The most widely read of the "qualities" was comfortably the *Daily Telegraph* (1.35 million), more than a million clear of the *Times* (282,000) and the *Guardian* (281,000). On Sundays, the racier titles also reigned supreme: *News of the World* (6.15 million), the *People* (5.56 million) and the *Sunday Mirror* (5.22 million), followed by the *Sunday Express* (4.46 million). Of the three weightier competitors, the *Sunday Times* (1.36 million) led by a distance from the *Observer* (881,000) and the five year-old *Sunday Telegraph* (650,000). Total average daily sales, which would decline to 14 million in 1975, were marginally down on 1961 – from 15.8 million to 15.6 million. The Sunday story would follow a similar path: 24.3 million in 1961, 24.2 million in 1965, 20.5 million in 1975.

As befits an event that would light the way ahead for broadcasters and sport in Britain, *Radio Times* and *TV Times* trumpeted their live coverage of the 1966 World Cup on their respective covers. The *Daily Mail*'s decision to introduce a *Sportsmail* section of four pages for the event's duration was considered radical, not least since this amounted to more than a quarter of the paper's average pagination. More typical was the *Guardian*, which decided to expand its sporting portfolio from 11 July, stretching one page to one and a half in a publication that frequently ran to twenty-two.

In 1966 England's sporting self-esteem was in steep decline. World Cups had been a washout thus far, ditto the fledgling European Nations Championship and the European Cup; Australia had held the Ashes since 1959; not since 1936 had a home entrant won the Wimbledon men's singles; not until 1969 would Tony Jacklin become the first English winner of golf's Open Championship since 1948. The past two Summer Olympics, 1960 and 1964, might have brought double glory in the long jump and long-distance walks, but Ann Packer had been the lone track athlete to strike gold.

With the exception of the 1958 World Cup (for which all four home nations qualified) and the 1960 Rugby League World Cup (won in a four-horse race), the teams representing Great Britain or the United Kingdom had been just as innocuous of late:

- Not since 1957 had the Ryder Cup been won, and it wouldn't be until 1985, by which time Continental reinforcements had been summoned.
- Not since 1936 had the Davis Cup been won.
- 27 of the past 29 tussles with the USA for the women's tennis Wightman Cup had been lost.
- Not until 1971 would the British Lions win a series in New Zealand for the first time.

After such a poor run scapegoats had to be found, if necessary before the fact. Thus Alf Ramsey became the first manager or coach of an England football team to suffer the slings and arrows of outraged sportswriters.

The *Guardian* could never quite decide how to refer to him, flitting between "Mr A. E. Ramsey," "Mr Ramsey" and, as the team flourished, "Alf Ramsey," though it was back to "Mr A. E. Ramsey" after the bitter quarter-final against Argentina. Small wonder that, with the exception of Jones and James, he regarded the press with a mixture of profound distrust and prickly disdain. "This is my day off," was his indignant riposte upon being greeted by a brace of reporters at the ITV studios in Borehamwood, scene of the squad's final party the day after the final. At Hendon Hall a few hours later, an eminent journalist approached him. "I just want to congratulate you, Alf," he said, "and thank you on behalf of all the press for your cooperation." Suspicious to the last, Alf was in no mood to drop his guard. According to the journalist, the manager's precise reply was "Are you taking the piss?"

In fairness, and unlike his predecessor Walter Winterbottom, he was obliged, on occasion, to face those confounded TV cameras. What viewers took away was a sequence of brisk platitudes delivered by an east Londoner who, like Yorkshire's Len Hutton, one of the country's finest cricket captains, had felt compelled to take elocution lessons. For a decade or more, teenage boys up and down the land would mock the way each clipped, teeth-gritted pronouncement would be prefaced by a needlessly posh "Most certainly."

In front of those prying lenses, Ramsey established the template for his successors: distant, unsmiling, stiff, a little bit gruff, forever on the defensive. Nor did he seek to endear himself. Indeed, after the draw against Uruguay, a simmering anger was unmistakeable amid the self-affirming, even reckless reassurances: "With regard to the mass hypnotism after the draw when everyone thought England was in an easy group, I said at the time that there were 15 others, and nothing was going to be easy. I still believe we are able to win the World Cup."

In *The Soccer Syndrome*, written in 1965, the Ramsey enigma was tackled by John Moynihan, who covered football for the *Sunday Telegraph* with affection and erudite insight and also served the paper as literary editor:

[Ramsey's] relations with the Press were often cool. 'He behaves like a R.A.S.C. captain' was how one critic described him bitterly. [His] cold, withdrawn expression, as impersonal and mysterious and vaguely hostile as a duty officer marching up to inspect a fire picket, hides a burning fanaticism and surely a trace of anxiety... Perhaps we of the press and all supporters of England would like rather more communication from him, and less of an attitude that the England side is his and his alone. It is not his alone.

Moynihan also recounted a brief encounter with the Dagenham pied piper:

On a train going north to Sheffield, Ramsey was the only other member of the restaurant car. As the landscape turned into the industrial tattoo of the North, [he] gazed out of the window at fields and factories, giving the waiter a slightly embarrassed smile when he was recognised. He was going to watch Sheffield Wednesday play Everton and the odds were that Temple, the Everton outside-left, was his key figure that afternoon. I asked Mr Ramsey if it was indeed Temple he was going to see. He looked up at me as if I was mad. The coffee cups tinkled and tried to spring across his table. He looked just as edgy. 'Could be,' he said in a slightly refined tone. 'Now, if you'll excuse me.' He rose and walked away towards his compartment.

Moynihan was anything but a snob, but note that slightly sniffy "slightly refined." Ramsey's attempt to bridge the class divide was not widely appreciated. The summary was Moynihan personified:

Alf Ramsey, the shrewd enigma, the terror of the press, awaits his destiny. We may hope that he avoids the fate Dostoevsky describes for a losing gambler: 'When once anyone has started upon that road, it is like a man in a sledge flying down a snow mountain more and more swiftly...'

More caustic was Brian Glanville, who would do more than most to give the *Sunday Times'* sports coverage an unmatched depth and authority. In January 1966, freshly arrived at the paper from the *Northern Echo* in Darlington, Harold Evans was instructed to revamp the sports pages – "the kiss of death" according to Mark Boxer, who had launched the paper's trailblazing Sunday colour magazine earlier that decade (word had it that Ken Compston, sports editor for the past seventeen years, terrorised management with his belligerence). One of Evans's first actions was to commission a column from an irreverent, witty, little-known Yorkshireman, Michael Parkinson. Literary editor Leonard Russell's enthusiastic reaction ("Damned good sports pages this week") quelled any brewing dissent. "All that was required," Evans would write, "was for England to win the World Cup."

In 1967, Compston was replaced by John Lovesey, a highly intelligent, imaginative and adventurous man for whom sport was about a great deal more than the final score. That the ailing octogenarian Glanville was still reporting football for England's best-selling Sunday "heavy" in 2015 tells you all you need to know about his undying fidelity to a game he has loved wisely, flamboyantly and never – thank goodness – dispassionately. All too typical was this fulminating critique in the aftermath of England's 3-2 defeat at home to a "modest" Austria in October 1965:

It was John Wilkes who said that the peace of Paris was like the Peace of God; it passed all understanding. He might just as well have been talking about Mr. Ramsey's England teams. Next Wednesday, against [Northern] Ireland, he fields the great bulk of the side which drew laboriously at Cardiff, and lost so shabbily at home to Austria. When one has made due allowances for consistency, generosity and the abysmal lack of talent in the League, his choice is still remarkable. Above all, in continuing to choose Stiles of Manchester United as the linking right half, he is

pursuing a course which is as obstinate as it is inexplicable, a
course which leads one seriously to doubt if the team is picked on
any rational basis.

Yet Glanville insisted in the same article that he had lost faith
in neither Ramsey ("despite these strange perversities") nor the
potential of his team:

During the long home season, Ramsey appears to become now
obstinate, now confused. Get him away to the relative tranquillity
of the Continent, give him the players to himself, and his talents
and qualities are better revealed. I think it is arguable that we
should not have abolished, in effect, the selection committee.
Perhaps a compromise could have been achieved, on the
Portuguese pattern, whereby there is a sole selector and a team
manager who pick the team together... But by July [1966] there is
ever hope that Ramsey will have made his errors, found a more
rationally conceived team and injected his players with his own
determination.

Of the 300-odd foreign players who descended on England for
the World Cup from late June onwards, Pelé was probably alone
in being instantly recognisable. Live TV broadcasts had been
impossible from the 1962 World Cup in Chile; the first Telstar satellite was launched a fortnight after the final, confining the BBC
– for whom Raymond Glendenning and John Camkin provided
live radio commentary – to recorded highlights in ragged black-
and-white. Midweek coverage of the three European club tournaments (all knockouts) had brought Eusébio, Mario Coluna and
Giacinto Facchetti into the nation's front rooms. But even if more
column inches had been available, the idea that any could have
been wasted on overseas league tables was unthinkable.

In an eve-of-tournament overview headlined "Why the world
needs an England win," Brian James, once again, personified the
unfounded arrogance that still coursed through English football:

England, as creators of the game, have both the right and the responsibility to readjust the balance between science and spectacle... England have the ability to do this despite having resorted to a dour, dulling defence insuring against all error. It was no joy to see Ramsey leading England along this path, yet he had no alternative... You cannot stop a stampede by standing in its path. You have to join the herd and lead it. Even so, when England pulled back forwards to mark other forwards, defenders were released as marks men. No country has more adventurous backs, or stoppers more likely to turn strikers... If England win the World Cup our football theories and practices will become a model for the world as in the past.

Four weeks later, on the morning of the final, a decidedly neutral piece led the coverage in the *Daily Mail*. On a page already crammed with golf, cricket and greyhounds – as well as a reasonably unobtrusive ad for "8mm Soccer Films" – came "a statistical survey, the most comprehensive ever structured on the tournament." Nor was it a ludicrous claim. This labour of love was nothing if not prescient, analysing everything from "headers off target" to "goals following throw-ins" and "average attempts per goal," minutiae that would take decades to become integral to the sports pages. Even though the last of these found West Germany streets ahead (8.46 to 15.7) the ensuing prediction was for extra time, even a replay.

A round-up of overseas newspapers brought unanimous support for a home win from Belgium, Brazil, Sweden, Hungary and even Germany, with Gerhard Reimann forecasting in *Der Tagesspiegel*, clearly in ignorance of Helmut Schön's new strategy: "If Hottges and Weber can hold Charlton this should open the way for Beckenbauer to get our forward line moving, but otherwise I see England winning by one goal."

The greatest conjecture from an English perspective surrounded Jimmy Greaves: would Ramsey recall his one world-class striker? "England to win – but who scores the goals?" wondered the *Daily Mail*; beneath ran an even louder headline next to a large photo highlighting the manager's bushy eyebrows, crisply parted hair and grouchy countenance: "Ramsey keeps world waiting." James urged a recall for Greaves, albeit hedging his bets on whom he might replace; his suggestions were Hunt, Ball or even Hurst:

> [Greaves's] skill is undeniable. Only his application has ever been suspect, and in a World Cup final, EVERYBODY works...

> Against Portugal... England played a confident team, and that confidence had to be turned into a weapon against them. The need then was pace and persistence: better ball players had to be encouraged to attempt their moves then shut out at the split second before their completion.

> Against West Germany, speed and stamina will be needed, too. But such qualities are not enough on their own. The Germans are as fast as England and certainly as fit. Today, for the first time in this tournament, England can only win if they are more skilful than their opponents...

In the *Guardian*, Eric Todd sounded a more pragmatic if long-winded note:

> I shall be very surprised indeed if any changes are made [from the side that beat Portugal] and more so if one such change involves the return of Greaves, who has declared himself fully fit. The England attack is certainly in need of more vitality in front of goal. Nevertheless, there is no reason to presuppose that Greaves can suddenly return and produce it. And it is far too late surely to experiment?

Hints of joy were predictably thin on the ground in J. L. Manning's typically magisterial *Daily Mail* column, "The Last Word." He struck a prescient chord:

World Cup 1966 has shown that by the accident of originating professional football and a public broadcasting service, Britain pioneered the most popular entertainment in the world.

When the BBC announces that 2,000 million have watched this thing one wonders what this thing is. Is it show business or sport? Is it the real thing or the wrong thing?

I answer that the theme is still sport, despite what has happened occasionally to cause one to doubt it…

What has been written across the face of this World Cup is promotion, discipline and skill. Its promotion has been astonishing. Its discipline, by which is meant its sportsmanship, has been disappointing. Its skill has shown, once again, that football has made little progress since the war.

Football's skills have spread more widely in the past 30 years, but those of the elite are not higher. North Korea's Asiatics and Portugal's Africans have increased the width of football, but England's and Germany's best players have not raised the peaks.

Eusébio and Pelé are not, even within British recollections, greater players or more vivid personalities than Alex James and Hughie Gallagher. Are Simoes and Emmerich better wingers than Alec Jackson and Stanley Matthews? Is Bene better than Bastin? Is Coluna more skilful than Willie Edwards? Is Yashin greater than Hibbs? They are not. Tactics are different and good technique has been more widely acquired. But the art of football, as in most team sports, has been dispersed among the ordinary and the mediocre.

Manning also noted that the tournament total of 1.5 million spectators (by way of perspective, the same number saw the group phase alone of the 2015 Rugby World Cup) had raised £1.5 million in receipts, whereas a global audience of 2000 million viewers had paid "only" £400,000 via their licence fees:

> Television fees should always be greater than the gate receipts, otherwise those who can attend subsidise those who must stay at home. Of course, millions must stay at home, but now they have the means of paying. This is not a question of profitability for a professional sport. It is a question of the world's richest sport helping its poorest constituents. The World Cup, properly organised and fairly paid for, could invest nearly £1,000,000 every four years in Africa and Asia where many countries' football needs development.

Did Joao Havelange hatch his plans for global domination after reading those sentiments (or having them translated)? It seems far from impossible.

At 11am on Saturday 30 July, Ramsey finally revealed his eleven, giving the evening papers a rare world exclusive. "ENGLAND MAKE IT SAME AGAIN," declaimed the front page of the London *Evening Standard*. Bernard Joy, the last amateur to play for England and the paper's long-time chief football correspondent, contended that Ramsey had made up his mind after England's "reserves" had beaten Arsenal in a practice game on the day of the semi-final against Portugal, a game wherein Greaves had netted twice, but "preferred to play a cat-and-mouse game with the announcement in the hope of wringing the utmost out of the situation." Accompanying Joy's musings came a further sign of the dying days of deference: a photo from Hendon Hall of a tie-free Bobby Charlton.

Percy Young, Wembley head groundsman since before World War II, and his dozen-strong team had reportedly been toiling since dawn:

> Light rollers swept the pitch from end to end, and the lines were freshly marked out. Said Mr Young: 'The pitch is in excellent

condition, although a little more yielding than it was yesterday due to the heavy rain. Considering the number of matches that have been played on the ground in the last three weeks, the turf has stood up to it remarkably well.'

Even the thoughts of a carpark attendant were deemed worthy of reproduction. "It's going to be like 10 Cup Finals rolled into one," chirped one, "as a coachload of Germans from Munich pulled on to the park." A few hours later, the compositors assembled the *Standard*'s front-page headline, white type on red background: "CHAMPIONS of the WORLD." Underneath lay that iconic photo of Moore on Wilson and Hurst's shoulders over an ad for Taylor's Port.

The most glowing tribute to Ramsey's achievement appeared in the *Guardian*. "I have never tried to jump on this crowded bandwagon," wrote Ian Todd with no little pride, yet "admiration cannot be suppressed for the manner in which he has made his players believe in him and themselves. Not for one moment can I be persuaded that they either enjoyed or understood the tactics they were asked to employ at the outset. Their adaptability is a tribute to Mr Ramsey's powers of persuasion and rhetoric."

Somewhat less enthusiastic was Hans Keller, the Austrian-born musicologist and iconoclastic cultural critic often seen on the BBC during this period (most illuminatingly when interviewing Pink Floyd, a sneer never far from his lips). To this admirer of the pre-war Austrian *Wunderteam*, Ramsey personified the "New Mediocrity." In a 1969 essay, "Sport and Art: the Concept of Mastery," he bemoaned that "there is little beauty in those tackles by Ramsey defenders which crunch so near the borderline that the boss hastens to their defence and identifies them, by way of verbal magic, as 'professional'." On the day before the final, writing in the *New Statesman*, he promised readers that, in the next issue, he would "describe how England won the World Cup, and what we can do about it."

"BBC SOCCER SPREE ANGERS THE TV WIVES." On 1 June, in a sign of both the evolving media landscape and the unchanging nature of the game's ingrained sexism, it was this banner headline that had led the pre-tournament build up in the *Daily Mirror*. The Corporation had announced that it would screen more than 50 hours of the World Cup ("an average of more than two hours per night, mostly during peak viewing time"); having restricted spending to £150,000, half the opposition's budget, the commercial channel would serve up less than a third of that. As a consequence, the BBC was apparently "standing by for a massive protest"; and heading the onslaught would be "Britain's housewives."

"Complaints? We'll just have to accept them," shrugged controller Huw Wheldon. Peter Dimmock, head of Outside Broadcasts, warned that there would be "many football-mad husbands who – for once – want to decide the viewing." This would "hit a lot of people," countered Juanita Francis, chairwoman of the Married Women's Association, "particularly women – who normally enjoy TV after a hard day's work. They will be bored to tears."

Sport already ate up a chunky portion of the schedules. On 5 May, of the fourteen hours of programming on BBC1, four hours and ten minutes revolved around balls: visits to Worcestershire vs West Indies and the Penfold & Swallow golf tournament followed by live coverage of the European Cup Winners' Cup final between Liverpool and Borussia Dortmund. Ahead lay day-long live broadcasts from Wimbledon, the British Open and the five-chapter Test series between England and West Indies.

While the 1966 World Cup was the last in black-and-white for British viewers (colour arrived on BBC2 the following year), it was the first to be broadcast via satellite. In the circumstances, from a South American perspective at least, this was not an unmitigated boon: a Bogota radio station would ask the British embassy to stop sending it recordings of matches during the tournament because of "the manifest and shameful attitude of the English football authorities against South American athletes."

BBC and ITV coverage had entered another stratosphere since

Chile. A full camera crew covered every match and the channels shared the same pictures from Eurovision, although nothing like every moment was screened as it happened: kick-offs were not staggered, and the quarter-finals were played simultaneously. The final, on the other hand, could be found on no fewer than three channels: the higher definition 625-line BBC2 as well as the 405-line services on BBC1 and ITV.

ITV really pushed the boat out. The commercial channel assigned commentators to every match and even devised its own title sequence, accompanied by a theme tune, *On The Ball*, performed by The John Schroeder Orchestra. The co-commentators-cum-prototype-pundits were managers, among them Dave Bowen (Wales), Bill Shankly (Liverpool) and Jock Stein (Celtic), who at the end of each game were entrusted with summing up events in front of a pitch-side camera. England's most-capped player, Billy Wright, was presenter Eamon Andrews' Man Friday. Doing duty for the other side were former Fulham teammates Jimmy Hill and Johnny Haynes, Tommy Docherty, Danny Blanchflower and Ron Greenwood. Snobbery and advert-phobia would appear to have been the main reasons the majority of the nation favoured the BBC.

The 1966 World Cup final remains Britain's most-watched broadcast – 32.3 million, a whisker ahead of Princess Diana's funeral thirty-one summers later: all the more remarkable given that only 15 million households possessed a TV at the time. "But nowhere was it discussed at the time as a television event," observed Martin Kelner in *Sit Down and Cheer: A History Of Sport On TV*. As yet, no one had "grasped the way reality, in the shape of sport, and television could interact." However, the *Daily Mail* did make a tentative early stab at a sort of TV sport column. In one, Geoffrey Nicholson criticised the BBC's "link man" David Coleman for not being "sufficiently vulnerable to be a good interviewer." Even so, "that same brisk assurance... makes Coleman particularly effective in handling a mass of facts and a jumble of lines to distant provinces." To Nicholson, in fact, the BBC's "thoroughness" made the competition "almost irrelevant." As Alistair Reid explained in *The New Yorker*: "The BBC appointed a team to work on phonetic recommendations, so that announcers and commentators might practice getting their tongues round the elusive names of Brazilian, Bulgarian, and Russian players ('The Brazilian Olegario Toloy de Oliveira is familiarly known as Dudu, or Doodoo')."

Reacting to events on the hoof was one matter; any substantive alterations to the schedule were off-limits. ITV declined to take its viewers to the England–Uruguay match until Coronation Street had finished, and paid the price; while the BBC transmission attracted 13.5 million, viewers for the soap opera, the biggest then drawn by either channel for a single regular programme, dwindled to 6.5 million – a third of its usual audience.

On the eve of the final, the BBC squeezed in an extra half-hour show, *World Cup Report*, at 7pm ("Meet the teams and the personalities who play tomorrow"); *The Hippodrome Circus, Great Yarmouth*, occupying the peak-time berth at 8pm, was afforded almost twice as much airtime. ITV didn't even bother with a preview, scheduling *Ready, Steady, Go* against the BBC effort. Nor, writes Kelner, "was there any great hoop-la" after Geoff Hurst had completed his hat-trick.

> The BBC granted Grandstand a whole twenty minutes extra, to round up the momentous events of the day. Had West Germany not equalised in the final minute, we should all have been enjoying the Laurel and Hardy short County Hospital on the BBC by 5.20... Even less time for post-match hosannas was allowed by ITV, who scheduled Robin Hood at 5.15pm – in other words, allocating the World Cup final slightly less time than Sky in 2012 would grant a mid-table Premier League match.

Some of the clearest-eyed observations of the tournament came from Arthur Hopcraft. "Football and Foreigners" is probably the most frank and illuminating chapter in *The Football Man: People and Passions in Soccer*, originally published in 1968 and effectively a compilation of his reports for the *Observer* and the *Sunday Times*. It was here that Hopcraft sought to shed light on what the World Cup said about the nation's relationship with football and "footballing foreigners," and Englishness itself:

> To begin with the competition released in our country a communal exuberance which I think astonished ourselves more than our visitors. It gave us a chance to spruce up a lot, to lighten the leaden character of the grounds where the matches were played, to throw off much of our inhibition of behaviour, particularly in the provinces, so that we became a gay, almost reckless people in our streets, which is commonly only how we conduct ourselves when we put on our raffia hats in other countries' holiday resorts. Except in the celebrations that greeted the end of the Second World War, I have never seen England look as unashamedly delighted by life as it did during the World Cup.

North Korea's conquest of North East hearts so gladdened Hopcraft's heart, one can forgive the outrageously patronising comment about football being "the one art the labourer fully comprehends":

> In a matter of days a dark, slant-eyed footballer with a name like a nonsense rhyme can be adopted as a personal representative by a Middlesbrough labourer just because he is expressing hope and liberation through the one art the labourer fully comprehends. It often sounds unduly pompous and pious when men talk ceremonially about football's role as a bridge across national frontiers. But that is because the occasions of such statements are usually pompous, and so turn a decent truth into a banality. East and West were undoubtedly linked at Middlesbrough.

The final found Hopcraft watching not from the pressbox but the stands. He cared little for what he saw and heard:

> I was struck well before the game by the unusual nature of some

of the crowd around me. They were not football followers. They
kept asking each other about the identity of the English players.
Wasn't one of the Manchester boys supposed to be pretty good?
That very tall chap had a brother in the side, hadn't he? There they
were in their rugby club blazers and with their Home Counties
accents and obsolete prejudices, to see the successors of the Battle
of Britain pilots whack the Hun again. Some of them wept a bit at
the end, and they sang Land of Hope and Glory with a solemn
fervour I have known elsewhere only at Conservative party
rallies. I suspect that if they had found themselves sitting among a
crowd of real, live football fans from Liverpool they might have
been amazed at the degree of treacherous support available to
Jerry. Some football fans prefer even German footballers to
plump-living countrymen exercising the privilege of money to
bag a place at an event thousands more would have given their
right arms to see – and understand.

For all his on-the-ball soothsaying about the future makeup of
sporting crowds, Hopcraft cannot have imagined how drastically
the media landscape would alter. In the admittedly unlikely
event of England reaching the 2018 World Cup final in Moscow,
that ludicrous term "over-hype" might even acquire a smattering
of meaning. It would be easier to elude snow in a blizzard than
avoid the bombardment of reports, YouTube videos, news, gossip,
blogs, columns, interviews, previews, profiles, pull-outs and stats
– let alone the "Joe Hart has a Whopper" billboards and "At Home
With the Rooneys" surreality shows. In the days leading up to the
match, to all sense and purpose, the rest of the world would stop.

Ah, but would we be wiser – about the game in question or in
general? For those immersed in this non-stop digitised planetary
infotainment, even for the anti-Murdochs among us, being del-
uged with footage and paying for the privilege is generally seen as
a fair trade. Being there retains a unique allure, but it is scarcely
proof of regression to live in a world where you can be on a train
3000 miles away and hiss "Yessss!" as you watch a goal on your

telephone. That we now know so much more about the participants cannot be a bad thing either, and not solely because, provided we're prepared to surf industriously enough, we can find
out pretty much everything there is to know about the remarkable rise of Iceland and Albania. Far more important, with money
exerting an ever-more-relentless grip, so the business of football
is now addressed as never before. Indefatigable souls such as
Andrew Jennings, David Conn and the *Sunday Times* investigations team hold the powerful to account, exposing the almighty
FIFA as every inch the squalid, grasping, systemically corrupt
equal of its brother-in-harmful-charms, the International Olympic Committee.

In an age, furthermore, when the distance between spectators
and spectated has never yawned wider, players and fans have
been reconnected by the mighty tweet. Sure, far too many holding midfielders are media-trained within an inch of their lives,
and one-on-one interviews are becoming as lesser-spotted as the
sabre-toothed tiger, but Twitter has granted these PR-dependent
young millionaires a vestige of control and a more personal, inti-
mate voice. Some, notably the questing if perplexing Joey Barton,
have used it to shine a torch on the game's darker corners. Others,
like Rio Ferdinand, have even dared use it to make political statements. For all its endless contributions to that bonfire of the
inanities we really ought to call anti-social media, the tweet has
served a noble purpose.

And now for the next trick: virtual reality, now with us in the
shape of the Oculus Rift headset, a bulky contraption equipped
with thousands of sensors. According to Mr. Facebook, Mark
Zuckerberg, who "acquired" Oculus Rift VR in 2014, the mission
is "to enable you to experience the impossible." And yes, the
way he sees it, a virtual seat at Wembley is comfortably within
the bounds of possibility. Insiders have predicted a forbidding
launch price – $350-plus (in addition to the accompanying PC) –
but once a smaller model comes to market…

"It puts you in situ in a sensory way that is beyond anything that's been done before," enthuses Jed Novick, my co-course leader of the BA Sport Journalism course at the University of Brighton. "I tried it when it was in its beta stage, during testing, and among the scenarios being tried was a rollercoaster at a fairground. It was extraordinary. One woman's balance went to such a degree she keeled over. Extraordinary."

As for the massed ranks of the commentariat, a tad more respect for the audience would be nice. Patronising readers and viewers is never a good idea, yet still broadcasters, especially, cling to the ancient snobberies about the IQ of the average football-lover. The inexorable rise of the punditocracy – whose magnetic attractions can be traced to ITV's panel for the 1970 World Cup, Derek Dougan, Malcolm Allison, Paddy Crerand and "Handsome" Bob McNab – bred an increasingly grotesque emphasis on personality and emotion at the expense of tactical and strategic insight, a balance now in dire need of redress.

Much the same can be said of the pressbox, whose days may not be as severely numbered as suspected. Never has the reporter enjoyed so much space. Increasingly late to the party in print, and with the advent of the transfer window killing off that Sunday staple, the who's-eyeing-up-who column, the web has been a saviour. The ubiquitous live blog, a multimedia twelve-inch remix of the old-fashioned running report still filed for midweek matches, has added immediacy as well as a younger, livelier, less reverent flavour. It is no simple matter deciding which was the more fascinating sign of the times: that Henry Winter, whose recent six-figure transfer from the *Daily Telegraph* to the *Times* captured almost as many headlines as his beloved Arsenal's latest match, should command more Twitter followers than the *Telegraph* has readers; or that, prior to starting his new job, his employer insisted he went on "gardening leave" for half a year, thus keeping him out of the opposition line-up for as long as the lawyers would permit. Reporters still sell papers.

The trouble is that match reports in the press focus on context and diminish the contest, the performance. Individuals and backstories are uppermost, relegating the strategic why and tactical how to cameos. Half a century ago, Desmond Hackett's reports in the *Daily Express* were accompanied by a star rating for entertainment; I can't remember the last time I read a match report that told me how *good* a game it had been.

The reasons are not complex: with so much more to report, and so many means of doing so, the focus on news – pumped out unstoppably by email and tweet, easy to copy and paste – is inevitable. Getting away with being a scoundrel isn't the piece of cake it was, yet something has been lost. Here, after all, is a world where sponsors and broadcasters must on no account be the teeniest bit offended and clubs are only too keen to ban reporters who dare to even hint that their "brand" might not be immaculate in every possible respect. Tell the readers their team lost because their offside trap malfunctioned and local journalists find themselves reporting the next home game from outside the ground.

Happily, one of the neglected benefits of Murdoch and his rapacious ilk has been to level the journalistic playing field. After all, round-the-clock broadcasts of matches and media conferences on multiple platforms mean one is no longer obliged to possess a press pass to have an informed, publishable opinion. That's why there are blogs, fan sites and webzines that now outstrip the conventional media for sophistication and breadth. Nevertheless, in these days of parasitical news aggregators such as the Huffington Post, Buzzfeed and Vice, it is all too often forgotten that, like the sociologists who pass Solomonesque judgement on David Beckham, the vast majority of aspiring opinion-formers rely entirely on second-hand sources at best. Despite the DIY merits of the web, it remains extremely unusual for these alternative voices (who are seldom restrained by professional or legal constraints) to have any mainstream impact beyond affirming what Michael Parkinson calls "the rule of the mob."

"I wonder if the papers still have an appetite for humour." So said Parkinson last year, robust enough to conduct an interview on his mobile phone while having his prostate examined. To him, the end of the liquid lunch in Fleet Street – no time or place for such collective refreshment now – has taken its toll, likewise the Twitterati and those no-holds-barred comments readers are now encouraged to leave at the bottom of a story in the ceaseless pursuit of hits and "likes."

The upshot has been a dumbing-down when enlightenment is required; a black-and-white world with no room for shades of opinion or nuances. Witness the argument, parroted *ad nauseam* on BBC, ITV, Sky and BT Sport by their assorted pundits that the secret to England's world conquest is more speed, extra power and added stamina.

With such insight passed off as post-match analysis is it any wonder that 1966 remains an act unfollowed?

Why England Won

Simon Kuper

IF NOSTALGIA FOR 1966 could be plotted on a graph, it probably peaked in February 1993. That month Bobby Moore died of cancer aged 51, and was mourned as the kind of gentleman winner that England no longer produced. The economy, England's footballing fortunes, and national morale were all then at a low. Only the crime-rate was buoyant. Twelve days before Moore's death, the murder of two year-old James Bulger by two other small boys had shocked Britain. The event "registered a growing presence of evil," said the Labour MP Frank Field. He called for children to be taught the "Bobby Moore morality."

The technicolour moment when a beautiful Queen Elizabeth handed a beautiful Moore the World Cup in the London sunshine serves as a constant reprimand to the English present. National decline is a powerful notion in modern English history, and England's failure to win a football tournament since 1966 seems to sum up that decline. That's why the English often turn 1966 into a symbol. The argument then goes that England won because Moore's "greatest generation" were giants compared with today's spoiled overpaid lot. However, if we want to know why England really won, symbolism doesn't get us very far. In an attempt to demystify 1966, I read the history and crunched data.

The first thing to say is that England in 1966 probably were slightly better than most subsequent England teams. A crucial caveat: the quality of England sides over time scarcely varies. This may sound improbable. Fans feel strongly about the qualities of managers and players. Periods of national euphoria alternate with periods of national pessimism (such as 1993 or 2014). The public tends to think the England team is either strong or a disgrace.

But in fact, England in almost any era pretty consistently wins about half its games, drawing or losing the rest. Contrary to all popular opinion, it may be that since the 1960s the strength of the England team has barely changed (which would make the vast apparatus of punditry attached to the team instantly redundant).

The chart across was made by the economist Stefan Szymanski, with whom I wrote the book *Why England Lose* (we renamed the later editions *Soccernomics*; the original title for some reason didn't appeal to English book-buyers). The chart shows England's cumulative win percentage from 1950 to 2013 (counting a draw as worth half a win). Apart from a few moments in the 1950s the win percentage has not risen above 70%, and it has never fallen below 67.5%.

The overall picture is one of steady but extremely slow decline, punctuated by two eras of exceptional performance. One of those eras was the late 1960s. The other period of clear improvement began in the early 2000s and continues today.

It really does look as if the only period in England's modern football history that can match the late 1960s is the present. Here is some more evidence – the win percentages of all post-war England managers:

Manager	Played	Won	Drawn	Lost	Win Percentage
Capello	42	28	8	6	0.762
Hodgson	42	24	13	5	0.726
Ramsey	112	67	28	17	0.723
Eriksson	67	40	15	12	0.709
Greenwood	55	33	12	10	0.709
Venables	24	12	9	3	0.688
Hoddle	28	17	4	7	0.679
Winterbottom	138	77	33	28	0.678
Robson	95	47	29	19	0.647
Taylor, G.	38	18	13	7	0.645
Mercer	7	3	3	1	0.643
Revie	29	14	8	7	0.621
McClaren	18	9	4	5	0.611
Keegan	18	7	7	4	0.583
Wilkinson	2	0	1	1	0.250
Pearce	1	0	0	1	0.000
Taylor, P.	1	0	0	1	0.000

(Note: Figures correct through 6 September 2015)

Match for match, the only England managers whose stats compare with Alf Ramsey's (in charge from 1963 to 1974) are the two most recent incumbents: Fabio Capello (2008–2012) and now Roy Hodgson. It seems that England this last decade have been stronger than usual, perhaps because today's English internationals spend their careers competing with the world's best in the unprecedentedly strong Premier League. (This would rather blow out of the water the idea that all those foreign imports are ruining the England team.)

Admittedly the differences between the top few managers in our table are small. In addition, it's hard to compare eras. Since the breakup of the USSR and former Yugoslavia, England play more small countries like Estonia and Slovenia. But then Ramsey's England spent a lot of time beating the little Home Nations. Moreover, most of today's stronger European teams – Spain, France, Holland and even Germany – weren't yet world-beaters in his day. In 1966 neither Germany nor West Germany had ever beaten England. At every single World Cup since, the Germans have outperformed England.

Defenders of Ramsey will object that what sets him apart is that he's the only England manager who (at least in 1966) won the big games that mattered. It's true that twenty-first century England teams have disappointed at World Cups and European Championships. Possibly they lack the moral fibre of Moore's men. However, here's an alternative hypothesis: at big tournaments, today's England players are simply more tired.

Ramsey's men were uncommonly fit by the standards of 1966. Before the tournament, the manager gathered his players for a training camp at Lilleshall and told them he wanted two months of sacrifice. "Gentlemen," he added, "if anybody gets the idea of popping out for a pint, and I find out, he is finished with this squad for ever." When the team's habitual drinkers did hatch a plot to escape "Stalag Lilleshall" for a night in the pub, Ramsey forestalled them. After eleven gruelling days in isolation at Lilleshall, England went on a rapid four-match European tour.

Ramsey's approach was radical in an age when footballers routinely lived it large. The French team in 1966 stocked up for their training camp in the Scottish town of Peebles with "litres of French wine." While according to the Dutch author Hans Molenaar the Argentines on their warm-up tour of Europe smoked straight after friendlies and training sessions, in defiance of their manager's edict. Professionalism of Ramsey's stamp wasn't the norm back then. The Swiss midfielder Philippe Pottier actually requested a week's leave from training camp to go on holiday. (This was a bit rich even for little Switzerland, and he was left at home.)

Ramsey's professionalism was total. "The players were even given lessons in how to cut their toenails for fear that a poor clipping technique would lead to a septic toe," writes Niall Edworthy in his history of England managers. England's 0-0 draw in their opening game against Uruguay was disappointing, but afterwards Jimmy Greaves said: "There can't be a fitter team in the tournament." Decades later, England's left-back Ray Wilson told Ramsey's biographer Dave Bowler: "We were fitter than most teams... In the last half hour we'd generally overcome most sides." Wilson said fitness mattered especially at Wembley, where players often cramped up on the springy turf. Playing every game in London also meant that England didn't waste any energy travelling.

The statistics seem to confirm England's superior fitness. Of the nine goals they scored in normal time at the 1966 World Cup, five came in the last fifteen minutes of matches. Then there were those two goals in extra time in the final. Wilson told Bowler: "We were much fitter than them [West Germany] in extra time. They were gone, they created nothing." George Cohen, the right-back, recalled: "When Alf came out at full-time, he said, 'Look at the Germans, they're finished.' And they were all lying on the floor. Alf made us stand up to show them how fit we were." In Dave Bowler's words: "The World Cup was won on the playing fields of Lilleshall."

Ramsey himself seems to have identified the physical as England's USP. "We were the fastest and the strongest side in the World Cup," he said in victory, "but I do not think we can ever match the individual techniques of the Latin-Americans or the Latin-Europeans."

Contrast the fitness of 1966 with England's modern summer fatigue. Now that the Premier League is the most physically demanding league on earth, English players typically arrive at

World Cups exhausted. (Wayne Rooney, for instance, flopped in South Africa in 2010 after being squeezed like a lemon by Manchester United that Spring.) Managers and players often point to tiredness as a reason for England's failures. Here, for example, is Capello telling FIFA.com why England don't win summer tournaments:

> They're the least fresh of any of the competing national sides, because their league doesn't have a break. It's like when you're driving a car: if you stop halfway to put fuel in then you'll definitely get where you want to go, but if you don't there's always the chance you'll be running on empty before you reach your goal. In my opinion the soccer played in the first half of the English season is much better than in the second half.

Such excuses are typically dismissed by angry fans, but supporting evidence comes from England's curious scoring patterns. Most goals at World Cups come after half-time. That is natural: in the second half players tire, teams start chasing goals, and gaps open up on the field. But England, in its eight big tournaments from 1998 through to 2014, scored twenty-eight of its forty-five goals before halftime.

England's fitness in 1966 was to Ramsey's credit. So were his brave decisions to dispense with wingers mid-tournament, and to pick Geoff Hurst ahead of the established star Greaves in the final. This manager made a difference.

But however good, fit and well managed his team were, they needed to be lucky. In a league, the best team generally wins. Over thirty-eight games or so, luck tends to even out. One week the referee will mistakenly give your opponents a penalty, but the next week he'll give it to you.

But luck matters more in much shorter World Cups. The 1966 tournament lasted just under three weeks. As Arsène Wenger has noted, any team in a league can top the table after three weeks. In such a short run, a few inches here and there on a couple of shots can be decisive. England in 1966 beat Argentina in the quarter-finals and Portugal in the semis by one goal each, and won the final only after extra time. Victory hinged on a few moments. Jonathan Wilson puts it well in his *Anatomy of England*: "One moment can shape a game, and one game can shape a tournament, and one tournament can shape a career. Football is not always fair."

It's even less fair than other ballgames. In Test cricket, each batting side has twenty wickets to fall, so an individual dismissal is rarely decisive; tennis Grand Slams are played over five sets, so a favourite can lose two and still triumph. In basketball and rugby, the team with territorial dominance tends to win. Football is more random. Nonetheless, we tend to tell the story of any World Cup with hindsight as if the winners were destined to win.

The last and possibly key reason why England won in 1966 and never since: they were at home. In *Why England Lose*, Stefan Szymanski and I calculated that in international football since 1980, home advantage has been worth about two-thirds of a goal per game. That in itself could be enough to propel a decent team like England – typically about tenth-best in the world – to the title. However, before 1980 home advantage was probably worth even more. Back then travel was more arduous, local fans often hostile and in-your-face, and conditions very different from home. Think of England in Mexico in 1970 being kept up all night by a crowd outside their hotel before they faced Brazil, and then Gordon Banks missing the decisive encounter with West Germany because of diarrhoea.

England hosted the World Cup at a time when hosting really mattered. Over the period 1930–1978, hosts won five out of eleven World Cups, while three of the other winning countries shared a border with the host. Contrast that with the much weaker performance of hosts since 1982: just one trophy out of nine. Admittedly that's partly because some modern hosts have been weak football nations. But even taking that into account, they have done poorly. No modern host except winners France in 1998 has even reached the final. Spain, Japan and the US didn't make the quarter-finals,

South Africa fell in the first round, and readers may recall Brazil's 1-7 defeat in Belo Horizonte, 2014.

The decline in home advantage has probably been starkest in international football, but the statistical website Fivethirtyeight. com has shown that it has also occurred in English domestic football:

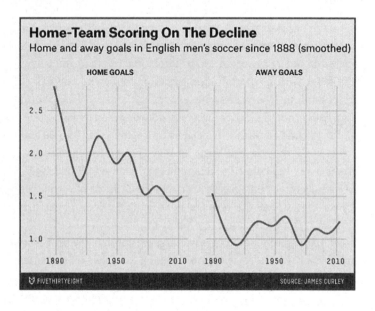

Home-Team Scoring On The Decline
Home and away goals in English men's soccer since 1888 (smoothed)

At the 1966 World Cup, visiting teams faced all sorts of obstacles. Argentina, a serious contender for the title, tried to fit in their own Lilleshall session, but, writes Jonathan Wilson, "the plan turned into farce as the Argentina bus got lost, taking two hours to cover the thirty miles from their base near Birmingham." Then, the evening before their quarter-final against England, Argentina weren't allowed their mandatory twenty-minute practice session at Wembley "on the grounds that it would have interfered with the evening's greyhound-racing," writes Wilson. (He adds that they could easily have been fitted in ahead of the dogs.) Setbacks like that just didn't happen to the hosts. There was homesickness, too. Argentina's captain Antonio Rattín listened to a cassette of his wife and children ten times a day, he told *Razón* newspaper. "If I could draw up my own contract for football at this level, I assure you I would put in a clause that said I could only play in Buenos Aires and would never leave my country again."

So many things went England's way. Eusébio always believed that the organisers had illegally moved the England–Portugal semi-final from Goodison (where Portugal had come to feel at home) to Wembley (where England had played all their games). In fact, he was wrong. In 1966 FIFA was free to decide which semi-final would be played at which venue. However, this was exactly the sort of decision that went in favour of the hosts.

Most refereeing decisions probably did too. In England's 2-0 victory over a weak France, the first goal was "blatantly offside," writes Edworthy, while the second came after Nobby Stiles "crunched Jacques Simon right under the nose of the referee with a challenge so late that it beggared belief." The ref ignored the foul, allowing England to go upfield and score, whereupon Simon was stretchered off. A subsequent cartoon in the French newspaper *L'Equipe* showed Bobby Charlton driving a Rolls-Royce while referees dressed as British bobbies cleared opponents from his route. Uruguayan and Argentine critiques along these lines were angrier.

In the final, the Soviet linesman Tofiq Bahramov was wrong to award England's third goal. The point isn't that later scientific studies showed that Hurst's shot probably bounced on the line. The point is that the linesman couldn't possibly have seen whether the ball bounced in or not. Given the uncertainty, as Dave Bowler writes, Bahramov "had to give the benefit of the doubt to the defending team. His decision was incorrect." But it's the kind of decision a linesman makes with a Wembley packed with Union Jacks behind his back.

There's a more general sense in which hosting favoured England. At the time, two different ethical codes were effectively fighting for dominance in international football: the Latin American code and the northern European code. In Latin America, playacting, shirt-pulling and bullying the ref were considered OK, but violent fouls weren't. "In northern Europe," writes Bowler, "the reverse was true, histrionics were frowned upon while heavy tackling was part and parcel of a man's game." FIFA had said before the World Cup that referees would crack down on violent fouls, but that didn't happen. This may have had something to do with the instincts of the crowds and referees. As Jonathan Wilson notes: "Of 23 listed referees, 18 were European, ten of them from Britain." And so Stiles was free to foul against Uruguay and France, while other Europeans kicked Pelé out of the tournament.

The triumph of the northern European code favoured England. With more Latin referees, Pelé might have had more protection and could have won Brazil their third straight World Cup, as the bookmakers had expected. Moreover, a Latin referee at England–Argentina mightn't have sent off Rattín for "the look on his face," as the German Rudolf Kreitlein did.

Afterwards FIFA fined Argentina £85 (the maximum permitted) and threatened to bar the country from the next World Cup. As Hans Molenaar has reported, outraged Latin Americans met while still in London to discuss breaking away and founding their own tournament. The Latins must have been particularly irked that England's cheating (as they saw it) was accompanied by lots of pompous rhetoric about "fair play." In truth, most English people of the day, certain of their moral superiority, probably couldn't have imagined that they themselves might be cheating.

Lastly, any analysis that compares England in 1966 with later England teams has to address the issue of penalty shootouts. Penalties – rather than any lack of moral fibre – may be the single biggest reason why modern England lose. From 1990 to 2014 England played in eleven World Cups and European Championships. They exited six on penalties. But in 1966, shootouts didn't yet exist. If they had, the exhausted West Germans in the final would surely have parked the bus in extra time and played for penalties. We can all guess how that would have turned out.

Still, at the end it was the England team waving a replica of the Jules Rimet Trophy from the balcony at Kensington's Royal Garden Hotel. (The real trophy had been taken into custody by policemen to stop anyone stealing it.) In the popular imagination, the men of 1966 now tower over all future generations of English footballers. Perhaps they were better, perhaps just fitter, perhaps they were the most sober team of their day, and perhaps they even possessed a never-say-die English spirit that has since been lost. However, it would be wrong to infer anything much from a narrow victory in a three-week tournament at home.

Memories are Made of This

Claire Westall

Dressed in red, white and blue,
He's World Cup Willie
We all love him too, World Cup Willie
He's tough as a lion and never will give up
That's why Willie is fav'rite for the Cup

— "World Cup Willie", Lonnie Donegan, 1966

Three lions on a shirt
Jules Rimet still gleaming
Thirty years of hurt
Never stopped me dreaming

—"Three Lions", Baddiel & Skinner, with the Lightening
  Seeds, 1996

We're tired of bragging about forty years ago...
Surely it's the right time
I wanna see you win it in my lifetime

—"Shout", Dizzee Rascal & James Corden, 2010

YES, YES. I KNOW. England won the World Cup in 1966. That is, one country within Great Britain won the bid to host the World Cup and went on to lift the Jules Rimet Trophy for the first and only time in its history, in front of our home support at Wembley. Despite Scotland, Wales and Northern Ireland failing to qualify for the finals, Britain maintained a strong iconographic hold on the event. Even the post-1996 reimagining of '66 as specifically English has remained tied to a British mode of nostalgia that inhibits England's national ambitions.

England is often described as the "home" of football despite sports historians explaining that football developed as a pan-European folk activity from the late-medieval period, with villages and other groups playing games in which they kicked an object, like a pig's bladder, towards a target zone. What England can claim, though, is an early institutionalisation of football – codification and formalised clubs, leagues and a football association (the FA) – as well as a role in disseminating the sport via the British Empire. Across nineteenth-century Britain the game helped bind industrial communities, especially the city-based working classes of London, Manchester, Liverpool and Glasgow. But in 1966 the geographical "home" of football was London alone, the capital of Britain (not England) and the seat of a British government that had backed the tournament with substantial grants. Importantly, World Cup London functioned as a British space of domestic exclusivity that, thanks to the size and income-potential of Wembley, bypassed the national claim to the England team made before and during the tournament, specifically Everton's Goodison Park being denied the promise previously made to host England's semi-final match.

In addition, British domestication of the tournament helped massify the consumptive power of football. Sizeable crowds and abundant television coverage helped link post-war pride and growing consumer power with the televisual penetration of domestic space. Sports historian Fabio Chisari has suggested that women became an obvious part of football's TV-viewing audience for the first time in '66 and that approximately half the British population over five years old watched the final. With fifty-six hours of BBC airtime, twenty-six hours on ITV and increasing TV sales, the World Cup invaded the British home in a way that no sporting event had before.

Strangely, for an event set entirely within England, the World Cup relied upon a British iconography that minimised England. First, and quite obviously, the Union flag of Britain was used for the official logo and mascot. The logo set the trophy and an FA badge encircled by "World Championship – Jules Rimet Trophy – England 1966" against a Union flag. And the first ever championship mascot, World Cup Willie, was a chesty upright cartoon figure whose union shirt said "World Cup." Writing about these symbols in his 1996 thirtieth-anniversary book *England's Glory*, Dave Hill explains that "the use of the Union flag to denote an event to take place exclusively in England illustrates a distinctly English attitude to other parts of the British Isles... But such considerations do not seem to have exercised the FA." The attitude Hill describes is one of superiority in which England sees itself as Britain. Hill seems right. England and the English often appear to stand for Britain, or the UK, especially in the eyes of the world. But this is also fundamentally problematic for England as it is subsumed within Britain and Britain's imperial presentation of Englishness while being actively denied its own sense of nationhood.

Across the tournament British insignia stood for England in a seemingly natural fashion. Then, as now, "God Save the Queen" was sung as England's anthem, and the British monarch opened the tournament and eventually presented the trophy to Bobby Moore. According to Roger Hutchinson in his book *66! The Inside Story of England's World Cup Triumph*, the Queen approved of the "red, white and blue" bouquet Moore presented to her at the start of the final because it had the "right" colours. Yet there is of course no "blue" in England's St George's flag, and though the colour is associated with the FA logo the Queen was surely referring to Britain's flag. This Union flag was ubiquitous throughout the tournament. As British Pathé images show there was barely a St George's Cross to be seen. Instead, the English crowd waved Union Jacks in abundance, particularly during the final. This was understandable given the generational proximity to VE Day celebrations, themselves a spectacle of British jubilance and flag-waving glory in victory. The World Cup celebrations were iconographically British, dominated by London and the South East, just as with the recent Olympic and Diamond Jubilee festivities of 2012. This

'66 British iconography was captured in the award-winning 2008 Hovis TV advert "Go On Lad" as one young boy carries bread through the major scenes of British history, from 1886 to the present. As he encounters the 1960s – after the spitfires and the Blitz – a car rushes past, adorned in Union flags, with men shouting "champions" into the streets. This moment of World Cup euphoria – fleeting and mobile – merged with World War II to become a pseudo-retro aesthetic. The ad captured two key tendencies in the memorialisation of '66. It pushed together England and Britain so as to obscure English national specificity, and it offered a reduced version of British history, a headline-history of clichés about a victorious and worldly, imperial, past.

Nothing captures the absorption of '66 into a truncated, breathlessly positive version of British history like the "Two World Wars and One World Cup" chant of some England fans – a chant that carries both a hard edge of English xenophobia and a supposedly softer "don't mention the war" humour. It is a chant that has become a defining feature of contemporary '66 nostalgia, helping to attach English football to an imperial mythology of Britain's world wars as successes, despite Allied troops determining the outcome of both conflicts. The England team's association with the 1963 film *The Great Escape* has reinforced this conflictual imperial connection. Since the mid-1990s, the England Supporters Band has played the film's signature track (originally composed by Elmer Bernstein) at England matches. However, as Peter Bradshaw, film critic for the *Guardian*, suggests, when fans play this jaunty tune there is "a tinge of despair and defeat in the air." The Hollywood retelling of Paul Brickhill's story – based on the Australian's own PoW experience in Stalag Luft III, the site near Sagan where the most famous escape attempt took place – merges the British officer class, associated with English decorum and class stability as portrayed by Richard Attenborough, with US stardom and individuality, embodied by Steve McQueen, to conjure up an idea of Allied pluck, perseverance and ingenuity. For Bradshaw there is something "depressing and hubristic about

smugly harping on... about that gallant defeat within victory."
Britain does this especially well, as evident in celebratory claims
to a Dunkirk spirit. In the film this is conveyed through the enormous number of men recaptured and killed. Of course it hardly
needs saying that the film has nothing to do with football either,
and that the only sporting referent is McQueen's baseball.

Perhaps *The Great Escape* comes to contemporary England fans
via another: the 1981 film *Escape to Victory*, the Michael Caine, Sylvester Stallone, Pelé, Bobby Moore and Ossie Ardiles picture in
which an Allied PoW team takes on and defeats a German side
before escaping in a crowd pitch invasion. Insisting on a collective sporting heroism and something akin to a working class
(anti-hierarchical) camaraderie amongst the "lads," the Allied
team is imagined as Britain's international England with their
red kits carrying the hallmark of football victory that the West
Ham reference (to Caine in character, but embodied by Moore)
reinforces. The film explicitly draws on the August 1942 "Death
Matches" in which former Dynamo and Lokomtyv Kiev players,
as FC Start, faced off against a German side and won (twice). But it
recodes this legendary over-turning of the occupying Nazi forces
by Soviet players into a tale of Anglo-escape. This World War II
escape motif has become fundamentally absorbed into the nostalgia surrounding 1966 and the unending puns used by tabloid
papers and in comedy homages as well as advertising campaigns.
For example, the 1999 Umbro advert for the new England strip
launch appeared to combine the two escape blockbusters by por-
traying current England players, including Shearer, Owen and
Seaman, as PoWs having to prove themselves worthy to wear the
shirt. More recently, Carlberg's 2012 "The Crate Escape" advert has
men trapped in their female partners' spa weekend escaping to
the land of beer just beyond. These examples, and a multitude of
others, all insist on remembering England's World Cup win as if it
is a phantom limb-like extension of Britain's war efforts – efforts
that could not stave off the decline of British imperial power.

Crucially, throughout its imperial history, Britain has been conflated with England, with both being incorrectly described as the "island nation." This is largely due to Britain's strong grip on an imperial Englishness, on the idea of the ethical and moral superiority of England providing the rationale for overseas invasion and colonisation. Britain used the idea of England as a special, protected and pure British heartland, so that its Englishness could remain untainted by imperial contact. Set against the post-war dawn of what Paul Gilroy has termed Britain's "postcolonial melancholia," this conception of Englishness as Britain's imperial residue hung over 1966 and has been inscribed into its popular memorialisation ever since. It helped minimise England's claim to nationhood and only came to be popularly and publicly questioned in the 1990s.

During the late 1990s, in the wake of Euro '96 and the 1997 death of Princess Diana, waving the flag of St George became a newly popular activity in England. In his book *The Politics of Englishness* Arthur Aughey writes of the English coming out of the "national closet" and England fans beginning to forge a visual "Republic of St George." Unsurprisingly, then, England's '66 triumph came increasingly to the fore of the collective imaginary. Since 1996, and thanks in no small part to the political fallout of post-1997 devolution and the ongoing moves towards Scottish independence, a resurgent interest in a national England has emerged, which first challenged new Labour's "Cool Britannia" and latterly continues to challenge Britain's conservative retro-heritage aesthetic.

A key moment for this mix of English fandom and English national self-assertion was Euro '96, and specifically the "Three Lions" anthem by David Baddiel and Frank Skinner with Ian Broudie of the Lightning Seeds. The optimistic insistence that "thirty years of hurt," of defeat and disaster, could be overcome offered a departure from the mood of worldly despondency and domestic malaise that had characterised the years of the John Major premiership. The song brought the glory of '66 to a new generation of fans with "that tackle by Moore," "Bobby belting the ball" and "Nobby dancing." The accompanying music video pushed the iconic '66 red shirt to the fore with Ian Broudie wearing a replica one to make the tea while Baddiel and Skinner sing out against the condemnation of England TV pundits peddle. But the TV itself sits under a Union flag as if England was still just a subsidiary of Britain. By the close of the video the threesome are in a pub and almost fail to recognise Geoff Hurst. These are the "lads" that helped cement the 1990s loaded-lad image but are really the unthreatening face of graduate, even literary, football fandom represented so fulsomely by Nick Hornby's bestseller *Fever Pitch*. By 1998 the new "Three Lions" video saw the same three fans leaving a rainy London for a World Cup stadium carpark in Paris where they have a friendly match against mock-German fans (with wig-mullets and comedy moustaches). Although on the TV commentary accompanying the video Jonathan Pierce describes England flags everywhere as Southgate misses his '96 penalty, by the close a St George's Cross and a Union flag are displayed on the fan bus, indicating that England can (still) only be imagined within the security of British union. Indeed, this is the only way in which an opposition to Europe and "the Germans" makes sense.

Baddiel and Skinner's anchoring lines are extremely close to the refrain in *1066 and All That: A Musical Comedy of English History* written in 1930 by Arkell and Reynolds. "We're going home, we're going home" is sung by a chorus of Roman Soldiers and later in a first-person form by a "Common Man." This text is a famed comedic abbreviation of English and British history littered with puns, misnomers and misleading connections between historic "fact" and ahistorical myth. Capitalising on the 1990s rise of English nationalism and in an explicit homage to *1066 and All That*, the BBC created *The Nearly Complete and Utter History of Everything 2000*, aired on 2 and 4 January 2000. Its "'66 Crunch Time for England" sketch overlaid 1066 with 1966, via contemporary BBC sports programming – primarily *Match of the Day* and *They Think It's All Over*, the 1995–2006 comedy sports quiz concerned with sporting gaffs, errors, excuses and the "feeling" of sportsmen. In the millennial sketch Rory McGrath is "Harold," a regal captain/ manager whose pre-match press conference sets the clichéd ground for England's battle against an invading France, narrated as footballing contest. Against France's 4-thousand, 3-thousand, 3-thousand formation stands Sir Geoffrey of Hurst, Lord Martin Peters, Master George Cohen and other English footballing and TV personalities. With the score a death count, the action is captured "live" by the women producing the Bayeux tapestry. Half-time brings an in-studio-tent Lineker and Hansen, with Hansen criticising the English defence for letting "too many arrows through." Actor James Fleet is William the Conqueror and, as the continental stereotype requires, he dives and wins a determining free "shot" – which turns out to be an arrow shot at Harold, staying behind a wall of defenders, who gets it in the eye. The end is a William win with the rematch set for Agincourt in 1415.

What is important about this sketch – besides how comically tight and effective it is – is the way it reinforces Britain's containment of England, and enables the short-cut version of British history to dominant a growing popular understanding of England. The layering of the comedy, as in *1066 and All That*, comes from a familiar understanding of the common tropes and clichés that haunt England, and English football, as they are used to bolster Britain's "greatness." There is an insistence on mocking nostalgic forms of memorialisation, but the mocking of stereotypes and clichés, even as they are reproduced by the BBC, is the key means by which the satirical content is allowed to stand as politically neutral, so that England is simply absorbed into a pre-existing union visually managed by the BBC.

When Lonnie Donegan sang "World Cup Willie," he helped initiate the phenomenon of the official World Cup song. In 1970 the England team sang "Back Home", insisting that they needed to again "prove" that they were "the greatest." After two failed attempts at qualification the 1982 effort claimed that "This Time" they'd get it "right." Thereafter 1986 brought "We've got the whole world at our feet." And 1990 came with "World in Motion" by New

Order featuring that rap from John Barnes. This track brought a kind of pop cool to the football song that was clearly new, and marked the rising Manchester-based music scene – a scene that would come to define the 1990s and enable an England outside of London to register culturally. 1998 came with "How Does It Feel To Be On Top Of The World," though it was overshadowed by the re-release of "Three Lions" and the release "Vindaloo" by Fat Les. According to Steve Redhead, writing in *The Ingerland Factor*, "Vindaloo" was part of a more inclusive vision of England's fan culture and footballing associations. It did, though, retain an obviously British frame of reference. This was lost when in 2000 Fat Les released "Jerusalem"; the amalgamation of voices – and seemingly classes – used sought to remake England's popular national song as one of inclusive and dynamic engagement. And by the World Cup of 2010 there was a musical insistence on moving beyond '66 as "Shout" by Dizzee Rascal and James Corden described a generation tired of "bragging about forty years ago." This decidedly ambitious pop-anthem combination of "No Diggity" by Backstreet (ft. Dr Dre and Queen Pen), originally released in 1996, and Tears for Fears' 1984 hit "Shout," insisted that success would come from real footballing teamwork, but still held on to a lad-like call to combat with its "Come and have a go if you think you're hard enough."

For World Cup 2014, BBC's Sport Relief orchestrated a Band Aid-like rendition of Take That's "Greatest Day" hit with ex-England players singing and a music video revolving around Geoff Hurst. Lineker announces his musical plan for the hit song at the end of *Match of the Day* by calling Gary Barlow. An idea of Britain and Ireland as the critical yet supporting cast for England is offered with Scot Alan Hansen complaining about the excessive focus on England, Welshman Robbie Savage chipping in and former Republic of Ireland International Mark Lawrenson giving his usual dismissively despairing expressions. The ambition that Lineker outlines for England – to win the World Cup – is repeatedly scaled back, as if a winning ambition is now amusing, hilarious even. The rest of the video is resplendent with England flags, shirts and references, and has Hurst as the lordly winning presence, with Sir Geoff standing in front of a poster that shows him post-final with the trophy in hand as his red shirt stands out in an otherwise black-and-white image. Hurst poses in front of the poster, in the same position, in his red replica shirt with a replica trophy, and closes the video with the question, reminiscent of '66, "is it all over?"

The mythological status of '66 has been at the heart of contemporary football-linked advertising campaigns, especially for lager. Saatchi & Saatchi's campaign "The World According to Carlsberg," running from 2006 to 2011, hit home with its "Probably the Best in the World" tagline. Their three minute ad-epic "Old Lions" presented ex-England "legends" as a pub team managed by Bobby Robson and banging in goals (as well as tackles) against their "Dog and Duck" opposition. With a white-van-man camaraderie, World Cup winners Alan Ball and the Charlton brothers play alongside a cross-generational group of other retired England players. In a 2010 follow-up "Team Talk" ad Stuart Pearce's psycho-passion is overlaid with a voiceover of dramatic footballing patriotism, targeting those "eleven English men" about to play "the rest of the world." According to Leo Benedictus of the *Guardian*, a "sentimental lunacy" arrives when famous sporting figures, like Steve Redgrave and Kelly Holmes, are screaming support in the tunnel. In the ad we even see Ian Botham in chainmail as a knight in shining armour supposedly lifting the spirits of the team. For Benedictus, the advert "overshoots patriotic cliché, screeches on through nationalism, and ends up somewhere in the latter stages of the *Question of Sport* Christmas party." There is also a rather uncomfortable resurrection of the deceased Bobby Robson and Bobby Moore. The team are told that "it's time to join the immortals" as they climb Wembley's stairs, below Robson's image, to meet a ghostly Moore in his '66 kit, standing alongside a lion, as if Moore is a footballing gladiator and playing for England is a death-in-life experience.

This fairly straight effort at patriotic iconography stands in contrast to the more typical tongue-in-cheek excesses. For example, in Carlsberg's 2012 "Fan Academy" ad, St George flags fly high and England supporters "learn to be great fans," with face-painting instruction, chanting practice, penalty-watching endurance and rain-chamber survival for the English summer. The best recruits "graduate" as English knights, wrapped in flags as the Red Arrows flyer overhead and a Maradona-like figure mops the floors.

In each of these lager-fuelled versions of English fandom, the claim to national pride is remorselessly positive, with hints of multicultural inclusion, and is set against any expectation that flag-waving for England is a dangerous display of xenophobia or small-minded prejudice. What is critical to this campaign's success, though, is how it plays with abbreviated history and nostalgic connection. What seems like simple football nostalgia in "Old Lions" is complicated when the referee books Jack Charlton, asking "Can I have your name please?" The advert ironises the equality of anonymity and any possible claim to ignorance (or forgetting). Charlton and '66 are built into the national and popular psyche so that any sense of unknowing can only be feigned, a fallacy of knowing humour.

The same motif, of feigned forgetting as nostalgic reconnection, was used in an episode of a Nickelodeon children's TV programme entitled *Renford Rejects*, which ran from 1998–2001 and presented a group of teenagers playing football together after being rejected by their school teams. The particular '66 episode sees the formation of the "Glasgow Rejects," a team of "ringers" that includes Geoff Hurst, Martin Peters, George Cohen and Gordon Banks. Not knowing these famous faces the "reject" children want to teach them to play football. The humourous premise is that each child player teaches their corresponding World Cup winner the skills needed for their shared position – and Hurst is seen to always be hitting the cross bar. The opposing manager thinks he recognises the famed players but mistakenly sees them as the aged winners of the Renford Youth Cup in 1964.

The ex-players wear England replica shirts and easily win. This comedic enforcement of memory is a fun cross-generational way to ensure that the heroic ideal of English success is passed down, but is also repositioned as British – as attached to Glasgow, with no sign of Scottish resentment or rebellion.

The World Cup victory has also been repeatedly read through father–son narratives of British familial reconciliation or re-union, including via fictional accounts of attendance at the final itself.

The BBC sitcom *Till Death Us Do Part*, which ran from 1965 until 1975, and also made into a 1969 feature film, provides an early example of familial reconciliation via memories of 1966. Alf Garnett is famed as a working class East End conservative – racist and arrogant – whose allegiance to Queen and country means he always stands for the anthem, even if he's naked in the bath. His support for West Ham became iconic and in one 1967 TV episode, "A Wapping Mythology," he wins tickets to watch his side away to Liverpool, the team of his socialist son-in-law Mike (while their wives watch the game, and specifically Bobby Moore, from home). As well as claiming that "West Ham won the World Cup," Garnett reiterates his hatred of the socialist "reds" that endanger Britain and claims that his team's defeat is caused by Labour Prime Minister Harold Wilson buying off the referee. This anti-red motif is repeated in the 1969 film as Alf insists that the kit is a conspiracy of colour set to enable the Labour government to take credit for England's performance. In the 1970 TV episode "Up the Polls" Alf even claims that England returned home early from Mexico to help defeat Labour in the General Election. When, in the film, Alf and Mike attend Wembley, their solidarity as England support-ers – in red-and-white scarves – supersedes political rivalry, but only in favour of British allegiance as both stand for "God Save the Queen," a first for Mike the supposedly socialist-republican. The match is the beginning of a familial resolution that sees Alf coming to terms with a move into Essex and reuniting with his household. This finale stretches Alf's London-based British unionism out into Essex, and thereby prefaces the conception of an English national space beyond the capital. And we should note that this End East/Essex overlap played a notable part in the 1966 campaign – with Alf Ramsey and Jimmy Greaves (Dagenham), Bobby Moore (Barking) and Geoff Hurst (Chelmsford).

In a notably different fashion, David Thompson's book *4-2* provides a ball-by-ball account of the final interspersed with the story of his childhood, and the bond football provided with his father. What is most appealing about the text is how the personal and the national are interwoven in a father-son dynamic set against the prominence of '66 for both of them. The narrative seems to be part of an adult re-membering of childhood and England that enables the narrator to enjoy the enormity of his affection for the '66 moment, and to reconcile himself with the unknowns of his father's life.

It is a child narrator in the 2006 film *Sixty Six* who presents the familial transformation sparked by a Jewish father and son attending the Wembley final on the day of the boy's dismal bar mitzvah. Paul Weiland's film recaptures the British iconography of 1966 as Bernie Reubens plans to use his upcoming bar mitzvah to become somebody in the eyes of his family and the world. Unfortunately, though, the date chosen clashes with the World Cup final. As England progress in the tournament the Reubens' family business collapses and their house catches fire. Consequently, Bernie's party is repeatedly scaled back until England reach the final and nearly all of his guests cancel. Throughout, Bernie's father has been an overly cautious and distant Jewish businessman. However, the father and son come together in a magical football union, as they rush to Wembley to witness the last minutes, and final goal, of the game. This is very much a contemporary representation of the need for father-and-son bonding. They don't love football, though, so they are football tourists, partaking in the event because it acts as a moment of inclusion. Yet there is no new social interaction or group to emerge from this. The film ends with the family in their garden, having fun but as an insular and separate group.

A different example of familial reconciliation is offered in the 2001 film *Mike Bassett: England Manager*, a comedic take on the farcical nature of English footballing cliché and tournament expectation. When Mike (Ricky Tomlinson), manager of a lowly Norwich City, becomes the only candidate willing to take on the England job, his working-class and supposedly old-school approach to lower-division football is revealed as hollow, unsophisticated and without merit – as the press repeatedly points out. Mike is continually criticised for playing a simple 4-4-2 formation. He tries to vary this, but clearly knows nothing about alternative formations. Ultimately, he insists on his 4-4-2 solidity, declaring that "if it was good enough for Alf Ramsey, it is good enough for me." This allusion to the '66 formation is worth noting because Ramsey was playing with his formation in the run-up to the tournament and during its early stages. As is often explained, 4-3-3 was itself something of a novel development in the mid-1960s and the arrival of 4-4-2 (England's formation for the final) was the most defensive-minded of formations used at that time. It was indicative of what is described in the official World Cup 1966 film *Goal!* as the "modern" mood, "the football of negativity," that relinquished attacking options in favour of possession and solidity. The emotional pull of the film, though, is provided by Mike's intense love of England and football, and the consequences of this commitment for his wife and son. Indeed, the situation becomes so tough – with his son bullied at school and the press camping outside their family home – that his wife leaves him. When, after a farcial start, England make it through the group stages and are only knocked out in the semi-final, Mike is greeted as a returning hero and he is reunited with his family.

A familial reworking of 1966 nostalgia fits into a British mode of memorialisation but at the same time also opens up the space for a more specifically English reaction to the World Cup win. The Mike Bassett character is explicitly English, rather than British, and the ordinariness of his allegiance to football and simple working-class tastes and tactics are mocked and embraced, almost in equal measure. Paul Gilroy's "postcolonial melancholia" emphasises the psychosis of melancholia, the failure to separate from the past, specifically a past loss, that inhibits growth, healing and forward momentum. The culture of nostalgia for '66 symbolises both a Britain holding on, melancholically, to its imperial past, and England's search for its mid-century place within it. For England itself the challenge remains to move beyond this process, to briefly celebrate a win as only one victory within many losses. To look to the future as a nation working to reform its relationship with its near neighbours. And to create a new footballing and popular political culture that is not reliant upon an old claim to worldly dominance.

Match Report: Quarter-Final

Argentina vs England

Marcela Mora y Araujo

Argentina Team Background

THE PERENNIAL DICHOTOMY of skilful artistry versus defensiveness is an established issue among Argentina's football-loving intelligentsia, and identified as such even across the ocean by erudites such as Brian Glanville who notes an Argentina "once famous for their ball artistry, now notorious for relentless defence." Diego Bonadeo, perhaps our country's answer to Glanville, echoes the sentiment, and describes the way our team are being asked to play "garbage football", dating back to mistakes made at World Cup '62. The "ideologue" of this process, according to Bonadeo, is none other than the Argentine manager at World Cup '66, Juan Carlos "El Toto" Lorenzo.

Lorenzo first took over the national team after a brief successful spell managing San Lorenzo, following his conversion from player to player-manager to manager at FC Mallorca, closing a career in Europe which spanned stints at Sampdoria in Italy, AS Nancy in France, and Atlético de Madrid, Rayo Vallecano and RCD Mallorca in Spain.

At Chile '62, Argentina were joined in the same group by England. Soundly beaten by England 3-1, Argentina failed to get out of the group. The feeling back home was that Argentina focused too much on tactics and strategy, copying a physical schematic European style with "our own" ways lost. Particularly, Lorenzo's request that Rattin man-mark Bobby Charlton was something critics found difficult to forgive, and even Lorenzo-advocates who argued the idea in itself wasn't a bad one, agreed in this instance it didn't work.

Matches against England had been established already as ones of great significance; at club level, English clubs would come to play in Argentina, amongst the earliest visitors Southampton in 1904, Nottingham Forest 1905 and Everton in 1909, leading some to assert that this is how the notion of "teachers" and "pupils" started. Internationally, a couple of friendlies in the early 1950s had etched indelible markers in football folklore: Argentina's goalkeeper Rugilo became known as "the Lion of Wembley" following a visit in 1951, and when England played in Buenos Aires in 1953 Oscar Grillo's goal from an acute angle was immediately labelled "the impossible goal." Some of these encounters were not without controversy: in 1956 when San Lorenzo visited Coventry, the ref awarded a penalty to local team City and José Sanfilippo, one of Argentina's most lauded forwards, physically attacked the official.

The Chile clash was less memorable by comparison, but nevertheless Argentina's failure to advance in the tournament was seen as an unmerited blow.

Following this fiasco Lorenzo left his job as national team manager. A handful of interim appointments proved unsuccessful, including Osvaldo Zubeldía, the symbol par excellence of the concept of anti-football. Zubeldía left the job too after his choice of assistant and his work plan – which included teaching the players English – was frowned upon by the Argentine Football Association (AFA). With little time left before the '66 World Cup would begin, Lorenzo was recalled.

"El Toto" is renowned for saying before a match "*plin-caja*," an onomatopoeic hybrid expression used when someone manages to take advantage of a situation which appeared disadvantageous by alluding to the sound the till makes when the cashier opens it. *Pling-till* would be the literal translation, and pling-till is indeed a rather perfect expression for the ideology behind Argentina's behaviour during the 1966 World Cup.

The joke that the Argentine psyche is rather full of itself, that we believe ourselves to be better than most, and that the entire

cosmos is colluding in a big conspiracy against us may well have
some foundation in reality. Psychoanalysis is rife in Argentina,
because digging within fascinates us. As such, we endeavour to
"kill the father," as the shrinks put it, and in football, the father is
England.

Rather than a straightforward enmity, the relationship is more
of a conflict of admiration and competition. The novelist and
sportswriter Juan Sasturain describes it thus: "England, in the
constitution of an Argentine national identity, historically, economically, is the one who subjugates us and at the same time
gives us things: it has given us Borges' literature and it has given
us football. Two things which are within our very essence."

The World Cup on English soil is therefore significant. Argentina have qualified top of their group, a campaign notable for two
strong home performances beating Paraguay 3-0 and Bolivia 4-1.
In 1964 they mounted a serious challenge to win the South American Championship in Brazil with no one much believing in them,
and finally won the trophy without losing a single game.

A confident squad therefore, perhaps a little over-confident,
travelled to the 1966 World Cup – an improved version of the
team that had played at Chile '62; much more offensive at least
on the counter-attack. Drawn in the group phase with Spain, Germany and Switzerland, the Argentine delegation – players, officials and journalists – are based in Birmingham, where the team's
unrest has become the main story. The players are bad-mouthing
the manager to anyone who will listen, the manager has been
engulfed by paranoia and his secrecy surrounding training loca-
tions and formations has the press corps playing a cat-and-mouse
chase that they resent. Beating Spain and Switzerland comfortably, the match against Germany is a dismal 0-0 draw that was met
by a booing crowd.

Dante Panzeri, the *maestro* of Argentine football writers, says
it is only when Germany beat Spain, meaning Argentina would
meet England instead of Uruguay in the quarter-finals, that a certain tranquillity took hold of "camp" Argentina, who feel playing

against the hosts at Wembley "guarantees a 'triumphant' reception back home. Against England the prefabricated role of martyrs has been secured."

Issue has already been taken with the fact that the World Cup Organising Committee has gone ahead and designated the referees without the Argentine delegation present. If we cling onto the cliché, the irony will not be lost that it was in fact the Argentine delegation who arrived late. Still, the conspiracists believe Stanley Rous could have waited. At any rate, the decision to appoint a German referee for the England–Argentina match and an English referee for the Germany–Uruguay match was taken, and neither Argentine, nor Uruguayan representatives were present when this happened. Something South America is not likely to forgive in a hurry.

So it is that facing England at Wembley comes as both a cause for pride and celebration as well as a good excuse for enhancing the feeling of being conspired against, with Argentina playing the role of the mistreated underdog.

Argentina vs England Match Report

Date: 23 July 1966
Kick-off: 15.00
Venue: Wembley Stadium
Argentina line-up: Roma (GK), Perfumo, Marzolini, Ferreiro, Albrecht, Rattin (C), Solari, Gonzalez, Artime, Onega, Mas
England line-up: Banks (GK), Cohen, Wilson, Charlton. J, Moore (C), Stiles, Ball, Charlton. R, Hurst, Peters, Hunt
Attendance: 90,584
Final score: Argentina 0 England 1
Goal: Hurst, 77

Enrique Macaya Marquez has travelled to England to file TV reports for Argentine Canal 7, and describes Wembley Stadium as filled with the chant of "Animals" directed at Argentina.

Having previously reported on the 1958 World Cup in Sweden as well Chile 1962 he notes the change in mood among our squad: "This is a very messy World Cup; the players have fallen out with Lorenzo, and the AFA president Valentín Suárez has had to travel to England as a matter of urgency."

Macaya is impressed however by one thing: having access to television in the hotels in England. So when the players complain of noise from a nearby motorway and other disturbances he says to them, "Do you have a telly back home? No? Then what are you moaning about!"

Canal 2, known as Tevedós, was launched in late June 1966, and has secured the rights for the World Cup, but as Argentina's technological infrastructure does not yet allow for live broadcasts the reels are being flown in after the matches and aired a couple of days later. For live coverage it is only the radio, and so most of the nation is glued to their transistors for the quarter-final.

My late grandfather Juan Mora Y Araujo, a sportswriter who passed away in January 1966, wrote about why football means so much for Argentina. "Forget the Greeks, the Romans, the English even... they may have invented the ball but, old man, it was here that football was re-born." His sense of ownership of the game was not so much personal as *national*:

> Football is made up of the dance of our land: it's tango, chamamé and milonga. A choreography that includes gambetas, elasticty, preciousness. Our whole earth is to be found in fútbol criollo, get inside it and you will see from within; the pampas and the sky, the mountains and the jungle, calm rivers and currents that drag, the music of the accordion on the boat cradling by the wharf.

According to him the mountain provides the sturdiness; the plains serene courage; the jungle, shrewdness; and in the city it all came together with a dash of *picardía*, cheekiness, and even nastiness. "Because in football, as in life, you cannot be good all the time. Now and again you have to open the door to the savage."

And so the game kicks off, with Argentina defending fiercely and effectively, an attempt by Onega to nutmeg Hurst, the English dazzling with their long balls. Up front Artime is almost invisible as so much of the game takes place deep in our own half. The German referee Keitler takes names in his notebook relentlessly ("he'll have a library before he's finished," remarks the English commentator) as the fouls from both sides interrupt the flow. In point of fact, as statisticians back home analysing the action establish post-match, the ratio of fouls is thirty-three by England to Argentina's nineteen.

Then once more Hurst attempts a run towards goal that is efficiently turned into a corner by the Argentine defender. There are chants of "Come on Argentina" audible from the terraces, and a big national oohh and ahh when Mas looks like he is about to score but can't. England put a lot of pressure on Argentina, and Rattin, our Captain, seems to be forever on top of the ref, arguing and gesticulating, particularly when he gets warned after a foul on Hurst.

Football history is written by the ball, so we follow its storyline. Perfumo carries out a dangerous tackle on Hunt and the ball is then kicked out of the Argentine six-yard box by goalkeeper Roma to Marzolini – Silvio Marzolini, a potent, tall, blonde defender who would forever be regarded as a gentleman back home. He then seems to initiate a one-two with Gonzalez but play has been interrupted by a fracas on the other side of the pitch.

It appears the referee is telling Rattin to leave the pitch. The Argentine captain is furiously gesticulating. "I am the captain," he tries to communicate. The German official takes it as an insult it seems, some sort of "up yours" and insists on pointing with his hand the way off the pitch. Rattin refuses, continues to argue. All the Argentine players and some of our officials are now crowding around the man in black. In the press box a number of commentators are mumbling that they can't see why Rattin is being sent off, on the pitch he claims he is requesting an interpreter because he doesn't understand what he's being told. For eleven minutes in total he will remain protesting, six of them spent refusing point-blank to leave the pitch. He walks provocatively slowly away, circling the field of play, finally wipes his hand on the corner flag, spits as he enters the tunnel.

Poet Chalo Lagrange's has a tale of the moment he hears of Rattin's dismissal on his radio:

My God, Argentina's elimination at the hands of the English! I still had the letter 'O' fresh in my throat from all of Artime's goals against the Swiss and the Spanish. The radio shook with each goal. I had the radio clamped into the cavity of my ear: you have to understand, Argentina vs England, the hosts, World Cup Quarter-finals. Bobby Charlton was a star even when just standing on the grass. When the radio said he had the ball, I would shut my eyes as tight as I could and convince myself that if I kept them shut a spider would rise up from the stadium itself and bite him. It didn't happen, not that day or any other. When Rattin was sent off I wanted the radio, my friend, to lie to me. Rattin was leaving the pitch amidst a scandal, the commentary said. Always with the radio in my hand I would pretend to summon the other kids in the neighbourhood to go and defend him from the bastard English. And even though the radio didn't say that Rattin was weeping, and it's true that he didn't weep, I could see him, literally see him, with the blue and white strip soaked by tears. Later, when Hurst's goal was scored, the one which made it 1-0 and England won, the one who cried was me.

Panzeri's match report:

The little football we could have expected ended there and the rest was a soporific prolongation of a ball moving very slowly among Argentines and very clumsily among the English, no longer fast or spirited. The English goal was the result of the only ball trapped by an English player, among those long balls they launched upfield. Nothing else can be said about football, because there wasn't any.

Macaya Marquez focusses on that chant of "Animals! Animals!" all around the stadium. He reports: "It's not a myth, indeed it went on for quite a while. It hurts, we felt very Argentine."

Panzeri's account is more self-critical: "Rattin refused to leave the pitch and the rest of the players started all manner of arguments and play-acting, playing the victim, with the intent of shaping out of it a response of Argentine salvation and heroics." He goes on to report what he saw with his own eyes:

> That during and after the match against England Juan Carlos Lorenzo discharged the entirety of his dictionary of insults against the match officials. That once the match was over Pastoriza threw a punch at the referee which according to my colleague Rodriguez Duval hit him in the face – I only saw him throw the punch. And that Lorenzo marched alongside the referee and behind his back gave him a series of little kicks.

Even Bonadeo, who has so often frowned upon the kind of "naphthalene clad, sterile commentary that announces only polemic moves; never a backflick, a nutmeg, a skilful curl. Always the doubt of whether or not it was off-side, of whether or not the infraction should have been penalised," was lost for any other description of the match apart from: "all that remains for history of that match is Rattin's sending off by Kreitlin."

In fact, all of those witnessing this match will recall this as the single salient event. And generations to come will also somehow acquire this remembrance of a pivotal landmark in the story of football, the product of this event, this seminal moment, which quite literally became a before-and-after moment for the game as a whole.

Arguably even down to ten men Argentina could have turned the game in their favour, and the defence deserves praise to the last, even when thirteen minutes before time's up Hurst finally manages to score. But all the details of what ensued are secondary to the drama and controversy of Rattin's rebellion. Panzeri foresees that the frantic gesticulating and insult throwing by players and delegates alike are an acting-out of what many "spokesmen of national opinion" claim: "The English have robbed us of this game like they robbed us of the Malvinas."

When the final whistle is blown Ramsey forbids his players from swapping shirts with our team. In the tunnel and in the dressing room, the Argentines spit, punch and continue to complain. Afterwards Rous and his FIFA people fine Argentina the maximum-allowable fine and threaten to ban them from future World Cups. The English crowd's and media's insult "animals" is then firmly implanted as evidence of the mistreatment received back home, and much to Panzeri's astonishment, there and then a version of events at odds with what he had witnessed starts to unravel:

> The shameless organised lie protecting the business, as the TV cameras register, for the consumption of thousands of journalists, Rattin's statement that he was merely asking for an interpreter. That this delegation was returning home as one of the most exemplary to emerge from the country.

Panzeri claims that "no Argentine team would ever dare to conduct themselves in Buenos Aires like this one has in London. The opposing fans would make it impossible and no referee would stand for Rattin's open rebellion in remaining on the field of play for so many minutes."

The Argentine What Happened Next

Back in Argentina in late June 1966 the presidential house had been stormed by the military, who took power under the guise of an "Argentine revolution" to restore "order" for the benefit of "national security and stability." It was neither the first nor the last military intervention in the governance of the country, but by way of background illustrative of the general state of the society.

Amidst civic and economic turmoil, on the brink of technological innovation, the ever-popular game of football was a welcome distraction to escape from all of that.

Onganía, who presided over the military government, was again neither the first nor the last to spin the events on the pitch and use it feed some nationalistic fervour: "Your brilliant campaign, your courage and battle spirit, make you worthy of the joyous reception with which the people and government of the Motherland await you," he told the players publicly.

While the actual final of the tournament was being played between England and Germany, (won by England with what Argentine history has written down as a "ghost" goal, and proof if any more were needed that the whole World Cup had been manipulated by the hosts with a cunning selection of match officials), Onganía's troops were marching into Buenos Aires University to forcefully silence student protests in an infamous, dark episode known as the "night of the long batons."

But that's another story.

In the pendulum swing from the extremes of left and right that engulfed our nation's political history, when I met Antonio Ubaldo Rattin many years later he was an aspiring politician (he later won a seat in Congress), campaigning hand in hand with an extreme right-wing candidate, Luis Patti, appealing to paranoia and fear, hoping to win a ticket on the back of promises to combat crime. "I love England!" Rattin told me, with a cheeky smile, "the English were always very kind to me, even after the match," he liked to boast. "I remember taking a taxi to Harrods and the cab driver was very friendly, even asked for an autograph." He is able to laugh the incident off, almost with pride.

Roberto Perfumo, by contrast, became a symbol of "left-wing football," a staunch defender of the beautiful passing game and a football pundit with an outstanding mind. He would advise Cesar Luis Menotti on the eve of the 1978 World Cup:

> I spent six years with the national squad and played two World
> Cups. As far as I'm concerned, a World Cup is comparable to a
> commando operation; it's completely different to any other
> tournament a player might be used to. The physical wear and
> tear is exhausting, and much more so the nervous one. It leaves
> you dead.

Silvio Marzolini, a potent tall, blonde defender forever
regarded as a gentleman back home, was a pin-up good-looker
in his youth and has become a much-liked man of football,
devoted to youth training and club development.

And "Toto" Lorenzo, by the time of his death in 2001, had
forged an almost legendary status, particularly at Boca Juniors where he had played two seasons before his move to
Europe but where his final imprint is without doubt his success as manager in the mid–late '70s winning several trophies
both domestic and international. By the end of his life his CV
included managing in Italy, Mexico and Colombia. Lorenzo is
still regarded as the forefather of the "anti-football" which his
successors such as Zubedlía took to infamous levels in the late
'60s with Estudiantes de La Plata.

The national team held on to the idea of being "best in the
world." It would take time before results on the pitch bore
resemblance to the ambition, but eventually two World Cups
would find their way to the trophy room of the Argentina FA.

In the immediate aftermath of '66 though, in preparation
for the next World Cup due to take place in Mexico 1970, the
notion that something so unacceptable as the Rattin-type incident could happen again forced the introduction of yellow
and red cards. TV transmissions were now live across the
globe and apart from anything else a delay of so many minutes
was – from a commercial point of view – absolutely not on.

And in 1974 Stanley Rous's reign over FIFA came to a close,
replacing him a young Brazilian businessman stepped up,

who vowed to protect South America and all the underdog nations of the world from European plotting and dominance in all matters football. The rest is history.

Second Half

A Question of Football

David Goldblatt

Mark Perryman: In your book *The Ball is Round,* you chronicled football's history as a global game. No other team sport's World Cup comes close to football's international representation. The closest might be the World Athletics Championship. What is it about football that has turned it into such a universal?

David Goldblatt: Athletics is a great sport, capable of evoking amazing moments of imagined community, but it cannot compare to the symbolic power of team games. Why football became global rather than say baseball or handball is a more complex question but I think that a combination of factors, some intrinsic to the character of the game itself and some that are the product of its long complex history and globalisation, are at work. Football remains a remarkably simple game, whose rules, like offside, are virtually intuitive. It can be played with a minimum of equipment on a variety of surfaces and retains essential ludic qualities with anything from two to thirty-two players. It is open to a vast variety of skills, talents, body shapes and sizes. Its combination of flow, uncertainty and three-dimensionality makes it an exceptional spectator experience. As for history, the British Empire via formal and informal means proved the most effective diffuser of sports in the late nineteenth and early twentieth century, conjuring the ground for football before many other sports could begin to make an inroad.

Football isn't unique in English culture with being drenched in nostalgia yet '66 is perhaps the most extreme example of the appeal and security of the nostalgic. What for you lies behind

the enduring appeal of 1966 as England's comfort blanket for football, and beyond?

I think the story begins long before 1966. 1950 is as good a place as any to begin, when England play their first World Cup, get beaten by the USA and are sent home from Brazil early. As with other signs of national decline this was brushed off by many, but when the Hungarians beat England at Wembley in 1953 – England's first defeat by a foreign nation at home and a comprehensive and unambiguous demonstration of the antiquity of English football – it becomes impossible to ignore. The fate of the national team and the narrative of global decline and what to do about it were fused and it is this that gave the 1966 World Cup such emotional power. For a short moment in the mid-1960s, the combination of Wilsonian technological optimism, rising prosperity and widened educational opportunities, plus a small but furiously creative arts and counter-culture, made it look like a successful post-imperial Britain might emerge and 1966's golden football moment just topped it all off.

I also think that our nostalgia for 1966 is part of a longer lament for the lost world of an industrial, working class Britain. All of those features of English and British society are stamped on 1966. The vast, crude unadorned stands at Wembley; the last hurrah for formal dress at the football; the contorted vowels of Alf Ramsey's post-elocution-lesson diction; a team of tough northerners and working class gentleman, and all of them were white. It is now impossible to imagine an England team without black players, and that, however one feels about it, sets 1966 deep in the past on the other side of a long period of tumultuous change.

Over the past fifty years since '66, Great Britain, the United Kingdom, the Union, England, each have changed in all manner of ways. In what ways is football a useful tracker of these changes, and is there a danger we over-estimate its significance in and around these kinds of issues?

The narratives surrounding the national football teams of these Isles are interesting elements in the ongoing process of imagining communities and nations. The enormous number of Union Jacks at Wembley '66 is testament to the then unreflective elision of Britain and England. The appearance of St George's flags at Euro '96 is an indicator of the slowly emerging notions of a popular English nationalism and identity. It remains the case that the England football team (and in minor voice the England cricket and rugby union teams too) is the only meaningful and popular English institution around which a modern civic nationalism can be invented – the Church of England, English Heritage, nor English National Opera will do. The Tartan Amy, which first emerged at Spain '82 and peaked in its scale and political resonance in the late 1990s, served as a very public identifier of emergent Scottish national identity, adding a bacchanalian and working class dimension to the middle class trinity of kirk, law and education. Their conscious decision to be the world's most amicable fans sharply contrasted with the anti-social behaviour of a minority of England supporters in the 1980s and 1990s.

Since then, and with remarkably few exceptions (like Charleroi at Euro 2000), England fans' behaviour on tour has been a lot more carnivalesque, opening up the possibility of imagining a different kind of England and Englishness. England fans are, without question, more diverse than in the past and, as shown by the English conga lines in Niigata at the 2002 World Cup and the fancy dress at South Africa 2010 and elsewhere, a lot funnier than they used to be.

You have helped to pioneer an argument that decisively roots football cultures within the social, economic and cultural framework in which they are situated. Does that argument help us to understand in any sense the scale of England's failure to come close to matching the 1966 golden moment?

But is it such big failure? According to the econometric work done by Simon Kuper and Stefan Symanski, since the shocks of not qualifying in the 1970s, England has done about as well at the World Cup as one might reasonably expect for a medium-sized country. Their model is admittedly rather crude, considering only the length of a nation's football history, its GDP per capita and its population – which hardly takes account of more complex issues of the balance of sports with an national sports culture – but it is a good and sobering starting point for the debate. Expectations have been unreasonably high both because of the way in which the press have constructed the narrative, aided and abetted by much of the public, and because for the last ten or fifteen years we have lived under the illusion that a successful elite professional league is still a reasonable guide to the form of the national team. It's the same worldview that thinks because the City of London is doing fabulously well then the rest of the country will do too. To use Galbraith's terms we have a problem of private opulence and public squalor where the gains of globalisation are sequestered by a few, and where elites, domestic and foreign, feel increasingly little allegiance to public and common projects. In that regard England's hapless performance at the last two World Cups, while a sporting disaster, has at least made this point transparently clear. I can't help thinking that the recent success of Wales and Northern Ireland – qualifying against the odds for Euro 2016 – who don't have as big a talent pool to draw upon, are reflecting and drawing upon a sense of Welshness and Northern Irishness that is much more communitarian than an individualised England.

You are an arch-critic of the mismanagement of modern English football. Are the errors made so entrenched they rob you of any hope for the England team in the next fifty years? And if not what are your resources of hope, and how might these impact on England getting anywhere close to winning a World Cup ever again?

In the short to medium term I'm not particularly hopeful. The current programme of reform that the FA is working on, and the government's review of sports policy, will I suspect leave the most important problem untouched – the decline in the sheer number of people of all ages playing sport in general and football in particular. The FA's renewed emphasis on coaching, and nurturing the education of these coaches, is tremendously good news, but until we can match the numbers of UEFA A-Grade accredited coaches in Germany (four times higher per head than here) developing footballing skills will not be sufficient to produce a world-beating football culture.

I remain hopeful however because I continue to believe that the core common sense assumptions and beliefs of football culture are social-democratic. There is an insistence that football is a common enterprise. That there is space and status for the individual, the talented, the genius, but that in the end it is the collective that makes their ascent possible. A culture that accepts that someone must pay for the circus, that some degree of commercialisation and professionalisation are necessary, but that can never be unhinged from social obligation and public regulation. I am always struck when watching Bristol Rovers that the meaning of the game simply cannot be reduced to winning, to glory, to victory, art or entertainment, but is powerfully about being and sharing, a rare sanctuary in our abominably narcissistic and introspective culture where the moment is about us not me. That gives me a lot of hope.

I also see a lot of really brilliant work being done in British football. The Scottish fans who stopped the "new" Rangers being given a free pass back to the top of the Scottish game are a fabulous example of the power of social media and the capacity of fans to make things happen. Of course, in the Scottish lower leagues, where unlike England there is virtually no TV money at all, the dependence of clubs on ticket income gives fans extra leverage. The supporters-ownership movement is also gathering momentum and diversity, from the part-ownership model at Swansea, to post-nightmare rescue co-ops at Portsmouth and Hereford, to the rip-it-up-and-start-again model at FC United of Manchester. The Holmsdale fanatics at Crystal Palace show that the Premier League hasn't yet killed the spontaneity and power of the English crowd, and their riposte to the Premier League's astronomical new TV deal – widely circulated banners excoriating greed – shows that there is a political edge to the change as well. The ingenuity and passion of the football-as-social-policy-and-development people – like Football Beyond Borders – is inspirational.

Will any of this help England win the World Cup again? Probably not, but I'm just not convinced that this is a priority just now. In any case, it is an ambition best served by deep long-term structural reform at the grassroots of the game.

Last year you helped put together an ambitious Fans' Manifesto to reform the English game. What would be your top ideas to help the England team get somewhere close to ending those fabled years of hurt?

A serious levy on the currently offshore betting industry on all their football winnings, and a proper deal with the Premier League, all this to be spent on youth, coaching and infrastructure. Make independent directors a majority on the FA board. Reform the FA Council and force the FA to be made subject to a Freedom of Information law.

To conclude with '66... and if England had lost?

Part of me would like to argue that it would have delivered the sort of "short, sharp, shock" that catalyses profound structural change. The defeat would have required a level of introspection in English football and external pressure to democratise, modernise and transform the game. But I think it is just my social-democratic fantasy, a world in which the Wilson programme worked, Callaghan called the election in 1978 and Thatcherism and the Premier League never happened. Maybe at the very edge of possibilities, the defeat might have catalysed the kind of rethinking that was already circling in some quarters, like Sir Norman Chester's 1968 report for the government on the decline of league football. Some of the youthful participative energies of the moment could have flowed into challenging the structures of power in the game rather than fighting on the terraces. Maybe in the strange interregnum that was the minority Labour government of 1974 Brian Clough could have taken a rebuilt England to the 1974 World Cup and won, and then who knows?

What Have the Germans Ever Done For Us?

Mark Doidge

WHEN GEORGE ORWELL WROTE that football was "war minus the shooting," he correctly identified the nationalist pride attached to both. Both England and Germany are in a small, select group of World Cup-winning nations: only eight countries have won the men's tournament and four the women's. For many England fans, 1966 has become the equivalent of war as a way of representing national superiority over our European neighbours. Yet as the German comedian Henning Wehn sardonically notes, it is always World War II that is used as a benchmark, not one of the more recent wars that Britain has been involved in. English national superiority in war and football is becoming a distant memory. 1966 has become a remote point of reference for England's footballing prowess. A victory on home soil for the founders of the modern game has become the epitome of the men's game. A semi-final for the men at Italia '90 represents the sum total of England's World Cup achievements since. In sharp contrast, Germany, both pre- and post-unification, have succeeded in becoming one of the most successful nations in the men's game. They are second only to Brazil, having won the men's tournament four times and been losing finalists four times. These supreme levels of global success for Germany are also replicated in the women's game. Fifty years of hurt? When Germany doesn't do well in a World Cup, the painful years in between a semi-final at least and reaching a final can be counted on one hand.

While Germany have been World Champions four times and European Champions thrice, England's men's successes have been reduced to one World Cup and three semi-finals (1968, 1990, 1996). Similarly, the German women's national team has won the

World Cup twice, been a losing finalist once, and losing semi-finalists twice (out of seven tournaments). They have won the European Championships eight times out of eleven! In contrast, the England women's team have failed to qualify for the World Cup three times, been quarter-finalists three times and lost in the semi-finals in 2015. They have a similar record in the European Championships, although they made it to the final in Finland in 2009 – guess who England lost to in that final? Though the lionesses made up for that at World Cup 2015 when they returned the favour with a victory in the third–fourth match. It is fair to say though, in men's or women's football, that the Germans are the dominant footballing nation in Europe.

The contrasting fortunes of Germany and England in international football reflect the role of socio-economic differences too. Mostly also to England's disadvantage. Although the two countries are often placed together, sharing an Anglo-Saxon model of political economy, it's these subtle differences that help explain the context for success and failure on the pitch.

Europe is currently immersed in a financial crisis that has impacted on various national economies in a variety of ways. When the global financial crisis emerged in 2007 and then erupted in 2008, a similar pattern developed. In the US and UK (and Iceland), a series of banking crises led to the collapse of a number of banks, including Northern Rock, Lehman Brothers and AIG. The crisis then spread across Europe and directly impacted economies within the Eurozone, the part of the EU that had the Euro as currency. Ireland, Greece, Cyprus, Spain, and Portugal were all affected. The European Central Bank, like many national central banks, purchased the debt to stabilise the market and restore confidence. What is important for this narrative is that Germany was the strongest economy within Europe and helped underwrite the ECB's actions. The German Chancellor, Angela Merkel, took a central role in the negotiations and came to symbolise the economic power of Germany. The Prime Minister of the UK at the start of the crisis, Gordon Brown, also took a leading role, but his subsequent election defeat in 2010, combined with the Euroscepticism of the incoming Conservative-led coalition, reduced the role of the UK in finding solutions to the crisis. As in football, England's position has become marginalised as Germany became central.

It is the wider social, political and economic cultures of Britain and Germany that help explain their relative success and failure at world football. In this case we can safely include Scotland, Wales and Northern Ireland with England for their collective failure to set the world of football alight. The German political model is characterised by consensus-building and a diverse economic base. In contrast, Britain has led the way in neoliberal economics. Since the 1980s, successive Conservative and Labour governments have followed policies that have explicitly reduced the state's involvement in the economy. This has led to widespread privatisation, de-industrialisation and a focus on the financial industries. Whilst the European Union has neoliberal values inscribed into its constitution, via the Maastricht and Lisbon Treaties, national governments have implemented these policies in vastly different ways. As a consequence, some nation states have retained a centralised role in how they regulate their economies. These cultures of state involvement are clearly reflected in football.

Historically, sport in England has been seen as a leisure activity that is outside the realm of the state. Throughout the Middle Ages, rival villages would play each other at football on religious holidays. Throughout this era the ruling classes attempted to control unruly mob football. By the nineteenth century, the emerging industrial classes were sending their (male) children to school. These public schools (so-called because the boys were taught in "public" not tutored at home), also attempted to control the boys' desire to play football. There was a continued moral panic about young men being engaged in anarchic activity. Thomas Arnold, the headmaster of Rugby School, permitted games to be played in order to allow the boys to run off these, and other, urges. The modern game originated when students from different schools came together at Cambridge University and realised they had slightly different rules. A typically English meeting took place in a pub, The Freemasons Arms; the outcome was the formation of the Football Association in 1863. A secondary outcome of no less significance was that these founding members established football clubs as private spaces, outside of the control of either state or society.

There was a specific class and imperial element to the early development of English football. The boys made the transition from public school to Oxbridge and then into the military or government. This was a time of Empire and physical activity was seen as the driving force of Britain's international success. These schoolboys were being schooled in how to run the Empire and football was part of this development. It may be apocryphal, but when the Duke of Wellington declared that "Waterloo was won on the playing fields of Eton," there was a clear link between sport in public school and military success. A cursory look through the early winners of the FA Cup shows these early class origins. Teams like Oxford University, Old Etonians and the Royal Engineers dominated the competition until the professional teams from the industrial north took over. Once again, there is a class element to this. Football was seen as a way of controlling the uncouth, rowdy working classes. The ideas of Muscular Christianity, of a healthy mind in a healthy body, ensured that football (and other sports) were encouraged to stop the moral deprivation of the urban industrial classes. Getting men playing football would get them out of the gin shops, pubs and gambling dens and provide spiritual fulfilment. Churches formed many of the early teams. Industrialists, many of them inspired by Muscular Christianity or their religious beliefs (like the Quakers) also encouraged works' teams. These church and company teams copied the practice of football clubs being private clubs.

In contrast to Britain, Germany has a more state-orientated approach to football clubs. The early sports clubs in Germany were primarily focussed on *turnen* or gymnastics. This reflected the different sporting traditions of Scandinavia and Prussia, but also helped to promote a more militaristic physical activity. Over time, gymnastics helped to differentiate Prussia from their nineteenth century economic rival, Britain. As football spread across Europe and Latin America, Germany sought to encourage a more Teutonic activity. Despite the middle class adoption of gymnastics, football's popularity was not to be stopped amongst the industrial and urban classes. Slowly football became incorporated into pre-existing gymnastics' clubs and this helps to explain how some German football clubs have foundation dates that predate English clubs, such as VfL Bochum 1848 and Munich 1860. Significantly, these private clubs were also mutual associations that incorporated a more democratic voice from the start.

After World War II all of Western Europe followed a broadly similar economic model. Underpinned by investment from the US in the shape of the Marshall Plan, The Western European post-war consensus consisted of an agreement to use state intervention within a capitalist economy to counteract uneven development; used Keynesian macroeconomics to achieve full employment; and encouraged state policies to redistribute economic surpluses through a welfare state. Across Europe from the late 1940s to early 1970s there were a range of economic "miracles," from *Il Miracolo* in Italy, to the *Trente Glorieuses* in France, and the miracle on the Rhine of the *Wirtschaftswunder*. Although Britain did not have a "miracle," post-war affluence greatly increased, leading Harold Macmillan to declare in 1957 that Britons "have never had it so good." Throughout this period football's popularity in England dramatically increased as more people had the money to attend games, and then to purchase the televisions that showed the matches.

It is in the context of this period that we should view England's victory in 1966. The '60s were in full swing. High wages and levels of employment were driving new forms of consumption (including football) and many people had greater opportunities. After the establishment of the welfare state under Clement Atlee, there followed a succession of aristocratic and Eton-educated Conservative Prime Ministers; Sir Winston Churchill, Sir Anthony Eden, Harold Macmillan and Sir Alec Douglas-Home. Labour Premier Harold Wilson represented a decisive break from this tradition, as he was a grammar school-educated boy from Huddersfield. Economic prosperity led Wilson to a narrow victory in 1964 and a greater majority in 1966, five months before the World Cup. Wilson's love of football (and Huddersfield Town) provided a populist appeal. Long before Tony Blair jumped on the "Cool Britannia" bandwagon, Wilson was photographed with the Beatles and always attended the FA Cup final. Sport was an important enough part of Wilson's politics, or perhaps his populism, that one of his earliest acts when he came to power in 1964 was to appoint Denis Howell as the first Minister for Sport.

It was during this period of post-war prosperity that German football also took off. Their desire to differentiate themselves from Britain in football's early days also explains another peculiarity of German football. The *Deutscher Fußball-Bund* (DFB, German Football Federation), actively resisted professionalism within the sport and powerful regional football associations maintained their own competitions. It was only in 1963 that the Bundesliga was formed to allow a national professional league.

Significantly, the Bundesliga was established by the DFB. This originally ensured that the league and the Football Association had the same values. In contrast, the English game has always been divided by internal politics. The class divisions in the early days of English football meant that there was continued conflict between the bourgeois amateur ethos of the early gentlemen's clubs and the professional demands of football clubs in the industrial centres of Britain. Working class players did not want to lose money by playing football, so agitated for compensation. Eventually the FA permitted professionalism, yet this increased the desire of club chairmen to have a regular competition to justify the wages. The intransigence of the FA led to the formation of the Football League in 1888. Once again, class divisions are at play. The founding teams of the FA hailed from the public schools and professions from the South. The Football League was founded by professional clubs in the industrial North. Here were the beginnings of two key factors that would shape the England national team's enduring failure.

Firstly, the arrogance of the FA meant they failed to appreciate the direction international football was heading in. This can be seen in their relationship with FIFA (both then and now). The FA did join the international governing body only a year after its inception. But then they withdrew (along with their fellow British members) after World War I when FIFA refused to exclude Germany, Turkey and Austria-Hungary. They re-joined in 1924 but resigned again because of disagreements over payments to ama-teur players – a decinsion that meant England did not take part in the first three World Cups. This haughty approach to interna-tional football further minimised England's involvement in com-petitive matches beyond the home nations and close neighbours. Whilst football spread across the globe and became a powerful force for many nations and clubs, England rested on its laurels. The challenge to the national psyche after the "match of the cen-tury" in 1953 highlighted how much England had failed to appre-ciate the development of the game abroad. England's 6-3 home defeat to the "Magnificent Magyars" was followed by a 7-1 humil-iation a year later in Hungary. This shouldn't have come as too much of a surprise as England's first venture into the World Cup in 1950 was greeted with an exit in the first round after defeats to the US and Spain. Four years later at World Cup '54 they pro-gressed to the quarter-finals, only to be defeated by the holders Uruguay. Uruguay in turn lost to the "Magnificent Magyars" who lost to West Germany in the final. A pattern emerges.

Secondly, the origins of England's failing national team can be traced back to the institutionalised conflict between the FA and the Football League. The open hostility between the two bodies ensured that little agreement could be reached about the future direction of the sport in England. By having a separate body gov-erning the professional league, the football clubs gained a significant amount of power to challenge the FA. Knowing that the clubs could withdraw at any moment provided a counterweight to any centralising tendencies within the FA. In contrast, the federations of Spain, Italy, France and latterly Germany all controlled their leagues. The strategies of clubs, leagues and federations were aligned more coherently than in England. This situation has only been exacerbated since 1992 with the formation of the Premier League. In an attempt to regain some control, the FA supported the formation of a breakaway elite men's league. Thanks to the agitation of the "Big Five" clubs in England's old Division One, coupled with the support of ITV's London Weekend Television, the Premier League was formed with the financial support of Sky Television. This effectively wrested control of elite men's football from the Football League, but instead of the FA filling that vacuum, power shifted to the clubs in the newly formed Premier League. As the television deals have significantly increased, the power of the clubs has only grown, the remit of the FA as a governing body steadily diminishing in return.

The Premier League approach explicitly comes out of the Thatcherite period of English political economy. The European post-war economic consensus collapsed in the 1970s with the oil crisis and introduction of neoliberal policies by Richard Nixon to mitigate problems caused by the Vietnam War. The global recession undermined James Callaghan, successor to Harold Wilson, and his Labour government. In his place Margaret Thatcher came to power in 1979. Britain's success in the Falklands War not only gave England fans something to sing about against Argentina in 1986, but also helped Thatcher to a greater majority in 1983. This allowed her to begin implementing her reforms, which included widespread privatisation and deregulation of the finance industry. The Big Bang in 1986 opened up a global banking industry. Private capital investment became the order of the day as new forms of financing helped create a new economic boom in global cities, but at the expense of localised production outside of these financial centres.

The Premier League reflects this market-orientated, deregulated approach to British political economy. Not only does the government not get involved in the regulation of football but the governing body, the FA, chooses not to impose, or even try to impose, any regulation either. What changes that have been implemented have come from negotiation, rather than central imposition. This was the ideology of New Labour, which adopted Thatcherite neoliberal economic policies but at least acknowledged that some of the consequences would not benefit everyone. In football, this New Labour approach led to the creation of the Football Task Force. Two months after Blair's landslide election victory of 1997, the Football Task Force was established to tackle the commercial effects of the Premier League: issues like rapidly increasing ticket prices, the resultant social exclusion of football's traditional working class support, and widening inequality between the elite men's clubs and everyone else. The impact of course on these key issues bordered on the non-existent.

One very welcome outcome of the Football Task Force however was that it created Supporters Direct. Yet while this is a cause for celebration what it also revealed was the impotence of New Labour and the FA. Supporters Direct was established to help fans set up trusts to save their clubs from financial crisis. Since the formation of the Premier League, over fifty clubs have entered administration. Whilst Supporters Direct do a fantastic job helping fans save their clubs from extinction, the lack of regulation ensures that the formation of a body to help fans is akin to using a sticking plaster to deal with a broken leg. The structural problems of the game remain. An explicit tenet of the Taylor Report after Hillsborough was to treat fans as customers. Clubs have adopted commercial strategies that seek to increase revenues from these customers and this has stretched the identification of fans with their clubs. Many clubs no longer represent their local community, and some are no longer in any meaningful sense English clubs either. The financial focus of football has attracted a wide range of foreign investment. The globalised neoliberal approach of the Premier League has resulted in foreign owners, players, managers and fans being involved with clubs who happen to be physically located in England. Whilst the fans of smaller clubs that have faced financial crisis may remain rooted in their local or national community, for the elite men's clubs in the Premier League, this is no longer the case. Why should a Russian owner of a West London club, managed by a coach who might be Portuguese, Dutch, Italian or Israeli but almost certainly never English, with a team of Brazilians, Spaniards, Serbians and Belgians, care about the fortunes of the England team?

The Premier League highlights what happens when a deregulated neoliberal model is adopted. The focus on financial profit ensures the growing marketisation of the game. The product has to be promoted to an ever-increasing global market to maintain financial viability. A club's history and culture is ruthlessly commodified; devoid of any of its original meaning and purpose; it becomes just another means to attract sponsors and investors. Those with the greatest resources accumulate more commercial income, and consequently invest more in their squads and marketing to further grow their fanbase and sponsorship. A two-, three-, four-tier top division emerges with next to no durable mobility between those tiers. Since the inception of the Premier League in 1992, only five clubs have won the title. One of those, Blackburn Rovers, only achieved this in 1995 thanks to the generous benefaction of their owner, Sir Jack Warner. Sir Jack was a domestic pioneer of how money can buy success, followed by Chelsea and Manchester City managing to break the dominance of Arsenal and Manchester United thanks to massive financial investment from their owners from Russia and Abu Dhabi respectively.

Whilst a similar pattern has emerged in Germany, it has not had the same negative effect on the prospects for smaller clubs, nor crucially the national team. Only Bayern Munich has truly followed the marketing principles laid down in the Premier League. Like Manchester United (who removed "Football Club" from the club's badge), Bayern removed "e.V." from theirs. This stood for *Eingetragener Verein*, or "Registered Club," and indicated that they wanted to be a global brand – FC Hollywood, as the critics dubbed the club. Bayern's historical tradition and catchment area has ensured international and national dominance. Yet for the remainder of the Bundesliga, greater redistribution of income ensures that at least there is more fluidity beneath the Bavarian giants.

It is fair to say that only Bayern Munich seems likely to regularly challenge for the Bundesliga title and to win the Champions League. This is not unique to Germany. Early victims of football's uneven development, the once-mighty Italian Serie A has already been reduced to the second tier of elite leagues and looks unlikely to recover anytime in the near future. Spain has effectively been a two-club nation since the 1930s, though like Germany below Barcelona and Real Madrid there is considerable fluidity with a variety of clubs competing for lesser domestic honours and occasional European spoils too. Paris St Germain was only founded as a club in 1970; it is the Qatari royal family that has bankrolled the club's recent French success and Champions League ambitions. When football was more regulated and less commercially driven during the 1960s and 1970s, there were a greater range of football clubs challenging for national league titles and European Cups. No one could imagine a Nottingham Forest, Ipswich Town, Celtic, Malmö or Hamburg competing in a European final any time soon. Deregulation benefits those who can attract the most resources and marginalises everyone else.

Part of the reason for the difference in Germany is their approach to regulation. In the aftermath of 1945 a new German constitution was drafted in conjunction with the US, UK, France and the Benelux countries. In a desire to prevent one person assuming control of the nation, certain checks and balances were imposed. The powers of the Reichstag were strengthened, as were the regional and local parliaments. Social responsibility was embedded within the constitution, and a focus on consensus-building was introduced. An obligation by German citizens and broader civil society to consider their social responsibilities is actively encouraged. This helps explain why trade unions remain strong in Germany as organisations of collective labour, but strikes are rare. It also helps explain the rationale for the ownership model of German football clubs. This approach is reflected in the economy as Rhenish capitalism is based on social solidarity, which is achieved through a strong state and bureaucracy. There is a consensus that there should be a social aspect to capitalism and the welfare state helps promote social inclusion. This is in stark contrast to the Anglo-American model which focuses on the individual and places shareholder value central.

Whereas English football clubs were set up as private clubs, German clubs are mutual associations. And consequently they have a greater democratic focus. As mutual associations all members have a vote and a say on the running of their club. While English fans become more distanced from their club and more exacerbated by the way English football has developed, the so-called "German model" has become the reference-point of choice. The "German model" is the "50+1" rule. This is where the fans own 50% of the shares of the club, plus one share. This prevents the club becoming the private property of an individual or corporation and ensures that the club works with its fans. There are two exceptions to this rule: Bayer Leverkusen and Wolfsburg. Both of these clubs have longstanding links to Bayer and Volkswagen as they were the original works' teams.

The "German model" has become a romanticised vision of another possibility for English football. It is not *the* "solution" as many English commentators, fans and journalists seem to think. What it does show though is the different approach to economics, politics and community in Germany and provides a way in which England could welcome greater regulation for the benefit of the many, rather than a wealthy few. The 50+1 rule is an important starting point, both for German and English clubs, and it highlights how valuable it is for the clubs to have a dialogue with their fans.

The 50+1 rule is actually a recent development. It is the German consensus response to the introduction of the "English Model." The success of the Premier League has piqued the interest of capitalists across the world. A success defined not by the improving fortunes of the national team but the rising commercial profitability funded by the television and sponsorship deals of the Premier League and the hyper-riches of the small number of elite men's clubs. This financial aspect has seen similar models adopted across Europe. After clubs were allowed to become public limited companies in England in the 1980s, similar deregulation occurred across Europe. The Sports Law allowed Spanish clubs to become private companies in 1990; Roma and Lazio floated on the Milan *Borsa* in the late 1990s. This desire for private capital investment also occurred in Germany. In 1998, the DFB permitted clubs to attract private investment. But thanks to fan resistance, and the consensus approach of German politics, the 50+1 rule was introduced to maintain fan involvement.

The 50+1 rule is actually therefore a symbol of German football introducing the English model, but it is being kept in check by the German approach to regulation. The worrying thing for German fans is that the exceptions of Wolfsburg and Bayer Leverkusen create potential ways to gain control of a club. The exception was made as these clubs could show twenty years of continued investment. As soon as other businesses demonstrate twenty years of support, they could start to challenge the 50+1 rule. These owners want to capitalise on the popularity of football. Anyone who has been to watch a German match will notice similar trends to England, with high levels of commercial sponsorship (it should not be forgotten that the first club in the world to have a shirt sponsor was Eintracht Braunschweig). The Bundesliga sells television packages globally and has a range of corporate partners, in the same manner as the Premier League. Furthermore, the Bundesliga has been operated by *Deutsche Fußball Liga* since 2000, when it was formed as a private company. Following the Premier League model, the league became a private company with each club being a shareholder of this company. These companies then market the league and sell the media, television and internet rights to the leagues.

The German model has however been successful in retaining certain controls over the national team. The 50+1 rule at least ensures that all fans have a say in the running of their club. The national team in Germany still occupies its rightful position at the pinnacle of the sport. After the failure of the national team at the 2000 European Championships, when like England they failed to get out of their group, the DFB held a wide-ranging review. Rather than copy what other leagues did in a superficial attempt to impact the national team, they focussed on developing their own talent. They invested €500 million in restructuring the youth-development system. This is centrally controlled and all thirty-six Bundesliga clubs have to operate youth academies that must have at least twelve boys from each annual intake who are eligible to play for the national team. Failure to do so will mean that they are not granted a licence to play in the league. By South Africa in 2010, Germany had the youngest squad with an average age of twenty-four. Four years later, they won the World Cup in Brazil. Central regulation for national benefit clearly outshines the toothless lack of regulation from the FA and the market-led approach of the Premier League.

Football, for all its faults and changes, remains a useful way to understand society. The uniformity of the rules ensures that we have a similar social activity to compare across and between nations. And when we look, we see the different ways that social and political life shape the world's most popular sport. As the Italian thinker Antonio Gramsci argued:

> Observe a game of football: it is a model of individualistic society.
> It demands initiative, but an initiative which keeps within the
> framework of the law. Individuals are hierarchically
> differentiated, but differentiated on the grounds of their
> particular abilities, rather than their past careers. There is

movement, competition, conflict, but they are regulated by an unwritten rule – the rule of fair play, of which the referee's presence is a constant reminder. The open field – air circulating freely – healthy lungs – strong muscles, always primed for action.

Neoliberal free-market economics became hegemonic in Britain first under Thatcher and then under Blair. This is reflected in English football where a small number of clubs compete for the money, fans and players. Conversely, Germany retains some regulatory control, even with Merkel as Chancellor. Clubs remain under the influence of fans, and despite Bayern other clubs have at least a chance of national success and occasional European glory.

Where Britain went to one extreme, Germany retained the capacity for centralised regulation, across society and in football too. Where the Premier League is economically successful and attracts fans, owners, and players from around the world, the Bundesliga retains a sense of competition, fan-involvement and national identity whilst still adopting commercial practices that make the German game richly profitable. Central regulation also ensures the pre-eminent position of national team in both German football and culture. The positive results, for Germany, are obvious. It is unlikely that England will be replicating their 1966 success anytime soon. Our only chance would mean swallowing our national pride and asking that country over the Channel which can boast four stars on their national team shirts to our measly and fading one to teach us a thing or two about how to run our game.

A Scottish Farewell to All That

Gerry Hassan

SCOTTISH FOOTBALL for most of its history has seen itself in relation to English football, and pivotal to this for the last fifty years has been how England's 1966 World Cup victory is remembered.

There are many other Scottish stories about football – the wearisome tale of Celtic and Rangers; the suffocating dominance of "the Old Firm"; the pioneering early days of Queen's Park and "the Scotch Professors"; Scottish club triumphs across Europe, and the exploits – highs and lows – of the national team and its supporters.

Yet the changing characteristics of the Scottish–English football relationship have provided one of the main pillars of how Scots have seen football, and also, critically, how English opinion has portrayed Scottish football. In this asymmetrical relationship, a wider set of anxieties, sentiments and feelings can be identified which illustrate the relative place of the UK in the world, Scottish and English national identities, and the evolution and future of the political and social union that is the United Kingdom.

England's 1966 World Cup victory has always been seen across parts of Scotland as problematic, even something to be antagonistic about. At the time, Scotland was, by numerous indicators, still very British. UK politics were for the most part largely heterogeneous, about Conservatives and Labour and national swings – with a then miniscule Liberal Party. The SNP were but a tiny dot on the electoral landscape. The constitutional question of Scottish self-government had never gone away, but was firmly in the margins of politics and public life, with Labour, most of the left, and trade-union opinion firmly against it, their faith and focus firmly on British politics.

31 March 1966 saw Harold Wilson win a landslide Labour victory and an overall majority of ninety-seven seats after governing for a year and a half with a slender majority. In Scotland, 1966 can be seen as the last unambiguous British election before it began to depart, first slowly, then dramatically, from the rest of the UK.

Scottish Labour that year won 49.9% of the vote, the highest vote the party was ever to win in its history – only ever exceeded by the Tory majority of 50.1% of 1955 (and remarkably just lower than the SNP's 49.97% of 2015 which produced such an electoral earthquake).

Scotland then was very British, unionist, traditional and conservative with a small "c." It was a country where authority, elites and institutions still mattered; where the Church of Scotland was a force in the land, with its General Assembly treated by civic life as the nearest thing to a national Parliament. Large parts of Scotland prided themselves on their radical traditions, but more powerful was a respectability combined with silence and omissions about many areas: historic discrimination against Catholics, abortion, homosexuality, and anything else to do with sex, sexuality and the body. The Labour Party, headed by Willie Ross, a dour Presbyterian former teacher, was well placed to articulate this mood: cautious, not very democratic, the so-called "hammer of the Nats," but always prepared to use the non-existent threat of the separatist bogeymen to win more concessions from Whitehall.

This is the Scotland that awaited England hosting the 1966 World Cup. It was a tournament in which England alone represented the UK, with Scotland, Wales and Northern Ireland having all failed to qualify. This gives some context to England that year presenting themselves as British. What is interesting is that in 1966 most of this passed in all four corners of the Union with little comment.

How did Scotland react to 1966 and England's victory? One immediate response in the media was to downplay it. Large sections of the Scottish press did not put it on their front pages or see it as a major event. Even allowing for football being less ubiquitous than today, this is telling.

On the Monday after England winning the World Cup, *The Scotsman* had as its top front-page story, "Lyceum to change play policy," concerning theatrical matters in Edinburgh. On the sports page, England's victory was given the same space allocation – two columns – as a Scottish inter-university golf tournament, while the football report by John Rafferty compared Wembley excitement to "the hysteria of Nuremburg rallies." The *Glasgow Herald* on the same day marked the occasion with a picture of the West German team returning home on its front page, with no photo of the English team. Their coverage the following year of Celtic winning the European Cup would be very different.

In wider society, reactions were more mixed and touched upon a number of strands from pride at British-English achievement, to disparaging England, and annoyance at what was perceived as English condescension of Scots and the world. My father, then aged thirty-three, maintained for the rest of his life that 30 July 1966 was "the second worst day of my life" – the worst being the day he and my mother separated.

Similar attitudes litter Scottish popular culture and public life after the event. Indeed, in many places and particularly in football and "Tartan Army" circles it became customary to embrace the "Anyone But England" mindset and see regular jousts with some of their favourite adversaries, Germany and Argentina, as the best times for expressing this.

Many Scottish football fans still show their annoyance about 1966, asserting that "England won't let it drop" and "they won't stop going on about it" – seeing this as some kind of football imperialism. This ignores the fact that England did win the World Cup, and that all "big" footballing nations and those that see themselves as such like to invoke their greatest moments. A comparable example to England would be Uruguay, who won the 1930 and 1950 World Cups and the best they've done since has been losing semi-finalists in 1970 and 2010. Do Uruguay fans sing "six decades of hurt never stopped us dreaming"? Possibly. And does it annoy some of their less successful neighbours? Maybe.

One problem in considering Scottish attitudes to 1966 is that, by their nature, most comments about 1966 came after the event. This is true of any historical occurrence, but in this case there is a need to be aware that post-1966 interpretations inform how this is seen as much as the event itself. Important in this is how English opinion chose to express itself post-1966 and the highs and lows of English football that followed, and how Scots reacted to this; and as a secondary theme, not all of this can be seen as just about football, but society, politics, and much more.

Less than one year after England's moment in the sun two further football matches had an effect on British football. One was Scotland playing England at Wembley in April 1967 with the Scots playing the English off the park, winning 3-2. This was England's first defeat since being crowned World Champions, and led to the Scots declaring themselves unofficially "Champions of the World." Decades later, in a 1994 essay "What Scotland Means to Me," Gordon Brown reflected on the euphoria of that day – "1967 was surely one of the greatest hours of the boys in blue."

More important was Celtic in 1967 becoming the first ever British team to reach the European Cup final and then to win it in style, defeating Inter Milan 2-1. The European success of Celtic's "Lisbon Lions" came at a golden moment for Scottish club football. While Celtic were in the premier European final, Rangers reached and lost the European Cup Winners' Cup final – with Glasgow becoming the first city to have two teams at the same time in European finals.

Such achievements reflected on the depth of the Scottish game, but tended to go unnoticed in England as Celtic manager Jock Stein often pointed out. The English football commentator Kenneth Wolstenholme of "They think it's all over, it is now" fame said when Celtic won their semi-final in 1967, "We've made it," claiming Celtic as a British club, causing Stein to reflect, "We became British that night."

Alongside the England World Cup win, 1966 can now be seen in retrospect as the last high point of British Labour and social democracy. Wilson's "New Britain," with its "Let's Go With Labour" energy and optimism, seemed at the time the politics of the future: challenging outdated, stuffy Toryism. Yet, by late 1967 this mood had completely changed in what turned out to be a deep-seated attitudinal shift few understood at the time. Beset by economic problems and a weak British economy with poor economic growth compared to its Western European neighbours, a balance of payments deficit, and an over-valued pound which made UK exports uncompetitive, the Wilson government lost its way.

The closing months of 1967 saw the Labour Government postpone for as long as it could the inevitable devaluation of the pound in relation to the dollar. The delay meant that Wilson was seen as being forced into acting, and therefore lost political capital, as well as seeing Britain's international status diminished.

Just before the devaluation finally happened, on 2 November 1967, the SNP's Winnie Ewing overthrew a 16,576 Labour majority in the seemingly impregnable Labour seat of Hamilton, winning by 1,779 votes on a 38% swing from Labour. The SNP had been until this point an irrelevance in Scottish politics, but this wasn't the case after Hamilton. It is not an over-statement to say that Scottish, and indeed British, politics would never be the same again.

A little over two weeks later, on 18 November, Wilson bowed to economic pressures and devalued the pound from $2.80 to $2.40. This cost the Labour Government not only immediate authority and confidence, but inflicted longer-term damage that Wilson's party never fully recovered from. By devaluing, Labour abandoned the idea of long-term national economic planning, and prioritising economic growth as a means of redistribution. Moreover, this traumatic event can be seen as the beginning of the end of British social democracy, a road that leads directly from 1967 to the IMF crisis of Labour in 1976 and to Prime Minister Jim

Callaghan's embracing of monetarism, and ultimately, to Blair-Brown's New Labour.

Four years after 1966, England went to the Mexico World Cup as Champions. This was a whole new experience, and again England were the sole British representatives. They qualified from their group stage, despite narrowly losing to Brazil (the eventual winners) and met West Germany in the quarter-finals. After going 2-0 ahead England were pulled back to 2-2 at full-time (as in 1966), only to lose 3-2 in extra time.

This game has been replayed almost as much as the 1966 final – goalkeeper Gordon Banks missing through illness, the role of his replacement Peter Bonetti in all three German goals, and manager Alf Ramsey's second-half substitutions when ahead. But it represented much more: "the revenge for 1966" and to Germans, the payback for the "Wembley robbery."

The outcome had ripples way beyond football, happening at the end of a UK general election that Labour were widely expected to win. After being hugely unpopular, Labour had regained some support by spring 1970 and Wilson decided to go the polls; pre-English defeat, everything was going to plan, with Labour between 7% and 12.5% ahead of the Tories. The election was a mere four days after the match, and produced a Tory lead of 3.4% and overall majority of thirty seats. Labour was stunned; many blamed the World Cup factor, however Wilson's lead had been steady but short-term, and the bad balance of payments figures were also key. But once again the national political debate and English football fortunes seemed inter-related.

The most ignominious English defeat post-1966 was still to come. In the qualifying rounds for the 1974 West Germany World Cup, England needed to beat Poland to get there. In the pre-match analysis, Brian Clough dismissed Poland, calling its goalkeeper Jan Tomaszewski a "circus clown in gloves," remarks that were to be remembered on a painful night as the Pole played a blinder, England drew 1-1, and Poland qualified, not England. This was a shock to rival England's humiliation at the hands of Puskás and

Hungary in 1953, and was even worse because the descent from World Champions had been so swift – the *Daily Telegraph* even commenting that England had been "relegated to a place among soccer's second-class powers."

But north of the border something was stirring. Scotland had failed to qualify for the last three World Cups but defeated Czechoslovakia in September 1973 and qualified for the World Cup in West Germany the following year. This achievement came in the month before England's public angst and doubt unfolded in front of people's eyes, and was then doubly enjoyed by a swathe of Scotland, starved of success and fed up about English commentators going on about 1966 with a sense of entitlement.

This shifting mood happened against a backdrop of national crisis, malaise and establishment worries about governability, which led Tory Ted Heath to fight an election in 1974 on the theme "who governs Britain?" against union militancy, and to narrowly lose to Labour. The certainties of the post-war settlement were being shaken to their very foundation, with the global economy shuddering as a result of the OPEC oil price hike after the latest Arab-Israeli war, and Western governments worrying about economic prosperity and prospects.

The UK had become an oil producer a few years previous, but was yet to see the financial benefits, although the issue had already ignited Scottish politics with the SNP running a popular campaign, "It's Scotland's Oil," which gained them more support. At the end of October 1973, the Royal Commission on the Constitution (the Kilbrandon Commission) which Wilson had set up post-Hamilton to park Scottish and Welsh nationalism, reported – recommending Scottish and Welsh devolution. Labour refused to accept its recommendations, and a few days later in a by-election on 8 November the SNP's Margo MacDonald seized another Labour stronghold, Glasgow Govan. Devolution and the Kilbrandon Commission had not been an issue, the SNP breakthrough coming about more because of the decrepit state of Scottish Labour's urban rotten boroughs.

In the two general elections of 1974 the SNP established themselves as a national electoral force, winning 21.9% in February and 30.4% in October, with seven and eleven MPs respectively. This was the beginning of the devolution debate that dominated British politics for the rest of the decade.

Another seismic event occurred between the two 1974 General Elections with ramifications for Scotland's image, how it saw itself, and its place on the international stage: for the first time ever it took part in the World Cup Finals as the sole representative of the UK. This was a coming-of-age moment for Scotland and for a generation of football fans who could barely remember the last time the nation had taken part in the World Cup (1958).

1974 was the first World Cup I was aware of, heightened by Scotland's participation. To mark this auspicious moment my parents bought a Sharp 26" colour TV and, for Scotland's opening match against Zaire, arranged the living room with theatre-style seats and invited the neighbours, to see Scotland win 2-0. Honourable draws against World Champions Brazil and Yugoslavia saw Scotland go out on goal difference, but as the only undefeated team in the entire tournament.

This was the start of Scotland's emergence on the international stage, qualifying for five tournaments in a row, and slowly disinvesting from the fixation of defining itself in relation to the then annual match against England. The 1978 expedition to Argentina embodied the worst of Scottish swagger and over-confidence that led to a collective embarrassment and hangover that some have never recovered from. Scots comedian Andy Cameron even got a top-ten hit out of all the hype, titled "Ally's Tartan's Army," which, while representing all the usual football lines, included, "We're representing Britain; we've got to do or die. For England cannae dae it, 'cus they didnae qualify." Subtle or attractive this wasn't.

In 1978 Scotland had only failed to qualify for the touyrnament knockout stages due to inferior goal difference, and the same happened again at Spain 1982. Qualification followed again for the World Cups 1986 in Mexico and 1990 in Italy.

In the course of the five-in-a-row, Scottish football changed in numerous ways, if not on the park. Scottish football fans, for long caricatured as hooligans and drunks, particularly in relation to the biennial trip to Wembley to face the Auld Enemy, became conscious of their profile on the international stage. Self-styled as "the Tartan Army," they became unofficial ambassadors for a stateless nation, conspicuously defining themselves as the opposite of English fans who were busy gaining a reputation much worse than Scots had ever earned.

This was not a perfect embodiment of national consciousness, for the "Anyone But England" element became more vocal, oblivious to how small-minded and petty they appeared. Followers of the national team in the early twenty-first century did not realise that when they cited 1966 as the reason they wouldn't support England, saying that "they won't stop going on about it," that those most obsessed with England's triumph were elements of the Tartan Army. Or even worse, using supposed insults to Scottish footballing prowess, such as Jimmy Hill's dismissal of Dave Narey's stunning goal against Brazil in the 1982 World Cup as "a toe-poke" that led to the long-running Tartan Army campaign: "We hate Jimmy Hill, he's a poof."

But despite these significant caveats, much of the Tartan Army's demeanour and profile became rather impressive. Under eighteen years of Conservative governments, they grew into a conscious expression of a very different nation, making their presence felt in the World Cup and other matches, showing their disgust at British military interventions, jingoism, or at the imposition of the poll tax (one banner at the 1990 World Cup stating: "We Have-nae Paid Any Poll Tax"). For a nation that was becoming more and more detached from the Thatcherite version of Britain, there was a sense of determination and dignity in football fans making these political statements globally and at a time when the UK was seen as isolated in Europe and in alliance with Reaganite US militarism. This gave Scottish football and the national football team an importance way beyond what happened on the park.

The Tartan Army was however only part of Scotland's football community, let alone the nation. The scant public opinion surveys of national sentiment on football showed a more nuanced picture. A 2002 Scottish Opinion survey quoted in the *Scotsman* ahead of the World Cup that summer found almost 33% of respondents supported England at football, while 16% supported England's opponents, and 53% did not mind who won. Eight years on, just before the World Cup 2010, a similar YouGov survey cited in the *Daily Mail* found 24% support for England, 24% for England's opponents, and 38% did not mind either way; support for England was highest amongst the over sixty-fives at 40% with a mere 2% supporting England's opponents; younger people were much more likely to cheer on England's opponents.

Some prominent figures get in a terrible mess because of the Scotland vs England rivalry: one being Gordon Brown. In a 1994 essay he celebrated the Scottish invasions of Wembley in 1967 and 1977, writing of the former, "You need only to recollect the scenes of delirium among the Scottish fans... when they tore up bits of turf to take home as a living memento – to realise that clearly there was a lot more at stake than the result of 22 men kicking a ball around." In a similar vein, he wrote that after seeing Scotland defeated in the 1990 World Cup, this had to be seen in "an historical context in which disappointments and defeats at the hands of the English are legion," and cited the examples of Flodden in 1513 and Culloden in 1745.

A decade on, Brown was quoted saying one of his most memorable football moments was Paul Gascoigne's goal against Scotland in Euro '96, describing it as "Gazza's great goal." He also supported England's bid to host the 2018 World Cup, which was uncontroversial, but then identified with England potentially winning the trophy rather than Scotland, forcing him to later hastily backtrack in a BBC news interview, "My ideal scenario is that Scotland play England in the final and Scotland win." Such were the personal confusions that Brown was happy to embrace on his long march to 10 Downing Street; with Brown it touched a deeper moral chasm and ambiguity than David Cameron confusing his football team, Aston Villa, with that club who also wear the claret and blue, West Ham.

Some non-football fans, and even football supporters too, will question whether any of this matters – it is only a game, and there is a need to lighten up and embrace confusion, contradiction and occasionally allow for unpleasant views. That might be true, but given its cultural, historical and financial muscle, football does matter, and provides an almost unique insight into the state of society.

1966 is now in the realm of history and a distant, almost non-existent Britain. The election that year was a nationwide, homogeneous contest on the surface, but underneath the tectonic plates were already beginning to weaken. Scotland began to dissent from the Westminster consensus within a year and half of what can now be seen as the final fling of British social democracy.

Fast-forward nearly fifty years to the 2015 UK election when the SNP changed the parliamentary map of Scotland, winning fifty-six of fifty-nine seats. Unlike 1966 this was an election that did not exist as a UK national contest, but instead as five or six different campaigns. The difference between Scotland and England in voting patterns was the biggest ever recorded – in Scotland, the SNP up 30.1%, Labour down 17.7%, Tories down 1.8%; while in England, Labour rose 3.6% and the Tories rose 1.4%.

1966 can also be seen in many respects as the last great British sporting moment. A moment when the collective country that is the UK was able to come together in a British-English celebration, and whatever the tensions and resentments, to mark and acknowledge it, allowing the dominant national account to be articulated. It was also a rarity in that other sporting moments of collective joy, such as the opening ceremony and subsequent hosting of the 2012 London Olympics, was for all its manufactured British ethos not a lasting national moment – instead it was something both transitory and mainly about London's rise as a global city-state.

In contrast the impact of 1966 can be seen in the long tail of its inadvertent influence, in living with the shadow of England as World Champions. Scottish football fans reacted with disgust to what they saw as English arrogance and entitlement post-1966, and saw the human discomfort and pain that flowed from English reverses afterwards as part of this. Much of this was accurate and grounded in hard experience, but some of it was also Scottish football fans wanting to find such attitudes, and wanting to be slighted – embodying a "chip on the shoulder" attitude and unhealthy obsession with England experiencing defeat.

Maybe without 1966 things would have been the same. We will never know. But the 1966 experience became part of the painful readjustment of English football to its long-term international decline; the Scottish national football team, it could be pointed out, has never scaled those heights to experience such a marked decline.

All of this reveals some rather interesting facts about Britain, England and Scotland. There is England's ongoing semi-detached relationship with the European Union, and its simmering resentment in places with German power, whether economic or on the football field. Scotland has at the same time increasingly defined itself as a European nation, but done so as the European project has become visibly anti-democratic, technocratic and divorced from progressive values.

Scotland has in recent decades shifted to what I have described elsewhere as an "independence of the Scottish mind," whereby Scotland sees, portrays and represents itself as a quasi-independent nation, decoupled from the notion of Britain and British politics. Some of this journey can be observed in the emergence of Scotland as an international force in the World Cups from 1974-90 and, particularly, the three under the Thatcher Government.

The United Kingdom, like Europe and much of the world, is undergoing major change and in a state of uncertainty and impermanence. In the near future it is possible to imagine a very different set of relations between the nations of the United Kingdom. Here's an idealistic thought. I would like to live on an island where I support Scotland and England and Wales and Northern Ireland at football. For that to happen, part of England has to change, as does part of Scotland and, I acknowledge, even a part of myself.

There are of course significant differences across sports. The footballing "Team GB" in the 2012 London Olympics was met with equal disdain from the Scottish, Welsh and Northern Irish football associations and many fans, English included. Other sports show less rivalry and tension, from rugby to curling, but there are often numerous sensitivities such as when Andy Murray won Wimbledon in 2013. Murray's victory came in the year prior to the independence referendum, and witnessed David Cameron and Alex Salmond (with his Saltire in the Centre Court) both competing to claim Murray as either a "British" or "Scottish" champion, with Murray attempted to navigate a path including both.

Twenty-five years ago academic Henry Drucker observed: "I think you will find that if Scotland were independent football would just be about football and Scots would treat it in a way people in properly independent countries do." In the intervening period Scotland has begun, imperfectly, to embark on that still incomplete journey, with as yet its final destination still unknown.

The 1966 anniversary is another *leitmotif* in Scotland's growing self-awareness, and in learning not to displace all our negativities and neuroses onto England and English attitudes. Of course for this to change, multiple other changes have to occur. One of these is that the English media and broadcasters have to develop a more diverse, multi-national and relevant portrait of these Isles which, given tradition and inequalities of size, would have to break with the dominant account provided by various versions of the British establishment.

Modern life though is full of anniversaries, and once one has passed another quickly comes along: the fiftieth anniversary of the famous 1967 3-2 Wembley victory and Celtic's European Cup triumph. How these are seen and marked will reveal something about Scottish football: the first a totemic but token victory, the second a huge moment in Scottish and European football.

And it is coincidence, but the same year will see even more watershed historic moments pass – with the anniversaries of the Wilson government devaluation and Winnie Ewing winning the Hamilton by-election for the SNP. The old Britain of Empire and arrogance began to visibly wither and shake that year, and fifty years on from these aftershocks, we have come near to the end of the road of the old British story. That's a very positive development, but we still have far to travel on these isles to mark out an alternative set of stories – of football, and more important subjects, such as politics, power and democracy. We can but hope that we have begun and are up to this task.

We Won't Mention the Score

Markus Hesselmann

I t took some time until Wolfgang Weber appeared on the scene. "Today? Really? I thought we were to meet on Friday..." he said when I called him on the phone to say that I was waiting for him at *Geißbocekhim*, the club house of 1. FC Cologne's training ground on the greenish outskirts of the Rhine metropolis, and wanted to talk to him about the World Cup 1966 and his role in it. "Oh dear I must have mixed something up in my diary. I'll be over in half an hour. Got to take a quick shower because I had a gardening job to do today." Weber did not mention that gardening jobs for him include picking up litter along the green banks of the River Rhine as a member of a local volunteer initiative.

Could you picture any of the stars or ex-stars of '70s or '80s football – not to speak of the stars nowadays – regularly picking up litter in their spare time? Wolfgang Weber is very much your guy-next-door even though he was a successful international, a technical, stylish defender who scored in the World Cup final at Wembley. And very good-looking he was on his autograph cards with his Beatles haircut. In that German team of 1966 Weber fitted in well and was surpassed only by an über-normal guy: Uwe Seeler, the team captain, famous for not accepting an offer of 1.2 million Deutschmarks in 1961 from Inter Milan because he did not want to leave Hamburg, his beloved hometown. Wolfgang Weber only played professionally for one club, 1. FC Cologne, Uwe Seeler did the same for Hamburger SV. (Few but the most diligent football-fact trivia collectors though would know that Seeler did play for one other club: and that was a single match for Cork City in 1978 where he scored both goals in a 2-6 defeat against Shamrock Rovers and later claimed that he had not known that it was a regular League game into which he was lured by kit-manufacturer and sponsor Adidas for whom he was working.)

Uwe Seeler was also renowned for his hanseatic, almost English, sense of fair play, having been sent off only once in his career spanning two decades. He stuck to his principles even in a decisive, career-defining situation: "The three youngsters in the team, Franz Beckenbauer, Wolfgang Overath and I ran to the linesman and protested," recounts Wolfgang Weber. "Then Uwe came and chased us away. He said: Stop protesting, the referee has made his decision. That was how the older players thought and reacted. But we were young and wanted justice." Weber is talking about *that* situation of course: the situation of situations in the 1966 World Cup final. As the defender closest to the ball he had seen – and maintains to this day – that the ball had not crossed the line. I'll leave this question at that – don't mention the goal – and come to a more sociological point. Even a mild protest like this involving only those three young players of the team was seen as disrespect. Instead a situation like that should be met with fairness and a stiff upper lip. No *furor teutonicus* was to happen on the Wembley pitch by the likes of Seeler, Tilkowski, Held or Haller. And only mild instances of "wanting justice" by the young Turks. "Just think of how well-behaved and harmless our reaction to the Wembley goal was. Can you imagine that today?" Weber takes pride in mentioning that "we did not have a single player sent off during the whole tournament. We did not have any deceitful or sneaky players in our team." And interestingly he chides English players like Bobby Charlton for play-acting while celebrating a goal that was not. "I told him: Stop it! What's the point?" Weber recounts. "Somebody must have taught the English players to raise their arms as early as possible in order to influence the referee." And this while many German fans still uphold the view that English players feign and protest less than continental ones do.

Weber, Seeler, Tilkowski. Theirs is an in-between generation. With the oldest guys in the team, Uwe Seeler and goalkeeper

Hans Tilkowski, born in 1935 and 1936 respectively, they were old enough to remember the war but not yet of the generation when footballers were treated like pop stars. 1966 was also the year in which the Federal Republic's second chancellor Ludwig Erhard, a Christian Democrat and father of the West German post-war *Wirtschaftswunder* (our economic miracle) but not a successful leader, had to give way to the first grand coalition between Christian and Social Democrats. That was however only a prelude to the few but important Willy Brandt years. Under Chancellor Brandt and his first Social Democrat-Liberal coalition, West Germany opened up to Eastern Europe via *Ostpolitik* and started to acknowledge and come to terms with German responsibility for Nazi atrocities. These were also the years of the '68 student revolt, which introduced new ways of political campaigning and whole new ways of life to a so far rather bourgeois West Germany. More glamorous or, up to a certain point, even rebellious players like Günter Netzer or Paul Breitner represented these shifts in German society on the football pitch as well. Beckenbauer did so at least with his flamboyant, always relaxed-looking style on the pitch. If Erhard was the politician in between chancellors Adenauer and Brandt, two defining politicians for West Germany, then Seeler was the sportsman in between the hero of our first World Cup win in 1954, Fritz Walter, and Franz Beckenbauer. Parallels between politics and football were never again that clear-cut.

The German media theoretician Norbert Seitz even devoted a book to exploring this analogy: *Doppelpässe, Fußball und Politik* (*One-twos, Football and Politics*). "A new era began, Germany was eager for experiments, repressed utopias were revived," Seitz wrote. "Visions of reform as well as new football aesthetics started to captivate German minds in a republic that was conservative and defensive up till then." Willy Brandt's slogan "To dare more democracy" also promised a more creative and offensive football, according to Seitz. My colleague Michael Pöppl, who wrote his dissertation on "Football in German Literature," references Seitz and concludes with respect to "football reform" that the new

Bundestrainer Helmut Schön "was now able to recruit the personnel for this football reform from a strengthened *Bundesliga*." It was only in the beginning of the '70s that Schön, who had succeeded our 1954 World Cup-winning coach Sepp Herberger in 1964 and epitomised a more democratic and *laissez-faire* approach to managing players, really became his own man. The Schön era therefore began at about the same time as the Brandt era. Both the great politician and the great manager were incidentally known for not exactly being cut out for the rough environments of politics and professional football. Instead they were softer, more modern men.

In 1966 Bayern Munich and Borussia Mönchengladbach, the defining teams of Germany's football miracle of the '70s, had only one player between them on the pitch in the final, Bayern's Beckenbauer. Both teams had been promoted to the Bundesliga only in 1965. Bayern Munich won the European Cup Winners' Cup two years later, anticipating what was to come in the '70s, when Beckenbauer's team won the European Cup three times in a row from 1974 to 1976. Meanwhile Mönchengladbach won UEFA Cups in 1975 and 1979 and lost against Liverpool in the 1977 European Cup final.

The 1966 team in the final was instead dominated by players from Borussia Dortmund – European Cup Winners' Cup winners of the same year after a 2-1 victory over Liverpool at Hampden Park. Dortmund was represented at Wembley by three players, Hamburg SV and 1. FC Cologne by two each. Dortmund, German champions in 1956, 1957 and 1963, only became champions again in 1995. In fact they were even relegated to the second level of German football in 1972 where they had to stay for four seasons. The great days of Hamburg SV, champions of 1960, only began again in the late '70s, winning the European Cup Winners' Cup in 1977, the German Championship in 1979, 1982 and 1983, culminating in their 1983 winning of the European Cup. 1. FC Köln were the first Bundesliga champions in 1964 and after 1966 also only became Championship contenders again when the first era of

Bayern and Gladbach started to fade, winning German Cup and Championship in 1978.

Compared to the cultural, political and football revolution that built up towards the end of that decade and the beginning of the next one, the mid-'60s were prosaic times. This was underlined by the aesthetics of football coverage in the media. Everything seemed to be done to avoid any comparison with the Nazi newsreel and radio reporting. In 1954 the legendary radio commentary on Germany's victorious final by Herbert Zimmermann might as well have occurred in exactly the same excited, exciting and partisan shouting style to describe far darker events and results ten or twenty years earlier. In contrast the TV reports in 1966 are marked by a longing for objectivity and modesty with next to no emotion and long stretches of silence that you may wish to occur in our overexcited times today now and then. This happened not only in defeat as in the 1966 World Cup final but also when a German team won and even while commenting on a very special achievement such as Reinhard Libuda's 1966 winner for Dortmund against Liverpool scored at Hampden Park in the hundred-and-sixth minute from almost thirty metres. This artistic feat was greeted with a more or less descriptive "Libuda's ball is a goal in the hundred-and-sixth minute of the match," by the commentator. He allowed himself to repeat "goal" twice and added a cautious "unbelievable," but that was it. It was dryness with a view.

Weber, Seeler, Tilkowski. Theirs is also a tragic generation. It seems reasonable to suggest that even if the class of 1966 had won that World Cup final they would still not be legends today on the scale of the 1954 or 1974 teams that came before and after them. 1954 stands for a post-war miracle, a feeling of coming back from the ruins that was in many ways jingoistic then but miraculously has lost most of that touch by now. What is left of it is a largely positive myth, infused by the 2004 movie *The Miracle of Bern* by Sönke Wortmann or earlier in the 1994 novel *The Sunday I Became World Champion* by Friedrich Christian Delius. "I had never felt so light," writes Delius in this autobiographical piece, "and beneath the pulsing emotion of victory was a deep desperate hint of what it would like to be liberated from the curse of a world divided between Good and Evil, liberated from the occupying forces, from an insatiable god, and perhaps also a hint of the limited duration of this happiness at being able to say one time an unchecked Yes!" Yes, it was that urgent, and the author got away with his pathos.

Both filmmaker and novelist are decidedly non-nationalist and more or less left-wing protagonists in their areas of work. Both works allowed a fresh view on Germany's past while the country was going through a post-unification phase of searching for a new national identity, which climaxed with the World Cup 2006 in Germany for which a new "soft patriotism" emerged that was no longer seen as a threat at home or abroad any more. *Easier Fatherland* is the title the author and former Berlin correspondent Steve Crawshaw uses for describing this unfolding process: "Memory is important for understanding and absorbing dark lessons in history – thus making it possible to move on." The final chapter in his book is called "And Now," where Crawshaw makes the point: "Another kind of memory deserves encouragement, too: the memory of miracles achieved."

Wortmann filmed for his official film of the 2006 Tournament, *Sommermärchen*, a new and young German team playing creative and non-destructive football reminiscent of the early '70s, which was celebrated although it did not win the World Cup. In an interview with *Der Speigel*, when asked why as a filmmaker associated with the German Left he was now also able to call himself a patriot, Wortmann said: "I have no problem with this word any more today." In his book *World Cup Diary* Wortmann tried to figure out how this was possible for somebody who grew up in a post-'68 Germany that was defined by coming to terms with its Nazi past. "I was sceptical about the German anthem and flag which was typical for my generation and had to do with German history and a feeling that its darker parts were still hushed up." When protagonists of the '68 generation took over, Gerhard Schröder and Joschka Fischer in their red and green coalition, Wortmann finally overcame his distance towards his own country. "I liked it that the Germans had voted a Green Party into government." His is a German variant of a "Progressive Patriotism," a term that Billy Bragg coined for his own "search for belonging" from an English viewpoint. Here we have the German perspective that is heavily laden by our history. Billy, you think you have problems.

Meanwhile, 1974 for Germany was about winning at home much like 1966 was for England. But '74 was also the grand finale and swansong for the Beckenbauer generation. Many people say that the German team that won the European Championship in 1972 was the better and particularly the more creative one, but a World Cup victory on home soil provides better stuff for legend as the English know only too well. Plus it was won as a victory over Holland, an aspect that became more and more important over the years. As much as 1966 has in retrospect been seen as part of a rivalry between England and Germany, 1974 functions in the same way for the rivalry between Germany and Holland. And both are not really accurate since Germany could have been no real rival to England in 1966 because they had not won a single match against them by then. In 1974 the Dutch had qualified for a World Cup for the first time since 1938. Their total football was a fairly recent phenomenon then. Even mentioning the war and joking about it and using it to base a football rivalry on was a later phenomenon, as Maarten van Bottenburg and Christopher Young have examined in the book *Favourite Enemies*. When Holland beat World Champions Germany 2-1 in 1956 in their first post-war friendly, "the war was not mentioned in any of the football reports," writes Marten van Bottenburg. "There were no traces of bitterness or glee against the German people in commentaries." Chris Young adds an English perspective reflecting on 1966: "Newspapers mostly eschewed militaristic rhetoric even though they allowed themselves some hints at the war"; adding that during the '60s and '70s, football matches between England and Germany "were seen as apolitical events most of all." The England vs Germany and Holland vs Germany rivalries only built up after those finals of 1966 and 1974, those finals hsve become redefined as a starting point only in retrospect.

According to Young the strong, politically laden rivalry between England and Germany really only began with Margaret Thatcher and her decidedly anti-German stance. And that rivalry has always been asymmetrical. Whereas Germany is a defining factor both for England's political and "military finest hour," World War II, as well as in football with the World Cup victory in 1966, in contrast England is a country that Germans do not seem to bear a grudge against. German football fans do like to beat England, especially after penalties, but at the same time they have a soft spot for the country for being the home of football and popular culture. Most Germans have a favourite English club next to their Bundesliga team. Union Jacks, mistakenly seen as the national emblem of England, have always been part of fan attire over here. You would even find them on grainy black-and-white photographs of stadium scenes from the old East German *Oberliga*. Whereas there is a liking for Dutch clubs only amongst fans of German clubs with a strong legacy of Dutch players or managers such as Schalke. "Germany is England's Holland," as Christopher Young puts it. And Holland is Germany's England.

Even the 1990 World Cup Winners, who are respected in Germamy as strong and successful players rather than worshipped as legends, would most probably be held in a higher esteem than those players if Germany had won in1966. Though of course there is a link between both squads that gives the story added appeal, Beckenbauer. *Der Kaiser*, the emerging young star of '66, the victorious manager of '90, his career coming full circle. What will become of the stature of the winners of Brazil 2014 is too early to judge. Grabbing the World Cup in South America, being admired for putting up the only real team effort among the big guns in that tournament. And beating the World Cup record-holding Brazil 7-1 on their home soil may be helpful for an enduring legacy.

The legacy of the 1966 German team and the 1966 final largely relies on it all having happened at Wembley on its holy lawn,

Heiliger Rasen von Wembley, right in the heart of football's motherland, *Mutterland des Fußballs*. "Wembley is the *Neuschwanstein*
of football," says Wolfgang Weber, name-checking the Bavarian
castle which draws up to 10,000, mostly foreign, tourists per day
to add an entirely new superlative to all the praise for this most
holy of grounds in our affectionately respectful German football
lexicon.

It may have added to the lack of legendary status that Germany
today attaches to her 1966 tragic heroes that a German team won
a trophy at Wembley thirty years later at Euro '96 while football
was supposedly coming home. Baddiel, Skinner and Broudie's
"Football's Coming Home" was added to the motherland-wor-
shipping repertoire and is still sung even today by German football fans. Not least because our team won that tournament.

And, without rubbing it in, there have been other recent footballing feats that put 1966 in the shade from a German perspective. There is beating England in the semi-final of the World Cup
1990 with a crying Paul Gascoigne and then going on to win the
tournament. There is the last game at the old Wembley Stadium
with a goal by Dietmar Hamann, who is ironically now more of an
English than a German hero. And there is England's first defeat at
the new Wembley, by Germany of course, even though you may
not find many German fans who pay much attention to this particular result to be honest. The supposed rivalry is just not such a
big deal over here.

And Wolfgang Weber? As if to underline his lifelong status as
an ordinary bloke from Cologne, his homecoming to the English
motherland was a road-trip in a camper van from stadium to
stadium to watch the Euro 1996 matches. The tragic hero of 1966
paid for his own tickets and sat in the stands like any other football fan.

All that's left of 1966 for us is the *Wembley Tor* which has shed
most of its emotional connotations and reminiscences and
became a more or less technical term. While Wolfgang Weber,
protagonist and by-stander at the same time, grew slightly tired

of it over the decades, the *Wembley Tor* became a set phrase that pops up instantly when a ball hits the underside of the bar and plunges towards the goal line no matter at what level a German team is playing, from amateur league to a World Cup. Of course at South Africa 2010, in the game between England and Germany, the English ball had indeed passed the line and no goal was given in a reverse of 1966 proceedings; all the talk back home was of our *Wembley Tor*. Don't mention the goal? I mentioned it once, but I think I got away with it.

Match Report:
Semi-Final

Portugal vs England

Frederico Duarte Carvalho

Portugal Team Background

IT IS OUR FIRST TIME.

Portugal has never before qualified for the World Cup finals. This historic moment for Portuguese *futebol*, nevertheless, is no fluke. There is a background of international achievement in recent years at club level, and most of all one outstanding player in particular. Eusébio, the "Black Panther," born in the Portuguese African colony of Mozambique; he is the key player for the hugely impressive Benfica team. Eusébio was in the Benfica team that won the European Cup in 1961, and then retained it the following year, beating Real Madrid in the final. And last year he was in the Benfica team who were the 1965 losing finalists, defeated by Inter Milan.

In our qualifying group for the 1966 Finals we faced Romania, Czechoslovakia and Turkey. We topped our group, ahead of the favourites, the Czechs, losing finalists at the 1962 World Cup. An excellent campaign, four wins, one draw – against Czechoslovakia – and just one defeat, the last one against Romania, when our qualification had already been secured.

At the Finals Portugal were placed in Group 3. The other countries were all far more experienced in the competition than us. Hungary had been the defeated finalists of the 1938 and 1954 World Cups. Bulgaria had made its World Cup debut at Chile '62. And Brazil were the reigning World Champions, twice over, from 1958 and 1962. Even so, we had great expectations for our team. Portugal's first game ever at a World Cup was on 13 July, at Manchester's Old Trafford Stadium against Hungary. A 3-1 victory for the Portuguese side. The next match, three days later, was against Bulgaria, at the same stadium, and Portugal once more scored three goals, winning 3-0 with Eusébio scoring his first goal in the competition, too. Our last group game was against Brazil. It was one of the most violent matches of the entire competition. Played on 19 July at Goodison Park, Pelé was marked out of the game by the Portuguese defender Morais who was accused of violent tackling. But it was a fact that Pelé had picked up a knee injury before the match and it was this more than an over-physical approach by any Portuguese players that undermined the Brazilian gameplan. Portugal won 3-1, Eusébio scoring twice. The Portuguese had topped Group 3, with Hungary second.

The quarter-final was then played against another group-stage surprise package, North Korea, who had finished second in Group 4, ahead of Italy and Chile and second to the Soviet Union. The Portuguese suffered from being overconfident when on 23 July we returned to Goodison Park to play against the unfancied North Koreans. But then we had just beaten Brazil at the same ground and were more than ready to do the same to North Korea. But after the first twenty-five minutes of the match, North Korea were winning 3-0. Portugal were about to be eliminated. Then Eusébio reduced the Korean lead to 3-1 in the twenty-seventh minute, and ten minutes later to 3-2, thanks to a penalty, on the stroke of a delayed half-time. When the Portuguese came back for the second half they were a different team. Eusébio scored the equaliser in the fifty-sixth minute and, finally, thanks to a second penalty in the fifty-ninth minute, Portugal were up for the first time in the game, 4-3. The final goal that ensured the Portuguese victory was scored by Torres in the eightieth minute, 5-3. Portugal would be England's semi-final opponents.

Portugal v England Match Report

Date: 26 July 1966

Kick-off: 19.30

Venue: Wembley Stadium

Portugal line-up: Pereira (GK), Conceicao, Baptista, Carlos, Festa, Coluña (C), Graca, Simões, Augusto, Eusébio, Torres

England line-up: Banks (GK), Cohen, Wilson, Charlton. J, Moore (C), Stiles, Ball, Charlton. R, Hurst, Peters, Hunt

Attendance: 94,493

Final score: Portugal 1 England 2

Goals: Eusébio, 82 (pen); Charlton. R, 30, 79

After this game the memory of the Portugal team will live on in England for a long time to come. At the end Eusébio's tears say it all: the Portuguese team defeated with honour intact on an English battlefield.

Portugal and England may share the longest diplomatic treaty still existing in the world – the Treaty of Windsor, signed in 1386 – but one of them has to lose. We may try to justify the defeat with the fact that our team was playing against the host nation. But that alone is not sufficient to ease the wounded pride of Eusébio and the other courageous Portuguese knights on their adventures in England. Face to face were the two best attacking sides of the competition, and the best defences too. In the end, the 1-2 result was fair because – and as all the commentators agree – this was the best match so far.

From the kick-off, Portugal played nervously. Eusébio was marked by an effective Nobby Stiles, giving him little space, so that Eusébio was denied the chance to show off his skill. Instead it was England who created the best chances. And, like we always say: those who don't score, sooner or later concede a goal. And what had to happen, did happen. Goalkeeper José Pereira was fundamental in ensuring the score stayed 0-0, but that would end in the thirty-first minute, when a long ball sent from the English left side of the field flew directly into the Portuguese penalty area, where Roger Hunt made a run for it, chased by our defender José Carlos. The ball was cleared by José Pereira, but it wasn't enough. The ball landed directly at Bobby Charlton's feet and with a combination of fast reflexes and a powerful shot, the ball was in the back of the Portuguese net.

1-0 to England with another fourteen minutes to be played before half-time. When the whistle blew for the break Portugal had failed to make a single effective attack into England's penalty area during the entire first forty-five minutes. The strategy was to try to get high balls onto the head of Torres – the "Tower." But every time the tactic failed because of the defending of Jack Charlton and Bobby Moore. Since the start of the tournament their goalkeeper, Gordon Banks, had kept a clean sheet in every game. On this evidence this didn't look likely to change in the semi-final.

The first Portuguese attack of any note finally took place in the fifty-fourth minute. Simões managed a successful run down the right side of the English defence. Simões was looking for Eusébio when he saw his pass to him hit the hand of Nobby Stiles. The Portuguese claimed a penalty. But the French referee would not accept the protests of Eusébio.

This was a team that, three days before, facing North Korea, had turned the North Koreans' three-goal lead into a 5-3 Portugal victory. The top scorer of the competition was on our side. One can only speculate what were the words that Portugal's coach Otto Gloria said to his players during his half-time speech, but the result was quite visible. The team was playing quite differently from the first forty-five minutes. A Portuguese goal could come, though the tactics remained the same, long and high balls up to Torres for him to knock down. Portugal's captain, Coluña, was too busy marking Bobby Charlton; Eusébio wasn't getting the supply of balls that would enable him to change the game.

Now there are just fifteen minutes remaining and England are on their way to the final. Both teams are showing some signs of fatigue.

But, even so, the game doesn't slow down. In the seventy-seventh minute Portugal get into England's penalty area with a move that starts with Eusébio and ends with a cross from Simões to the centre, but the English back line cover the threat to their goal.

Once more, a team who doesn't score, concedes a goal. In the seventy-ninth minute, a long pass up-field to Hurst who manages to shrug off the Portuguese defenders inside our penalty area before passing the ball neatly to Bobby Charlton's feet, who scores his second goal of the match. There was no way Portugal's goalkeeper could stop a shot at such short range. England have the game under control.

As we contemplate near-certain defeat we are reminded of the words of João Havelange, President of the Brazilian Football Confederation, a few days ago, in Lisbon, when the Brazilian team made a stopover returning home sooner than expected: "I saw manoeuvres with the intent to change the spirit of our sport." And, as an example, Havelange mentioned the fact that the match between Portugal and England was initially planned to be played at Goodison Park and it was then immediately "transferred" to Wembley, in London. Is it possible that there would be a different score line if Portugal were playing at Goodison, the same place where, just three days ago, we scored five goals after being three behind? That, we will never know.

What we do know is that when Bobby Charlton scores his, and England's, second goal they are still not in the final, not yet. The crowd is singing "Oh When the Saints Go Marching In." But two minutes later the tactic of sending high balls looking for Torres does get the desired result. Simões once more crosses the ball and Torres sends it goalwards. We will never know if this would have been enough, as Jack Charlton uses his hand to stop the ball.

Unlike the first time, Stiles' handball, there is no way now England can escape the penalty. And Eusébio calmly scores his eighth goal of the tournament and England's first goal conceded of the entire competition. The solemnity of the moment is very visible when the Portuguese striker goes to pick the ball out the back of the English net and, before jogging back to the centre spot, gently taps Banks as if he's saying: "Sorry about that, my friend. But I had to do it. You were brave but someday it had to be over. It was now."

The match isn't over though and England aren't yet in the final either. With seven minutes more to go, Portugal can still get an equaliser to take the game into extra time where, maybe, maybe, the "miracle" of our Goodison Park comeback might happen again, this time with the extra ingredient of being up against the home team and in their capital. England aren't shaken though and they could have made it 3-1 when Bobby Charlton strikes again, but this time he is denied thanks to the defending of José Carlos.

Then, on the counter-attack, Simões scares the English defence enough to force a corner kick. Five minutes now left to be played and our Captain Coluña starts a run that ends in their penalty area and a header aiming goalwards. The Portuguese claim for another handball. This time it was not so visible to the French referee. What Frenchman would want to go to into the English history books as the man who gave two penalties against their team at Wembley?

And then the game is over. Our fellow journalists from all over the world give us their independent opinion: What a game! The best match so far in the tournament. Eusébio's tears at the end are not of sadness for not getting to the final nor for the joy of Portugal, and himself, getting so far in this, our first World Cup. It is the honour that he conquered for Portugal. The National Pantheon, our most special place where only the greatest of Portuguese are buried, has a place for men like him.

The Portuguese What Happened Next

After the semi-final, Portugal played against the other defeated semi-finalists, the USSR, in the third-place match, Portugal winning 2-1. Portugal had emerged as the surprise team of '66 to finish third the first ever time they participated in the competition. Eusébio scored his ninth goal and became the tournament's top scorer. After this World Cup however, the Portuguese team had to wait eighteen years before qualifying for the final stages of another international competition again, Euro '84 in France. The Portuguese did well but once more had to play the host nation, France, in the semi-finals. And also once more they lost, this time 3-2 after taking the game into extra time.

Since the 1966 World Cup, Portugal have played England in six competitive matches to date. And England have never won. The first clash between the two national teams following 1966 was eight years later, on 20 November 1974, at Wembley. It was a qualifier for the 1976 European Championships and the result was 0-0. The return game was in Lisbon, at the Alvalade Stadium, on 19 November 1975, another draw, 1-1.

It was another eleven years until Portugal and England would be face to face once again. The two teams were in the same group at the 1986 World Cup in Mexico, Portugal's second appearance in the World Cup Finals. On 3 June at Monterrey's Estádio Tecnológico, the Portuguese beat England 1-0; Carlos Manuel scored the solitary goal. It was our first match in Group F, a group which also included Poland and Morocco. After such a good start, getting out of the group looked easy, but we lost against Poland 1-0. A draw against Morocco would still have been enough to qualify but instead we lost again, 3-1, leaving Portugal bottom of the group. England finished second, beating Paraguay in the last-sixteen knockout stage before controversially losing to Maradona's Argentina, the tournament's eventual winners, in the quarter-finals.

Portugal returned to England for Euro '96, topping Group D, which also included Croatia, Denmark and Turkey. We lost in the quarter-finals to the Czech Republic, who made it all the way to the final before also losing, to Germany.

At Euro 2000, in Belgium and the Netherlands, Portugal and England met each other again. Both teams were placed in Group A, along with Germany and Romania. On 12 June, Portugal and England played their opening group game against each other. In the third minute Paul Scholes put England 1-0 up with Steve

McManaman adding a second in the eighteenth minute. England were looking like easy winners but then Luís Figo began to show some of his skills, scoring in the twenty-second minute, followed by a João Pinto goal in the thirty-seventh minute. All square at half-time and then in the fifty-ninth minute Nuno Gomes scored the winner, 3-2 to Portugal. The Portuguese also defeated Romania 1-0 and Germany 3-0. Portugal topped the group, Romania second, both above Germany, who finished bottom, and England were eliminated. Portugal beat Turkey in the quarter-finals but lost 2-1 against France, reigning World Champions and eventual winners of Euro 2000 too, in the semi-finals.

Four years later, Portugal was the host for Euro 2004. Portugal and England met in the quarter-finals, at Benfica's Estádio da Luz, on 24 June. Michael Owen opened the scoring in the third minute, 1-0 to England. That one goal lasted almost until the end of regular time, but Helder Postiga took the game into extra time when he scored the equaliser in the eighty-third minute. In extra time, the hundred-and-tenth minute, Rui Costa's goal put Portugal into the lead for the first time in the match. But only for a short time, Frank Lampard scoring England's equaliser just five minutes later. 2-2 at the end of extra time, penalties. David Beckham missed his and Rui Costa missed too. Portugal's goalkeeper Ricardo saved Darius Vassell's attempt and then scored the decisive and winning penalty for Portugal himself. Eusébio was there, sitting next to the goal, emotionally shouting his encouragement to the Portuguese players. It was if he was living the 1966 game all over again. Portugal went on to the final against Greece after defeating the Netherlands in the semi-final. We lost the final 1-0.

Two years later, and 40 years on from the 1966 semi-final, came the most recent match before the fiftieth anniversary of '66. Portugal played England in the 2006 World Cup quarter-finals, in Germany, 1 July, at the Gelsenkirchen Stadium. After a 0-0 draw and extra time, the game went again to penalties and, like two years before, the Portuguese were better penalty-takers than the English. Portugal would then lose once more against France in a semi-final. Just like '66 we played the third place match, but unlike '66 when we defeated the USSR to finish third, this time we couldn't get a win. Playing against the hosts Germany proved too much and we lost 3-1 to finish fourth.

Eusébio died on 5 January, a few days after his seventy-second birthday. Fulfilling the wishes of all Portugal fans from 1966 and ever after, his body was moved to the Portuguese National Pantheon on 3 July 2015.

Extra Time

A Dialectical Game

Steve Redhead

MODERN FOOTBALL dialectically contains within it the key elements of anti-modern football, its polar opposite. This is what in yesteryear was called the dialectical process, a kind of leftist language more familiar in 1966 than it is now. In this sense 1966 was both the beginning of modern football culture, but also the beginning of what we refer to today as "anti-modern football."

Within not much more than a decade of that golden moment of victory, the post-war settlement was over and Thatcherism was in charge. The effect on football culture was profound and produced its own fan-led resistance. Against mercenary and overpaid players, prohibitive ticket prices, sterile stadiums, the alienation of traditional supporters who wish to stand safely, rich oligarchs calling the tune and owning bloody everything, all this today is to be "against modern football," against the relentless commodification of the game. This opposition to modern football began almost as soon as the 1966 World Cup was over. Satirical, critical football magazines like *Foul* emerged, pre-figuring the football fanzine movement of the 1980s and 1990s. These were football fans who were ironic, jokey, privileging style over substance, playing with football's "signs" as the entire game threatened to go down the pan via Heysel, Bradford and Hillsborough. It was as if modern football had turned into a nightmare before our eyes and we could do nothing about it.

Italia '90 represented a crucial moment of hopeful optimism, *No Alla Violenza* and New Order's *World in Motion*, but it was, after a while, revealed to be not much more than a stopgap illusion. Postmodernism is "always already" within modernity, a modernity that has multiple facets, or modernities – cold modernity, dangerous modernity, creative modernity, original modernity, and so on. As neoliberalism emerged with its full force in the late 1970s, a much more dangerous modernity beckoned after the "hot" modernity of the mid-1960s. Today we are still living with this via a neoliberalism hardly disrupted by the watershed event of the international financial crisis of 2007–08. Football culture is ever-more implicated in this global process as transfers, corruption and sheer greed spiral. Paul Virilio has argued that we are moving from "cosmopolis to claustropolis." I would add that we are on the brink of "claustropolitanism," a post-crash condition where we feel that all we want to do is urgently get off the planet as what Slavoj Žižek calls "the new dark ages" beckon.

In 1966 I was fourteen and my family had been living in Blackpool in the North West of England for a decade. I grew up watching and playing football from the age of four in the North West of England. My primary school regularly showed black-and-white film of the whole of the "Matthews" Wembley FA Cup final from 1953 between Blackpool and Bolton Wanderers, which will always be associated with Stanley Matthews despite it being Stanley Mortensen who won that game thanks to his hat-trick. After flirting briefly with the idea of being a train driver (or a cowboy), I decided, aged seven, when I went to Bloomfield Road for the first time, that I only really wanted to be a professional footballer (and, no brainer, cricketer in the summer, opening the bowling and batting, for Lancashire naturally). My father, who grew up in Lancaster, was a lifelong Blackburn Rovers fan – for him it was a geographical choice between Preston and Blackburn (both a bus ride away) and Rovers won out. He took me during the late 1950s and early 1960s to games as a child and young teenager all over the North West – to Blackpool, Preston, Liverpool, Everton, United, City, Stockport, Burnley, Blackburn, Oldham, Bolton. I grew up thinking "Lancy, Lancy, Lancy, Lancy, Lancashire" was a hymn. He was a stoical, taciturn man, a staunch old-school socialist who kept himself to himself but he seemed to me in my innocence (a pervasive quality of the times) to know everyone at these grounds. He talked liberally about football to complete strangers as soon as we made it past the turnstiles onto the terraces, something he otherwise never did in his everyday life. The conversations carried on throughout the game. Ninety minutes of talking football and politics. It was a wondrous, magical experience; what else of any worth could there be beyond the touchline? It only seemed a matter of time, in my deluded pilgrimage to all these grounds, before I ran out there too as a fully kitted-out, fully paid-up player.

And this wasn't just local, it was international football culture. Football culture even in the 1960s was a passport to the world. At the 1966 World Cup Finals my father took me to two of the greatest games in the history of the competition, both played at Goodison Park, Everton's historic ground. On a gloomy Friday night, I watched from behind the goal defended by Communist-red shirts in the first half, entranced as Brazil (with Tostao but without Pelé, who had been brutally kicked out of the competition by Portugal) played Hungary (with glorious striker Florian Albert and flying winger Bene). This unforgettable contest ended 3-1 to Hungary, strongly supported by Everton, Liverpool, City and United fans in the crowd who, mainly standing, vastly outnumbered the Brazilian samba band contingent sat in the seats. Merseyside at that time had a strong trade union and diverse Socialist and Communist tradition, which often manifested itself on the terraces of Anfield, Goodison and Tranmere Rovers' Prenton Park. At that time Liverpool's rank-and-file shop-steward movement was second to none when it came to militancy and factory-floor organisation. The crowds at these games reflected this mass, radical labour movement of the area. That Friday night on Merseyside, Hungary, briefly, recalled their majesty of the 1950s and their talisman Ferenc Puskás: an era when English football's imperialism was turned upside down by two huge defeats in the early 1950s before Stalinism created its 1956 havoc, crushing the Hungarian revolution while sending the best of its players, including Puskás, into international exile.

More was to come. On a sunny Saturday afternoon Communist North Korea played Portugal in the World Cup quarter-final. After the Koreans had gone 3-0 up in the first twenty minutes, Portugal (well, Eusébio, actually, the so-called Black Pearl, who got four on his own) ran out 5-3 winners. Again Merseyside (and wider North West) football fans at the game manically cheered on North Korea, continuing the North East fans' staunch support at Ayresome Park, Middlesbrough earlier in the competition, where North Korea had sensationally eclipsed Italy. North Korea's football team, never mind its polity, people and culture, would never again enjoy this kind of optimistic and popular interest. The Cold War? Not during the ninety minutes of a simple football game.

Within a year of 1966, football fandom in Britain was manifestly changing. Skinheads, or "hard mods," started to "take ends" (other fans' kops or main terraces) while academics wrote of "soccer deviance." It is in this sense that the 1966 World Cup was the highpoint of the "cool modernism" of professional football. 1963–66 was a mod (literally "modernist") period in music and fashion. And it applied to football too. The mod fashions popular in football (later an inspiration for football casuals) contained the core elements of an "accelerated culture." It felt like everything, history, media, politics, culture, was first taking shape then in an instant disintegrating at a furious pace. The iconic political events – from Mao's 1966 Cultural Revolution in China, to the January '68 Tet Offensive in Vietnam, May '68 in both Western and Eastern Europe, and the civil rights and anti-war movements in the USA – were to speed up political, social and cultural change just as England was getting over the joyful excesses of winning a World Cup.

Today the football fandom of 1966 has all the appearance of an innocence abroad. The global football culture that I witnessed at those World Cup games at Goodison Park had an unfamiliar originality, something most fans marvelled at while being entirely unfamiliar with it. Standing, watching at Goodison Park, it hit you in the solar plexus. We should not underestimate the popular impact of what Baudrillard calls the "hyperreal" of attending live football games in England back in the 1960s. This was a purely visceral experience. Since 1966 of course fandom has remained pivotal to football, and this still means that the football industry cannot just free-marketise the whole damn thing simply because it feels like it.

For Badiou, Žižek and others it is possible to reimagine a non-capitalist future for the world just as it was in the mid-1960s at the time of England winning the World Cup. How could the so-called "beautiful game" become so dirty, sordid and greedy, yet still hold the attention of a mass audience that provides it with that well-worn moniker "the people's game"? Perhaps this is because of a more general political shift, holding fast to an image of a past rooted in collectivity and locality. When fans resist the homogeneity of football then the politics of football culture is starting to mean something again. In this sense the dialectic of '66 remains vitally important. We should celebrate England's World Cup win while positioning the importance of 1966 not in terms of the national team's endless search for an end to the years of hurt, but the event's crucial position in the development of the movements for "modern" and "anti-modern" football.

Have Tickets Will Travel

Stuart Fuller

THE ENGLAND SQUAD that travelled to the 1962 World Cup in Chile had to endure a flight with two separate changes to Lima where they played a warm-up game against Peru before moving on to Santiago, then Rancagua where they would play their group games and then bus to their base at the Braden Copper Company staff house in Coya, some 2500ft up in the Andes. The journey of over 7500 miles would have taken them more than twenty-four hours. Hardly an ideal preparation for the tournament. Very few fans could afford the high cost of travel (around £4000 in today's money) or the five-refuelling-stop flight to the Southern Hemisphere on a BOAC Comet, meaning that England played their games in the Estadio El Teniente in Rancagua in front of less than 10,000 locals. Today, that same journey would take thirteen hours and cost as little as £500, with no stops. On the basis of England's travelling support in the past twenty years several thousand would follow the team should they ever play Chile away in the near future.

When Walter Winterbottom's squad left these shores for Chile in 1962 it was from the Oceanic Terminal at London Airport. Four years later, when the squads for the 1966 tournament landed on English soil, the airport had a more familiar ring to it – Heathrow. It would be from departure points like this that the shift in our boundaries as fans would start. The travel revolution was still a couple of decades away when the 1966 World Cup kicked off on 11 July with England taking on Uruguay in front of nearly 88,000 fans, but there is no doubt that the staging of the tournament in England changed the perceptions of whole communities in terms of overseas visitors, the likes of which many English people had never seen before. If the North Korean, Argentine and Mexican

fans could travel halfway around the world to support their countrymen then so could England football fans from Consett, Corby
and Chatham.

It would however be a further sixteen years before England
fans got the opportunity to really experience what it was like
to be a football tourist. Four years after the tournament in England, Mexico offered better opportunities for the travelling fan
than Chile ever did, but still the cost and the misguided perceptions created by the media of what visiting foreign countries
was really like restricted the number of supporters prepared to
travel to Central America. However the 1970 World Cup did see
the first attempt to create an official England supporters' travel
club for those now intending to follow the team overseas. The
England Football Supporters' Association offered members
who wanted to travel to Mexico the opportunity to travel on an
organised trip to watch the tournament, with transport, hotels, a
full English washed down with pints of Watney Ale. The downside? Fans would need to part with between £230 and £250 per
person for a three-week trip, or around eight weeks' money for
someone on the then average UK wage of £32 per week, around
£7500 in today's money. Britain was on the verge of a recession,
after the "never had it so good" '60s. The typical demographic of
football fans at the start of the decade was more likely to spend
their money on a new Ford Cortina or Teasmade for their semi-
detached in suburbia.

English football in the intervening years between 1970 and our
next appearance in Spain in 1982 went through a radical change.
To many, the watershed moment in the development of a culture
of following club and country came two years earlier at Italia '80
when England qualified for the new-look European Championships. Thousands of fans travelled by plane, train and automobile
to the group games against Belgium, Spain and hosts, Italy. This
was a new generation of football fans who had not previously had
the opportunity to watch their nation play in an international
tournament. Many of these fans, only used to the passionate, if

sometimes unruly, terrace culture of England simply weren't prepared for the way the Italian authorities treated them. With few having experience of watching football abroad, many didn't adapt their behaviour and, faced with a new foe in the Italian police and the locals too, the English responded by running riot.

Despite the experience of being tear-gassed, or worse, two years later even more English fans headed to the 1982 World Cup in Spain. For some the appeal would be to repeat the Italian experience, while for others just like the Scots and Northern Irish they would bring their very English version of carnival football to the World Cup for the first time since 1966. Spain '82 was the first major tournament where a differentiated British national identity would come to the fore. All four home nations had previously qualified for the 1958 World Cup in Sweden but the travelling support for each was negligible in numbers, so no such impact occurred back then. In Spain, whilst the English fans would still doggedly wave the Union Jack, the Scots and the Northern Irish defined their support as "anyone but England" and would continue to do so from that point on. Spain was the founding moment for the Scots' Tartan Army, whilst the mainly Unionist Northern Irish support would put their politics aside and proudly wear their own Northern Irish Green in Spain and ever since. The Scots and Northern Irish, perhaps not weighed down with the expectations of a nation on the pitch, made the most of their time in the sunshine off it, while the troublesome reputation that wrapped itself round England at Italia '80 was resurrected once more across the tournament at Spain '82 too.

That reputation stayed with England and their travelling support for a number of years, and was one of the main reasons why the nation's group games in the 1990 World Cup were held on the island of Sardinia. The Italian police felt that containing the fans in one place for the first part of the tournament would be a benefit for all. Despite a tepid start and scraping through the group on goals scored, England woke up in the knock-out stages and gave the fans belief that nearly twenty-five years of hurt could be put to rest. Of course penalties were our undoing in the semi-final but the national team had acquired a new and potently positive identity amongst the fans, many new to the game, and crucially amongst the media too back home.

A few years later the creation of the Premier League and the commercialisation of the game started to take hold against the backdrop of new stadia and this new generation of post-1990 fans. Interest in following England abroad grew off the back of another impressive performance in the 1996 European Championships held in England. "Football's Coming Home" was the soundtrack of the summer and with the next two major tournaments taking place a stone's throw over the English Channel in France in 1998 and then Belgium and Holland in 2000, thousands of new fans started to use this new-fangled internet thing to take advantage of airline revolutionaries such as EasyJet, Ryanair and Buzz.

By Euro 2004, held in Portugal, the last remnants of trouble were ebbing away and England visiting overseas shores was no longer a case of bar owners having to lock up their daughters, as well as their beer. England fans began to be spoken of in the same tones as the hitherto friendlier Scottish and Irish fans, both Northern Ireland's and the Republic's too at Italia '90 and USA '94. Whilst there was the odd minor incident responded to by over-zealous policing, it was the England team who often let the side down rather than the fans when they travelled to the four corners of the globe. Part of that is due to the globalisation of the beautiful game, a far cry from the footballing fare the average fan had to watch or read about some fifty years ago.

Televised football has moved on from an hour on a Saturday night to weekends full of televised games. There will come a Saturday very soon when our Premier League will have no 3pm kick-offs anymore, with games moved for the convenience of global audiences rather than the fans who live down the road. Kids no longer play football in the street. Today it is all about FIFA 15 on the Xbox or PlayStation. English youngsters are as likely, in fact more likely, to wear a Barca or Real Madrid shirt than a United or Chelsea one thanks to globalisation. And those that still prefer a domestic replica kit will have their number and name of their club's hero, a Spaniard or Frenchman, Ivorian, Serb, almost certainly anyone but an Englishman on the back. There's a popular familiarity with La Liga, Serie A, Bundesliga and Ligue 1 via our TV screens which simply didn't exist in '66. And increasingly the same is true of other non-European leagues and nations too, Africa, North and South America, the Australian A-League and more. In the not-too-distant future virtually every professional game around the world will be accessible to watch through some means or another.

In 1966, as English football fans eagerly awaited arguably the biggest sporting event this country has ever hosted, what did most of them know about the teams who arrived on these shores for the greatest show on earth? Very little. But our sceptical, almost xenophobic, view of anyone from overseas prior to the tournament was replaced by a welcoming attitude in many areas, and to this day, people who lived through the tournament will tell tales of how local communities took these footballing nations into their hearts. The story of how the North Koreans were taken into the hearts, minds and kitchens of Teeside remains a legend that is both enduring and potently expressive of a very different type of Englishness to the one we are perhaps more used to recalling from this era.

There was some doubt whether the North Koreans would be allowed to take part in the tournament at all. Following the Korean War the British Government refused to recognise North Korea as a country and it took the intervention of FIFA, back when they were really for the "Good of the Game," to smooth the diplomatic ripples. After travelling by land, sea, air and finally rail, the North Koreans arrived in Teeside, speaking no English and having a press officer, a local journalist by the name of Bernard Gent, who spoke no Korean. They trained in front of 30,000 employees at the ICI Chemical works and went into their first group game as rank outsiders against Russia. Nobody batted an eyelid when they lost but a few days later a last-gasp equaliser against Chile meant they wouldn't be returning home empty-handed. Italy's defeat to Russia meant that a North Korean win in the final group game could take them through, assuming that Chile didn't beat Russia. However, nobody gave the Koreans any hope. The locals came out in force to support Korea. With the score still 0-0, Italy suffered a blow when Bulgarelli was carried off with a knee injury. With no substitutes allowed at the time, Italy faced an hour with ten men. Then with four minutes left in the half, one of the defining moments of world football occurred.

Today between the manicured lawns of the housing development where Ayresome Park once stood is to be found a bronze cast of an imprint of a football boot. It is a sculpture by the artist Neville Gabie and marks the exact place from where Pak Doo-Ik took the shot that resulted in the only goal of the game. The North Koreans still had to wait until that evening for Chile to blow their chance to beat a second-string Russia to take their place in the next round. Such was the popularity of the Koreans that over 3000 Teeside fans headed to their quarter-final with Portugal at Goodison Park a few days later.

Fifty years on and that open-minded affection for and interest in all things foreign among the majority of English football fans has hardly dissipated; instead it has been magnified over and over again to become a central part of the identity of our fan culture. Despite the way they have been treated by foreign police, demonised by the media, and on occasion disowned by their own Football Association, at the merest hint of a friendly – never mind a competitive match – somewhere abroad, hundreds, sometimes thousands, sometimes tens of thousands (for a European Championship or World Cup) of fans will be logging on to flight-comparison websites and finding the cheapest, if not always the most direct, route and booking it "just in case." More often than not these rumours turn into truth and the earlybirds can crow about picking up a bargain. In truth, when following England these days, it is relatively irrelevant where the final destination is – in fact for many the more inaccessible and unfamiliar the place, the more attractive the trip.

Compared to the 1980s and 1990s today's England fan is more mature both in temperament and age. And whilst the unfortunately-still-too-familiar suspicion and aggression can often be seen from the local police and community, sparking the same in return from our fans, by and large the reputation and behaviour of England fans abroad has improved beyond recognition.

However international football travel it is not just about following the Three Lions abroad. Today, it costs less to fly to virtually anywhere in Europe than to get a train from one end of England to another. There are literally no boundaries to where we can go to watch our fix of weekend football. The rise of the budget airlines has given us the reason, or if you prefer, excuse, to try something new. There are very few countries in Europe (and even North Africa) that cannot be reached by budget airlines from the UK every day.

On a trip to the Balkans a few years ago, over the course of one weekend a group of friends and I managed to see four local derbies in two countries including the infamous Belgrade derby. A £40 flight to Zagreb and a visit to the Maksimir Stadium was followed by an overnight train through Croatia, Bosnia and finally arriving in Belgrade at silly o'clock. At each border point armed police with dogs ventured onto the train to check our documents. Imagine a roasting hot compartment containing four blokes who had demolished the best part of two crates of cheap Croatian beer. By the last border crossing even the dogs were refusing to set foot in the carriage. A local guide, met through his love of the beautiful game on our football forum, took us to his home where his mother cooked for us, and plied us with some homemade gin before we enjoyed a day of football, culture and friendship in Belgrade. The whole trip cost less than a couple of tickets at the Emirates.

Taking in Barcelona or Real Madrid at home has become a rite of passage for me and my many fellow football-internationalists, but a trip to Madrid is no longer just about visiting the Bernabau. Of course, everyone should make the pilgrimage there but there are dozens of smaller clubs that ring the city. A trip to watch the hipsters of Rayo Vallecano is now the thing to do, where tickets cost a fraction of that to watch Bale and Ronaldo, leaving you more Euros to spend on tapas and cañas.

Fancy watching the closest local rivalry in Europe? Then head to the village of Spakenburg, southeast of Amsterdam. There, the blues of SV Spakenburg play the reds of Ijsselmeervogels twice a season in the third tier of Dutch football. This is the biggest amateur game in Europe, if not the world, where the whole village turns out to watch. The grounds almost touch each other, with both trying to outdo the other in terms of facilities and spectacles, which have included live pigs being released onto the pitch and an overhead shower of toilet brushes from an airplane.

By air, less than ninety minutes on a good day from the sanitised atmosphere of the Premier League lies the passion of a whole new community of football, travel and overnight hotels for less than the cost of a decent ticket at most Premier League grounds.

A few years ago I wrote an introduction to the book *The Football Tourist*, responding to the claim that modern football was rubbish. Whilst plenty will claim the game today has been hijacked by money, technology also has given us opportunities to follow football in a way that have never existed before. From my introduction:

> Modern football is crap. How many times have I heard that throwaway comment in recent years? There have even been a couple of books that eulogise about times gone by and how much better the beautiful game was when we only had three TV channels, sand for pitches and steak 'n' chips with light ale on the side for a pre-match meal. But it's not really crap is it? That's actually a load of rubbish. In fact it's bloody wonderful.

Technology means that the global game is now in the palm of your hands. At this very moment I'm writing these words for my publisher on an iPad as my train passes under the English Channel. I have the fixtures for every league in the world at my fingertips for plotting my next little trip, whilst Twitter is keeping me up to date on the Ebbsfleet United versus Macclesfield Town pitch inspection. On Sunday I will be able to sit in my armchair at 10am and watch live football from Italy, Germany, Scotland, England, France and then South America without moving a muscle.

Modern football is crap? Rubbish. A trip to the football no longer means getting on a Football Special. Those foreign stadiums we used to see on BBC Sportsnight, built up by the host David Coleman to be such places of mystery and wonder, are now within a £20 flight (with tax, luggage charge and environmental levy on top of course) from an airport near you. The Internet has given us a wonderful opportunity to broaden our horizons and experience the true meaning of the phrase 'The Beautiful Game'.

Possibly the most successful international football tournament ever held coincided with the fortieth anniversary of '66. The 2006 World Cup in Germany featured twelve stadia in twelve cities which were either completely rebuilt for the tournament or were constructed especially for it at a cost of over $2 billion, including the outstanding Allianz Arena in Munich, all of which are still used today, with an average of 49,000 fans visiting them on a bi-weekly basis. The German Bundesliga is unsurprisingly still the most popular destination for today's football tourist, with cheap tickets, outstanding stadiums filled with atmosphere, great food and the ability to have a beer whilst watching a game. On a typical weekend, budget airlines fly from the UK to more than twenty regional airports across Germany, meaning that almost every corner of the country can be reached within a couple of hours of home.

There have of course been a number of key factors that have broadened our horizons. The liberalisation of the skies, with budget airlines now making travel overseas not only affordable to the wealthy but to us all. The internet has placed everything we need to travel on a laptop, tablet or smartphone. The bloodied Balkans post-'89 seem a faraway memory now, political and cultural stability means that few places seem too risky to visit and despite the crash the European economies are stable enough too for a flight and hotel booking not to be too big an ask either. It all means that fans no longer view football overseas as something mad, bad, dangerous, or all three. Today's savvy football traveller doesn't need a guidebook, a map or knowledge of local language; they're all there via a Wi-Fi connection. Travel has not only broadened our horizons but also changed our perceptions. Football has become the universal cultural currency. As long as we stick to the football we can converse with locals in backstreet bars of Lisbon, Lima and Limassol without knowing a word of the local language. We no longer fear our fellow overseas fans but embrace them in a way that politicians and the media often struggle to understand.

A decent proportion of twenty-first century football fans have discovered the joys of overseas away trips and have never looked back. Our attitudes and perceptions have changed as we have experienced what football and travel is like across the Channel, and beyond too. Social media has allowed us to share our experiences, ask advice from fans thousands of miles away and, of course, show off our photos. Today, unlike in '66, watching international football in the countries and the leagues from which those foreign teams came is just a click away and few of us would want it any other way.

Politicians have struggled for years to find the key to internationalism, yet it isn't economic or political change that has had the biggest popular impact. It's been the mix of globalisation, football and travel. Never mind high culture or diplomacy; if you want to know what a popular cosmopolitan culture might look like, look no further than today's football tourist.

Two Tribes

Nick Davidson

THERE'S THE BEGINNINGS of a flow of radical, progressive ideas between football fans in Germany and those on *die Insel*. The original "Kult" club, FC St. Pauli, marked its centenary in 2010 with a friendly match against FC United of Manchester. Non-league Dulwich Hamlet has established a firm friendship with another Hamburg team, Altona 93. These two clubs were both founded in 1893 and played a friendly match in Germany in 1925, although the relationship was only recently rekindled, born out of a ground-hopping trip to Germany and shared values of anti-racism, anti-sexism and anti-homophobia. Dulwich and Altona met again at Dulwich's Champion Hill ground in July 2015 for a friendly match ninety years on from the original fixture, and there are plans for Dulwich to, once again, travel to Hamburg in 2018 to celebrate both clubs' 125th anniversary. Then there's Clapton FC, whose Scaffold Brigada ultra group draw inspiration from various left-wing fan groups and who displayed a "Free Valentin" banner at their home game against Enfield 1893 in August 2015, expressing solidarity with an anti-fascist Werder Bremen fan who was arrested by police following clashes with local neo-Nazis.

From the wreckage of modern football there is emerging a different type of fan who wants something more than the Premier League can provide. It is proof that globalisation can work both ways, that it doesn't just have to equate to the centralisation of talent, money and resources in the self-proclaimed "Best League in the World." Via cheapish train and air travel across Europe, plus the internet and social media, globalisation has helped shape an internationalist resistance. Well-organised, committed fans who far from just being "Against Modern Football" are proposing an alternative, trying to shape the football culture of the future.

Globalisation and co-operation are important drivers behind these new forces for change in modern football culture, but there's a backstory too.

A radical, anti-authoritarian football culture is perfectly illustrated by the Christmas Truce of 1914. Sure, it was the German troops singing "*Stille Nacht*" (aka "Silent Night") on Christmas Eve that first united two sets of predominantly working class soldiers from both sides of the trenches in a spontaneous celebration. But football provided the facilitator to turn this into their coming together in No Man's Land.

After another World War, there was Bert Trautmann – a German prisoner-of-war turned Manchester City goalkeeping stalwart, best remembered for playing the last fifteen minutes of the 1956 FA Cup final with a broken neck.

There's an even earlier instance too, September 1908, when, Leipzig-born Max Seeburg made his one and only appearance for Tottenham Hotspur, becoming the first European-born player to play professional football in England. He went on to make a number of appearances for Leyton, Burnley and Grimsby Town.

It would be a while longer before an Englishman played in the German League. But when it happened, it happened in style. In the summer of 1977, Kevin Keegan became Liverpool's second-most-famous export to the city of Hamburg when he landed "head over heels" at Hamburger Sport-Verein. Unlike the Beatles, Keegan was already a household name when he arrived in the city on the banks of the Elbe. He was financially astute too; a release clause in his Liverpool contract kept his transfer fee at £500,000, allowing him to trouser a reported £250,000-a-year salary (including endorsements). But it wasn't the money that sent shockwaves through English football, it was the fact that Keegan had turned down offers from the established European superpowers in Spain and Italy and instead opted for northern Germany and HSV. True, they'd won the Cup Winners' Cup in 1977, but they were hardly a European powerhouse or even the first name that rolled off the tongue of English fans quizzed about West German football at the time. In the school playgrounds of Britain that honour fell upon Borussia Mönchengladbach, partly for their success in European competition throughout the 1970s but mostly for their tongue-twister of a name. In those days they, together with Bayern Munich, were the only German club that most football fans in England had heard of. What Keegan achieved on the pitch in his three seasons in Hamburg is well documented, but culturally he achieved almost as much in terms of raising the awareness of West German football amongst fans back home in England. Others followed, although it was more of a trickle than a flood. Perhaps most famously, after Keegan, was Tony Woodcock who had two spells with 1. FC Köln and a stint at crosstown rivals Fortuna. In a time before widespread TV coverage of European competition, it was news of these trailblazing exports along with the crackly commentary of Bryon Butler, Ron Jones and Jimmy Armfield on Radio 2's *Mid-Week Sports Special* that taught us all we knew about German and, indeed, European football.

It was nearly twenty years before Germany sent a player of equal stature to Keegan back to England. Jürgen Klinsmann arrived at Tottenham Hotspur in 1994, one of the first marquee signings in the all-new Premier League era. Universally derided as a "diver" on arrival in England, he won fans round in a similar fashion to Trautmann all those years before. He both confirmed and contradicted long-held German stereotypes. His "German efficiency" in the box saw him average a goal every other game in his time at Spurs, but he also subverted that other lazy stereotype of Germans having no sense of humour by making the "Klinsmann dive" his trademark goal celebration. The sheer volume of international superstars that followed Klinsmann to the Premier League somewhat diluted the uniqueness of his cultural legacy, but it was another gentle nod to the strength of German football, as if the German national team's success at international level wasn't enough already.

These individual players moving between England and Germany and vice-versa are significant in as much as they raised awareness and piqued interest in football in each other's countries at a time when you had to squint at European scores in the results sections of the newspaper or wait on the arrival of that month's *World Soccer* for a league table and a bit more insight. Yet, even back in the 1970s, it wasn't just Keegan and Woodcock who moved between England and West Germany; ideas and inspiration were flowing too.

It is not clear what impact the atmosphere inside the stadiums at the 1966 World Cup Finals had on the relatively small number of fans visiting from West Germany. But according to Thomas Kozinowski of St. Pauli's *Der Übersteiger* fanzine, notable games in the early years of European football that helped frame this appreciation of each other's fan cultures included: the European Cup Eintracht Frankfurt vs Glasgow Rangers in 1960; Hamburg vs Burnley in the quarter-final a year later; the Cup Winners' Cup final West Ham vs Munich 1860 at Wembley in '65; followed by Liverpool's defeat to Borussia Dortmund in the '66 final of the same competition. Cumulatively these, and other matches too, had a definite impact on German fans who travelled to their side's games in Great Britain, and the many more who listened to them on the radio, watched on TV or read the match reports in a newspaper.

We should also perhaps pay our respects to Archibald Leitch and others, as stadium architecture played its part too. In the 1970s and '80s most grounds in Germany were multipurpose stadiums with a running track, distancing fans from the action. This contrasted sharply with stadiums in England where, aside from a few lingering greyhound tracks, fans were tight to the pitch, creating an intense and sometimes intimidating atmosphere. It is a point noted by Uli Hesse, author of *Tor! The Story of German Football*, who told me, "I come from Dortmund and we were always proud when people said our ground was like an English ground and our fans like English fans... Dortmund and Kaiserlautern were different, so people often compared us to the English." There was a definite deference to the English style of support, with the Anfield Kop frequently referenced as an example of everything that was good about English support. Kozinowski emphasises the point:

> German football fans always had a huge admiration for England as the birthplace of modern football and particular British clubs as its 'ambassadors', something still that could be seen on the jeans vests – the Kutten – in the form of badges of a particular British club or pieces in Union Jack style.

Of course, English (or British) terrace culture was an influence and an inspiration, but it wasn't reproduced as a facsimile in German grounds, it was adapted and mixed with other influences. Uli Hesse points out that after the 1974 World Cup on home soil, German fans increasingly developed their own style, many developing the *Kutten* into a full-on metal-head look; also songs and klaxon horns were imported from West German ice-hockey. Nevertheless, and despite the organised and relentless chanting of German ultra-groups these days, English football fans still retain a certain mystique when it comes to singing. According to Hesse:

> As late as 2001, when Liverpool played Alavés in Dortmund, many Germans were literally in awe when the English fans started to sing. Maybe they don't do it as often and as loudly anymore as they used to, but boy – the English can still sing their hearts out better than anyone else.

By the 1980s, another aspect of English fan culture was mirrored in West Germany: hooliganism. Football had a bad reputation in the 1980s, so much so that when viewed alongside the success of Boris Becker and Steffi Graff there was a popular desire that tennis, not football, should become West Germany's national sport. In 1990 West German clubs voted to reduce the Bundesliga to sixteen teams because they feared the game wasn't popular enough to sustain eighteen clubs. Quite incredible when, in England, Italia '90 is seen as the turning point in the popularity of English football and led directly to the creation of the Premier League.

Whilst it is too simplistic to say that football hooliganism was less obviously political and more tribal in England, the influence of neo-Nazi groups was more overt on West German terraces in the 1980s. Uli Hesse recalls his experience supporting Dortmund:

> Well, I stopped going to away games, because the hassle was just too much... And this atmosphere, I regret to say, was also prevalent during home games. We had a really notorious right-wing supporters group in Dortmund, the *Borussenfront*, and you had to try and find ways of staying away from them.

Uli Hesse's account is similar to that of Sven Brux, founder of St. Pauli's *Fanladen*. Sven had been a 1. FC Köln fan as a youngster, but on discovering punk he found it harder and harder to attend games at the Müngersdorfer Stadion for fear of being set upon by right-wing fans angered by his different way of dressing. Sven moved to Hamburg to serve his *Zivildienst* (a type of community service that was an alternative to military conscriptioon) and his involvement in the city's punk scene soon led him to St. Pauli's Millerntor Stadion where he established the club's fan project, organising transport to away matches, and helped ensure St. Pauli became a club that stood firmly against these neo-Nazis that held sway on the terraces of other clubs at the time.

Why was German fan culture in the 1980s politicised in a way that was much rarer in England? Context is important here. Germans were still living in a divided country, they were at the very epicentre of a Cold War that was being played out in front of them. More and more American nuclear weapons were being located in West Germany and this as a result galvanised the peace movement and led to the growth of the Green Party. As Uli Hesse notes, "It was just the natural thing to do for a young German male or female during this era to, well, care about things. It was very difficult to *not* be political if you came of age in the 80s."

If the downside of this radicalisation was neo-Nazi groups on the terraces then the upside, as the decade drew to a close, was the response from other, progressive fan groups. Inspired by the fanzine movement – English fanzines like *When Saturday Comes* were an important stimulus but so was expertise derived from the German punk and alternative music-zine scene – fans became organised and began to win the battle against right-wing groups. Uli Hesse illustrates the point:

> Realising that you could do something like that with football was certainly a crucial moment for German fan culture, because in those pre-internet days you had to find a way of getting in touch with like-minded people just to become aware of how many like-minded people there were! Until I delved into that football fanzine scene, I had no idea that thousands and thousands of fans all across the country were fighting for the same things.

The tide began to turn. Real progress was made on the terraces.

Sönke Goldbeck, another FC St. Pauli fan, identifies the importance of this change coming from the fans themselves:

> The fact is that those responsible for limiting the power of right-wing groups in the stands were mostly the supporters themselves and this was only possible because of the organised, active support. It was an approach to fight it from the 'below' rather than the 'top-down' tactic that was used in England. There the 'unwanted' elements were driven out by higher ticket prices and extremely strict rules, removing most of the 'good guys' from a working class background as well.

It is was this difference in approach that began to signal a parting of the ways between German and English football culture.

Football in England had experienced the terrible tragedies of Bradford and Hillsborough that then forced the modernisation of all-seater stadiums. That's not to say that the German football authorities didn't consider following English football's example and a move towards all-seater stadiums. Today, Borussia Dortmund's "Yellow Wall" is held up as an example of how terracing works, but Uli Hesse recalls:

> Most people don't realise how close we came to losing the terraces. Today, the people who run Borussia Dortmund are proud of the south stand and probably give themselves a pat on the back every day for having had the good sense to first preserve and then actually enlarge the terrace. But we, meaning the fans, had to plead with them to do this! In the 1990s, there were regular meetings between club representatives and fan delegates. And those delegates had to use all their powers of persuasion to stop the club from making the ground all-seater.

One of the strengths of German fan culture has always been the effective networking across fan groups, bypassing traditional club rivalries, and good nationwide organisation. This has allowed German fans to campaign effectively against not only the removal of their much-loved terraces but also ticket pricing, match-day policing and kick-off times. In 1993, *BAFF* (Alliance of Active Fans) was formed as an alliance of various different fan groups, and has campaigned relentlessly ever since against racism and fascism in German football alongside other important issues including the fight against sexism, homophobia and the campaign to legalise pyrotechnics in stadiums. In 2001, another alliance of active fans came together under the banner "Pro 15:30" focussing principally on the single issue of games kicking-off at their traditional 3.30pm on a Saturday afternoon. As in England, the more money television companies paid for the rights to screen games the more they wanted control of the kick-off times.

The Pro 15:30 movement has evolved into an organisation called ProFans and in 2009 they published an eight-point plan outlining their defence of fan culture. It stated that: fan culture was indispensable to the game; fans were not criminals by virtue of just being football fans; more needed to be done to reduce police oppression and violence; terracing remains vital to a vibrant fan culture in the same way that the 50+1 rule protects clubs from becoming the plaything of big business; fans deserve freedom of expression inside the stadium, not harassment and confiscation of banners; a sensible discussion needs to take place regarding the use of pyrotechnics in the stadium; everyone should be welcome to join ProFans except those groups with far-right connections; and finally that they should be able to engage in honest and constructive dialogue with the football authorities and the police.

Apart from these national fan campaigns there are at individual clubs dedicated "Fan projects" (institutions with a degree of autonomy from the parent club that work on engaging the local community and supporting fans with anything from ticketing to legal services) and the highly organised ultra-groups (virtually all German sides have at least one ultra-group – in this context: highly motivated and organised fans who lead the singing in their section of the stadium and produce the incredible displays of choreography on show in stadiums prior to kick-off, and that often, though not always, have acknowledged political leanings). Collectively German fan groups are organised, established and visible.

Yet despite their fans being renowned across Europe for the incredible atmosphere inside the stadiums and the Bundesliga respected for keeping ticket prices affordable, there are still those in positions of authority in German football who look enviously towards England and the "Premier League model." A model that generates almost limitless income through ever-improving TV deals, tempts the best (or at least the highest paid) players in the world, and attracts investment from billionaire overseas owners.

Average Bundesliga attendance broke above the 40,000 mark back in the 2005–06 season and has not fallen below since, but as Roland Reng, author of *Matchdays – The Hidden Story of the Bundesliga*, points out, "the money made from selling those tickets played a smaller role than ever. By now, gate-receipts accounted for only about 30% of club budgets." Television is king, and the rights deals negotiated by the Premier League remain the envy of the football world. There are, of course, massive concerns amongst German fan groups about the direction football in the country is heading. The continual subtle erosion of the 50+1 rule threatens to tip the balance in favour of those like Karl Heinz Rummenigge who clearly favour aligning German football to the lucrative English model. The continued success of clubs backed by large corporations like TSG 1899 Hoffenheim (backed by the Dietmar Hopp, owner of SAP software giant) or FC Ingolstadt 04 (promoted to the Bundesliga in 2015 and backed, since their creation via a merger in 2004, by car manufacturer Audi) has done nothing to quell the desire for the loosening of ownership rules.

With even the robust German model under threat, in what state do we find the radical fan scene on *die Insel?* Football in England appears at the top level to have an almost magical ability to dodge the omnipresent politics and effects of austerity that have dominated everyday life in the UK since 2008. In the Premiership TV deals are ever more flabbergastingly extravagant; the same goes for money spent on transfer fees. Ticket prices continue to completely out-strip inflation and yet attendance in the Premiership continues to rise (in 2013–14 the average top-flight attendance of 36,695 was the highest since 1950, with grounds showing a 95.9% seat-occupancy rate). In short, there is no sign of the Premier League bubble bursting. On this evidence, the conditions for an alternative, progressive fan culture don't seem particularly favourable. And yet, a radical and very different form of football support and governance, heavily influenced by the German fan scene, continues to grow. It represents the closing of the circle –

German fan culture initially inspired by the atmosphere at English stadiums in the 1960s and '70s is now a source of inspiration and hope for emergent fan groups across the United Kingdom.

It is a development that has made Uli Hesse smile:

> I always say that this is the most bewildering development in my life as a football fan: when I was a kid, we all wanted to be like the English, now the English want to be like us. The mind boggles. I think a major reason why so many English fans are so fascinated by German football is that great English character trait – nostalgia. I took two Villa fans to Dortmund's Südtribüne and they both said it reminded them of how English football used to be before it turned totally corporate: affordable tickets, crowded terraces, electric atmosphere, watching a game with a beer in your hands.

In Manchester a story has unfolded that shows the potential for turning an occasionally over-romanticised nostalgia for an imperfect past into action to create a better tomorrow: the formation of FC United of Manchester. Disillusioned Manchester United fans, unhappy with the takeover of their famous club by the American Glazer family, took the drastic step of setting up their new club founded on the principle of "one member, one vote." Giving every member a say in the future direction of the club is a powerful tool but, of course, not every fan wishes to get bogged down in the minutiae of running a football club – atmosphere, fan culture and the actual *football* continue to play an equally, in fact for most, more, important part in FC United's popularity.

There are two sides to the rejection of modern football in England. There's the "nostalgic" angle, wanting to be free of the restrictions placed upon football fans in the mainstream, the desire to have a beer and to stand on a terrace and sing. Then, there's the desire for governance, the feeling that for too long greedy and opportunistic club chairmen have been able to asset-strip our football clubs for their own gain. It's a phenomenon that has seen the rise in supporters trust-owned, phoenix clubs. Hereford FC, AFC Rushden & Diamonds, Aldershot Town and countless others represent a fan-owned alternative to clubs run as private businesses with only the most cursory of "fit and proper" checks on those taking over a football club.

Increasingly there is a third dimension: those football fans who crave a radical political football-fan culture, in the style of FC St. Pauli and other German clubs such as SV Babelsberg 03 from Potsdam. FC United covers all three bases to varying degrees. The fan ownership is there, as is the intense, ultra-style support from the terraces; the club is also, broadly speaking, left-wing. Edmund Barrett, who writes the *FCUM A.D.* blog, is perfectly positioned to comment, being both a FC United and FC St. Pauli fan who lives in Dortmund, and travels regularly to watch both teams. He believes:

> FC United is a political club although much of that is just a whiff of leftwing politics due to us being in a leftwing-ish city. If you go to a match you will encounter a crowd that doesn't tolerate racism, at least questions sexism and where lesbian and gay fans have always been welcome. Most fans aren't overtly political, they aren't overtly anything other than FC United fans. Those who are overtly "political" – fanzines with left-wing content, the Refugees Welcome banner, antiracism messages – are rarely challenged and it seems to have generally been met with enthusiasm and positive feedback.

Again, the mix is important; not all fans have turned their back on mainstream, modern football, they don't want to change the world, many just want to have a good time, or as Edmund Barrett puts it:

> I don't really feel the need to change football, or only have fan owned football. All I know is that whatever FC United has

achieved over the last 10 years has allowed me to stand with my mates, at cheap prices, in an environment of lefties and have a great time. And when I've felt the need to speak up or dip into football politics, at least I have had the chance to do it.

In the top two divisions groups such as Aston Villa's Brigada 1874, Crystal Palace's Homesdale Fanatics and Red Faction at Middlesborough are well-supported fan groups with antifascist leanings that have also tackled issues like racism and homophobia in football. But on the whole it is further down the football pyramid in England that the spaces are more open for an alternative, politicised fan culture. There are fewer restrictions placed on fans regarding alcohol and standing but also it is possible for these fans to be numerically important and therefore change the prevailing atmosphere (or, indeed, create an atmosphere from scratch) at a club. This has happened in a number of cases, the most widely known example currently being Clapton FC. The Clapton Ultras or "Scaffold Brigada" occupy a rickety stand constructed, unsurprisingly, out of scaffolding and plastered with left-wing campaign stickers from all over Europe. Working class fans rub shoulders with hardened activists and members of the Polish immigrant community who have adopted Clapton as their own. Attila the Stockbroker, a fan of St. Pauli as well as his hometown club Brighton and Hove Albion, wrote in the *Morning Star* about what Clapton means to him:

Clapton are one of the latest clubs to benefit from fans' disillusionment with modern football and I joined the hundred-strong and growing Scaffold Brigada at the Old Spotted Dog ground for an afternoon of pyrotechnics, banners, beer on the terraces and basically everything you aren't allowed to do at league football these days. I had a great time.

Rather than battling to change the institutions (a Premier League or Championship club, the Premier League, the FA, right up to UEFA and FIFA) fans are creating a fan culture in their own image and on their own terms. It's not about changing football as a whole, but instead about living out an alternative, albeit in miniature. If the Occupy Movement was about creating a public space to both discuss politics and live out an alternative, then are the examples of FC United, Clapton and Dulwich football's equivalent? Why form a protest group about the lack of terracing at football matches, when you can just stand? Why campaign against the Glazers owning "your" football club when you can create your own? Supporting a football club doesn't have to conform to the existing power structures. It can be radical, it can be democratic and it can be fun.

From small beginnings – there's nothing much more grassroots than Sunday League football – there is almost no limit to the imagination once fans start on this journey. Easton Cowboys in Bristol is a community sports and social club established in 1992. They play a variety of sports in local Sunday leagues but also take part in numerous anti-racist tournaments around the world, including the hugely popular *Mondiali Antirazzisti* (Anti-Racist World Cup) tournament. They've toured Mexico and played against the Zapatistas. Republica Internationale in Leeds is a Sunday League side that was founded by a collection of people involved in fund-raising and community activities; they fight intolerance and promote equality through football. In November 2014, a joint Easton-Republica women's team toured Palestine aiming to build solidarity under the slogan "Freedom through Football."

Across Europe networks have helped sustain and nourish a radical fan culture which localised initiatives increasingly see themselves as part of. Networking, aided by social media, has begun to enable like-minded football fans in the UK to come together and to organise – using the internet, Facebook and Twitter in the same way that fans in the 1980s would share and swap fanzines to com-

municate. Fans are realising they are not alone in their dissatisfaction with modern football. FAN (Football Action Network) was
established to create a network of football activists and intends
to "focus upon what unites rather than divides us and use this
as a starting-point for collaborative, innovative, provocative but
humorous, eye-catching activities and protests across the football
community." Along with a new generation of fanzines like *STAND*
we are beginning to see a coming-together of fans with common
aims. Whether it is greater fan representation, an "ultra"-style
atmosphere, or a radical focus on social issues, there are forces
now at work in England challenging the prevailing culture of
blandness that has engulfed English stadiums for a generation.

And if the authorities' regulations and restrictions limit the
chance to generate these kinds of initiatives in the higher reaches
of English football then fans have shown a willingness to recreate
this vibrancy elsewhere instead. Anyone who has visited Dulwich
Hamlet FC's Champion Hill ground could hardly fail to notice the
passion, politics and humour of their fans. At Dulwich these fans
have achieved a unique and difficult balance. They have taken
the club's existing support along with them for the ride. They've
actively engaged with the local community and it has paid dividends. Over 3000 fans turned up for the final home game of the
2014–15 season against Maidstone, an unprecedented attendance for football at this level, the Ryman Premier League, three
divisions below League Two. The humour of all remains every
bit as, probably more, important than the political motivations
of some. Altona 93 might be the inspiration but, at Dulwich, the
atmosphere and the radical politics all come with a large helping of very English self-depreciation. To get all sociological for a
moment, the prefigurative is combined with situationist *détournement*. The active supporter base at Dulwich, The Rabble, are creating a real alternative to modern football. In fact, as the pink and
blue banner proudly proclaims, Dulwich are actively "For Future
Football" – it's a positive spin backed up by action, but one done

with that flourish of punk *détournement*. This is exemplified by the ComFast Chapter supporters' group. In an interview on *vice.com* website, Robert Molloy-Vaughan from the group set out their utopian vision:

> Let's get robots, automated factories and 3D printers doing all the labour. Let's have – at most – ten-hour working weeks. Let's have more leisure time for people to spend watching Dulwich Hamlet. That, for me, is hopefully what the future of football will be.

It's brilliant on every level – both a genuine hope for the future and an outlandish imagined vision. I hope they can make it work.

German and English fans have always had far more that unites us than divides us. Fans from *die Insel*, wary of how much ground they themselves conceded to the Premier League and television, stand shoulder-to-shoulder with their German counterparts as they fight against the creeping tentacles of commercialism that threaten to engulf the Bundesliga. It is a cause particularly keenly championed by those British fans who travel regularly to watch football in Germany; for them German football is both a window to the past and a mirror to the future. It reminds us how good watching football from the terraces used to be, but also how good it *could* be again. If German football can resist commercialism on a Premier League scale and if English fan culture can continue to draw inspiration from Germany, then the circle of cooperation and influence will be complete.

Football from Below

Sanaa Qureshi

"I enjoy making revolution! I enjoy going to football!"
— Antonio Negri

I DON'T REMEMBER how old I was when I went to my first football match. I don't even remember who was playing. I do know that it was at Villa Park and I also know that I have not been able to forget how a full stadium felt, the way it rose and fell with the rhythm of play. The chorus of gasps and groans, the way people around me leapt and cheered and hugged strangers in unbridled, collective ecstasy. The spectacle of twenty-two men chasing a ball, sharing the burden of thousands of eyes and the weight of an imagined community, moved me to open-mouthed wonder as a child and continues to do so today.

The politics of access and participation featured almost as soon as my love affair began. Starkly aware of crowds that looked nothing like me and football facilities that failed to accommodate my burgeoning interest, the beautiful game became the formative ground upon which I first grappled with what it meant to be visible, to take up space and to play. It brought me my first experiences of collective action, something that translated later into political organising, as a potent tool of resistance to hegemonic systems.

Antonio Negri, a Marxist sociologist and political philosopher, is adamant that football cannot be separated from politics and the world around it but one should be used as a means of understanding the social relationships in the other. As I grew into myself, I was able to use football as a unique point of exploration to interpret and unpick the inequalities and injustices I encountered up close and from a distance. From the occupation of Palestine to the exploitation of low-paid labour and the lingering effects of colonialism, football has provided me with fresh perspectives on systems of power and how to resist them.

My activism with Football Beyond Borders (FBB) has allowed me to bring all of this together into practical, substantive action through campaigning, writing, researching and supporting young people via the medium of football. FBB has played a pivotal role in linking the determined political work of Palestinian solidarity activists with football fans to bring to the fore the myriad ways politics was violently interacting with football in Palestine and why this mattered.

In August 2015 a match between Al-Ahli and Shujaiyeh, two Palestinian football teams from the West Bank and Gaza respectively, briefly overcame the violence of the Israeli occupation to produce the kind of ecstasy and belonging that football is famed for. The first leg was a historic moment as Al-Ahli travelled to Gaza for a goalless draw was played out in front of a jubilant and packed crowd at the Yarmouk Stadium. Two weeks later, Shujaiyeh played the second leg in the West Bank. After fifteen years, Israel, in an uncharacteristic show of leniency, had allowed footballers to travel between the West Bank and Gaza. Al-Ahli won 1-0 but as Ahmad As-Salayme (a youth player with Al-Ahli) noted, there are no losers between brothers. That the games went ahead was momentous in itself, the scoreline merely a footnote in the wider struggle to reclaim a homeland.

Football is unrivalled in its power to unite people and communities. But it remains rooted in the structural and social inequalities that continue to plague society, and in the process, rather than challenging them, too often it reproduces them. The nature of football in occupied Palestine is perhaps the most salient reminder of this.

FIFA was one of the first and is still one of the only truly international organisations to recognise Palestine as a legitimate state. It is on football's global sporting stage that Palestinians have been able to reaffirm the existence that is so routinely denied them elsewhere. However, the fate of Palestinian football is rather predictably still tied up in the volatile political situation that surrounds it. The continued occupation is accompanied by an array of violent and restrictive measures that ensure footballing joy is at once exhilarating and fleeting.

Under the occupation, Palestinian footballers have been shot at checkpoints, their feet and legs the explicit targets. They continue to be regularly detained without charge, their homes bombed, lives in tatters and their footballing careers marked almost irrelevant up against the tides of death. The Israeli focus on repressing Palestinian football is intentional. With some meaningful international recognition and as an ever-emboldening symbol of resistance, Israel is aware of the resonance of football. Crushing the Palestinian football team means crushing an avenue to express joy and demonstrate resilience.

This is particularly pertinent when considering the actual dynamics of Palestine's national team. With a diaspora unable to return home and an occupation that prevents free travel between communities, the Palestinian football team exists as a crucial symbol representing the global Palestinian experience. The national team features players from various parts of Palestine, including the West Bank and Gaza, players forced to ply their trade abroad, players from diaspora Palestinian communities and players of Palestinian heritage. The Palestinian national team embodies both physical and political unity to a global audience of millions.

The Palestinian women's football team sits at the very unique nexus of not only having to overcome the obstacles of occupation faced by the men's team but also having to navigate the acute patriarchy of the world's most popular sport. Considered primarily a men's game, women's football teams are often relegated to a sideshow, with poor support, funding and facilities the norm across countries where the men's game is a multi-billion dollar industry. In Palestine, this is exacerbated by the cruel movement restrictions imposed by Israel that mean they are only able to meet in full on foreign soil while at home they are forced to hold training sessions on concrete handball pitches. Despite this, the women's team have a stadium to play in, a dedicated contingent of support, and a women's league that features women desperate to represent their beleaguered country and inspire resistance.

International football tournaments are now amongst the most-watched sporting events in the world, so it should come as no surprise that this mediated terrain has been expertly exploited by governing bodies and sponsors to promote their brands and products with great success. With an unrivalled global audience, millions of pounds are spent securing television rights, buying sponsorships and advertising space during football's World Cup. The same audiences that might bear witness to a Palestine forged by their football team competing in a World Cup-qualifying campaign have also been the recipients of Israel's public-relations onslaught that intends to whitewash their ongoing occupation.

The failure to impose any kind of sanctions on Israel of the sort Apartheid South Africa faced during the 1970s and 1980s from FIFA demonstrates Israel's successful acquisition of international legitimacy for its deadly punitive actions, and wholesale discrimination, against Palestinians and the complicity of those in power for supporting a settler-colonial state. The backing of Israel has been steadfast, despite repeated calls to suspend them for deliberately targeting Palestinian football activities through physical and logistical violence.

In 2013, Israel arrived as a host nation on the world football stage when it hosted the UEFA Under-21 European Championships. A multi-million-pound budget was provided to organise the tournament and to prove to the international community that Israel was a safe, vibrant and exciting place to visit. Elsewhere the awarding of international sporting events is now followed by mass evictions, increased state surveillance, social cleansing and the privatisation of public space. In Israel all of these features were already in place. By awarding this tournament and refusing

to heed calls to BDS (Boycott, Divest, Sanction), UEFA was signify-
ing its willingness to ignore the ongoing brutal and lethal treatment of Palestinians.

Israel's inclusion as a UEFA member state came about after two
decades of a nomadic existence after exclusion from the Asian
Football Association in 1974. In the Asian Games of the same
year, Kuwait and North Korea refused to play against Israel, thus
setting in motion a political exile that continues to this day. That
countries in the AFA were able to exploit the machinery of world
football to comfort their consciences is testament to the some-
times-messy intersection between the sporting and diplomatic
worlds. Owing to security concerns and the ongoing belligerence
of Israel, it is unlikely that this situation will change. This not
only denies Israel any genuine chance of World Cup qualification
but also a chance to really test the soft power wielded by football.
A return to the AFA and competitive fixtures against their neighbours may put pressure on Israel to at the very least ease restrictions on Palestinian football. However, this raises the crucial
question of whether encouraging normalised football relationships will ever undo or mitigate the merciless Israeli occupation.

Although Sepp Blatter was instrumental in the recognition of
Palestine by FIFA, he also worked hard to depoliticise the conflict
through the avenue of football. By calling for a "peace match"
whilst the Palestine FA were lobbying to have Israel suspended
for their actions towards Palestinian footballers, Blatter demonstrated his desire to disengage with the Palestinian struggle in
favour of empty PR. His attempts to negotiate with Israel and Palestine on an equal footing belie the very unequal ground upon
which they sit, as occupier and occupied respectively.

As illegal Israeli settlements increase at a pace and Israel's violent occupation shows no signs of abating, football for Palestinians will remain political, as a collective expression of national
identity and as a tool of resistance. This is whilst Israel asserts
its own national identity through the exact same avenue. It is an
instance where we are exposed not only to the specific contradic-

tions present when football is used to consolidate and build on a national identity, but more broadly, the complexities of the game, as a source of both great promise and destruction.

Despite an increasingly globalised world, where in the last ten years, football clubs such as Manchester United, Real Madrid, Barcelona and Bayern Munich have become global brands, international football remains understandably pinned to the idea of triumphant nation states. Thus state orders are reinforced and a popular nationalism is commodified. As part of this, England's World Cup win in 1966 remains, justifiably, a great source of national pride. The memories of that victory continue to fuel contemporary ideas of what success for the national team looks like.

In 1996, thirty years after the famous win, England hosted the European Championships and St George's flags, for the first time in my short life, were inescapable. Perhaps it was because England were facing Scotland in the group stages or because England were hosts, but somehow, the Union flag, with all those colonial traumas stitched into its fabric, was replaced by the St George's flag as the English patriot's symbol of choice.

However, somewhere amidst the fervour of late 1990s "Cool Britannia" and New Labour, the St George's flag also became the divisive symbol of the bullish, racist nationalism of the British National Party. Virtually no broadcast or news story about the BNP came without the familiar sight of the red and white flags or supporters adorned in England football shirts. With the far-right party picking up council seats and their candidates contesting parliamentary elections and holding on to their deposits, their rhetoric became mainstream. Thus, the St George's flag became synonymous with modern English fascism. Moreover, the formation and subsequent rise of the English Defence League (EDL) was closely linked to a subculture of football fans coming together against their imagined enemy of Islam. Members often seen draped in football paraphernalia, specifically England shirts, routinely take part in violent street demonstrations.

It is undeniable that English nationalism, footballing or otherwise, is viscerally bound up with an aggressive racism that demarcates who belongs and who is the unwanted Other. Invariably, there are groups of people, particularly those who have been targets of the BNP or EDL, that are reluctant to embrace the English national team and the associated aggressive patriotism.

Yet despite, or perhaps because of, how vigorously England, the St George's flag and the support of the national team has been hijacked by the isolating politics of nationalism, people believe the potential for subversion is even greater. Individuals and groups from minority communities in Britain have sought to reclaim the idea of Englishness from the far-right and to broaden the understanding of what it means to identify as English. Progressive ideals have been situated underneath a banner of nationalism that purports to be inclusive, welcoming and multi-cultural. England shirts have been worn proudly, the red and white a signal of support for a new, refreshed demonstration of Englishness.

Movements to reclaim and rebrand words and cultural associations have been favoured as a means of asserting alternative theories and ideas, albeit incrementally. However, it is difficult to assess how useful or sustainable this attempted reclamation can be without the accompaniment of the wholesale reframing of the issue, in this case, the concept of the English nation state. Further, can it be considered realistic for people of colour to reform an identity whose values are intrinsically bound up with whiteness?

Feelings of alienation are often exacerbated when international football tournaments come around and the success of the nation state appears to be so heavily hinged on the success of the national football team. Fifty years on England's famous victory football has irrefutably shaped what English national success looks like and at the same time continues to provide a tool to interrogate what Englishness looks like. The commodification of nationalism through international sporting events thus serves as a useful means to understand how collective identities are fractured, formed and expressed through football.

The relationship between nationalism and football is complex and often fraught with reactionary politics. However, the sport also serves an important role in the formation of collective national identity in post-colonial states. Famously, Algerian players in the French league formed the Front de Liberation Nationale (FLN) in 1958, a team that exported the desire for Algerian self-determination and liberation from the French throughout North Africa, the Middle East, parts of Europe and Asia. Similarly, the Iraqi national team's achievements in the 2007 Asia Cup were set against a backdrop of continued violence, occupation and logistical difficulties. Victory brought together an often fragmented country and a sense of Iraqi national pride was keenly felt throughout.

French success in the 1998 World Cup, which was also held on home turf, was heralded as a defining moment in the previously difficult narrative of integration. With a team led by the inimitable Zinedine Zidane, French-born to Algerian parents, and composed of players whose backgrounds told a story of French colonialism, this was supposed to be a turning point in French race relations. Instead, it has come to signify the shallow understanding of racial, economic and social inequality that continues to plague French society. The World Cup victory of a multi-cultural France allowed the French state and media to temporarily plaster over deep fissures without addressing the root causes of discontent. Owing to the universal nature of the game, the cohesion and success of a football team can be very easily translated into populist notions of unity and togetherness. Likewise, these concepts are often inspired by the collective spirit integral to team sports.

Despite its limitations, international football is situated in a unique position, where individual relationships with the state coalesce into either a collective sense of belonging or unbelonging. To be able to understand how people and communities relate to their national football team is to gain an insight into how they relate both to themselves and where they live.

The burgeoning cultural and financial potency of world football has benefited from an increasingly networked, globalised world. Football has grown in stature as a worldwide game, transcending borders, languages, races and religions. The simplicity and the aesthetics of play have contributed to its ascendant popularity, whilst free-market economics have encouraged both the corporatisation and commodification of the game.

Investment in stadium infrastructure in England was kickstarted by the birth of the Premier League and the virtual end of live-televised league football on free domestic channels. Ultimately, the transformation of how the sport was both accessed and managed lay in the increased exposure provided by Sky TV. Principal income streams switched from match-day takings, including tickets and merchandise, to the ever-growing sums from TV deals, while the football stadiums became sites for executive boxes, naming rights and touchline-to-touchline advertising and sponsorship.

In line with neoliberal economics, the influx of new money did not remove inequality but instead exacerbated it. Well-established football clubs that already had money were able to tighten their financial grip on professional football, whilst those at the lower end of the spectrum continue to drift further away, facing administration and a future of financial uncertainty. As television money pours into the English Premier League, the maldistribution of wealth is a salient reminder of the society it is situated in.

Alongside the increase in capital flows, labour flows have also predictably broadened, bringing players from all over the world to the top European leagues. This mobility of labour not only diversified talent but also undoubtedly improved the standards of football across the world, especially Europe where many of these players sought to forge careers. However, with this movement arose ample opportunity for exploitation, particularly of young Africans, who were trafficked on false promises to jobs that didn't exist. With such vast quantities of money thrown around at the highest levels of professional football, the potential for injustice is amplified, particularly in the search for social mobility and economic security. From countries still in recovery from the economic and social destruction suffered under British colonialism, professional football in Europe is considered a viable route out of poverty for many young men in Africa. Not dissimilar from the movement of migrant labour into often precarious, low-paid work in bad conditions in Western Europe, football is not exempt from its role in oppressive labour practices, nor is it very far removed from the spectre of colonialism. Flows of labour from the African continent also mirror neo-colonial resource-extraction models, with players viewed as raw materials that have their value added in the European academies. With fortress-Europe recklessly weaponising borders as a means of deterrence to incoming migrants, it is likely that this will only worsen in coming years, with only the most economically profitable allowed entry.

In England, the very foundation of the Premier League is the well-functioning football club, complete with the consistent exploitation of the lowest-paid workers, from club cleaners to catering staff. Despite the millions pocketed by star footballers, those at the other end of the spectrum, those who make matches possible, often scrape by on minimum wage. The astronomical increases in player wages and commercial revenues have not yet trickled down in any meaningful manner. After a lengthy and well-fought campaign by the Living Wage Foundation, the Premier League committed to ensuring all top-flight clubs will pay workers a living wage. However, this was stipulated to just include directly employed workers, excluding contracted staff, who are also often on precarious, zero-hour contracts. This short-sightedness on the part of Premier League Chief Executive Richard Scudamore demonstrated a real lack of desire to effect lasting change in labour policies not just in football but as an example to all employers. With burgeoning social and cultural influence both in England and the rest of the world, campaigners should use the football industry as a soapbox from which broader social change can be encouraged. Furthermore, for football to remain the most popular sport in the world, it should be willing to recognise its complicity in upholding systems of oppression, especially those from which it directly profits.

Amongst all the debates about whether football can be subverted to achieve social justice or if there is even a space for radical politics in a multi-billion-pound industry, one key thing stands out. Belonging. Whose game is it? Who should be most invested in the redemption of this beast? Those who are the architects of the spectacle or those who watch on, delighted? Numerous campaigns and movements speak about returning football to its roots, nostalgic for a time when football was the preserve of the working classes. Although it is true that football has been made successful through working class labour, the sport has always been controlled by the wealthy, capitalist classes. Codified in public schools, football was initially introduced to working class men as a means of civilising them. It is clear therefore that any reclamation of the game cannot take place at the top level – community-focused, fan-owned clubs are outliers, exceptions. To accept that this global game is too powerful, an uncontrolled monster, is not to give up on it. Instead, it allows us to focus on our communities, our local teams, our supporters groups, to direct our resources where we find utility. It offers up the potential for strength and solidarity beyond tribalism, to join up movements of resistance, from Palestine to Algeria to the militarised borders of Europe. It gives people a space in which to create a game in their own image.

Football is not separate from the society that supports it; rather it is irrevocably tied up with the most unjust systems of racism, patriarchy, homophobia, transphobia and capitalism. This, however, is precisely why the potential for resistance is so huge and necessary. The collective spirit in football, whether it's on the street or in the stadium, is unparalleled. This is what must be harnessed to unsettle and destabilise systems of power, to liberate occupied peoples and to imagine a game that we can be proud of.

In *The Wretched of the Earth*, Frantz Fanon's classic account of colonialism, he wrote:

> If sports are not incorporated into the life of the nation, in the building of the nation, if we produce national sportsmen instead of conscious individuals, then sports will quickly be ruined by professionalism and commercialism.

If it is too late for football to be used to build, we must be willing to use it to destroy.

Match Report:
The Final

West Germany vs England

Sven Goldmann

Germany Team Background

IN STOCKHOLM, a year before the final, Germany played a vital qualifying game against Sweden. The German manager, Helmut Schön, took a couple of huge risks by selecting the twenty year-old debutant Franz Beckenbauer, as well as Uwe Seeler, who was recovering from an Achilles tendon tear. Victory justified his decisions: Beckenbauer was outstanding and Seeler scored the winning goal in a 2-1 triumph.

Twelve months later, in England, Beckenbauer was the World Cup's biggest discovery of a new, young talent. With his elegance, technique and vision, he was the fresh face of a new German team that stood for beautiful football. He scored two in the 5-0 win over Switzerland in Germany's first group game, and even though his performance dropped a little in the 0-0 draw against a tough Argentinian side, he was one of the best players again in the 2-1 win against Spain. This game saw one of the most spectacular World Cup goals ever, when the Dortmund player Lothar Emmerich smashed the ball into the net from an extremely tight angle.

From then on, Emmerich was a regular in the side, but in the quarter-final against Uruguay in Sheffield, he and his teammates were a little lucky that the referee didn't see a handball on the German goal line by Karl-Heinz Schnellinger which if he had would have given the Uruguayans a penalty. Instead Siegfried Held scored a lucky opening goal thanks to a deflected shot, the South Americans lost their nerve. At the start of the second half, first Horacio Troche was sent off for fouling and slapping Uwe Seeler, and five minutes later, he was followed by Héctor Silva after an attack on Helmut Haller. Against nine Uruguayans,

Germany ran riot, finishing 4-0 winners with a goal each from Beckenbauer, again, Seeler and Haller.

The semi-final in Liverpool against the Soviet Union was a much closer game. The decisive phase at Goodison Park came just before the break, when Haller scored the first goal, and then Igor Chislenko was sent off for a foul on Siegfried Held. Germany used their numerical advantage, and Beckenbauer made it 2-0 midway through the second half but the legendary Soviet goal-keeper Lev Yashin didn't cover himself in glory when he failed to stop his long-range shot. The final minutes of the game were suddenly very exciting after a mistake by the German goalkeeper Hans Tilkowski. The Dortmund man let a harmless cross slip out of his hands and Valeriy Porkuyan tapped it in to make it 2-1. Ana-toliy Banishevski came close to scoring a Russian equaliser, but his header went just over the bar.

Franz Beckenbauer was extremely lucky. After a completely unnecessary foul on Josef Szabo, he received a second booking, which meant he was suspended for the final. FIFA however gener-ously allowed a post-match cancellation of the booking, and the German team and our young star were ready for our appearance at Wembley.

West Germany vs England Match Report

Date: 30 July 1966

Kick-off: 15.00

Venue: Wembley Stadium

West Germany line-up: Tilkowski (GK), Höttges, Schnellinger, Schulz, Weber, Beckenbauer, Haller, Overath, Seeler (C), Held, Emmerich

England line-up: Banks (GK), Cohen, Wilson, Charlton. J, Moore (C), Stiles, Ball, Charlton. R, Hurst, Peters, Hunt

Attendance: 96,924

Final score: West Germany 2 - England 4 (aet)

Goals: Haller, 12; Weber, 90; Hurst, 18, 101, 120; Peters 78

What a dramatic afternoon in London! At Wembley stadium, that cathedral of football, the German national team lost the World Cup final on Saturday, but in another sense, they are also the victors following the huge public outpouring of sympathy for this team, as human beings as much as simply players. It finished 4-2 after Germany had heroically first gone ahead then behind and finally levelled the score as full time almost came to an end. What a game! The English only triumphed after extra time, such a cruel way to finish a game and one of their decisive goals was so controversial that not one of the almost 100,000 spectators in the stadium could say with any degree of certainty that it actually was a goal.

This goal, scored by Geoff Hurst in the first half of extra time to make it 3-2, will be the topic of many discussions for some time to come. The striker from West Ham United turned and shot high and hard at goal; Germany's goalkeeper, Hans Tilkowski, may have even got his fingertips to it. The ball thundered against the crossbar and rebounded back down – and the question is whether it bounced on or behind the goal line. The Swiss referee Gottfried Dienst initially did not think it was a goal, and con-sulted his linesman, Tofiq Bahramov from the Soviet Union. He had apparently seen the ball behind the line, so Dienst changed his mind and pointed to the centre circle: goal, 3-2 for England!

The English broadcaster BBC had fourteen cameras in use for the final, but none of them recorded the controversial scene from an angle that could remove all doubt. Maybe, in the distant future, it will be possible to place a camera in the goal and thereby resolve such contentious scenes. Until then, however, the referee carries the sole responsibility, and the players must comply.

As controversial as the decision was, the German players accepted it with admirable sportsmanship. Heated protests from the young firebrands Wolfgang Overath, Wolfgang Weber and Franz Beckenbauer were dismissed by the captain, Uwe Seeler, with an energetic gesture that could be interpreted as "Accept the referee's decision!" It was this sense of fairness that earned the highest respect from the English spectators. On their lap of honour, the German team received almost as much applause as the English did when Queen Elizabeth II presented the English captain Bobby Moore with the Jules Rimet Trophy.

Yes, this English team, with its outstanding individual talents of Moore, Bobby Charlton and Alan Ball, are worthy World Champions. But Germany were worthy finalists too, a young team that both plays wonderful football but also represents our nation in the best possible manner – and that is more than could have been hoped for before this tournament, just twenty-one years after that appalling war that England has not yet forgotten.

It could have been even better. Germany began playing in this final with such a carefree fashion that no one could have guessed that the game was against their bogey team, against whom they had never won a game in the history of international football. The trainer, Helmut Schön, deployed his first-choice team – including the Dortmund goalkeeper Tilkowski, even though he picked up a bad injury to his left shoulder in the semi-final against the USSR.

Again and again, Tilkowski was drawn into aerial battles with an English side that is full of such excellent headers of the ball. After just seven minutes, he went to ground following a duel with Hurst and needed treatment for a couple of minutes. The German players held their breath, because an injury to Tilkowski would not have meant that the Bremen sub goalkeeper Günter Bernard could have entered the fray. The FIFA statutes declare that an out-field player has to take over the goalkeeper's duties. Germany would therefore have had to complete the game with a numerical disadvantage – in the final of the World Cup! Perhaps FIFA should consider rethinking their own rules, and, for the next World Cup in four years' time in Mexico, approve the use of one or two substitutes for each team?

Happily, Tilkowski recovered quickly and was called into action two minutes later for a long-range shot from Martin Peters. The players in front of him could sense the security he offered, and were free to push forward. The first chance was missed by an over-hasty Siegfried Held, but the second dangerous situation, in the twelfth minute, put Germany into the lead. This is how it happened: Held's cross sailed from the left-half position into the English penalty box, the defender Ray Wilson headed it clear, but only as far as Helmut Haller. The man from FC Bologna shot immediately with his right boot on the turn, and goalkeeper Gordon Banks had no chance as the ball went into the left corner. It was Haller's fifth goal of the tournament.

It was the first time in the tournament that the English had gone behind, and their response was rather confused. The German team appeared to be in control, and the approximately 10,000 German fans in the stadium sang *"Ri Ra Ro, England ist KO!"* It was a little premature. The Germans missed a chance to add to their lead, and only six minutes after the opening goal, Overath committed an unnecessary foul on Moore. The English captain took the free kick himself, aiming directly for Hurst, who was completely unmarked in the penalty box and headed home to make it 1-1. Hurst only made it into the team in the quarter-final, following an injury to their first-choice striker Jimmy Greaves, and he has kept his place ever since. Tilkowski's appeals for offside were in vain, but unlike a later goal from England, this wasn't such a clearly wrong decision by the referee.

It was now an open game. The diminutive Seeler leaped higher than the tall English defenders to meet a cross from Karl-Heinz Schnellinger, but Banks parried his header. At the other end, Tilkowski reacted just as well to a header from Hurst. Then it was the Germans' turn again: in the space of a few seconds Overath and Lothar Emmerich were denied by Banks. Then Tilkowski threw up his fists to punch away a shot from Liverpool's Roger Hunt, and just before the end of the first half Seeler forced Banks into another risky parry from a long-range shot.

In the second half, there were not as many high-class moments, but the English took more and more control in the German half of the pitch. This was perhaps a result of a risky tactical move by Helmut Schön. The trainer had tasked the young Beckenbauer, the star of the tournament, with keeping an eye on the English playmaker, Bobby Charlton. The twenty year-old from Munich performed his duties well, but didn't completely neutralise Charlton. It was, however, decisive that Beckenbauer's artistry was missing in the attack. He had made the number-four shirt famous all over the world, but in the final he played well within himself. Helmut Schön would have been better advised to entrust Beckenbauer with the role of Hamburg's Willi Schulz who was allowed to play as a central defensive figure but without an opponent to mark. As such Beckenbauer would have been in a much better position to put his technical and strategic talents to good use.

Now England went into the ascendancy with the intelligence of Bobby Moore, the ferocity of Nobby Stiles and the improvisation of Alan Ball. The German team gave their best, but Helmut Haller and Wolfgang Overath were tiring, Beckenbauer was occupied with defensive tasks, and, if that weren't enough, Lothar Emmerich on the left wing was a dead loss. The Dortmund man scored possibly the most spectacular goal of the tournament in the first round against Spain, but was anonymous in the semi-final against the Soviet Union. Albert Brülls of AC Brescia was raring to go for the final, but Schön, just like his opposite number Alf Ramsey, adhered to a golden rule of football: Never change a winning team! For England, this mantra worked with Hurst, but for the Germans with Emmerich, it didn't. In the final, he was the weakest link, dogged by technical errors, and if he took a shot, it invariably flew towards the corner flag. It was on his left flank that the English were at their most dangerous thanks to the tricky dribbler Alan Ball and the right-back George Cohen.

The English superiority was becoming more and more evident, and twelve minutes before the end, they finally took advantage. In comparison to what had come before, it was a rather banal moment. Hurst took a shot from the edge of the box, but Bremen's Horst-Dieter Höttges was in the way. What he had planned as an uneremonious clearance ricocheted into the path of Martin Peters, and the midfielder from West Ham United had an easy task to tuck the ball in from close range for a 2-1 lead.

Was that the decisive action of the game? No! One more time the German side pushed forward with energy that they didn't know they had. They were a little lucky that Hunt, Charlton and Peters missed their chances on the counter-attack, and then they had one last chance. The English protested angrily when referee Dienst awarded a ninetieth-minute free-kick after a foul by Jack Charlton on Siegfried Held. Emmerich thundered the ball at the goal, it took a deflection and fell to Held, who forced it into the centre, where suddenly Wolfgang Weber appeared – Weber of all people, whose job it is to prevent goals rather than score them. The man from Cologne slid the ball into the goal on his eighteenth international appearance.

Goalkeeper Banks protested wildly – he had seen a handball by Schnellinger – but Dienst would not be influenced. Shortly afterwards, he blew the final whistle and gave the teams five minutes to catch their breath before extra time.

Were the English shocked? Possibly. But the Germans, in particular, were exhausted. The game had completely taken it out of them, and the short break before extra time said it all about the teams' energy levels. While the weary Germans Höttges, Weber, Schnellinger and Beckenbauer received massages, the English were already scurrying around the pitch as though they couldn't wait to get started again. And so the game resumed.

The history books will note that the endeavours of this German side cost them a great deal of energy. In extra time, it was really only the English team that was capable of playing. Their first chance was missed by the little redhead Ball – his shot was turned over the bar by Hans Tilkowski. Then, Bobby Charlton was unlucky to only hit this post. And then, the inevitable happened – even if it was highly controversial.

It was once more that rascal Ball, who slipped free on the right-hand side and crossed to Hurst while running at full speed. Willi Schulz was just a little too far away to intervene, and could only watch as Hurst stopped the ball, turned towards the goal and shot. And then... who knows? The ball hit the underside of the crossbar and bounced up. Weber headed it away but the Englishman Roger Hunt was already celebrating and wasn't at all concerned with chasing the rebound.

Goal or no goal? In the press box, every reporter crowded around the BBC's screen, but they couldn't see anything. In America, there are slow-motion replays at American-football and ice-hockey games – television images that repeat and slow down the action. Football hasn't come that far yet, so we can but speculate. The referee Dienst awarded a goal, and that was that.

The German team didn't create a single chance in extra time. England simply had more energy and scored a fourth goal in the hundred-and-twentieth and last minute, and once more it was Geoff Hurst. The game was as good as over, and some fans had run onto the pitch – an irregularity, of course, but it didn't make any difference. England are worthy World Champions, Uwe Seeler and co represented Germany outstandingly, and all that remains is hope for the future. The next World Cup will be in 1970 in Mexico, and nothing would be sweeter than seeing Germany meet England again – preferably in a knockout game.

The German What Happened Next

In the summer of 1966, Germany felt as though its national team was at the beginning of a new era of success – one that would be adorned with many trophies. It took a few years, however, before the team could fulfil these expectations, but when they did, Franz Beckenbauer was almost always involved.

Next up though there was a huge disappointment: the failure to qualify for the final rounds of the European Championships in 1968. At fault was an embarrassing 0-0 draw in Tirana with Albania for which Beckenbauer was an injury-enforced absence, and which nearly cost the trainer Helmut Schön his job.

For the World Cup in 1970 in Mexico, Schön convinced the thirty-three year-old Uwe Seeler to make a comeback, and, in the quarter-final, the Hamburg man scored a famous equaliser with the back of his head to make it 2-2 against England. In extra time, the Germans won 3-2, but lost the semi-final 3-4 against Italy, also after extra time, in a match later dubbed The Match of the Century. Beckenbauer dislocated his shoulder early in the game, but since the Germans had already made two substitutions, he had to play on and finished the game with his arm in a sling. The *Evening Standard* praised him as a "wounded, beaten but proud Prussian officer."

The German national team played perhaps the best football in its history in the 1972 European Championship in Belgium. For the 3-0 win over the Soviet Union in the final, there were only two players of the Wembley eleven on the pitch: defender Horst-Dieter Höttges and Franz Beckenbauer, who in the meantime had invented the new position of *libero* for himself.

Two years later, 1974, Germany won the World Cup for the second time, this time on home soil. Beckenbauer was the team captain and had by now become known as the "Kaiser." The 2-1 win over the Netherlands in the final was Helmut Schön's last triumph – he retired after Germany had a disastrous World Cup '78 in Argentina. Beckenbauer had also departed by then, and without him, there was no chance. He was once more the decisive figure when Germany won the World Cup for the third time, this time in Italy in 1990. As Manager, Beckenbauer gave the orders, and became only the second man after Brazil's Mario Zagallo to win the Wold Cup both as player and coach. In 2006, he had a third triumph: as the head of the tournament-organising committee, Beckenbauer brought the World Cup to be played on German soil for a second time.

The German team in 2006, however, wasn't as successful as expected and went out in the semi-final against Italy. The fourth star on the jersey for winning a fourth World Cup would have to wait eight more years, until Brazil 2014 – and this time, the win, for the first time since 1966, was entirely without any involvement by Franz Beckenbauer.

Post-Match

Fifty Years of Hurt Charted: 1966–2016

Philip Cornwall

IT WAS 10 JULY 1994, New Jersey pretending to be New York. There were fifteen minutes left on another painfully humid day. When I think of the moment of silence coursing around Giants Stadium after Stoichkov's free-kick hit the back of the net, the hairs on my neck still rise. And when I remember that I have never enjoyed a similar moment watching England, they fall again.

Four years before Bulgaria's captain put them on the way to beating Germany at USA '94, Italia '90 should have been my first World Cup. I had motive, means and opportunity, even the language (courtesy of a Paolo Rossi inspired A-Level choice). But as I tried to find a way into journalism at *When Saturday Comes*, staying in London represented a chance to prove my worth beyond tea-making and packing T-shirts.

Somewhere along the line it paid off and four years later I went to the World Cup for *WSC*, even though Graham Taylor's England didn't make it. We watched two quarter-finals. In the first, consistent challengers and 1982 winners Italy beat perennially unlucky Spain in Massachusetts; and then we drove south to watch Bulgaria, who had never won a match in five final tournaments until their group successes against Greece and a Maradona-deprived Argentina, play the defending champions, Germany.

Just after half-time, Lothar Matthaus put Germany on course to face Italy for a place in the final, scoring from the penalty spot – just as he had done for West Germany in the Italia '90 quarter-final, and in the Turin shootout with England. At Giants Stadium Matthaus, Jurgen Klinsmann and co did not add to their tally but few thought they would need to. This was Bulgaria; Bulgaria do not reach World Cup semi-finals. And then, with fifteen minutes left, there was a foul twenty-five yards out, to the right of the D as Bulgaria attacked.

Hristo Stoichkov had three goals already in the Finals but had taken countless free-kicks without scoring from one. Yet here he was, pointlessly lining another effort up against the champions. No one knew *exactly* what would happen – would it smack into the wall, or would it sail harmlessly over? But we all knew what wouldn't happen – Bodo Illgner would *not* be picking the ball out of his net.

Watching it again on YouTube, the split second of silence is drowned out by the commentary. But it was there. It is impossible to know what Stoichkov himself was thinking, whether he truly thought he would score. Did he, too, have to erase his disbelief? Perhaps the Germans were equally bewildered as just three minutes later Yordan Lechkov's diving header gave the underdogs a lead to cling to. And they clung. At the whistle crowds of Americans, their faces painted in the colours of the match favourites, were celebrating the underdogs' success; such was the fickle nature of Soccer USA. And who cared, as long as they didn't beat me in the rush to buy a souvenir Bulgaria T-shirt?

Stoichkov's side were not the only unexpected semi-finalists. Four days later on the west coast, I saw Sweden lose narrowly to the eventual winners, Brazil, opponents they had previously held to a draw in the group stage.

Italy, Brazil, Sweden, Bulgaria: the first quartet of sides to match the achievement of Bobby Robson's men four years earlier. Maybe England's turn would come in 1998.

At least, buoyed by the almost-glory of Euro '96, they qualified for France; but on a memorable night against Argentina in Saint-Etienne, David Beckham lost his head and his remaining team-mates lost England's second World Cup shootout, this time in the last sixteen. Sven-Goran Eriksson went one round better than Glenn Hoddle in both 2002 and 2006, narrowly losing quarter-finals, for which the Swede was widely excoriated while being chased out of the job two years early. But after the disastrous reign of Steve McClaren ended in failure to reach Euro 2008, Fabio Capello's side slipped back to be overrun in the last sixteen of the 2010 World Cup and Roy Hodgson could not even get that far in 2014, with England's first World Cup group-stage exit since 1958.

Quarter-finals, last sixteen, first round with a match to spare. The longer England go without another World Cup semi-final, the further short they fall, the less likely they look to reach one, the more my Italia '90 regret grows.

At one level, we remain members of a select bunch. Spain, in 2010, became the eighth and most recent different nation to win the World Cup (if we rightly award reunified Germany, 2014 winners, the trio won by West Germany). But now only a dwindling number of people at home and abroad can actually remember England winning ours. Eriksson's era of quarter-finals (including one at Euro 2004) looks a poor return for an allegedly golden generation, but one quarter-final at global or European level since is product of a far baser metal.

Past failure is not actually a guarantee of future poor performance; otherwise all but a handful would give up playing any team sport at all. It can, though, offer a guide, a dose of realism in a world where hope too often gets the better of you.

The question needs asking, therefore: just how bad are England, not in any given moment but over time? Too many of the matches have made painful viewing; some bare statistics add to the grief but also give it a rational grounding. Since 1990, our post-'66 high point, fourteen different nations have reached the World Cup semi-finals at least once. Add in the five World Cups between our victory and our only other semi, and the number who can also boast at least one last-four spot rises to sixteen.

We could make ourselves more miserable by including European Championships, despite Terry Venables' shootout defeat when football so nearly came home. In our fifty years, Czechoslovakia won one Euro and, though there was a sizable Slovakian contingent in 1976, twenty years later the Czech Republic reached

the final of Euro '96. Denmark (1992) and Greece (2004) recorded
deeply improbable continental victories, too. The USSR lost finals
to the 1972 West Germany and to Marco van Basten's Holland in
1988 (after both had beaten England in the group stages). Portugal's loss to Greece at home in the 2004 final must ache, yet we do
not even have runners-up medals to throw away in disgust.

But, sticking to the World Cup, let's try to answer as objectively
as possible, by going tournament by painful tournament, where
England have stood since Bobby Moore lifted those twelve inches
of not actually solid gold.

There are some immediate difficulties in comparing achievements at different World Cups: the number of finalists has doubled from the sixteen of 1970–78 to the thirty-two since 1998, with
twenty-four for the four finals from 1982 to 1994. While 1970 had
quarter-finals and semis, a second group stage in 1974 and 1978
meant that there was only one actual knockout match – the final –
plus the third-fourth play-off. Spain '82 still had two group stages
but with four groups of three producing semi-finalists. Getting
out of an initial group meant being in the last eight up to 1978, the
last twelve in 1982 and the last sixteen from 1986 onwards.

Immediately objectivity is undermined, then, unless you award
points only to the last four, and to do so would be to ignore some
considerable achievements and deprive the continent of Africa
of any place in our final table. It would also give too much credit
to one particular host nation who in eight other attempts have
only once escaped their group, but went all the way to the semis
in 2002 with the aid of some generous refereeing. Meanwhile –
though I watched Sweden put four past Bulgaria in the 1994 game
– no weight can generally be given to the third-fourth match,
contested between sides with greatly varying degrees of interest.
Semi-finalists should be treated equally. But a scale of 2pts for
quarter-finalists, 4pts for semi-finalists, 7pts for runners-up and
13pts for the winners offers sufficient gradation and allows room
for a couple of tweaks.

Home advantage hasn't been penalised. In our fifty-year period of twelve World Cups hosts have only won in 1974 (West Germany), 1978 (Argentina) and 1998 (France); and if they didn't make it that far, they were losing semi-finalists in 1990 (Italy), 2002 (South Korea), 2006 (Germany) and 2014 (Brazil). But given the World Cup's overall history some allowance should be given to teams competing outside their own hemisphere – after all, in 2014 Germany became the first European team to win in the Americas and Brazil at Sweden '58 are the only South Americans to win in Europe. A South American side reaching the last four in Europe should gain 0.5pts, with a full 1pt for the final, and vice versa for European sides in the Americas. Apart from South Korea, and that was as hosts, no Asian nation has made it to the semi-final stage to date, no African nation has done so, thus the award of points for "away" hemisphere rather than for "away" continent seems fair and accurate. At least for now.

From 1986 to 1994, the six initial groups eliminated only one third of the teams, as four third-placed sides reached the last sixteen. On the other hand, group winners have done more at the finals than runners-up and also-rans. There are more group winners in later years, but we should acknowledge that the World Cup has expanded not simply for commercial and political reasons but because the quality of global football has risen. While thumpings were regular occurrences in the '70s and '80s, there are fewer true minnows, as Costa Rica proved in Brazil: the alleged makeweights in a group containing three former World Cup winners came out on top. So there are 0.5pts for winning a group in the era of sixteen-team tournaments, and 1pt subsequently.

Any ranking scheme when teams do not simply all play each other home and away has an arbitrary edge to it; look at the scepticism that greets every announcement of the FIFA rankings. But just as England should never give up trying at the World Cup, we should not give up trying to measure how bad, post '66, they have been, relative to their own performances and those of other countries.

If we cannot acknowledge our realistic place in football's world order then we are condemned to more frustration, more dashed expectations – and more shock and surprise when teams such as Costa Rica can get the better of us. If we can broadly accept that a raft of countries have left us far behind, we will perhaps be more willing to implement the policies that have led to their success. And if – because of the clash of interests between our globally focused clubs and the national team – we are unwilling to reform, then we may at least embrace such lesser successes as we can achieve.

Notes on the Tables

Tables are cumulative, beginning with 1970 and adding each team's points successively through to 2014.

Teams in **bold** scored points in this tournament; teams not in bold show points scored in previous tournaments.

Points scheme: winner = 13, runner-up = 7, semis = 4, quarters = 2, group-winner = 0.5/1, away hemisphere = 0.5/1

Mexico 1970

England's decline from the status of World Champions was not as swift as, say, France's, eliminated winless and goalless in the first round in 2002 (albeit as European champions). Instead, 1970 is one of our great, improbable what-might-have-beens: Gordon Banks laid low by food poisoning and replaced by Peter Bonetti, a two-goal lead lost, Bobby Charlton substituted at 2-1 to save him for the semi-final, a Geoff Hurst equaliser in extra time mysteriously disallowed as West Germany won 3-2. Still, at least Alf Ramsey's team pick up a couple of points in this analysis for having got this far, along with Peru and the hosts, Mexico.

On their own in fifth sit the Soviet Union, quarter-final losers but also winners of their group, with 2.5pts. It is one of the oddities of the global game that while one superpower barely paid attention to the world's number-one sport during the Cold War, the one that did largely flattered to deceive. And Russia have continued to do so, as Putin's putative World Cup looms (we can live in hope there is yet time for a change in 2018 venue).

Uruguay, twice World Cup winners, lost a semi-final to Brazil best remembered for Pelé's extraordinary dummy on the goalkeeper; they earn 4pts in our first table. West Germany's reward for their epic semi with Italy, in which Franz Beckenbauer played on with a broken clavicle, is 5pts as they also won their group and reached a semi in their "away" hemisphere. Italy lost 4-1 in the final, but the scoreline is remembered more than the fact that they took this greatest Brazil into the final quarter of the game level, four days after the draining 4-3 extra-time thriller with the Germans. Dino Zoff and co earn 8.5pts, as European runners-up in the Americas after winning their group. Which leaves only Brazil, picking up and keeping the Jules Rimet Trophy and claiming 13.5pts, including their bonus for taking the group, as well as the cup, off England.

	Overall ranking 1970	Points	Group winner bonus	Hemi-sphere bonus	Subtotal	Carried forward	Total
1	Brazil	13	+0.5		13.5		13.5
2	Italy	7	+0.5	+1	8.5		8.5
3	West Germany	4	+0.5	+0.5	5		5
4	Uruguay	4			4		4
5	USSR	2	+0.5		2.5		2.5
6=	England	2			2		2
6=	Peru	2			2		2
6=	Mexico	2			2		2

West Germany 1974

The finals in West Germany were as good as it got for communist football nations. Of the eight point-scorers in these rankings, three were from Eastern Europe. The least of these was Tito's Yugoslavia, who edged out Brazil (and third-placed, unbeaten Scotland) on goal difference, thanks to a 9-0 mauling of Zaire, but finished bottom of the second group stage. Still, that's worth 3pts in our scheme, as were East Germany's efforts, winning Group One thanks to Jurgen Sparwasser's goal, which secured victory over West Germany in the only competitive meeting of the nations divided by the wall. (In February 1990 the pair were drawn in the same group for Euro '92 qualifying, but the wall had already tumbled and football's plans were overtaken by reunification.)

And then there was Poland: Kazimierz Deyna, Grzegorz Lato, Jan Tomaszewski and all. The conquerors of England in Chorzow then held on for that crucial draw at Wembley. Seven years, two months and seventeen days after winning the World Cup there, Sir Alf Ramsey's last competitive side could not secure the win they needed to reach the finals.

But when you analyse England's 1970s failures, it's worth remembering that the sides they lost to all went on to achieve something memorable. West Germany lost the 1970 semi but won the 1974 tournament on home soil as 1972 European champions, after scorching England at Wembley in the home and away quarter-finals. Poland, meanwhile, won their group at the 1974 finals, ahead of Argentina, and contested what was in effect a semi against the hosts, losing in appalling conditions that did not suit the 1972 Olympic champions' game. England would go on to fail to qualify for Euro '76 – but that was won by the side that beat them, Czechoslovakia. And that's before you get to the Italy side that Don Revie's team had to face in the battle to reach the next World Cup.

To mention Argentina '78 yet would be to get ahead of ourselves, though. Back in '74, the Poles take 4.5pts as group winners reaching the last four. The other point-scorers start with Argentina and Sweden, with 2pts for reaching the last eight. Brazil lost their crown thanks to a 2-0 win for the best team in the tournament, Holland; the South Americans made the last four, though, to add 4.5pts to those from their 1970 title.

Alas for total football, Holland fell short amid a certain amount of controversy. England did have one finalist, the referee Jack Taylor, who correctly awarded the Dutch a first-minute penalty but more dubiously balanced that out with one for West Germany, for whom Gerd Muller added a second and decisive goal. Holland as group-winning runners-up have 7.5pts, but 13pts tie West Germany with Brazil overall, on 17.5pts. England, stuck on 2pts, are already ninth equal overall.

Overall ranking 1970–74	Points	Group winner bonus	Hemi-sphere bonus	Subtotal	Carried forward	Total
1= West Germany	13			13	5	18
1= Brazil	4		+0.5	4.5	13.5	18
3 Italy					8.5	8.5
4 Holland	7	+0.5		7.5		7.5
5 Poland	4	+0.5		4.5		4.5
6 Uruguay					4	4
7= East Germany	2	+0.5		2.5		2.5
7= Yugoslavia	2	+0.5		2.5		2.5
7= USSR					2.5	2.5
9= Sweden	2			2		2
9= Argentina	2			2		2
9= England					2	2
9= Peru					2	2
9= Mexico					2	2

Argentina 1978

And things did not get any better at Argentina '78, as once again England (in the words of the Scottish song) didnae qualify. Ron Greenwood presided over the last rites after Don Revie had conceded too big a goal difference advantage to Italy. But, yes, it was Italy, not makeweights: past failures had put England in the same qualifying group as the 1934 and '38 champions and 1970 runners-up, who did well enough at these finals to beat the eventual winners, Argentina, in the group stage. They pick up 5pts, as last-four finishers outside their hemisphere and group-winners.

Other point-scorers included Peru, despite their not scoring a single goal and conceding ten in the second group stage. The conquerors of Scotland were the last South American team outside the big two to make the final eight until Paraguay and Uruguay in 2010. Like Austria and Poland, group-winners who did not reach the last four, they gain 2.5pts – 0.5 more than the defending champions, West Germany who having lost 3-2 to Austria in the second group stage exited the tournament.

Brazil, cost a place in the final by scheduling that allowed Argentina to know the margin of victory they required against Peru, were second to Austria at the group stage and in the Americas so gain only 4pts – but that's enough to regain their overall lead from the Germans. Holland, the width of the post in the final from a late winner that could have brought down the Argentinian junta and changed the course of British political history (well, maybe), take 8pts as European finalists in the Americas. And, begrudgingly given the rule manipulation and the antics that kept the Dutch waiting, we give Argentina 13pts.

And absent England? Overall, now down to thirteenth, while Brazil break the tie with Germany to move 2pts ahead at the top.

	Overall ranking 1970-78	Points	Group winner bonus	Hemi- sphere bonus	Subtotal	Carried forward	Total
1	Brazil	4			4	18	22
2	West Germany	2			2	18	20
3	Holland	7		+1	8	7.5	15.5
4	Argentina	13			13	2	15
5	Italy	4	+0.5	+0.5	5	8.5	13.5
6	Poland	2	+0.5		2.5	4.5	7
7	Peru	2	+0.5		2.5	2	4.5
8	Uruguay					4	4
9=	Austria	2	+0.5		2.5		2.5
9=	USSR					2.5	2.5
9=	East Germany					2.5	2.5
9=	Yugoslavia					2.5	2.5
13=	England					2	2
13=	Sweden					2	2

Spain 1982

For someone who was not yet three when England lost their crown in Mexico, seeing the national team in the World Cup Finals was a long time coming. That it took just twenty-seven seconds for Bryan Robson to put England ahead against France made it seem worth the wait, but the end was agony: unbeaten after five games but edged out in the second group stage. Still, it was another last-eight finish, as group winners, and with the Finals expanded to twenty-four sides that's worth 3pts – which is what Brazil picked up, too.

Earning 1pt each, as initial group-winners who finished bottom in their three-team second sections, are Northern Ireland and Belgium. With 2pts, in the top eight without winning their group, are the Soviet Union and – despite the disgrace of the "Anschluss game" against West Germany – Austria.

France were beaten by England in their opening match but ultimately undone only by weak refereeing and poor penalties, as the West Germany goalkeeper Harald Schumacher stayed on the pitch, despite his challenge knocking the French defender Patrick Battiston into a coma, to win a semi-final shootout. The French pick up 4pts points, one fewer than Poland, beaten by Italy in their semi but initial group-winners.

The Italians had almost gone out in the group stage but instead emerged as overall winners, inspired by Paolo Rossi, rehabilitated after a match-fixing ban. They beat West Germany 3-1 in the final. The winners take 13pts, the runners-up 7pts.

That is enough for West Germany (28pts) to overtake Brazil (25), the previous leaders, and Italy (26.5) split the pair. England, after their first Finals in a dozen years, overtake Peru, Uruguay, Austria, the USSR, East Germany and Yugoslavia, shooting up from thirteenth to seventh – but with barely half the points of Poland in sixth.

	Overall ranking 1970–82	Points	Group winner bonus	Hemi-sphere bonus	Subtotal	Carried forward	Total
1	West Germany	7	+1		8	20	28
2	Italy	13			13	13.5	26.5
3	Brazil	2	+1		3	22	25
4	Holland					15.5	15.5
5	Argentina					15	15
6	Poland	4	+1		5	4.5	9.5
7	England	2	+1		3	2	5
8=	Peru					4.5	4.5
8=	Austria	2			2	2.5	4.5
8=	USSR	2			2	2.5	4.5
11=	France	4			4		4
11=	Uruguay					4	4
13=	East Germany					2.5	2.5
13=	Yugoslavia					2.5	2.5
15=	Sweden					2	2
15=	Mexico					2	2
17=	Belgium		+1		1		1
17=	Northern Ireland		+1		1		1

Mexico 1986

Back in Mexico, back in a genuine quarter-final. There was no 1970-style squandered lead against Argentina, instead England trailed to a pair of dramatically contrasting Diego Maradona goals before not quite pulling off a stunning comeback once John Barnes was on the pitch.

That is 2pts in our system, because Morocco won the group – one of a trio to top their section but go out in the last sixteen, along with Denmark and the Soviet Union, and take 1pt. England are matched on 2pts by Spain, who thumped the Danes 5-1 but then succumbed to a Belgium team on an all-time high. Brazil and Mexico both won their groups and exited the quarter-finals on penalties to take 3pts each.

Six of the Belgians who would face England in the last sixteen four years hence were in the side that lost the semi-final to Argentina and collect 4.5pts, for being in the semi-finals in the Americas. France match that achievement, but felt rather less good about a second straight last-four loss to West Germany, a damp squib after the win against Brazil and the building up of the semi as revenge for Battiston.

As for the Germans, their 8pts for being losing finalists in the wrong hemisphere extended their lead over Brazil but Argentina – winning a second World Cup in eight years – overtake Italy.

And England? Pushed down to eighth by France, despite Gary Lineker winning the tournament golden boot as top scorer.

Overall ranking 1970-86	Points	Group winner bonus	Hemi-sphere bonus	Subtotal	Carried forward	Total
1 West Germany	7		+1	8	28	36
2 Argentina	13	+1		14	15	29
3 Brazil	2	+1		3	25	28
4 Italy					26.5	26.5
5 Holland					15.5	15.5
6 Poland					9.5	9.5
7 France	4		+1	5	4	9
8 England	2			2	5	7
9 Belgium	4		+1	5	1	6
10 USSR		+1		1	4.5	5.5
11 Mexico	2	+1		3	2	5
12= Peru					4.5	4.5
12= Austria					4.5	4.5
14 Uruguay					4	4
15= East Germany					2.5	2.5
15= Yugoslavia					2.5	2.5
17= Sweden					2	2
17= Spain	2			2		2
19= Morocco		+1		1		1
19= Denmark		+1		1		1
19= Northern Ireland					1	1

Italy 1990

One of the oddities about Italia '90 is that despite its near mytho-logical status in England, to many independent judges it was the World Cup's nadir in terms of the quality of football. The officiat-ing was awful at times, with a decision to use referees as linesmen leading to especially poor offside decisions. There were red cards from start to finish but there should have been more, and the calls for reform in the game's laws were enhanced by the cynicism on show. There was an all-time-low goals-per-game ratio of 2.21, and both semi-finals had to be settled on penalties.

To the English it all looks so different: Pavarotti, Platt, Gazza, and a second World Cup semi twenty-four years after the pre-vious one, with Chris Waddle's shot against the post and then penalty into stratosphere the difference between heaven and... well, an enduring warm glow that is far from hellish. Plus 5pts, as semi-finalists and group-winners.

That total was matched by Italy, and surpassed by an Argentina side that deserved worse than being runners-up but could easily have won the whole thing, and pick up 8pts including one for being South American finalists in Europe. West Germany scored two penalties and one free-kick in their final three matches to be underwhelming winners for a lead-extending 13pts.

On their own with 3pts stand Cameroon, Africa's first quarter-finalists, who would have gone further with better finishing against an England side that almost froze under the burden of being favourites to reach a semi-final. Czechoslovakia and the Republic of Ireland get off the mark with 2pts as losing quarter-fi-nalists, matched by Yugoslavia, while Spain and Brazil pick up 1pt apiece as group-winners who went out in the last sixteen.

And so, at the midway point between 1966 and today, England have stacked up 12pts – one fewer than they would have started with if we had included that victory. And overall, they trail all the winners – Brazil, West Germany, Argentina and Italy – plus Holland, and are level with Poland. The worst is yet to come.

Overall ranking 1970-90	Points	Group winner bonus	Hemi-sphere bonus	Subtotal	Carried forward	Total
1 West Germany	13	+1		14	36	50
2 Argentina	7		+1	8	29	37
3 Italy	4	+1		5	26.5	31.5
4 Brazil		+1		1	28	29
5 Holland					15.5	15.5
6 England	4	+1		5	7	12
7 Poland					9.5	9.5
8 France					9	9
9 Belgium					6	6
10 USSR					5.5	5.5
11 Mexico					5	5
12= Peru					4.5	4.5
12= Austria					4.5	4.5
12= Yugoslavia	2			2	2.5	4.5
15= Uruguay					4	4
16= Cameroon	2	+1		3		3
16= Spain		+1		1	2	3
18 East Germany					2.5	2.5
19= Sweden					2	2
19= Czechoslovakia	2			2		2
19= Republic of Ireland	2			2		2
22= Morocco					1	1
22= Denmark					1	1
22= Northern Ireland					1	1

USA 1994

Of the eight quarter-finalists at USA '94, seven were from Europe — and the odd team out were the ones to lift the trophy. Brazil, holding firm on penalties against Italy in the final, also won their group to pick up 14pts. Roberto Baggio and co — in the middle of a run of losing a semi, a final and then a quarter-final on penalties — had almost gone out in the first round but instead, as European finalists in the Americas, take 8pts, while those improbable semi-finalists Sweden and Bulgaria take 4.5pts each.

Holland were floored by a Branco free-kick after recovering from 2-0 down against Brazil. Romania's outfielders were worth a place in the last four but their goalkeeper was not, and Sweden advanced as a result. This pair of quarter-final losers, plus Germany, won their groups so get 3pts. Spain should have had a late penalty for an elbow-blow that led to an eight-match ban for the perpetrator, Mauro Tassotti, and cost the victim, Luis Enrique, half a pint of blood; Italy went down the other end and scored the winner. Spanish misfortune yields another 2pts, while Mexico and Nigeria – group-winners who lost in the last sixteen – pick up 1pt apiece.

	Overall ranking 1970-94	Points	Group winner bonus	Hemi-sphere bonus	Subtotal	Carried forward	Total
1	Germany	2	+1		3	50	53
2	Brazil	13	+1		14	29	43
3	Italy	7		+1	8	31.5	39.5
4	Argentina					29	29
5	Holland	2	+1		3	15.5	18.5
6	England					12	12

(continued)

Overall ranking 1970–94	Points	Group winner bonus	Hemi-sphere bonus	Subtotal	Carried forward	Total
7 Poland					9.5	9.5
8 France					9	9
9 Sweden	4		+0.5	4.5	2	6.5
10= Spain	2			2	3	5
10= Mexico		+1		1	5	6
10= Belgium					6	6
13 USSR					5.5	5.5
14 Mexico					5	5
15= Bulgaria	4		+0.5	4.5		4.5
15= Peru					4.5	4.5
15= Austria					4.5	4.5
15= Yugoslavia					4.5	4.5
19 Uruguay					4	4
20= Cameroon					3	3
20= Romania	2	+1		3		3
22 East Germany					2.5	2.5
23= Czechoslovakia					2	2
23= Republic of Ireland					2	2
25= Morocco					1	1
25= Denmark					1	1
25= Northern Ireland					1	1
25= Nigeria		+1		1		1

France 1998

At least England were back. The 1998 campaign – which finished with a defeat to Argentina featuring Michael Owen's goal, Sol Campbell's disallowed one, ten men battling so hard after David Beckham's (deserved) red card – was a bitter-sweet experience. The bitterness grew following the disintegration of Glenn Hoddle's short-lived reign as England manager. And losing on penalties to Argentina in the last sixteen without winning the group is worth zero points in our scheme.

Romania, who had topped England's group, were also last-sixteen losers but pick up 1pt for that earlier achievement, likewise Nigeria for the same feat. Denmark beat Nigeria but were quarter-final losers and are awarded 2pts. Italy's penalty shoot-out nightmare continued in the quarter-final they lost against France, while Argentina were done by a piece of brilliance from Dennis Bergkamp that relegates Owen's effort to the second best scored past Carlos Roa in these finals. The big surprise was that along with Italy and Argentina, Germany were also picking up only 3pts, as group-winners going out in the last eight.

Croatia self-destructed against the Germany at Euro '96, but took full advantage of a red card five minutes before the end of the first half of their quarter-final and ran out 3-0 winners over the Germans. They even led France in the semi, but had to settle for finishing third overall – and claiming 4pts. Holland lost to Brazil again, this time on penalties, but take 5pts as group-winners.

Which leaves Brazil and France. The hosts had never got beyond the semis; they were without Laurent Blanc, sent off against Croatia thanks to a foolish flick and Slaven Bilic's play-acting; and they were in effect playing without strikers. But Zinedine Zidane left his mark on the final with two goals, and Brazil were in crisis over Ronaldo's health. The champions capitulated, conceding the first three-goal defeat in the final since Pelé and co beat Italy in 1970. France 13pts, Brazil – in their away continent – 8pts.

Overall, the French triumph took them clear of England, while Brazil, Holland, Germany, Argentina and Italy all improved their lead too.

	Overall ranking 1970–98	Points	Group winner bonus	Hemi-sphere bonus	Subtotal	Carried forward	Total
1	Germany	2	+1		3	53	56
2	Brazil	7	+1	+1	9	43	52
3	Italy	2	+1		3	39.5	42.5
4	Argentina	2	+1		3	37	40
5	Holland	4	+1		5	18.5	23.5
6	France	13	+1		14	9	23
7	England					12	12
8	Poland					9.5	9.5
9	Sweden					6.5	6.5
10=	Spain					6	6
10=	Mexico					6	6
10=	Belgium					6	6
13	USSR					5.5	5.5
14=	Bulgaria					4.5	4.5
14=	Peru					4.5	4.5
14=	Austria					4.5	4.5
14=	Yugoslavia					4.5	4.5
18	Uruguay					4	4

(continued)

Overall ranking 1970–98	Points	Group winner bonus	Hemisphere bonus	Subtotal	Carried forward	Total
19= Romania		+1		1	3	4
19= Croatia	4			4		4
21= Denmark	2			2	1	3
21= Cameroon					3	3
23 East Germany					2.5	2.5
24= Nigeria		+1		1	1	1
24= Czechoslovakia					2	2
24= Republic of Ireland					2	2
27= Morocco					1	1
27= Northern Ireland					1	1

South Korea & Japan 2002

Given that the talk after the qualifying group home defeat to Germany in the wake of a disastrous Euro 2000 was of England not even making it to World Cup 2002, that they did get to the South Korea & Japan tournament was laudable; that it came via the famous 5-1 in Munich the more so. They also survived an awful finals group draw to eliminate Argentina. And then Denmark were swamped 3-0 inside the first half – as in Munich, even Heskey scored. When Michael Owen put them ahead against Brazil, anything was possible.

Except being England, it wasn't. In the end an injury-hit side failed to make a second-half impression even after the match-winner, Ronaldinho, had been sent off. Sven-Goran Eriksson's side take 2pts, the same as the USA, with their best finish since being

1930 semi-finalists, and Senegal, Africa's second quarter-finalists. Three group-winners – Mexico, Sweden and co-hosts Japan – take 1pt apiece.

Spain's latest tale of woe was a linesman deciding the ball had gone out of play before a cross that was successfully converted, this time to the benefit of South Korea, who had also received favourable decisions against Portugal and Italy, and now became the eighth different team to make the last four since Italia '90, just before Turkey – in their first World Cup Finals since 1954; they've not qualified again to date either – became the ninth.

That pair, 4pts each, fell to Germany – in their first semi-final as a united country – and Brazil, respectively, setting up a first final between two of the World Cup's most successful teams. A fumble by Oliver Kahn, the player of the tournament less than a year after that spanking by England, led to Ronaldo's first, and Brazil had a fifth victory, 2-0.

Their 13pts takes them to 66pts overall; Germany, despite 8pts, are overtaken as the leaders, 2pts behind.

Overall ranking 1970–2002	Points	Group winner bonus	Hemi-sphere bonus	Subtotal	Carried forward	Total
1 Brazil	13	+1		14	52	66
2 Germany	7	+1		8	56	64
3 Italy					42.5	42.5
4 Argentina					40	40
5 Holland					23.5	23.5
6 France					23	23
7 England	2			2	12	14
8 Poland					9.5	9.5
9 Spain	2	+1		3	6	9

(continued)

Overall ranking 1970–2002	Points	Group winner bonus	Hemi- sphere bonus	Subtotal	Carried forward	Total
10 Sweden		**+1**		**1**	**6.5**	**7.5**
11 = Mexico					6	6
11 = Belgium					6	6
13 USSR					5.5	5.5
14 South Korea	4	+1		5		5
15 = Bulgaria					4.5	4.5
15 = Peru					4.5	4.5
15 = Austria					4.5	4.5
15 = Yugoslavia					4.5	4.5
19 = Turkey	4			4		4
19 = Romania					4	4
19 = Uruguay					4	4
19 = Croatia					4	4
19 = Denmark		**+1**		**1**	**3**	**4**
24 Cameroon					3	3
25 East Germany					2.5	2.5
26 = USA	2			2		2
26 = Senegal	2			2		2
26 = Nigeria					2	2
26 = Czechoslovakia					2	2
26 = Republic of Ireland					2	2
31 = Japan		**+1**		**1**		**1**
31 = Morocco					1	1
31 = Northern Ireland					1	1

Germany 2006

If reaching a quarter-final in 2002 felt like an achievement, Sven-Goran Eriksson's failure to break England's penalty-losing streak at Euro 2004, a limp qualifying campaign and an appallingly prurient interest in a single man's sex life meant that the Swede was on his way out, come what may in Germany. And what came was another quarter-final, and another penalty defeat to Portugal. This one was with ten men after Wayne Rooney's absurd stamp on Ricardo Carvalho. Another 3pts for England, with the Portuguese winners another team to add to the list of post-Italia '90 semi-finalists.

Portugal's neighbours, Spain, were one of two group-winners, along with Switzerland, to lose in the last sixteen. While Switzerland's goalless, penalty-shoot-out defeat to Ukraine was probably the worst game of the Finals, Spain had another classic tale of misfortune: with the scores at 1-1, Thierry Henry took a dive to win the free-kick for the first of a pair of France goals in the last ten minutes. When would Spain's pain end? 1pt for them and the Swiss.

Ukraine lost their quarter-final to Italy, as expected. But the other two games carried on South American sides' poor records in Europe: Argentina losing on penalties to Germany, and Brazil falling to a resurgent France. 3pts each for the group-winning losers.

In the last four, Portugal went down limply, to France, while Germany – for whom that 2002 final was an anomaly in what proved to be a period of sustained mediocrity – rose to the occasion as hosts but fell to two late extra-time goals for Italy, as penalties beckoned. 5pts for the group-winning losers.

Just as in 1998, Zinedine left his mark on the final – but this time with a red card in his final competitive game, for a head-butt on Marco Materazzi. Italy, too, finally broke their run of penalty disasters. France take 8pts and the winners 13pts.

Overall, Germany claw back the 2pt deficit and now share their lead with Brazil, Italy have more than three times England's total and France are looking good, too.

Overall ranking 1970–2006	Points	Group winner bonus	Hemi-sphere bonus	Subtotal	Carried forward	Total
1= Germany	4	+1		5	64	69
1= Brazil	2	+1		3	66	69
3 Italy	13	+1		14	42.5	56.5
4 Argentina	2	+1		3	40	43
5 France	7			7	23	30
6 Holland					23.5	23.5
7 England	2	+1		3	14	17
8 Spain		+1		1	9	10
9 Poland					9.5	9.5
10 Sweden					7.5	7.5
11= Mexico					6	6
11= Belgium					6	6
13 USSR					5.5	5.5
14= South Korea					5	5
14= Portugal	4	+1		5		5
16= Bulgaria					4.5	4.5
16= Peru					4.5	4.5
16= Austria					4.5	4.5

Overall ranking 1970-94	Points	Group winner bonus	Hemi-sphere bonus	Subtotal	Carried forward	Total
16= Yugoslavia					4.5	4.5
20= Turkey					4	4
20= Romania					4	4
20= Uruguay					4	4
20= Croatia					4	4
20= Denmark					4	4
25 Cameroon					3	3
26 East Germany					2.5	2.5
27= USA					2	2
27= Senegal					2	2
27= Nigeria					2	2
27= Czechoslovakia					2	2
27= Republic of Ireland					2	2
27= Ukraine	2			2		2
33= Switzerland		+1		1		1
33= Japan					1	1
33= Morocco					1	1
33= Northern Ireland					1	1

South Africa 2010

A first African World Cup – and for the first time the hosts failed to make it out of their group. Still, more painful fates can happen than the one that befell South Africa.

Ask Ghana, for whom Asamoah Gyan missed a penalty against Uruguay that would have given the continent their first semi-finalists. Instead the South Americans – playing in the last four without the man who gave away the goal-saving penalty, Luis Suarez – reached the semis for the first time since 1970.

Or ask England, victims of a weird humiliation in the last sixteen, losing 4-1 to Germany despite scoring twice, the second being a Frank Lampard equaliser that the officials did not see had sailed over the line.

Of course, Ghana get 2pts and England – denied first place in their group by ineptitude and a late goal for the USA – get none.

There were three group-winning quarter-finalists eliminated, with 3pts awarded to each, all from South America: Paraguay narrowly by Spain, Argentina in emphatic fashion by Germany, and Brazil by Holland, Wesley Sneijder's double exacting a measure of national revenge for the 1998 semi-final defeat to the same team.

In the last four, the Dutch edged out Uruguay 3-2 and Spain won 1-0 for the third straight game, against Germany, to leave the losers with 5pts. For the Germans, that is enough to give them a 2pt overall lead.

The final, alas, was a letdown for everyone but the Spanish, who won 1-0 once again, against ten men in a game scarred by some horrendous Dutch clogging. Holland's third final ended with neutrals pleased they had lost, in contrast to '74 and '78.

The Dutch still get 7pts, the Spanish 14pts – the latter more than enough to overhaul England as they added the world title to the European crown, ending decades of letdowns.

Overall ranking 1970–2010	Points	Group winner bonus	Hemi-sphere bonus	Subtotal	Carried forward	Total
1 **Germany**	4	+1		5	69	74
2 **Brazil**	2	+1		3	69	72
3 Italy					56.5	56.5
4 **Argentina**	2	+1		3	43	46
5 **Holland**	7	+1		8	23.5	31.5
6 France					30	30
7 **Spain**	13	+1		14	10	24
8 England					17	17
9 Poland					9.5	9.5
10 **Uruguay**	4	+1		5	4	9
11 Sweden					7.5	7.5
12= Mexico					6	6
12= Belgium					6	6
14 USSR					5.5	5.5
15= South Korea					5	5
15= Portugal					5	5
17= Bulgaria					4.5	4.5
17= Peru					4.5	4.5
17= Austria					4.5	4.5
17= Yugoslavia					4.5	4.5
21= Turkey					4	4
21= Romania					4	4

(continued)

Overall ranking 1970–2010	Points	Group winner bonus	Hemi-sphere bonus	Subtotal	Carried forward	Total
21= Croatia					4	4
21= Denmark					4	4
25= Cameroon					3	3
25= Paraguay	2	+1		3		3
25= USA		+1		1	2	3
28 East Germany					2.5	2.5
29= Senegal					2	2
29= Nigeria					2	2
29= Czechoslovakia					2	2
29= Republic of Ireland					2	2
29= Ukraine					2	2
29= Ghana	2			2		2
35= Switzerland					1	1
35= Japan					1	1
35= Morocco					1	1
35= Northern Ireland					1	1

Brazil 2014

Since deposing England as World Champions in 1970, the Germans had already established themselves at the top of our tree before they reached Brazil, albeit by a narrow margin. What followed demonstrated the gap between the 1966 finalists in emphatic style: England failing to get out of their group for the first time since 1958, Germany becoming the first European team to win the World Cup in the Americas and doing so via a demolition of the hosts that will scar a generation of fans of the second best team in these rankings. England opts, Germany 14pts.

All four losing quarter-finalists were also group-winners: Colombia, France, Costa Rica and Belgium pick up 3pts each. France were already ahead of England and the others were not close enough to catch them. But semi-finalists Brazil – despite a humiliation for the ages – gain another 5pts and Holland 5.5pts, while Argentina pick up 8pts for losing the final.

→

Overall ranking 1970-2014	Points	Group winner bonus	Hemi-sphere bonus	Subtotal	Carried forward	Total
1 Germany	13	+1	+1	15	74	89
2 Brazil	4	+1		5	72	77
3 Italy					56.5	56.5
4 Argentina	7	+1		8	46	54
5 Holland	4	+1	+0.5	5.5	31.5	37
6 France	2	+1		3	30	33
7 Spain					24	24
8 England					17	17
9 Poland					9.5	9.5
10 = Uruguay					9	9
10 = Belgium	2	+1		3	6	9
12 Sweden					7.5	7.5
13 Mexico					6	6
14 USSR					5.5	5.5
15 = South Korea					5	5
15 = Portugal					5	5
17 = Bulgaria					4.5	4.5
17 = Peru					4.5	4.5
17 = Austria					4.5	4.5
17 = Yugoslavia					4.5	4.5
21 = Turkey					4	4
21 = Romania					4	4

Overall ranking 1970-94	Points	Group winner bonus	Hemi-sphere bonus	Subtotal	Carried forward	Total
21 = Croatia					4	4
21 = Denmark					4	4
25 = Cameroon					3	3
25 = Paraguay					3	3
25 = USA					3	3
25 = Colombia	2	+1		3		3
25 = Costa Rica	2	+1		3		3
30 East Germany					2.5	2.5
31 = Senegal					2	2
31 = Nigeria					2	2
31 = Czechoslovakia					2	2
31 = Republic of Ireland					2	2
31 = Ukraine					2	2
31 = Ghana					2	2
37 = Switzerland					1	1
37 = Japan					1	1
37 = Morocco					1	1
37 = Northern Ireland					1	1

The Fifty-Year View

It was the Germans who lost the 1966 final, the Germans who knocked out the World Champions in 1970 – and the Germans who outlasted Bobby Robson's side at Italia '90. For us that is a high point; for the Germans a losing semi would be a missed opportunity.

Overall, the Germans go out in the last eight about as often as England do; the difference is that when they don't lose a quarter-final, they usually reach the final, while we are lucky to make the last sixteen.

On the one hand, England are technically part of an elite club of World Cup winners. On the other, only Uruguay – a country with a population smaller than Scotland's – of those has fared worse in the past forty-eight years and even they can boast one more semi-final, bookending a long barren spell. And while the Dutch have never quite delivered in the final they have an emphatically superior record (bolstered by that European Championship win in 1988).

In the six finals up to Italia '90, England failed to reach two World Cup finals at all – but they made the last eight each time they did qualify, going one better in Italy. In the six finals since Gazza's tears, they have failed to qualify only the once – but on three of the occasions when they have made it, they failed to earn any points in our chart.

Since Italia '90, all the teams other than England who had previously won a World Cup have at least reached the semi-finals: Italy, Brazil, Germany, Uruguay and, in 2014, Argentina. Of that quintet, only Uruguay have not reached the final itself; instead France (won one, lost one), Spain (won one) and Holland (lost one) take the number of finalists in the past twenty-four years to seven, and it is these seven teams that head England in the table.

Sweden, Bulgaria, Croatia, Turkey, South Korea and Portugal join Uruguay in being semi-finalists. The fact that success has been so widely spread has an odd effect on our table: England have dropped only from equal-sixth to eighth. But our total of 5pts since Italia '90 is bettered emphatically by the seven teams above us, as well as narrowly by Sweden, while being matched by Uruguay, South Korea and Turkey. A further nine teams – Romania, Denmark, Senegal, Ukraine, Ghana, Paraguay, Colombia, Belgium and Costa Rica – can also claim our high point of a losing quarter-final. We have not quite slipped into the pack, but we are deeply unconvincing leaders of it.

We can analyse many of England's failures and point to a freakish or knife-edge element – two shootouts in which England needed just one more decent penalty-taker; Campbell's (not unreasonably) disallowed goal in '98; Lampard's (absurdly) disallowed goal in 2010, in the only World Cup Finals game England have lost by more than one since the 1962 quarter-final. But the trend is unmistakeable and before the unfortunate exits we never impressed in the manner of Spain – for so long the victims of ill-luck until their 2008–12 run of two European Championships and a World Cup.

Only once since 1970 have we reached a quarter-final as favourites, against Cameroon in 1990, and we almost made a hash of that one. The group-stage victory against Argentina in 2002 was the one time in World Cup Finals that we have won a match as underdogs since – well, arguably forever. Sometimes we punch our weight, but we never punch any higher.

You could make an optimistic case through rose-tinted spectacles that had the team gone further in '82, '86, or '90, this would have been a correction to some sort of norm, and that the '70s were serial misfortunes of the kind that afflicted Spain. Since Italia '90 and especially Germany 2006, though, increasing failure has knocked off those glasses and stomped on them. An England success now, whether continental or global, would smack not of a rightful return to the top but more of the sort of anomalous moment of European Championship triumph enjoyed by Denmark in 1992 and Greece twelve years later.

Does the past offer any grounds for hope? If you look far

enough back. England had not reached a semi-final before 1966, either, with just a couple of convincing quarter-final defeats to go with the farce of losing to the USA in 1950 and the 1958 brave battle in the shadow of genuine tragedy, the Munich air disaster, that robbed England of a number of certain star-players at that tournament. The circumstances in 1958 were horrifically unique, but the fact remains that it was only eight years between England failing to get out of their group and being World Champions. 1966 can seem inevitable with hindsight but no host nation had won the tournament since 1934. After the 2018 bid debacle (with the slight consolation of the subsequent disintegration of Sepp Blatter's FIFA) there is no home World Cup for England remotely on the horizon, but we could get to play the conclusion of the transcontinental Euro 2020 at Wembley if we can navigate our way around the mainland. There has been no true shock-winner of a World Cup since West Germany beat the mighty Hungary in 1954, but the European miracles of Denmark and Greece are a reminder that knockout football will always have an unpredictable element.

We can, therefore, still dream. But the lesson of the past fifty years, and especially the past two decades, is that it is only a dream – and unless something fundamental changes it will remain so.

Technical Area

The 1966 Final Scoreboard

Asif Burhan

A RECORD SEVENTY NATIONS entered the qualification tournament from which fourteen countries emerged to join England, the hosts, and Brazil, the holders. Portugal and North Korea were making their debuts at the World Cup Finals. Sixteen African nations boycotted the tournament in protest at FIFA's qualification process but North Korea was the first Asian team to reach this stage since neighbours South Korea in 1954.

The format of this World Cup exactly mirrored that of the previous edition in Chile: sixteen finalists were split into four geographical round-robin groups, the top two in each group qualifying for the quarter-finals. Where teams were level on points, Goal Average was used to split the teams as in the Football League at the time. During the knockout stages, if matches were still level after extra time, a coin toss was used to decide who would progress, apart from after the final where the match would be replayed. The Uruguay vs France game in Group A was moved to White City because Wembley was already booked that night for a greyhound meeting. On the advice of the Foreign Office, the FA decided that the national anthems of the competing teams would only be played prior to the opening match and the final. It was subsequently revealed that this was a subterfuge to prevent North Korea's anthem being played and the Communist State being afforded international diplomatic recognition.

Group 1

England eventually qualified comfortably as Group 1 winners but began poorly in a drab encounter with two-time champions Uruguay. France missed the chance to grab the initiative in the group when they failed to defeat Mexico after falling behind the following day and despite taking the lead against Uruguay in their next match at White City, France's defeat left them needing to beat the hosts in their final match. England once more looked unconvincing against Mexico until Bobby Charlton's long-range goal finally awoke them, the second from Hunt putting England ahead of Uruguay on Goal Average. Uruguay – never eliminated at the group stage of a World Cup – ensured qualification with another 0-0 draw against Mexico, before England won the group with another two goals from Hunt against a French side playing with ten fit players, and reduced to nine after Stiles' aggressive challenge on Simon.

1	Played	Won	Drew	Lost)	Goals For	Goals Against	Points	Goal Average
England (Q)	3	2	1	0	4	0	5	∞
Uruguay (Q)	3	1	2	0	2	1	5	2
Mexico	3	0	2	1	1	3	2	0.3
France	3	0	1	2	2	5	1	0.4

England   **0-0**   **Uruguay**

11 July — Wembley Stadium, London — 87,148

France   **1-1**   **Mexico**

Hausser (62)   Borja (48)

13 July — Wembley Stadium, London — 69,237

Uruguay   **2-1**   **France**

Rocha (26)   De Bourgoing (pen. 15)

15 July — White City Stadium, London — 45,662

England   **2-0**   **Mexico**

Charlton. R (37)

Hunt (73)

16 July — Wembley Stadium, London — 92,570

Mexico   **0-0**   **Uruguay**

19 July — Wembley Stadium, London — 61,112

England   **2-0**   **France**

Hunt (38, 75)

20 July — Wembley Stadium, London — 98,270

Group 2

The last European winners of the World Cup, West Germany, qualified impressively ahead of the South American champions, Argentina, and European Champions, Spain. Argentina joined them in the last eight, finishing second ahead of Spain, whom they beat in their first match, but won few friends in doing so, defending aggressively and having Albrecht sent off against West Germany. The Germans, with twenty-one year-old Franz Becken-bauer looking imperious, began superbly, scoring some wonder-ful goals against Switzerland but played cautiously against Argentina. Spain could not recover after losing their opening match and despite coming from behind to beat Switzerland needed to defeat West Germany to qualify ahead of them. They took the lead through Futse but Emmerich soon equalised. A late goal from Seeler, scoring in his third World Cup, ensured West Germany won the group ahead of Argentina on Goal Average thereby avoiding England in the quarter-final.

2	Played	Won	Drew	Lost	Goals For	Goals Against	Points	Goal Average
West Germany (Q)	3	2	1	0	7	1	5	7
Argentina (Q)	3	2	1	0	4	1	5	4
Spain	3	1	0	2	4	5	2	0.8
Switzerland	3	0	0	3	1	9	1	0.11

West Germany	**5-0**	**Switzerland**
Held (17)		
Haller (21, pen. 77)		
Beckenbauer (40, 52)		

12 July — Hillsborough Stadium — Sheffield, 36,127

Argentina	**2-1**	**Spain**
Artime (65, 77)		Pirri (67)

13 July — Villa Park, Birmingham — 42,738

Spain	**2-1**	**Switzerland**
Sanchis (57)		Quentin (31)
Amancio (75)		

15 July — Hillsborough Stadium, Sheffield — 32,028

Argentina	**0-0**	**West Germany**

16 July — Villa Park, Birmingham — 46,587

Argentina	**2-0**	**Switzerland**
Artime (52)		
Onega (79)		

19 July — Hillsborough Stadium, Sheffield — 32,127

West Germany	**2-1**	**Spain**
Emmerich (39)		Futsé (23)
Seeler (84)		

20 July — Villa Park, Birmingham — 42,187

Group 3

Reigning World champions, Brazil began with two stunning free-kick goals in a win over a defensive Bulgaria but an injury sustained by Pelé hindered the rest of their campaign. Portugal, playing in their first World Cup, surprised many by scoring after a minute and defeating the talented Hungarians against the general run of play in Manchester before easily disposing of Bulgaria in their next match. It was Hungary, not Brazil, who would join them after the match of the tournament at Goodison Park. Without Pelé, Brazil lost their first World Cup match since losing to the same opponents in the 1954 tournament and this new generation of Magyars seemed to be turning the clock back. Brazil almost certainly now needed to beat Portugal in their final game but after a returning Pelé was injured again by a rugged challenge from Morais, that never looked likely. Eusébio looked every inch the new Pelé, scoring a spectacular goal to the acclaim of the highest attendance outside London. The next day, Hungary confirmed Brazil's first-round elimination, coming from behind to beat Bulgaria with Bene scoring for a third match in succession.

3	Played	Won	Drew	Lost	Goals For	Goals Against	Points	Goal Average
Portugal (Q)	3	3	0	0	9	2	6	4.5
Hungary (Q)	3	2	0	1	7	5	4	1.4
Brazil	3	1	0	2	4	6	2	0.67
Bulgaria	3	0	0	3	1	8	1	0.13

Brazil   **2-0**   **Bulgaria**

Pelé (13)

Garrincha (63)

12 July — Goodison Park, Liverpool — 47,308

Portugal   **3-1**   **Hungary**

José Augusto (1, 67)   Bene (60)

Torres (90)

13 July — Old Trafford, Manchester — 29,886

Hungary   **3-1**   **Brazil**

Bene (3)   Tostão (14)

Farkas (64)

Mészóly (pen. 73)

15 July — Goodison Park, Liverpool — 51,387

Portugal   **3-0**   **Bulgaria**

Vutsov (og. 17)

Eusébio (38)

Torres (81)

16 July — Old Trafford, Manchester — 25,438

Portugal   **3-1**   **Brazil**

Simões (15)   Rildo (70)

Eusébio (27, 85)

19 July — Goodison Park, Liverpool — 58,479

Hungary   **3-1**   **Bulgaria**

Davidov (og. 43)   Asparuhov (15)

Mészóly (45)

Bene (54)

20 July — Old Trafford, Manchester — 24,129

Group 4

Group 4 began predictably with the Soviet Union outmuscling the North Koreans to win easily and Italy gaining revenge for their defeat four years earlier in the Battle of Santiago by beating Chile in Sunderland. North Korea looked to be heading out in their next game, trailing Chile for over an hour to a penalty, before a stunning late volley from Pak Seung-zin kept them in the finals. The next game in the group was supposed to decide who would win, a single goal from winger Chislenko gave the Soviet Union an unexpected victory over Italy in a tight game. However Italy still only needed a draw against North Korea in their final game to qualify but lost their captain Bulgarelli to injury in the first half. Pak Doo-Ik then shocked the Italians by scoring just before half-time – Italy's ten men could not find an equaliser and were eliminated. Chile could have still qualified ahead of North Korea but were unable to defeat the powerful Soviet Union in their final match. Two goals from Porkujan ensured the Soviet Union were one of only two teams to maintain a 100% record throughout the group stage.

4	Played	Won	Drew	Lost	Goals For	Goals Against	Points	Goal Average
Soviet Union (Q)	3	3	0	0	6	1	6	6
North Korea (Q)	3	1	1	1	2	4	3	0.5
Italy	3	1	0	2	2	2	2	1
Chile	3	0	1	2	2	5	1	0.4

Soviet Union   **3-0**   **North Korea**

Malofeyev (31, 88)

Banishevskiy (33)

13 July — Ayresome Park, Middlesbrough — 23,006

Italy   **2-0**   **Chile**

Mazzola (8)

Barison (88)

14 July — Roker Park, Sunderland — 27,199

Chile   **1-1**   **North Korea**

Marcos (pen. 27)   Pak Seung-zin (88)

15 July — Ayresome Park, Middlesbrough — 13,792

Soviet Union   **1-0**   **Italy**

Chislenko (57)

16 July — Roker Park, Sunderland — 27,793

North Korea   **1-0**   **Italy**

Pak Doo-Ik (42)

19 July — Ayresome Park, Middlesbrough — 17,829

Soviet Union   **2-1**   **Chile**

Porkujan (28, 85)   Marcos (32)

20 July — Roker Park, Sunderland — 16,027

Quarter-Finals

World Cup newcomers, Portugal and North Korea, produced
the highest-scoring match of the Finals that ended with the
expected result but not before a sensational opening twenty-five
minutes that saw the Koreans leading 3-0. North Korea showed
no fear, throwing themselves at Portugal from the start and
taking an early lead, Pak Seung-zin finding the top corner from
the edge of the area. Portugal stretched North Korea's goalkeeper, Li Chan-myung, three times but it was North Korea who
scored again when Perreira was left in no-man's land after
misjudging a cross and Li Dong-woon volleyed in at close range
from the pullback. Moments later, Yang Seung-kook waltzed
through a scattered defence to make it three. European Footballer of the Year, Eusébio almost immediately reduced the
Koreans lead, racing through onto José Augusto's pass to score.
Shortly before half-time, Eusébio scored from the penalty spot
after Torres was felled in the area. The second half was one-way
traffic. Eusébio's third was similar to his first, this time from
Simões' through-pass, his fourth, another penalty when he
himself was chopped down after a coruscating run down the
left. In the eightieth minute, Eusébio's corner was headed back
across goal by Torres leaving an unmarked José Augusto to head
home from close range. Portugal head to Wembley for the
semi-final, North Korea go home, but their contribution to this
match will never be forgotten.

	Portugal	**5-3**	**North Korea**
	Eusébio (27, pen. 43,		Pak Seung-zin (1)
	56, pen. 59)		Li Dong-woon (22)
	José Augusto (80)		Yang Seung-kook (25)

23 July — Goodison Park, Liverpool— 40,248

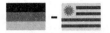

In the clash of the former World Champions in Sheffield, the scoreline does not begin to tell the story of a match disfigured by two Uruguayan dismissals. It was the South Americans who began on the front foot. Tilkowski touching Cortes' sensational strike onto the bar before full-back Schnellinger produced an equally good save on the line from Rocha's goal-bound header. English referee, Finney, failed to award a penalty and the Uruguayans' sense of injustice was heightened moments later when Held's weak shot was deflected past Makurkiewicz by Haller. Uruguay continued to look the better side, regularly testing Tilkowski until captain Troche was sent off for retaliation on Emmerich off-the-ball. Shortly after, Silva was also sent off for violently kicking Haller. Thereafter, West Germany were in control but it took until the seventieth minute before the elegant Beckenbauer glided through, playing a one-two with Seeler and side-stepping Makurkiewicz. Seeler then rifled the ball into the top corner before Haller side-footed home after a defensive slip.

West Germany   **4-0**   **Uruguay**

Haller (11, 83)
Beckenbauer (70)
Seeler (75)

23 July — Hillsborough Stadium, Sheffield — 40,007

The Soviet Union withstood a late siege from Hungary to progress to their first-ever World Cup semi-final. Hungary were made to pay for two goalkeeping errors by Gelei. The first after only five minutes, in allowing a tame shot by Porkujan to slip under his body where Chislenko pounced to poke in from almost on the goal line. The second at the start of the second half, when he misjudged the flight of a left-wing Khusainov free kick leaving Porkujan with the simple task of finishing from close range. Bene, freed by Mészóly, scored for the fourth game in a row soon after and Hungary then dominated. Porkujan blocked a fierce Mészóly volley, Szepesi fired narrowly wide. An acrobatic overhead kick from Mészóly struck the angle of post and bar before Yashin made a flying save from Sipos' free kick. Had he been in the Hungarian goal, the result may have been very different.

Soviet Union	**2-1**	**Hungary**
Chislenko (5)		Bene (57)
Porkujan (46)		

23 July — Roker Park, Sunderland — 26,884

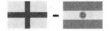

England scraped into the semi-finals of the World Cup for the first time in their history at the expense of one of the World Cup favourites but made hard work of defeating a side playing with ten men for nearly an hour. The hosts began on the front foot, Bobby Charlton nearly scoring direct from a corner and Geoff Hurst, in for the injured Greaves, testing Roma with a long-range effort after a quick exchange of passes. Thereafter, Argentina stifled England, indeed Mas nearly caught out Banks in the nineteenth minute, hitting the side-netting with a surprise volley. In the thirty-sixth minute, Argentinian captain Rattin was sent off by German referee Kreitlein for persistent dissent, Rattin's persistent refusal to accept the decision held up the game for over ten minutes. Early in the second half, Roma again denied Hurst from point-blank range but clear chances were at a premium as England struggled in the heat. Mas nearly caught England out, breaking behind Jack Charlton, but he was unable to hit the target after taking the ball wide. The breakthrough eventually came twelve minutes from time, Wilson finding Peters on the left wing whose near-post cross was flicked home by his West Ham teammate Geoff Hurst. It was a rare moment of quality from an unexpected source and enough to decide a poor match.

England   **1-0**   **Argentina**

Hurst (78)

23 July — Wembley Stadium, London — 90, 584

Semi-Finals

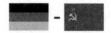

West Germany reached their second World Cup final after making heavy weather of beating a Soviet Union team reduced to ten men before half-time when Chislenko, their best winger, was sent off for foolishly lashing out at Held. The Germans had dominated the first half with only Yashin denying them but it took until the forty-second minute for them to score, Schnellinger robbing Chislenko and striding out of defence before sliding a fine pass to Haller who struck the ball first time past Yashin at his near post. Beckenbauer almost extended the lead in the second half when his long-range shot hit the side-netting. Midway through the half, the same player glided past his marker before driving home superbly with his left foot past a startled Yashin. The Soviet Union unexpectedly pulled one back when Tilkowski, earlier injured diving for a shot, dropped the ball under pressure straight to Porkujan who volleyed into the roof of the net. Porkujan then headed over when well placed and the Soviet Union's chance to force extra time was gone.

West Germany	**2-1**	**Soviet Union**
Haller (42)		Porkujan (88)
Beckenbauer (67)		

25 July — Goodison Park, Liverpool — 38,273

England deservedly won a place in the 1966 World Cup final after a fine match at Wembley, Bobby Charlton scoring two goals in perhaps his best performance in an England shirt. Early long-range efforts from Peters and Charlton tested Portuguese goalkeeper Perreira before Wilson's long ball fell kindly for Roger Hunt racing forward. Perreira rushed out to clear but Charlton, following up, swept the ball home from thirty yards. Portugal responded with Coluna shooting from long-range and Eusébio volleying powerfully to test Banks. In the second half, England maintained their lead and in the seventieth minute, Cohen looked for Hurst down the right of the penalty area. He won the ball by outmuscling his marker Carlos and laid the ball off perfectly for the onrushing Charlton to drive the ball across Perreira and into the net. Almost immediately, a Simões cross from the right evaded Banks and Torres' goalbound header was flicked away by Jack Charlton's hand. Eusébio scored his eighth goal of the finals from the penalty spot and Portugal pressed for an equaliser, Coluna forcing Banks into a save, but England had done enough to win.

England   **2-1**   **Portugal**

Charlton. R (30, 80)   Eusébio (pen. 82)

26 July — Wembley Stadium, London — 94,493

Play-off for Third Place

The largest crowd of the finals at a match not involving England saw Portugal become the first team since Germany in 1934 to finish third on their World Cup debut. The tournament's leading goalscorer, Eusébio, stretched his lead over Helmut Haller and moved closer to the £1000 prize for the tournament's top goalscorer by opening the scoring with his fourth penalty in three games. After a Soviet defender handled a Festa free kick destined for Torres' head, Eusébio again struck the ball high to the goalkeeper's right, his ninth goal of this World Cup. The Soviet Union equalised just before half-time, Malofeyev poking in from close range after Perreira spilled a straightforward Metrevelli shot. The second half produced fewer chances and extra time looked likely until José Torres flicked on a long Hilario cross, which was headed back to him to volley home spectacularly past Lev Yashin. Yashin's final act was to stop a drive from José Augusto and at thirty-five this was surely the former European Footballer of the Year's last appearance on the world stage.

Portugal   **2-1**   **Soviet Union**

Eusébio (pen. 12)   Malofeyey (43)

Torres (89)

29 July — Wembley Stadium, London — 87,69

The Final

In a match full of drama, controversy and no little skill, England became the fifth country to win the World Cup, after extra time at Wembley Stadium. England began brightly with Peters and Charlton testing Tilkowski, who suffered an injury to his shoulder in a collision with Hurst. After twelve minutes, England were shocked when Wilson's weak header was seized upon by Haller who opened the scoring for the third match in a row. England struck back quickly, captain Bobby Moore first won and then took a free kick from which an unmarked Hurst glanced home the equaliser. England had the better of the second half and deservedly took the lead in the seventy-eighth minute. Ball forced a corner which he took, Hurst worked some space on the edge of the area and his shot deflected up in the air, Peters reacted fastest to volley home from close-range. A last-minute free kick allowed the Germans one final chance. England failed to clear as the ball ricocheted around the penalty area and Weber slotted it into the net before Wilson and Banks could intervene. In extra time, England tried to force the pace, Charlton hitting a post before Ball's cut back allowed Hurst to turn and shoot powerfully against the underside of the bar. The linesman from the Soviet Union adjudged the ball had bounced over the line, to the chagrin of the Germans. In the final minute, with the Germans committed up-field, Bobby Moore brought the ball out of defence and released Hurst once more, running free, his left foot strike found the top corner of Tilkowski's net to confirm his hat-trick and England's place in history.

England	**4-2**	**West Germany**
Hurst (18, 101, 120)		Haller (12)
Peters (78)		Weber (89)

30 July — Wembley Stadium, London — 96,924

The '66 England Team:
What Happened Next

Asif Burhan

1. Gordon Banks
1966 tournament record: Played 6 matches, 3 goals conceded

Set a new World Cup record going 442 minutes without conceding a goal, which stood until Peter Shilton surpassed it in 1982. England's number one for the next six years and voted Footballer of the Year in 1972, he was involved in a car accident that year which cost him the vision in his right eye, effectively ending his top-level career.

2. George Cohen
Played 6 matches

Started all six games and remained ever-present until 1967 when a serious knee injury sustained against Liverpool curtailed his career. He was the last Fulham player to play for England until Bobby Zamora in 2010. After a five-year battle with cancer George Cohen has become a tireless campaigner for a number of cancer charities.

3. Ray Wilson
Played 6 matches

Another who played every minute, it was Wilson's uncharacteristic mistake that presented Helmut Haller with the opening goal in the final. First choice through to the 1968 European Nations' Cup, Wilson then suffered a training-ground injury that summer which ended his England career. After retiring in 1971, he joined his brother-in-law's undertaking business.

4. Nobby Stiles
Played 6 matches

Stiles failed to impress in England's opening games and gained notoriety for a mistimed challenge on France's Jacques Simon that earned him a booking and a reprimand from FIFA. The FA asked Ramsey to drop Stiles but he refused, threatening to walk out on the job. Stiles was retained and starred in the semi-final, neutralising the threat of Eusébio. He played for England for another year before being replaced as Ramsey's first-choice defensive midfielder by Alan Mullery. In 1968 he again got the better of Eusébio at Wembley as Manchester United became the first English club to win the European Cup. He was part of the squad in 1970 but did not play. After two serious cartilage operations ended his time at Manchester United he went on to coach Vancouver Whitecaps before returning to join the youth-team coching staff at Old Trafford.

5. Jack Charlton
Played 6 matches, 1 assist

Part of a rock-solid centre-back partnership with Moore throughout the tournament, Charlton's header against France led to Roger Hunt's second goal. His deliberate handball against Portugal caused England to concede a penalty, their first goal conceded of the tournament, in the semi-final. Charlton was replaced as first-choice centre-back by Brian Labone in 1968 but travelled with the squad to Mexico '70, playing one game. He later managed the Republic of Ireland, including against England in the 1990 World Cup where they famously reached the quarter-finals.

6. Bobby Moore
Played 6 matches, 2 assists

Imperious throughout the tournament, he was close to missing the final due to tonsillitis but recovered in time. Moore won the FIFA award for Player of the Tournament, memorably assisting England's first and last goals in the final. Arrested in Bogotá for an alleged jewellery theft, shortly before the 1970 tournament, on the pitch he went on to perform flawlessly. Months after the tournament he was finally cleared of all charges. England's record appearance holder for sixteen years until overtaken in 1989 by Peter Shilton, he still holds the joint-record for most England appearances as captain with Billy Wright. He died in 1993, aged 51, after suffering from bowel cancer.

7. Alan Ball
Played 4 matches, 1 assist

Started the tournament against Uruguay but did not return until the change of formation for the quarter-final. Better suited to 4-3-3, he excelled in the final where he was the youngest player on the pitch. It was from his run and cross that Geoff Hurst scored the decisive and disputed third goal. Capped seventy-two times and twice moving for record transfer fees, Ball went on to manage various clubs. He died suddenly from a heart attack in 2007, aged sixty-one.

8. Jimmy Greaves
Played 3 matches, 1 assist

Unable to score in the group games, despite laying on Roger Hunt's goal against Mexico, England's record goalscorer suffered a shin injury against France following a kick by Joseph Bonnel which required four stitches. Declared himself fit for the final but was not picked. Only played three times for England thereafter, scoring once. Battled with alcoholism for years before becoming a successful television pundit.

9. Bobby Charlton
Played 6 matches, 3 goals

Came out of the World Cup as arguably the greatest footballer in the world after proving instrumental in England's success. His energetic goal against Mexico in their second game shook England from the lethargy of the team's poor opener with Uruguay and his two goals in the semi-final were the highlight of his '66 and England's best performance of the tournament. It is testament to his ability that West Germany's best player, Franz Beckenbauer, was chosen to man-mark him in the final yet he still managed to hit a post. Charlton went on to regain his position as England's leading goalscorer in 1968, a record that stood for forty-seven years until surpassed by Wayne Rooney, scorer to date of one lone goal at the World Cup Finals, in 2015. On the board of Directors at Manchester United since 1984, he remains England's greatest and most decorated footballer of all time.

10. Geoff Hurst
Played 3 matches, 4 goals, 2 assists

The unlikely hero. Uncapped until four months before the World Cup Finals, Hurst was unused in the tournament until Greaves' injury against France forced a reshuffle. Hurst proceeded to be a revelation, involved in all but one of the seven goals that England scored in the knockout stages. His intelligent link-up play was decisive in setting up Charlton's winning goal in the semi-final and his hat-trick in the final, still the only one in history, consisting of a header, a right-foot strike and a left-foot shot. Hurst scored for England in three consecutive tournaments in '66, Euro '68 and Mexico '70, a record not equalled until Alan Shearer scored at Euro '96, France '98 and Euro 2000 at the turn of the century. Briefly a manager at Chelsea and an insurance salesman, Hurst is now an ambassador for various sponsors of the game.

11. John Connelly
Played 1 match

Started the tournament in a front three and came closest to breaking the stalemate against Uruguay, hitting the bar and post. Connelly was replaced for the next game and never played for England again. Released by Manchester United that summer, he played for Blackburn and Bury before retiring to run a fish-and-chip shop, "Connelly's Plaice." He died in 2012, aged seventy-four.

12. Ron Springett

Springett never saw action in the Finals and never played for England again after appearing in the pre-tournament game against Norway in Oslo. Uniquely swapped for his brother when he moved to Queen's Park Rangers in 1967, he went on to become involved in a gardening business. He died in 2015, aged eighty.

13. Peter Bonetti

Third-choice goalkeeper in 1966, Bonetti was thrust into the limelight for only his seventh cap when Gordon Banks came down with food poisoning on the eve of the 1970 World Cup quarter-final. Criticised for his performance as England went out to West Germany, he never played for England again but enjoyed a stellar career with Chelsea as a Cup-winning player and latterly as goalkeeping coach.

14. Jimmy Armfield

England Captain at World Cup 1962, a broken toe prevented Armfield from playing in the 1966 World Cup. He never represented his country again but helped Blackpool win promotion to the First Division in 1970. Managed Leeds United, taking them to the 1975 European Cup final before becoming a respected journalist and radio pundit, still regularly appearing as a match summariser on BBC Radio 5Live.

15. Gerry Byrne

Never played for England during or after the 1966 World Cup. A one-club man, he continued to represent Liverpool with distinction until injury forced him to retire in 1969. Thereafter, Byrne briefly joined the coaching staff. Suffering from Alzheimer's Disease, he passed away aged seventy-seven in November 2015.

16. Martin Peters
Played 5 matches, 1 goal, 1 assist
Came into the team after the disappointing opening game and

never lost his place. He supplied the near-post cross that helped break the deadlock in the tight quarter-final with Argentina before scoring what so nearly proved to be the winning goal in the final. Famously labelled "ten years ahead of his time" by Alf Ramsey in 1968, Peters was not always as respected by a critical media. Yet he continued to play for England for another eight years, scoring twenty goals from midfield. Peters became England's first £200,000 footballer when he moved from West Ham to Tottenham Hotspur in part-exchange for Jimmy Greaves who went in the opposite direction. After retirement he worked in insurance and is now employed providing matchday hospitality for paying guests at White Hart Lane.

17. Ron Flowers

Another who never played for England during or after the tournament, Flowers finally left Wolves in 1967 after fifteen years at the club to become player-manager at Northampton Town before leading Telford United to the FA Trophy final. After retiring, he opened a sports shop in Wolverhampton, "Ron Flowers Sports," which still trades today.

18. Norman Hunter

Hunter remained Bobby Moore's understudy for much of his England career, winning twenty-eight caps. His only World Cup appearance came as a late substitute in the 1970 defeat to West Germany. Finally picked ahead of Moore for the vital qualifier against Poland in 1973, it was Hunter's error that led to the Polish goal in a 1-1 draw and England failed to qualify for World Cup '74. He won numerous honours at Leeds, earning the distinction of becoming the first-ever PFA Player of the Year in 1974. After various coaching and management roles, he joined the after-dinner circuit before working for BBC Radio Leeds.

19. Terry Paine

Played 1 match

One of three wingers who Ramsey rotated in the group stages, Paine's chance came in the second match against Mexico, his nineteenth and last England cap during which he was concussed but forced to play on. Made a record 801 appearances for Southampton over seventeen years and was their record goalscorer until overtaken first by Mick Channon and then Matthew Le Tissier. His career total of 819 league appearances has only been surpassed subsequently by Tony Ford and Peter Shilton. He emigrated to South Africa to become a football coach and now works there as a TV presenter. He was an ambassador for South Africa's successful 2010 World Cup bid.

20. Ian Callaghan

Played 1 match, 1 assist

Callaghan replaced Paine for the final group game against France and crossed for club-mate Roger Hunt's opening goal. When Ramsey opted to forsake his wingers in the quarter-final, Callaghan was dropped for Alan Ball and he did not play for England again until eleven years later, a record gap. In the meantime, Callaghan re-invented himself as a midfielder and won every honour available except a League Cup Winner's medal. Retired to set up an insurance business and today he remains Liverpool's record appearance holder, president of their official fan club and, alongside Bobby Charlton and Nobby Stiles, one of only three Englishmen to win both the World Cup with England and a European Cup with their club.

21. Roger Hunt

Played 6 matches, 3 goals, 1 assist

Played every game and finished the group stage as joint-top scorer with three of England's Group One goals. In the knockout stages it was Hunt's run that created the opening goal of the semi-final and may have scored a goal in the final had he chosen to follow up Geoff Hurst's shot against the bar in extra time that was of course credited to Hurst. Hunt only scored two more goals for England in the next three years. He left Liverpool in 1969 but remains their all-time highest scorer of league goals. Retired in 1972 to work in the family haulage business and for a while formed part of the Football League Pools Panel.

22. George Eastham

Never played for England again after scoring in the final game of the pre-tournament Scandinavian tour. Left Arsenal for Stoke in the summer of 1966 and spent seven years there, scoring the winning goal in the 1972 League Cup final and briefly managing the club. Emigrated to Johannesburg in 1978 and set up a sportswear company. An opponent of apartheid, he coached black children and is now president of the South African Arsenal Supporters' Club.

Manager: Alf Ramsey

A year after the World Cup, Ramsey became the first football manager to be knighted. He led England to third place at the 1968 European Nations' Cup and was confident of retaining the World Cup in Mexico two years later. A quarter-final defeat to West Germany was followed by another two years later to the same opposition in the Nations' Cup. Failure to beat either Wales or Poland at Wembley in 1973 meant England did not qualify for the 1974 World Cup and Ramsey was sacked by the FA shortly after. Following a brief stint as manager of Birmingham City and serving as Technical Director at Greek club Panathinaikos, Ramsey retired in 1980. Following a stroke in 1998 and suffering from Alzheimer's, England's only World Cup-winning manager passed away after a heart attack in April 1999.

A 1966 Kitbag of Further Reading and Resources

1966 *and Not All That* is meant to be a serious book to be enjoyed. Not always an easy mix to achieve, so to that end we have purposely avoided the academic convention of footnotes, endnotes and bibliographies to allow the flow of reading chapters in whatever order the reader prefers. Instead, in this section books and other resources are listed in thematic groups so if an intellectual, or other, fancy has been tickled by what you read, the ideas and incidents covered can be followed up.

1966 World Cup History

The best book to date (!) on 1966 is *England's Glory*, written by Dave Hill for the thirtieth anniversary in "real-time" style. Roger Hutchinson's *66! The Inside Story of England's World Cup Triumph* is the most detailed account of the team and their victorious campaign. David Thomson's *4-2* is a brilliant elegy to all that 1966 came to represent for one fan. *An Amber Glow* by Peter Allen deals with much of the politics and organising of the tournament. The book *1966 Uncovered* by photographer Peter Robinson and designer Doug Cheeseman magnificently creates a visual history of the 1966 World Cup. Dilwyn Porter's essay "Egg and Chips with the Connellys: Remembering 1966," published in the journal *Sport in History*, Volume 29, number 43, 2009, is a really good account of the social history of '66. A counterfactual history of "What Happened Next" is provided by Kim Newman's "The Germans Won" in the thirtieth-anniversary 1996 collection of writing, *A Book of Two Halves*, edited by Nicholas Royle. The real version, in terms of what happened to the England team, is recorded by Simon Hattenstone in his book *The Best of Times*, published for the fortieth anniversary in 2006.

1966 England Players' Biographies

Home tales from the '66 squad are provided by two autobiographies, each published just a year after the tournament: Alan Ball's *Ball of Fire* and Jack Charlton's *For Leeds and England*. Geoff Hurst's *The World Game* appeared a year later in 1968. *Goals from Nowhere!* by Martin Peters was published in 1970. Jeff Powell's *Bobby Moore: The Life and Times of a Sporting Hero* was published shortly after Bobby Moore's death as an unapologetic tribute volume. *Jack and Bobby*, by Leo McKinstry, is a superb biography of the World Cup-winning Charlton brothers, while Matt Dickinson's *The Man in Full* seeks to uncover what it was that made Bobby Moore such a special player and England captain. Alan Tomlinson and Christopher Young's chapter "Golden boys and golden memories: Fiction, ideology, and reality in *Roy of the Rovers* and the Death of the Hero" from the collection *A Necessary Fantasy? The Heroic Figure in Children's Popular Culture*, edited by Dudley Jones and Tony Watkins, puts a lot of the myth-making contained in the idea of footballer as hero, fictional or non-fictional, into perspective.

The Manager

For more on the playing side of the '66 victory, both Dave Bowler's biography of Alf Ramsey, *Winning Isn't Everything*, and Leo McKinistry's *Sir Alf* provide essential insights into how England did it. Jonathan Wilson's *The Anatomy of England* analyses the evolution of England playing styles, before and after Ramsey, while Niall Edworthy's *The Second Most Important Job in the Country* gives a wider perspective on the problems England managers have faced to build on the '66 success. Tony Pawson's *The Football Managers*, published in 1974, is a very '70s view of football management. Jimmy Greaves took a while longer to go into print with his own view of Sir Alf and other England managers; his book, with Norman Giller, *Don't Shoot the Manager: The Revealing Story of England's Soccer Bosses*, was published in 1993. A more instant assessment of Ramsey's achievement was "Sir Alfred Ramsey – The Man

Who Must Win – and Did" by Brian James, in Lesley Frewin's *The Saturday Men: A Book of International Football*, published in 1967.

The Legacy of '66

The significance of '66 culturally is explained by John Clarke and Chas Critcher's chapter "1966 and all that: England's World Cup victory," in *Off the Ball: The Football Word Cup*, edited by Alan Tomlinson and Garry Whannel. And again by Chas Critcher, in his chapter "England and the World Cup: World Cup Willies, English Football and the Myth of 1966," in the collection edited by John Sugden and Alan Tomlinson, *Hosts and Champions: Soccer Cultures, National Identities and the USA World Cup*. Two essays by sports historian Tony Mason further broaden an understanding of the historical significance of the tournament: "England 1966: Traditional and modern?" in *National Identity and Global Sports Events: Culture, politics, and spectacle in the Olympics and the football World Cup*, edited by Alan Tomlinson and Christopher Young; and "England 1966 and all that," in Kay Schiller and Stefan Rinke's edited collection, *The FIFA World Cup 1930-2010: Politics, Commerce, Spectacle and Identities.*

'66 in Popular Culture

A number of films provide some kind of sense of where 1966 lies in English popular culture. The delightful *Sixty-Six* is the only one actually set in 1966. *The Great Escape* of course has nothing actually to do with football but has become emblematic of a certain version of Englishness that hopelessly mixes World War II with World Cup adventures. *Escape to Victory* served to perpetuate this very particular confusion; having Sylvester Stallone in goal didn't help matters either. The comedy *Mike Bassett: England Manager* is gently self-mocking about England's failings, perhaps marking that moment when we finally learned to laugh at ourselves. Arthur Aughey's book *The Politics of Englishness* is also useful in helping us to navigate ways to link these popular-culture images of England with the dawning political reality that the Great Britain that England in '66 was the dominant part of may no longer exist.

English Football '66 and before

The experience of being a top-flight footballer, and member of England team, in the 1960s is recorded by Johnny Haynes in his autobiography from the period, *It's All in the Game*. The essay by Martin Johnes and Gavin Mellor, "The 1953 FA Cup Final: Modernity and Tradition in British Culture," covers the preceding decade, published in the journal *Contemporary British History*, Volume 20, Number 2, 2006. Ronald Kowalski and Dilwyn Porter covered the most seminal England game of that decade in their essay "England's World Turned Upside Down? Magical Magyars and British Football," published in the journal *Sport in History*, Vol 23, Number 2, 2003. Essays that use two different clubs to record the changes in post-war English football are: "Professional Football and local identity in the Golden Age: Portsmouth in the Mid-Twentieth Century" by Nick Phelps in *Urban History*, Vol 23, Number 2, 2005; and Matthew Taylor's "Football, History and Memory, The Heroes of Manchester United," published in *Football Studies*, Volume 3, Number 2, 2000. This period is also expertly described by Andrew Ward and John Williams in their book *The Football Nation*. John Williams covers the economic and social history of one club and its city in his biography of Liverpool FC, *Red Men*. Joyce Wooldridge describes how post-war footballers wrote about their own lives in her essay "The Sporting Lives: Footballers Autobiographies 1945-1980," published in *Sport in History*, Vol 28, number 4, 2008. John Moynihan's *The Soccer Syndrome: From the Primeval Forties* was published in 1966 and is a viewpoint on the game framed by the period. Hugh McIlvanney's *McIlvanney on Football* includes his writing from the period too. James Corbett's *England Expects* is a comprehensive and very well written history of the England team that takes us from 1870 to 1966 before continuing on to World Cup 2006. Simon Kuper and Stefan Szymanski's "Why England Lose" chapter in their book *Soccer-*

nomics is the ultimate in empirical analysis, explaining England's failings as a football team, before 1966 and ever-after.

Britain in '66

For 1966 beyond football, Richard Weight's *Patriots: National Identity in Britain 1940-2000* is a magnificent social and cultural history of wartime and post-war Great Britain. Covering the period immediately prior to '66, have a read of David Kynaston's *Modernity Britain: A Shake of the Dice 1959-62*. Dominic Sandbrook's two books *Never Had it So Good*, covering 1956–63, and *White Heat*, spanning 1964–70, neatly sandwich '66. Jon Savage's *1966: The Year The Decade Exploded* explores the music of that year and its connection to art and fashion as well as increasingly radical politics. Ben Pimlott's biography *Harold Wilson* is essential for understanding politics in and around 1966. In addition Arthur Marwick's *The Sixties: Social and Cultural Transformation in Britain, France, Italy and the United States, 1958–1974* gives a broader, more international picture of the period.

England Fan Culture

The troubled past of England away is carefully chronicled by Clifford Stott and Geoff Pearson in *Football Hooliganism: Policing and the War on the English Disease*, and again by Geoff Pearson in his book *An Ethnography of English Football Fans*. Bill Buford's *Among the Thugs* is a hooliganism insider account from the late 1980s, including Italia '90. On how race impacted on football, particularly in the 1980s and 1990s, *The Changing Face of Football* by Les Back, Tim Crabbe and John Solomos is very good. Edited by Daniel Burdsey, *Race, Ethnicity and Football* helps bring the analysis up to date. By the same editor, *British Asians and Football* is specifically about the relationship between the game and the under-representation of a community. For a broader survey of racism vs anti-racism in the 1960s and after, read Satnam Virdee's *Racism, Class and the Racialised Outsider*. Carrie Dunn's books *Female Football Fans* and *Football and the FA Women's Super League* are excellent on the growth both of women fans and the women's game. Follow her **@carriesparkle**. Edited by Jayne Caudwell, *Women's Football in the UK* gives an idea on how far the women's game has developed compared to when it was formally banned by the FA back in 1966. The Jimmy McGovern film *Hillsborough* is an incredibly moving portrait of the tragedy that was Hillsborough '89. How fan culture changed in the late 1980s and early 1990's is covered by Steve Redhead's book *Football with Attitude*. Mark Peryman's *Ingerland: Travels with a Football Nation* is the definitive account of the changing culture of England's in the 1990s of the last century and into the 2000's. The best England fan travel blog is Mark Raven's www.englandbrighton.blogspot.co.uk.

World Cups 1966-2014

Books about England's World Cup campaigns, and others' too, perhaps both cheer the English reader up a shade as well as put any failure in the context of the tournament as a whole. A recommended list of such books, not including '66, would include Jeff Dawson's *Back Home* about England at Mexico '70. *All Played Out* by Pete Davies is regarded by many as the finest ever football book; it covers England's Italia '90 campaign, and the documentary film *One Night in Turin* is also based on the book. Don Watson's *Dancing in the Streets* covers USA '94 from the Irish fans' point of view. Edited by Hugh Dauncey and Geoff Hare, *France and the 1998 World Cup* is a collection of academic essays reviewing the impact, nationally and globally of France '98. *No More Buddha Only Football* is a superbly funny account of what it was like to follow England to World Cup 2002. Jamie Trecker's *Love & Blood* is an American-eye view of World Cup 2006. *Africa's World Cup*, edited by Peter Alegi and Chris Bolsmann, consists of an impressive range of critical viewpoints on the actuality of South Africa hosting World Cup 2010. American writer George Vecsey's *Eight World Cups* covers tournaments 1982–2010, with an afterword on World Cup 2014. Part travelogue, part history, with a particular emphasis on the rise and rise of the USA team, this is a very good

World Cup overview of an over thirty-two-year period from the point of view of someone who was there, throughout. To begin at the beginning go back to *The Game of their Lives* by Geoffrey Douglas, about the USA team who beat England at the 1950 World Cup. And for the long view therew's none better than Brian Glanville's *The Story of the World Cup* is updated to coincide with each World Cup; it remains the definitive history of the tournament as a whole. For the statistical breakdown of every game in every World Cup, visit www.planetworldcup.com.

German Football

David Downing's *The Best of Enemies* is a history of the England vs Germany footballing rivalry. How England vs Germany fits into the world of football, and more particularly the media representation of it, is the subject of "Crossing the Line: The English Press and Anglo-German Football, 1954-1996," Christoph Wagner's PhD thesis, De Montfort University, Leicester. Raphael Honisgstein's *Englischer Fussball* is a German view on the curious clash of football and the making of Englishness. By the same author, *Das Reboot* tells us how Germany recovered from what seemed to us the briefest of years of hurt to become World Champions, again. Uli Hesse's *Tor!* is a superb history of German football. Lee Price's *The Bundesliga Blueprint* and Ronald Reng's *Matchdays* tell in their different ways the story of the German model. The best way of all however to appreciate Germany's World Cup success story is to begin at the beginning, sit back and enjoy the film *The Miracle of Bern*, a fictionalised account of their first World Cup victory in 1954.

Latin American Football

On Latin American football, the stories in *The Football Crónicas* edited by Jethro Soutar and Tim Girven include Mexico, Uruguay and Argentina. Andreas Camponar's book *Golazo!* is a more conventional approach to the same subject concentrating on events on the pitch. The collection *Football in the Americas*, edited by Rory

Miller and Liz Crolley, consists of academic essays explaining the social and cultural significance of football in the region. David Downing's *World Cups and other Small Wars* deals specifically with the England vs Argentina football rivalry.

Scottish Football

Gerry Hassan's website www.gerryhassan.com is an excellent way to keep up with Scottish politics, culture and sometimes football. His book *Caledonian Dreaming* is a very good portrayal of what an independent Scotland would look like. Ian Black's *Tales of the Tartan Army* tells the story of the Scotland fans who follow their national team. Graham McColl's *'78: How Scotland Lost the World Cup* is a brilliant account of perhaps the biggest Scottish World Cup misadventure. Richard Gordon's *Scotland '74* does the same very well for the previous World Cup. Of several histories of the Scottish team, amongst the best are David Potter's *Wizards and Bravehearts* and Archie McPherson's *Flower of Scotland*.

Other National Footballs

For how two of England's '66 opponents have got on since, see first the late-twentieth-century rise and rise of the French national team, covered in the collection *Le Foot*, edited by Christov Rühn. And for Portuguese football, Phil Town is easily the best-informed English-language writer and an invaluable source of information; his website is www.footballportugal.com.pt and you can follow him on Twitter too **@footballport**. The documentary film *The Game of Their Lives* is a wonderful portrayal of both the North Korean team's achievements at World Cup '66 and the friendly reception they received in England wherever they played. This achievement is also carefully documented in Jong Sung Lee's PhD thesis, "Football in North and South Korea c.1910-2002: Diffusion and Development," from De Montfort University, Leicester.

World Football and Globalisation

Franklin Foer's *How Football Explains the World* is a highly readable use of football as what the author describes as "an unlikely theory of globalisation." David Goldblatt's *The Ball is Round* is an essential global history of football. An earlier approach to the same subject is Bill Murray's *Football: A History of the World Game.* David Held's work is amongst the best for a more traditional way of explaining of globalisation; his book with Anthony McGrew, *Globalization/Anti-Globalization,* is a useful introduction to this key debate. Richard Giulianotti's *Football: A Sociology of the Global Game* is the classic and easy-to-read introduction to what an -ology has to do with football. Jamie Cleland's 2015 book *A Sociology of Football in a Global Context* is a more recent approach to the same subject.

Modern Football

For a daily round up of critical thinking on modern football follow Philosophy Football's twitter feed **@phil_football**.
The best insights into the modern game are provided by the monthly magazine *When Saturday Comes* and the quarterly journal *The Blizzard.*

Two books that cover the marketisation of English football, especially following the formation of the Premier League, are David Conn's *Richer than God* and David Goldblatt's *The Game of our Lives.* Steve Redhead's *Postfandom and the Millennial Blues* single-handedly introduced postmodernism to football. His latest book *Football and Accelerated Culture: This Modern Sporting Life* continues with the mission. Steve's work can be followed at his website www.steveredhead.zone. For up-to-the-minute opinion on all things football follow **@barneyronay** and for the business side of the game follow **@david_conn**. To keep up-to-date with academic research on football and other sports follow **@sport_research**. Stuart Fuller's *The Football Tourist* is the best introduction to combining travel with taking in a game, or three. The follow-up volume is titled, naturally *The Football Tourist – The Second Half.*

Alternative Football

Efforts towards a manifesto for English football include Mark Perryman's Fabian Society/*When Saturday Comes* version, *Football Unite: New Labour, The Task Force and the Future of the Game* from 1997 and by the same author for the Institute for Public Policy Research, *Ingerland Expects: Football, National Identity and World Cup 2002*. Most recently the 2015 Football Action Network Fan Manifesto at www.thefan.org.uk. For a grassroots coaching view of how to save English football from itself see Matthew Whitehouse's *The Way Forward: Solutions to England's Failings*, while Chris Green addresses specifically the issue of youth football in *Every Boy's Dream. Punks, Pirates, Politics* is Nick Davidson's impassioned account of what St Pauli represents. Martin Cloake seeks to apply this spirit of resistance to the English game in *Taking Our Ball Back*. Will Simpson and Malcolm McMahon's *Freedom through Football* takes such an ambition to anarchic limits via the story of the Easton Cowboys and Cowgirls football teams. There is plenty of very well-informed critical thinking and writing about football online, for amongst the best follow **@gameofthepeople** and **@twoht**. For a picture of the increasingly attractive alternative offered in non-league follow the match reports provided @ **beautifulgame15** and the photo-essays of **@centrecirclepub**. For campaigning initiative and imagination www.footballbeyondborders.org set the standard. Seeking to provide an ideological overview for all this activity, and others too, isn't easy but *Fan Culture in European Football and the Influence of Left Wing Ideology* edited by Peter and David Kennedy has a good go.

Fifa and Football Governance

Football Worlds: A Lifetime in Sport by Stanley Rous is his own view of how international football should be administered. Alan Tomlinson's FIFA: *The Men, the Myths and the Money* is a modern, and critical view. Denis Howell's autobiography *Made in Birmingham* includes his experience as the British Government's first Minister of Sport. Useful explanations of the connections between football and party politics are included in *Football and the Commons People*, edited by David Bull and Alastair Campbell.

Football in the Media

Reading Arthur Hopcraft's *The Football Man*, originally published in 1968, is a very good way to understand how the game was reported in the 1960s. Roger Domenghetti's *From The Back Room to the Front Room* is a most useful history of how the media has covered football, mainly in the newspapers. Martin Kelner's *Sit Down and Cheer* provides a history of football, and other sports, on TV.

Changing Sport Culture 1966-2016

Played in London by Simon Inglis gives readers an idea how the environment in which we watch and consume our sport has changed over the past fifty years. Visit the website www.played-inbritain.co.uk for other books in this excellent series. For further background read Rob Steen's *Floodlights and Touchlines*, a comprehensive history of spectator sports and the spaces in which we watch them.

English National Identity

For an introduction to the work of Stuart Hall in the 1980s read *The Hard Road to Renewal*, Eric Hobsbawm's writings in the same period are collected in his *Politics for a Rational Left*. Hobsbawm's essay "The Apogee of Nationalism 1918-1950," in his book *Nations and Nationalism Since 1780* is a good introduction to how nationalism evolved in the first half of the twentieth century. Mark Perryman's edited collections, *Imagined Nation: England after Britain* and *Breaking up Britain: Four Nations after a Union*, cover the implications of increasingly independent Scotland, Wales and Northern Ireland and the emergence of a distinctly Englidh national culture and polity on what used to be a United Kingdom (sic). David Winner's *Those Feet* explores the very particular relationship between football and English national identity.

And...

If that little lot isn't enough, or maybe if it is way too much, there is really only way to relive and re-examine 1966. Watch *Goal! The Official Film of the 1966 World Cup*, England fan or not, for a truly great celebration of that golden summer of football.

Notes on Contributors

Mark Perryman is one of the pioneers of an England fan-friendly culture and a regular media commentator on the politics of sport as well as writing for the *Guardian, Huffington Post*, the *Morning Star, Counterfire*, the journal *Soundings* and others on the same subject. Author of a number of books on supporting England, including *Ingerland: Travels with a Football Nation*, Mark has also written on English national identity in *Imagined Nation: England after Britain*. A Research Fellow in Sport and Leisure Culture at the University of Brighton, he is in addition the co-founder of Philosophy Football, self-styled "sporting outfitters of intellectual distinction." Until parenthood stepped in Mark went to all of England's games at Euro '96 and was a travelling fan through qualifying campaigns and to tournaments from France '98 to Euro 2012. Aged six and a half in '66, he has no actual memory of England winning the World Cup. **@phil_football**

Amy Lawrence is a football writer, mostly for the *Guardian* and the *Observer*, and is the author of occasional books, most recently *Invincible: Inside Arsenal's Unbeaten 2003-3004 Season*. She went to Italia '90 by train and ferry with a sleeping bag and enough money to buy tickets for a couple of matches, and has been fortunate enough to cover World Cups as diverse as France '98, South Korea & Japan 2002, Germany 2006 and Brazil 2014 as an enthralled journalist. **@amylawrence71**

Asif Burhan is an itinerant blogger on international men's and women's football for Kick it Out. He follows England home and away, attending three World Cups and five European Championships as well as seven Champions League finals. Along the way

Asif has watched games in seventy-five different cities across forty countries. **@AsifBurhan**

Joe Kennedy is a Teaching Fellow in Literature and Cultural Studies on the Gothenburg Programme at the University of Sussex. For Euros and World Cups he runs and edits the football and theory blog straightoffthebeach.wordpress.com. His book about football, neoliberal culture and authenticity is published by Repeater Books in August 2016. Half-Scottish Joe chooses to follow Scotland, his favourite World Cup memory being John Collins' equalising penalty against Brazil in the opening game of the '98 World Cup, a game Scotland went on to lose, of course. **@joekennedy81**

Richard Weight is an author specialising in the history of Britain since the nineteenth century. His books include *Patriots: National Identity in Britain 1940-2000*, which was shortlisted for the Orwell Prize, and *Mod: From Bebop to Britpop, Britain's Biggest Youth Movement.* He presents or contributes to documentaries for the BBC, Channel Four and Sky and writes regularly for the magazine *History Today.* He has been following England as a supporter since the 1980s, including travelling to the World Cups of South Africa 2010 and Brazil 2014. **@richard_weight**

John Williams is Senior Lecturer in Sociology at the University of Leicester. His books include most recently, with Andrew Ward, *Football Nation.* John carried out extensive field research tracking changes in England fan culture from the 1980s to Germany 2006. In 1966, John, aged eight, stood among Russian sailors smoking foul-smelling fags at Goodison as he watched CCCP's brilliant Lev Yashin try, unsuccessfully, to keep West Germany at bay on a chilled Merseyside night.

Alan Tomlinson is Professor of Leisure Studies, currently in the chool of Humanities, University of Brighton, and renowned as an expert on the politics of FIFA having written a number of books on the subject, most recently *FIFA: The Men, The Myths and the Money*. A regular contributor to *When Saturday Comes*, the *Financial Times*, *New Statesman* and the *New York Times* covering FIFA's mismanagement of world football, Alan is also the only contributor to this collection who was actually at the 1966 World Cup final. @ **AlanTomlinson1**

Claus Melchior was born in August 1954, missing the Miracle of Berne by a week, though he's been around to watch and enjoy Germany winning the World Cup on three other occasions to make up for this early disappointment. Claus works as a bookseller in Munich and writes about football, mainly for the magazine *Der Tödliche Pass*, as well as books about TSV 1860 München, and baseball and basketball in the USA. He watched the 1966 final on television and likes to believe that even at the ripe old age of twelve he was mature enough to acknowledge England as the better team.

Leonardo Haberkorn is a journalist and the Associated Press correspondent in Montevideo. In 2011 Leonardo's book on the war between the state and the Uruguayan urban guerrilla movement, the Tupamaros, *Milicos y Tupas*, won the prestigious Bartolomé Hildago and Libero de Oro awards. He contributes to a range of leading Latin American magazines including in Colombia, Mexico and Peru. Ahead of World Cup 2014 Leonardo's wrote a chapter in *The Football Crónicas*, an English-language anthology of Latin American writing on football. @**leohaberkorn**

Carlos Calderón Cardoso is a journalist, historical researcher and writer for television. The author of thirteen books on the history of Mexican football, his writing on the development of the sport in Mexico is featured in the FIFA Football Hall of Fame permanent exhibition. Carlos is also a Professor of Sport at both the

Universidad de Periodismo y Arte en Radio y Televisión and *Universidad Iberoamericana* in Mexico City. **@CarlosCalderonC**

Philippe Auclair is a writer based in London as the English football and international football affairs correspondent for *France Football* and English football correspondent for RMC Radio in France. He also writes for a range of other publications including the *Guardian, 8X8, Green Soccer Journal,The Blizzard* and *FourFourTwo* as well as being a regular studio guest for the BBC World Service, BBC Radio 5Live and talkSPORT. Philippe's book, *Cantona: The Rebel Who Would Be King,* was the 2014 Sports Book of the Year in France; other books of his include *Thierry Henry: Lonely at the Top* and *FIFA Gate: How Qatar 2022 Caused the Downfall of the Blatter System.* **@philippeauclair**

Simon Inglis is the author of the classic work *The Football Grounds of Britain* and, most recently, *Played in London,* which was shortlisted for the 2014 William Hill Sports Book of the Year. He is editor of the series Played in Britain, books about the nation's sporting heritage. During the 1990s, through his membership of the Football Licensing Authority, Simon played a leading role in the implementation of the Taylor Report and the updating of the *Guide to Safety at Sports Grounds.* In 1966 Simon was eleven years old and living in Birmingham. He particularly recalls seeing the German squad having a kick-around in a local park, in bare feet. **@The_SimonInglis**

Rob Steen has covered football for several national publications, ranging from the *People* and the late, unlamented *News of the World* to the *Guardian,* the *Sunday Times* and the late, much lamented *City Limits.* He is currently Co-course Leader and Senior Lecturer in Sport Journalism at the University of Brighton. Rob has also written and edited more than twenty books on sport, most recently *Floodlights and Touchlines: A History of Spectator*

Sport, which was shortlisted for the 2014 William Hill Sports Book of the Year. Aged eight, after the Steen family had watched the '66 final on the TV, Rob walked six houses up the road to the modest home of former England manager Walter Winterbottom, in the hope of conveying his congratulations. He was out; the idea that the old boy might have been invited to Wembley hadn't occurred.

Simon Kuper writes a column in the *Financial Times*. His books include *Football Against the Enemy*, winner of the 1994 William Hill Sports Book of the Year, and *Ajax, The Dutch, The War: Football in Europe During the Second World War*. Simon's book *Soccernomics*, co-authored with Stefan Szymnanski, opens with the chapter headed "Why England Lose," the definitive explanation of the team's post-'66 decline and fall. Born three years after '66, despite being English and living in Paris, Simon chooses to support Holland, which from 1974 on provided him with decades of moral superiority over friends who favour England, until the autumn of 2015, when the Dutch team experienced their own version of hurt too, failing to qualify for Euro 2016. @**Kupersimon**

Claire Westall is a Lecturer in the Department of English and Related Literature at the University of York. She has a long-standing interest in football, specifically its performative aesthetics and its place in English popular culture. Claire's research includes work on the relationship between sport and literature and she has written extensively on this as it applies to cricket. She is co-author, with Michael Gardiner, of *The Public on the Public: The British Public as Trust, Reflexivity and Political Foreclosure* and also contributed to *The Cambridge Companion to Cricket*.

Marcela Mora y Araujo is a writer and broadcaster. In the late 1990s she was co-editor with Simon Kuper of the groundbreaking football-writing journal *Perfect Pitch*. Marcela's journalism has appeared in the *Financial Times* and the *Guardian*. She has also worked widely in radio, TV and film as researcher, reporter and producer. Marcela was part of the production team, working on media liaison, for *La Coupe De La Gloire*, the official film of the 1998 World Cup. A baby of just thirty weeks, Rattin's sending-off in '66 passed her by; instead Marcela's first memory of the World Cup had to wait a further twelve years, until Argentina in '78 when amidst the oppressive political climate she can remember partying for a month. **@marc_cart**

David Goldblatt is the author of no less than three seminal books on football: *The Ball is Round*, a global history of the game; *Futebol Nation*, a footballing history of Brazil; and *The Game of Our Lives*, the winner of the 2015 William Hill Sports Book of the Year Award, which explains the meaning and making of English football. David writes on sport for the *Guardian,* the *TLS* and *Prospect* magazine amongst others, as well as making sports documentaries for BBC Radio. He teaches the sociology of sport at a number of institutions including Bristol University, De Montfort University, Leicester and Pitzer College, Los Angeles. **@davidsgoldblatt**

Mark Doidge is a Senior Research Fellow at the University of Brighton. He is an expert in European football fan cultures and the author of *Football Italia: Italian Football in an Age of Globalisation*. Mark has undertaken numerous football research projects across Europe, including studies on discrimination, pan-European fan organisations, ultras and community engagement, as well as reporting for UEFA on anti-racist football initiatives in Poland, Germany and Italy. He works closely with the campaigning organisation Football Supporters Europe, based in Hamburg. **@markdoidge**

Gerry Hassan is a political commentator and researcher who has written and edited twenty books on social change in both Scotland and Britain, including the widely referenced *Caledonian Dreaming: The Quest for a Different Scotland*. His latest book is *Spirit of Independence: How Scotland becomes a New Democracy*.

Gerry has visited all of Scotland's forty-two senior grounds, and is currently slowly working his way through the junior (in England these would be called non-league) football grounds. All this helps to pass the time until he can see Scotland play in a major international tournament again. When it happens, should this be in his lifetime, he will be there. **@gerryhassan**

Markus Hesselmann has been Editor-in-Chief of the online edition of the daily Berlin newspaper *Der Tagesspiegel* since 2009. He was Sports Editor of the same title's paper edition during World Cup 2006 in Germany, and London Correspondent too, 2007–2008. With Christopher Young, Markus edited *Der Lieblingsfeind* (*The Favourite Enemy*), a collection of essays and interviews comprising international views about German football and German national culture, including from England, Holland and Austria. He somehow knew that the '66 third-goal's ball wasn't in but wasn't really bothered until he was asked to contribute to this book. **@hesselmann**

Frederico Duarte Carvalho is an investigative journalist and writer whose investigations include US spy rings in Lisbon, the city where he lives and works, and most recently the Bilderberg Group. He writes for a range of publications including *O Primeiro de Janeiro*, *Tal&Qual* and *24 Horas*. Frederico is also the author of a biography of Benfica player Vítor Batista. Born in 1972 he grew up listening to others' memories of Portugal's glorious 1966 World Cup campaign while enduring the long wait until the next one was finally ended by Portuguese team qualifying for Mexico '86 to brighten up Frederico's adolescence. **@fduartecarvalho**

Steve Redhead is Professor of Jurisprudence and Head of CSU Law in the Faculty of Arts, Charles Sturt University, New South Wales, Australia. He has written widely on a number of theorists' work including Jean Baudrillard and Paul Virilio. Steve's book *Football with Attitude*, published in 1991, helped explain and justify their fandom to a generation of football-obsessive academics in this period. His most recent book is *Football and Accelerated Culture: This Modern Sporting Life*. In his youth Steve was a spectator at two 1966 World Cup games at Goodison Park, Brazil vs Hungary and Portugal vs North Korea. **@steveredhead**

Stuart Fuller heads up Global Commercial Operations for one of the world's largest online brand-management companies, but come 3pm on a Saturday (and 7.45pm on the occasional Wednesday) he is the Chairman of fan-owned Lewes FC. He has just completed writing *The Football Tourist – The Second Half*, in which he continues his journey around the world watching some of the biggest as well as the most bizarre games of football. Stuart first made his name in the football travel-guide market over a decade ago with his self-published *Budget Airline Guide to European Football*. For three years in the mid-2000s Stuart managed the England Fans Vets Away team including an infamous game in Skopje broadcast live on Macedonian TV as a cheapo alternative to the proper international match. **@theballisround**

Nick Davidson works as a teacher. The rest of the time he writes some of the best books there are on fan resistance including *Modern Football is Rubbish*, which with no sign of improvement he followed up with *Modern Football is Still Rubbish*. His account of the cult St Pauli football club and all it has come to represent, *Punks, Pirates and Politics*, has become almost a handbook for supporters committed to building an alternative football culture of their own. In 1981, aged nine years old, Nick attended Geoff Hurst's Soccer School; on graduating it was the World Cup hat-trick scorer who awarded him his certificate. Peaking perhaps a bit too early, this remains the high-point of Nick's career as a player. **@outside_left**

Sanaa Qureshi is a community worker in London. She joined Football Beyond Borders in 2012, organising the campaign's first film festival, Clipped 2014, and is now the proud captain of the FBB Warriors women's football team. Sanaa is also an occasional match-day reporter for the *Morning Star*. Despite owning an England shirt with Shearer on the back, Sanaa's only meaningful national allegiance is to the Pakistan cricket team, thus spectacularly and defiantly failing the Tebbit Test. **@sanaa_mq**

Sven Goldmann is a regular contributor to the magazine *Fifa Weekly*, as well as the International Football Correspondent for *Der Tagesspiegel* in Berlin. Since 2005 he has covered for the paper the Bundesliga, the Champions League and the German national team, including their victorious World Cup 2014 campaign from Brazil. Ahead of World Cup 2006 he took part in forums with England fans to introduce them to German football culture. Born in 1966, he is unsure how many of his fifty years qualify as hurt. @ **SvenGoldmann**

Philip Cornwall is Production Editor for the sport sections of the *Guardian* and the *Observer*. He has been a regular contributor to the magazine *When Saturday Comes* for the best part of twenty years and has written chapters on football, particularly the England team, in half a dozen books including *The Ingerland Factor* and *Going Oriental: Football after World Cup 2002*, both edited by Mark Perryman. Philip has followed England since 1985 as a fan from Barcelona to Bloemfontein, travelling to six European Championships and four World Cups, with or without the national team.

Acknowledgements

Without Philosophy Football it would have been hellishly difficult to assemble our line-up of writers. Via Philosophy Football's
T-shirts and events, networks were developed and contacts and
friendships were made and maintained with virtually all the contributors to this book. Thanks to Philosophy Football co-founder
Hugh Tisdale and Dispatch Manager Jacquie Rich for keeping the
show on the road while *1966 and Not All That* was being compiled
and written.

The Dangerous Times Festival provided a platform to test out
some of the ideas of *1966 and Not All That*, as did the Politics,
Power, Media and Sport module and the Football, Culture, Community module at the University of Brighton. FA Technical Director Dan Ashworth's contribution to the latter module was an
essential half-time inspiration during the process of putting this
book together.

The *Guardian, Morning Star, Counterfire, Huffington Post, Left
Futures, Compass* and others have provided Mark Perryman with
the space to develop his ideas on England.

Activities by members of the England Supporters Club show
the potential for a fan-friendly fan culture on England away trips.
The support of the FA for this venture as well as the Raise the Flag
initiative at home games are practical contributions towards a
better England. Thanks in particular to the FA's Helen Nicolaou
for her support for Raise the Flag and to the FA's Harpreet Robertson for her support for fan-friendly activities on England away
trips. Thanks are especially due to the fans involved, including
Raise the Flag stalwarts Ken Jackson, Mandi and Michelle Dovey,
the Leicester crew Jos Johnson, Roy Cole and Steve White, Steve
Enticknap, as well as those England fans involved with organising
the away-trip activities including Simon Harris, Mark Knapper,

Ed Rhodes, Dane Cloke and Dave Beverley. Without all of them and many others, the years of hurt would be even more painful. On trips to World Cup 2010 and Euro 2012, as well as Bulgaria and Montenegro away, the new addition of Edgar Coddington-Perryman to the Perryman and Coddington travelling party opened eyes to what the future for England might hold; may the next fifty years be less hurtful for Edgar.

Two most useful inspirations for this book were David Bull's monograph *Harold Wilson's Winning Ways – Mexican Myths with Major Meanings?* And an anecdote from Paul Jonson recounting his paper round in Stourbridge on the afternoon of the World Cup Final when at every address he delivered to the entire household were sat round the TV entirely oblivious to what he'd dropped through the letterbox.

It goes without saying that despite our gratitude to others, the responsibility for and views expressed in *1966 and Not All That* are entirely the responsibility of the editor and contributors. Thanks does not imply endorsement.

Without the memories of those who were there in '66, Amy Lawrence's oral history of the tournament would have been impossible to write. Amy is most grateful to all those who wrote in with their personal accounts of that golden summer and to Paul Campbell, Community Co-ordinator for sport at www.theguardian.com, who did so much to make her appeal for these a success.

Like many contributors Richard Weight was taken to an England game by a parent, his late father Philip Strong, and Richard thanks him for an experience that has lasted a lifetime.

Documents quoted from Sir Stanley Rous's personal papers were sourced from Alan Tomlinson's personal collection of these materials, courtesy of Rose Marie Breitenstein.

Hans Peters provided Claus Melchior with invaluable comments on an early draft of his chapter.

Tim Girven of Ragpicker Press advised on contributions sought from Uruguay and Mexico, recommending and liaising with

Leonardo Haberkorn as well as co-ordinating the translation of Carlos Calderón Cardoso's chapter by David Swift. In addition Leonardo also thanks Marcela Haberkorn and Garbriel Portos for assistance with his chapter.

Rob Steen's research into how the media covered '66 at the time was made possible by the kindly, smiley staff at the British Library Newsroom, St Pancras.

Ana Pereirinha put Frederico Duarte Carvalho in touch to provide a Portuguese match report for the semi-final.

Markus Hesselman persuaded Sven Goldmann, his colleague on *Der Tagesspiegel*, that writing a report of the final from the German side would not be too traumatic. Stephen Glennon translated Sven's chapter.

None of the collective efforts behind *1966 and Not All That* would have amounted to very much without a publisher. Tariq Goddard of Repeater Books responded instantly and enthusiastically to a speculative idea. As a publisher Repeater left us alone to get on with it while providing insightful advice when needed, and a final edit by Phil Jourdan and Alex Niven with skilful typesetting by Jan Middendorp ensured a book of our '66 dreams met that ambition. Thanks.

About Philosophy Football

Philosophy Football, the self-styled "sporting outfitters of intellectual distinction," was founded in 1994, not a good year for English football. Never mind. Taking inspiration from the words of Albert Camus, Nobel-prize winner for literature and goalkeeper for Algeria – "All that I know most surely about morality and obligations I owe to football" – we had our eye on loftier matters than the ignominy of failing to qualify for a World Cup. Camus' name and squad number on the back, words to the wise on the front, this unique line-up soon enough featured the T-shirted thoughts of Jean Baudrillard, Nietzsche, Wittgenstein and Gramsci, plus Jean-Paul Sartre and Simone de Beauvoir running the channels with a style more Left Bank than North Bank. The brainchild of Mark Perryman and Hugh Tisdale, Philosophy Football don't sell T-shirts, we promote ideas and ideals with 100%-cotton simply our preferred platform. The Harold Wilson '66 shirt is one of Philosophy Football's all-time favourites, squad Number Ten, naturally.

www.philosophyfootball.com or follow **@phil_football**.

Index

Repeater Books

is dedicated to the creation of a new reality. The landscape of twenty-first-century arts and letters is faded and inert, riven by fashionable cynicism, egotistical self-reference and a nostalgia for the recent past. Repeater intends to add its voice to those movements that wish to enter history and assert control over its currents, gathering together scattered and isolated voices with those who have already called for an escape from Capitalist Realism. Our desire is to publish in every sphere and genre, combining vigorous dissent and a pragmatic willingness to succeed where messianic abstraction and quiescent co-option have stalled: abstention is not an option: we are alive and we don't agree.